LITHUANIA: THE OUTPOST OF FREEDOM

Library of Congress Catalog Card Number: 76-596

International Standard Book Number: 0-912760-17-6

PUBLISHED BY

The National Guard of Lithuania in Exile
in cooperation with
Valkyrie Press, Inc.

LITHUANIA: THE OUTPOST OF FREEDOM

BY

DR. CONSTANTINE R. JURGĖLA

PREFACE

It is with mixed feelings that this work, largely written in 1974, is presented to the reader just after the Helsinki event.

The statesmen signing the Helsinki Document were fully aware that the principles of sovereign equality, territorial security, non-interference in internal affairs, nonaggression and the definition of aggression, etc., were all incorporated in the treaties and conventions sponsored by the Soviet Union and signed with the Baltic States. Both prior to the Hitler-Stalin deal and thereafter until the Helsinki show of 1975, the Soviet Union exhorted about the sanctity of the treaties signed by Moscow. Unlike the Helsinki Document, the treaties concluded by the Soviet Union with the Baltic States are parts of written International Law. Seemingly decent statesmen found no courage to face or speak the truth and to demand freedom for the last colonies in Europe — Estonia, Latvia and Lithuania. Our State Department explains away the Helsinki Document as a sort of non-obligatory code of ethics of détente, while Brezhnev claims that the part sanctioning the "present frontiers" is obligatory, and that the other "baskets" are subject to bilateral arrangements.

The reader should remember the Lenin dogma that treaties are signed by governments, that the central committee of the Communist Party signs no treaties, and that the government is not responsible for the Party — which controls the government. Lenin signed treaties in his capacity as head of the government, and simultaneously, as head of the Party, directed Party activities to contravene such treaties.

The Atlantic Charter and the wartime pledges to the captive peoples of Europe are not parts of the Helsinki Document: they were abandoned within a week after the Captive Nations Week observed in the United States under a Presidential Proclamation authorized by Congress. The Helsinki Document means a tacit amnesty to the Soviet Union for its part in the Conspiracy against Peace and Humanity for which Moscow's partners, the Nazis, were tried and hanged, and an amnesty to the Soviet Union for the abduction of millions of freemen from the annexed areas and their enslavement in forced labor camps in the Arctic.

The talks regarding the mutual and balanced reduction of armed forces in Central Europe remain unconcluded, even though the Helsinki affair was supposed to be contingent on progress in these talks.

The geographic center of Europe is in the Vilnius-Trakai area of Lithuania. These talks for a reduction of the armed forces actually affect only the fringe of Western Europe, since the Soviet bases in Czechoslovakia are midway between Europe's center and Portugal. As for the SALT talks, the Soviet delegation is headed by Vladimir S. Semyonov, one of the architects and supervisors of the absorption of Lithuania in 1940 and of East Germany later. The Soviet troops are to stay in Berlin but the other victors of World War II lost their jurisdiction over Germany within the frontiers of 1937.

Decent people will not abandon the Lithuanians and their good Baltic neighbors suffering untold persecution in their indomitable quest for freedom, for their human rights and for the restoration of their sovereign states pledged by the Atlantic Charter.

The reader will find in these pages the moving story of the Lithuanian people's experiences in their relations with Muscovy, later known as Russia and presently as the Soviet Union. I am most grateful to Dr. Samuel Eliot Morison, "always a friend to Lithuanian freedom," who encouraged me to write this story and assured me that "phoenix-like" Lithuania will rise again. I am particularly grateful to the veterans of the Lithuanian National Guard for publishing this work, and to their special committee headed by Jonas Švoba whose members ably assisted with their suggestions as individual chapters were being written. I am also grateful to my dear friends and scholars — Dr. Alexander Broel-Plateris, Joseph B. Laučka and Kestutis Čižiūnas — for their valuable observations as they read the manuscript.

I lived several years among the wonderful people of Lithuania and was privileged to know the rank and file people, a great many of their cultural, political and military leaders, as well as some of the leaders of the renaissance, both in Lithuania Proper and in Prussian Lithuania. I had been privileged to share in their unselfish activities, in their sufferings and triumphs, and — with my two brothers — in their armed struggles. Back in the United States, for over five decades I was active among the decent, honorable and unselfish Lithuanian Americans who remain true to the best traditions of their ancestral people. And it has been my rare privilege to meet and befriend some of the leaders of the insurrection of 1941, of the Supreme Committee for Liberation of Lithuania, and several postwar freedom activists, including Simas Kudirka — the steadfast freeman who readily forgave the Americans who had been ordered to surrender him to the Russians, and who, after surviving his imprisonment in hard labor camps, advocates all possible assistance to Russian dissidents, "the Giants" in his words, who opted for freedom by their own reasoning. I also recommend that the reader read the statements of Liudas Simutis, who in his petition to the Supreme Soviet, outlined his reasons for taking up arms. I like to associate these people with the insurrectionists of 1862-1864 whose beliefs are cited in these pages.

Constantine R. Jurgėla

August 1975
Bethesda, Maryland

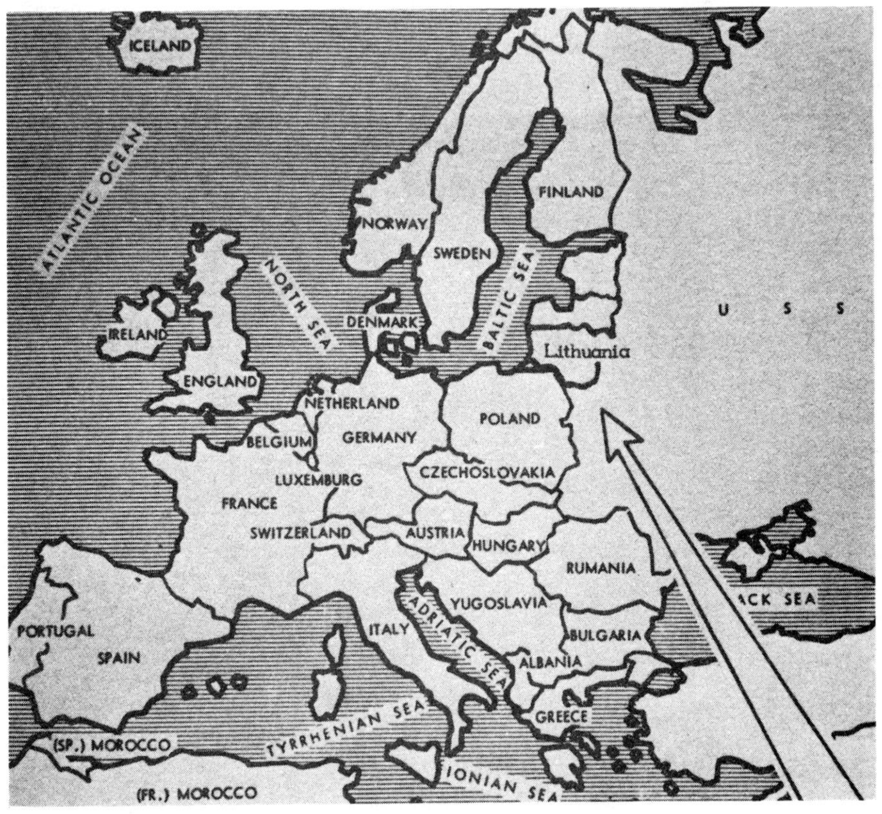

LITHUANIA AND HER NEIGHBORS.

TABLE OF CONTENTS

Page No.

FOREWORD

A CRY TO THE FREE WORLD'S CONSCIENCE

The Lithuanian National Guard was founded at the same time that Lithuania was fighting for its freedom and independence. Its purpose was and still remains the defense of Lithuania's freedom and the fight for its independence by whatever means necessary. Thus the central board of directors of the Lithuanian National Guard in Exile decided to publish the book, *Lithuania: The Outpost of Freedom*, by Dr. Constantine R. Jurgėla. The publishing committee believes that this book will be an effective tool against the Soviet imperialistic and genocidal policies. This book will show that czarist as well as communist Russia seeks to enslave all nations under its imperialistic arm. This book is one occupied nation's cry to the conscience of the Free World.

The author bases this book on true and documented facts and later events. In publishing *Lithuania: The Outpost of Freedom*, the committee also wishes to emphasize Lithuania's resistance to the czarist and present communist regimes. It brings out Lithuania's difficult and courageous fights for its rights, freedom, independence, and continued existence as a nation.

We cannot understand how Russia, calling herself the Soviet Union, can be a member of the United Nations since she doesn't carry out the precepts of the United Nations, remaining an imperialistic and a colonializing country, occupying many non-Russian nations.

Let this cry to the Free World's political conscience not perish as a futile cry in the wilderness. Rather, let it be heeded! Let it stimulate thought and strong resolutions in the minds of those champions of liberty who wish to see freedom for all nations and peace throughout the world!

Lithuanian National Guard in Exile
Publishing Committee

GENERAL OBSERVATIONS

MEMORABILIS.
Et perinde ſtupenda de cru
DELI MOSCOVITARVM
Expeditione narratio, è Germanico
in Latinum conuerſa.

DVACI.
Ex Typographia Iacobi Boſcardi,
Typographi iurati Regiæ
Maieſtatis.

MEMORABILIS ET PERINDE
ſtupenda de Moſcouitarum expeditione
narratio, è Germanico in Latinum
conuerſa.

Moſcouitarum exercitus ſuperioribus ſeptimanis agrum Polonicū inuaſit, & Polotzki, alias Pleſkj (Lituaniæ oppidum, quod ſedecim miliaribus à deſertis ſitum eſt) validiſsima manu, ſex incurſionibus expugnauit, diripuit, & dimiſsis ignibus ſolo equauit: eóque loci ſupra viginti hominum milia, triſti admodum ſpectaculo primum demenbrari, ac poſt ſtrangulari iuſsit. Nec vllis ſanè verbis queat exprimi, quāta in Matronas, in Virgines, in Pueros, Tyrannide graſſatus ſit. E propinquis & vicinis inde locis ſexaginta & amplius hominum milia in Moſcouiam abduxit: Matronas & Virgines veſtibus exuit, & omnes (vti nudæ, ac ſine amictu erant) vinctas in captiuitatem abſtraxit. Inter alios ve-

The prototype newspaper published in Venice in 1563 told the story of the Muscovite invasion of Lithuania and the seizure of Polotsk by the troops of Grand Knyaz Ivan IV the Terrible. Its 20,000 inhabitants were said to have been hanged after the amputation of their limbs. Some 60,000 people from the surrounding area, including matrons and maidens stripped naked and tethered, were driven into captivity. According to Dr. Vanda Daugirdaitė-Sruogienė, this story was reprinted in "The Russian invasion of Poland 1563, being a translation of a contemporary account in Latin, Edinburgh, 1884." The story may have been exaggerated, yet it generally conformed to the pattern of Muscovite behavior since the conquest of Great Novgorod in 1478.[1]

Back in 1371 King Algirdas remonstrated with the Orthodox Patriarch of Constantinople that Metropolitan Alexis named by him for the

[1] "... the Kremlin spread the tidings that the Novgorodians were 'pagans' determined to destroy Orthodox Christians. ... As Orthodox Christians... the Muscovites took honest pleasure in punishing these armed marauding pagans, in cutting off their noses, splitting their mouths and killing them. It was even more satisfying to loot the rich warehouses of the northerners, to pursue and possess the northern women, running around squawking like frightened fowls." Harold Lamb, *The March of Muscovy*, Garden City, N.Y. 1948, 73-74. Dr. V. Daugirdaitė-Sruogienė, *Lietuvos Istorija*, Chicago 1956, 431-2.

Russias was inciting the Muscovites against Lithuania. He added: "The Metropolitan should bless the Muscovites to aid us, because we are fighting for them against the Germans."[2] He and his co-ruler brother Kęstutis were obliged to chastise Moscow thrice. In 1380 the Lithuanians under King Jogaila and his cousin Vytautas marched again, this time as allies of Khan Mamay. They arrived at the designated meeting place just after the Muscovite victory over Mamay at Kulikovo near the Don River. The Muscovite ruler Dmitry was thence named "Donskoy," even though, according to Teutonic Knights chronicler Posilge, he had slept inebriated during the battle and his troops were actually led by two rebellious Lithuanian princes, Jogaila's brothers Andrew and Kaributas Demetrius. The Lithuanians attacked the Muscovites, seized their booty and marched home. Muscovy remained under the hegemony of the Tatar Golden Horde.

Following a period of mutual suspicions and an uneasy truce, the Muscovites invaded Lithuania in 1449. They were repelled, and an "eternal peace" was signed, one of a series to follow. Muscovy, now free of the Tatar hegemony, was harboring ambitions to become the "Third Rome" (after the Roman and Byzantian empires), and to bring under its rule the Whiteruthenian and Ukrainian possessions of Lithuania as an alleged patrimony of the Rurik dynasty. The Metropolitan of Moscow soon claimed for himself the title of Patriarch with a jurisdiction over the "Russian" Christians of Lithuania, and the Grand Knyaz claimed the title of Tsar of all the Russias.

Military and political fortunes varied. The unceasing menace of Muscovy drove Lithuania to form a confederation or union with Poland ruled by the Jogailan branch of the Lithuanian dynasty of Gediminas since 1386. The Poles had repeatedly elected Lithuania's rulers to the Cracow throne, and thus there had been several periods of personal union under the same monarch. A permanent confederation was finally negotiated at Lublin in 1569, soon after Lithuania had acquired most of Livonia (presently Latvia and Estonia) and had to defend it from the Muscovites seeking a "window on the Baltic sea." In 1582, by the treaty of Zapole, Muscovy renounced its claims to Livonia. Later, during the civil war in Muscovy, Lithuania joined in the Polish venture and participated in the occupation of Moscow. Michael Romanov, descendant of

[2] *Acta Patriarchatus Constantinopolitani*, Ed. Miklosich et Müller, Vindobonae, vol. I, 1860, II, 1862, reproduced in *Pamiatniki Drevne-Russkago Kanonicheskago Prava*, vols. 6 & 26 of *Russkaya Istoricheskaya Biblioteka*, Sanktpeterburg 1908, and in E. Golubinsky, *Istoriya Russkoy Tserkvi*, vol. II, part 2, Moskva 1917, pp. 7-11.

an immigrant Lithuanian family, was elected by the Muscovite boyars to the throne in 1613. However, two years earlier they had elected Prince Ladislas, son of King Sigismundus III Vasa of Poland, Lithuania and Sweden. A mixed army under Grand Hetman John Charles Chodkiewicz "Katkus" of Lithuania marched with Ladislas and besieged the Kremlin. A 16-year truce was negotiated in 1618. The war flared up again and another "eternal peace" was signed in 1634 at Polyanovo: Ladislas renounced his election and recognized Michael's title of Tsar of Muscovy, who renounced claims to Livonia and assumed to pay an indemnity to Ladislas.

Soon thereafter Muscovy cast its hungry eyes on the Ukraine, by then a part of Poland, and ultimately at Pereiaslav in 1653 induced the Kozaks to switch their loyalty from Poland and/or Turkey to Muscovy. Muscovite and Kozak armies, in conjunction with Sweden, invaded Lithuania and, in 1655, the capital city of Vilnius fell to a hostile army for the first time. For several weeks the Muscovites burned and looted the city. Tsar Alexis arrived in Vilnius and demanded allegiance to himself as the alleged Grand Duke of Lithuania but, being hopeful of gaining the royal Polish crown, he soon disabused his Lithuanian title. Vilnius was liberated only in 1661. The Kozaks rebelled again and Muscovy agreed to a truce signed at Andrussovo in 1667, gaining Smolensk from Lithuania. One clause provided that the Orthodox believers would not be oppressed in the Commonwealth of Poland and Lithuania, and that Muscovy would not oppress Catholics. Thereafter Muscovy claimed that this clause granted to it a protective power to interfere in the internal affairs of the Commonwealth. It may be noted at this point that, under the Pacts of Union, Lithuania handled most of the "Eastern" affairs and Poland handled most of the "Western" and "Southern" affairs or relations of the Commonwealth.

The final peace with Muscovy was signed in 1686, and state frontiers remained unchanged until 1772. However, since the accession of Peter I who claimed the title of Emperor of Russia and quarreled with Charles XII of Sweden, Russian armies continually crisscrossed Lithuania on their way to war fronts, and brought plagues. Lithuania Proper had lost 46% of its population in 1648-1667, one-third in 1698-1719, and again one-third during the Russian wars against Napoleon in central-western Europe and the French invasion of Russia. These calamities were followed by intensified German colonization of Lithuanian areas in East Prussia and the slavonization of Eastern Lithuania. These three periods of war, occupation and plagues within a century and a half, explain why the Lithuanians dwindled to 3 or 4 million, as their Polish and Belorussian neighbors had grown.

In 1772 Russia, Prussia and Austria dismembered the Commonwealth, and Lithuania lost some Latvian, Ukrainian and Belorussian areas. The second partition of 1793 brought the Russian frontier to ethnographic Lithuania. The third partition of 1795 split Lithuania along the Nemunas River: the left bank became New East Prussia until the Tilsit Peace of 1807 when it was joined to Napoleon's Grand Duchy of Warsaw and, since the Congress of Vienna of 1815, remained within the "Congress" Kingdom of Poland under emperors of Russia until 1915. In 1817 and again in 1842 a narrow belt of Lithuania's coastland was annexed to Courland and thus descendants of the Teutonic Knights achieved a German bridgehead between Prussia and Livonia. When Lithuania regained its independence by 1918-1923, four separate codes of law were in force: the Russian Code in most of the country since 1840, the Code Napoleon and the Gregorian calendar in Sudavia, the Courland Code in the Palanga township, and the Prussian Code in the Klaipėda District.

I.
THE RUSSIANS ARRIVE

In 1794 the Lithuanians joined in the Kościuszko Insurrection in an attempt to retain their independence within the dual Commonwealth of the Kingdom of Poland and the Grand Duchy of Lithuania. The Russians were expelled from Vilnius and Lithuania Proper and, for a brief period, the Lithuanians held the ports of Liepaja and Ventspils in Courland. Between April and mid-August the Lithuanians held the Russian armies at bay and blocked them from sending reinforcements to Poland. Finally, in the face of overwhelming odds, the Lithuanians made diversionary incursions toward Daugavpils in the north and eastward into Belorussia, while their main forces in three columns hacked their way into Poland, losing some 3,000 men en route. Some Lithuanian cavalry units took part in Kościuszko's last battle at Maciejowice on October 10, 1794. Five to seven thousand Lithuanians died in the defense of Warsaw on November 4, 1794 at Praga, among a total of some 18,000 defenders and inhabitants of that suburb. Suvorov's artillery had destroyed the bridge over the Vistula, thus blocking an escape route to Warsaw. Lithuanian generals James Jasiński and Paul Grabowski, and Diet Deputy Thaddeus Korsak perished, General Meyen was among the few surviving captives.

The following are brief unbiased eyewitness accounts of the massacre.

Russian Colonel Leo Engelhardt writes: "When Denisov ordered us to rush to the left through a swamp, we charged the trenches wading waist-deep through water and chasing the Poles, and we entered Praga in an orderly manner. We found our troops there in terrible confusion amid violence, murders and looting. . . . To realize the true horror of this storming, one had to be an eyewitness after it was over. On each step up to the Vistula bank there lay murdered and dying people from different classes; corpses of soldiers, civilians, Jews, priests, friars, women and children were heaped in piles along the riverbank. Viewing all this, the heart fainted inside a man and indignation swelled in one's soul over the hideousness of the scene. A man feels no mercy within himself and becomes ferocious during battle, yet murders after the battle are debasing."[3]

[3]*Zapiski Lva Nikolaievicha Engelhardta*, Moskva 1866, 177-8; Kazimierz Bartoszewicz, *Dzieje Insurekcji Kościuszkowskiej*, Wiedeń, n.d. (1909), 358-9; Mieczysław Grydzewski, *Na 150-lecie rzezi Pragi*, Londyn 1845, 15.

The profiteering Prussian provincial commissioner Friedrich Nufer relates: "The scene in Praga was horrible: people of both sexes, the old and infants at their mothers' breasts, lay murdered in heaps; blood-spattered naked bodies of soldiers, broken wagons, carcasses of horses, dogs, cats, even pigs. Here and there arms or legs were still quivering. The entire city of Praga was aflame in smoke and roofs were collapsing loudly to the tune of ululating cossacks, the cursing of the enraged soldiery. The loot was piled in stacks by the victors. . . . No one dared to show up in Praga; a few profit seeking Jews had come, but the cossacks grabbed them by their legs and smashed their heads against walls or sidewalks until their brains spewed, and then divided the money found on them. I paid 35 rubles for 35 gold and silver watches. I obtained a hatful of broken silver for 2 rubles. Shortly I loaded my rowboat and returned to Warsaw where Jews were waiting for me on the bank and they purchased nearly all I had. My third trip was not as profitable. Murders continued. Deafening shrieks of children pierced my ears and brought me to a courtyard. A multitude of Jewish children had fled there and the cossacks amused themselves by impaling these poor creatures on their lances. I paid a gulden per each child and saved 35 unfortunate victims. I hastened with them to Warsaw where sober-minded Jews at once reimbursed me. I lost only 4 guldens in this trade, because as many children fled from me into the dense crowd when we were landing."[4]

A Russian staff officer J. G. Seume serving as the German secretary to Russian plenipotentiary ambassador Igelström, recalls after his release from detention by the insurrectionists: "After the storming of Praga the Russians blemished the glory of that day by cruelty, as they murdered the helpless old people, women and even children. . . . The horrified Colonel Lieven, who commanded one regiment during the storming and later was the commandant of Praga, told me that near the end of the massacre he personally saw a Russian grenadier wandering with a fixed bayonet and stabbing every encountered Pole, with no exceptions, not sparing even the badly wounded, and then with a hatchet he carried on his person he split their heads. The colonel admonished him for such cruelty, yet he replied: 'Hah, what of it, they are dogs who had fought against us, and all of them must die.' "[5]

[4] *Friedrich Nufers Schicksale* während und nach seiner Gefangenschaft in Warschau unter den Polen und Russe, Posen 1795, 27-32, cited also by Bartoszewicz and Grydzewski.

[5] *J. G. Seumes Sämmtliche Werke,* Leipzig 1837, 405, Compare this with the scene in Great Novgorod in 1478, our footnote 1 on page15— and the massacre at Cherveń in June 1941.

[Civilian] General Thomas Wawrzecki, the Lithuanian successor to Kościuszko's supreme command, retreated from Warsaw with the remnants of the Polish and Lithuanian units. On November 18, 1794, he, one Polish and three Lithuanian generals surrendered and, still allowed to keep their swords, they were brought before Suvorov in Warsaw. Disregarding the conditions of the capitulation, Suvorov demanded that, if they wished to retain their personal freedom, they must sign "reverses" promising to abstain from ever fighting Russia and her allies. The generals balked, but on Wawrzecki's authorization they signed the papers. He himself would not sign, and was detained and sent to St. Petersburg. Russia, Prussia and Austria bickered over their respective loots. King Stanislas Augustus Poniatowski abdicated in 1795. On January 31/20*, 1796, Governor General Nicholas Repnin (1734-1801) proclaimed to the people of Lithuania the annexation of their country, north and east of the Nemunas River, to the Russian empire.

The Russians had arrived.

*. . . The date with the double numbers, shown on this page and on others in subsequent chapters, results from the calendar adjustment by many Western European countries in 1582. The inaccurate old Julian calendar had gradually been drifting away from the seasons. A more accurate calendar, the Gregorian, was adopted and was adjusted by the dropping of ten days, October 5 through October 15. Russia and other nations under her control, did not make the change until 1918, when many more days of inaccuracy had accumulated.

TO SIBERIA, by Artur Grottger.

General Jokūbas Jasinskis / James Jasinski, 1759-1794.

— Durny Lithography

II.
PEASANTS BECOME "REVISIONARY SOULS"

Inequity and selfishness in the social, economic and political developments of 18th century Lithuania stunted the growth and stifled the home rule of cities and towns, and hardened the lot of peasants, especially of those on private estates. Nevertheless, the poorest subject remained a human individual protected by the law and state institutions. The peasant did not own the land allotted for his use. However, the corvées of labor and crops and service levies which the peasant owed to the public or private estate were fixed in statutory inventories: he was not a chattel of his landlord or a slave unconditionally bound to the land. Noblemen of various classes owed a military duty in person when called by the Diet. However, professional armed forces of "salaried men," soldiers, consisted of foreign and domestic mercenaries including peasant volunteers. A feeble attempt to levy "recruits" in the insurrection of 1794, failed. Voluntary conversion of serfdom into contractual tenant relationship between emancipated peasants and landlords, made significant progress from the mid-eighteenth century: in 1795 freedmen constituted 28.4% of the peasantry.[6] Peasants along with nominal nobles, the landless "*bajorai*" or "*szlachta*," attended schools and became clergymen, army officers or professionals. Lawrence Stuoka-Gucevičius (1753-1798), the great architect of the cathedral of Vilnius and other monumental structures and the head of the insurrectionist militia of Vilnius in 1794, was a serf's son. John Rustem (1751-1835), former servant of the princes Czartoryski, became a noted painter, professor and the dean of arts of the University of Vilnius where this chair was on par with other disciplines — a unique phenomenon in contemporary European universities.[7]

Muscovite serfs steadily fled to Lithuania regardless of unsatisfactory social conditions there. Governor Sievers of Novgorod reported to his empress Catherine II in 1763 that 50,000 fugitive serfs from the Smolensk area were being sheltered in the Mstislav palatinate of Lithuania and that he lacked data from other places. He noted that "Russian landlords motivated by insatiable cupidity are overburdening their sub-

[6] Jerzy Ochmański, *Historia Litwy*, *Wrocław* 1967, 153.

[7] Halina Bartnicka, *Polskie szkolnictwo artystyczne na przełomie XVIII i XIX w. 1764-1831*, Ossolineum, Wrocław 1971.

jects with excessive duties and taxes, and thousands of Russian fugitives are therefore fleeing to Lithuania and Poland." After the first partition of 1772, masses of peasants fled from the territories annexed by Russia. In its notes of March 9, 1793 to Austria and Prussia, Russia justified its claims to Lithuanian and Polish areas as compensation for the property damages suffered: "Fugitive Russian subjects, borderland area inhabitants bound to the land and constituting a part of their lords' property, are received by Poles and are spoiled by them; their number is estimated at 300,000 heads exclusive of their descendants since the time of this insane emigration; it must also be taken into consideration that a large part of these fugitives is not accounted for by evidence." Catherine's ambassador in London similarly explained the matter to King George III in 1795.

Already in 1794 "preventive censorship" was imposed in Lithuania by Catherine's plenipotentiary, future Governor General Nicholas Vassilevich Repnin. State latifundia and confiscated church and rebel estates were lavishly distrubuted by Catherine II to Fieldmarshal Alexander Suvorov and her other favorites—Platon Zubov, Rumyantsev, Lanskoy, etc. Zubov rapidly advanced to generalship, countship (and a Prince of the Holy Roman Empire) — received the largest "economy" of Šiauliai in 1795, and he at once raised the labor corvées from 2 to 6 days per week. Other grantees followed suit, and they were emulated by some native renegade gentry. Per capita taxes were levied 50% above the level prevalent in Russia. Even the Gregorian calendar, in effect in Lithuania since the fifteen eighties under King Stephanus Báthory, was replaced by the old style calendar as of 1800, as decreed by the ukase dated July 28, 1799. Gradually the Russian system of bonded serfdom and "recruit" levies was extended throughout the newly acquired dominions.

Taxable units in the Grand Duchy of Lithuania had been the acreage (*valakas*, the hoof) and the family ("per chimney"). In Russia taxes were assessed per capita on male serfs listed in the periodic census every fifteen years: the census was called "revision" and the taxable units, serfs, were "revisionary souls." The noblemen were personally tax-free. Per capita taxes during the fifteen-year periods were assessed on the basis of the last previous revision, regardless of the actual situation caused by births, deaths and runaways. Catherine's ukase of January 17/28, 1765 had authorized landlords to sell their "souls" individually or en masse, with the land or separately. The serf-owning "*pomieshchik*" could gamble his "souls" away in card games, separate children from parents, husbands from wives, exile them to Siberia and recall them at will, sell serf maidens into Oriental harems or houses of ill fame, give away or sell men into "recruits" and seize their possessions.

"Revisionary souls" had nowhere to turn, and appeals to the sovereign were made punishable crimes: for the first offense — one month's incarceration at hard labor; the second offense — flogging and exile to a hard labor camp for a year; the third offense — public flogging and exile for life into the Nerchinsk area of Siberia, and the landlord was to credit such exile to his quota of recruits. When these penalties failed to stop complaints — the ukase of August 22, 1767 allowed exiling of first offenders to Nerchinsk. All this at the landlord's whim, with no judicial review. The Pugachov Rebellion was the outgrowth of this inhumane system.

In 1775 Catherine II extended the sale of serfs apart from land to her newly acquired dominions. Governor General Chernyshov had pointed out to her that such sales were not "customary" in former Lithuanian areas, except for occasional sales on the Russian frontier involving fugitives from Russia and "not embracing local inhabitants." The empress answered that she could not deprive her Lithuanian landlords of "the rights enjoyed by Russian landlords." [8]

Russian officials were baffled by statutory inventories which limited corvées and other duties to the estates in Lithuania. Emperor Paul I by an ukase of April 5, 1797 attempted to ban holiday labor and to fix weekly quotas at three days of labor. The ban was ignored in Russia and there were no institutions to enforce the order. On May 16, 1801 the "secret committee" of Tsar Alexander I considered "a minor item" — a proposal to ban sales of "souls" apart from land. The deliberation produced a decree banning newspaper announcements of such sales — lest Europe should learn.

Alongside the loss of human status and degradation into "revisionary souls," Lithuanian peasants were presently burdened with the "recruit" system. The Tsar's ukases levied annual or special quotas of recruits per fixed number of revisionary souls and city guilds. The ratio varied. The ukase of September 1, 1794 levied one recruit per 200 "souls" for 20 years of military service, and this quota was extended to Lithuania in 1795. Landlords were to select men to fill their quotas and to deliver them to the military. Jews and artisan guilds were allowed to pay 500

[8] Augustinas Janulaitis, *Lietuvos Bajorai ir jų Seimeliai XIX amž. (1795-1862)*, Kaunas 1936, P. 11, citing M. Yablochkov, *Istoria dvoryanskago soslovia v Rossii*, Sanktpeterburg 1876, 526-7, and the Collection of Laws.

rubles in lieu of each recruit due from them. Military duty was later extended to 25 years.

There was also the "postal duty" — to provide transport for government officials, prisoners and mails, and the road maintenance duty. Russia needed military roads — at the expense of the inhabitants. Much road construction was done in Lithuania in 1818-1820. A total of 2,332,978 labor days and 1,480,944 carting days were consumed, accompanied by accidental injuries and the neglect of tillage and harvesting, and the resulting shortages of food and fodder.

III.
PAUL I WAVERS

It may be noted at this point that at least one-half of the population of Lithuania Proper in 1795 were freemen—landed and nominal nobles, clergy, Tatars, regular troops, rural freedmen, burghers. Landless hereditary nobles predominated in administrative services and professions.

In connection with the allocation of recruit quotas, the Russian officialdom was at a loss regarding elements unknown in Russia — free peasants and landless noblemen engaged in tenant farming or as servants, artisans, professionals. Noblemen were a tax-free caste in Russia — other castes were "the tax-paying strata." Revenue collectors wanted more cash, the military wanted more able-bodied recruits. However, in the former Grand Duchy of Lithuania there were large masses of seemingly poor people who claimed they were tax-free noblemen, and the gentry vigorously opposed attempts to tax their tenant-noblemen or to include free peasants among the "revisionary souls" in asserting recruit quotas. In 1797 an ukase authorized recruitment of freemen "if they agree." This provision tempted serf-owning lords to seek mercenaries among unemployed freemen to fill their recruit quotas. Indeed, some freemen consented to become recruits upon payment of a 25-ruble bonus.

As early as 1796 Platon Zubov was the first satrap to suggest to Catherine II that up to a million Lithuanian tenant noblemen be resettled in the Ukraine, Crimea and the Caucasus in military settlements, and he proposed to start with 4,000 yeoman families. On June 5/16, 1796 Catherine approved this idea which was seconded by her secretary , at various times Governor and Cabinet Minister, the poet Gabriel Romanovich Derzhavin. Some people were forcibly moved or were about to be resettled when Tsar Paul I on March 6/17, 1797, countermanded his late mother's order. His ukase of April 3/14, 1797, indicated what he believed to be a better method "regarding the multitude of idle and landless noblemen." They were to be drafted as non-commissioned officers for the army, and "those of elegant manners and appearance" were to be sent to St. Petersburg for service in the imperial mounted Bodyguard (Leibhussar) squadrons and the Cavalierguard corps of noblemen — an employment which "will provide not only sustenance for them, but will allow them to lead useful lives." [9]

[9] Janulaitis, *Lietuvos Bajorai, supra,* 69-70, citing *Polnoye Sobraniye Zakonov Rossiiskoy Imperii* — the Full Collection of Laws of the Russian Empire.

Paul I ascended to power in a backward state embracing unreconciled non-Russian populations and held together by autocracy and armed force. He released most of the captive Lithuanians and Poles who had defended their Commonwealth's independence, and he restored some estates to former rebels. The two departments of Vilnius and Slanimas (Słonim) became one Lithuanian Gouvernement with its administrative center in Vilnius — until 1801, when Alexander I again established two departments — of Vilnius and Gardinas (Grodno). Paul reinstated the Lithuanian Statute and the Supreme Lithuanian Tribunal which was renamed the Lithuanian Supreme Court whose judgments could be appealed to Imperial Senate. His ukase of March 18/29, 1797 banned forcible religious conversions and proclaimed a "freedom of embracing Orthodoxy." The former Uniates — Roman Catholics of the eastern rite —at once petitioned en masse for a return to the Union. Paul was puzzled over this desertion of the Orthodoxy for which they had allegedly striven under his mother, and he ordered the governor of Minsk to verify the reason. Finally he authorized free transfer from one religious denomination to another.

Russia had acquired more than half a million hereditary noblemen in Lithuania — more than there were in Russia Proper. Reinstatement of the Lithuanian Statute revived the vigorous participation of noblemen in county and departmental dietines, and the frequent elections of delegations to present various grievances. This exercise of traditional liberties clashed with Paul's centrist and absolutist tendencies. Unlike his mother, Paul I disliked delegations, except those of Russian peasants who deified him. He decreed that delegations must obtain permission from their respective Governors, and later he held that it was enough for delegates to meet their governors to transmit their petitions. He made the civil service open only to noblemen who had served in the armed forces.

In addition to per capita taxes for their "revisionary souls," Paul I made the gentry pay for the maintenance of various administrative institutions and officials. Annual quotas were to be proposed by governors and nobility marshals. Furthermore, the gentry were to make "voluntary contributions" to the construction of garrison barracks and to subsidize cities. The Courlanders in 1797 refused to "donate" funds, and soon army units were quartered on the estates to live off the land. Paul emulated Prussian army methods and, while revoking the death penalty provisions of the Lithuanian Statute, he promoted "the twig" and exile to hard labor camps as "educational methods." The flogging was made applicable to noblemen, traditionally free from corporeal punishment, after sentences had stripped them of their status as nobles.

Elective offices among the nobility were gradually reduced to a minimum. All enrolled noblemen continued to elect the few county officials, but gubernatorial dietines (assemblies) were limited in membership to County Marshals and their deputies. The dietines were largely reduced to ceremonial sessions, religious services and elections of a few officials. Noblemen's institutions were deprived of the right to ennoble any one: Paul held this to be the sovereign's prerogative. Proofs of nobility were demanded from 1797 when all electors were to be listed in "hereditary nobility rolls." Paul also ordered marshals of the nobility to prepare atlases of the coat of arms. No such proofs had been required from the enfranchised nobility under the former Lithuanian republican democracy of the gentry. Documentary evidence was hard to get since the removal of the State archives, the Lithuanian Matricula, to Russia. This difficulty enabled Russian governors to separate and to drive a wedge between the landed gentry and nominal hereditary noblemen, yet they preferred that this be done by the gentry itself. When the Governor General tried to induce county marshals to engage the landless or tenant noblemen for salaried administrative offices — forest wardens, centurions and other duties, the marshals answered that the country's laws retained by the Emperor "do not allow any forcible measures against noblemen" and no nobleman could be forced to accept any office. In essence — they held that it was up to the government to *dis*prove the noble status of their petty yeomanry *(bajorai, szlachta)* colleagues.

Paul's absolutism gradually alienated the Russian landed gentry. His abrupt reversal of the anti-French policy of war and his frank admiration for Napoleon was the last straw which led to his murder by the praetorian military elite — said to have been abetted by Sir Charles Whitworth of England and a Spanish agent. Indeed, the news of the Tsar's demise reached London extraordinarily soon. Lord Nelson's ships were again able to replenish their fresh water and other supplies in Estonian ports, and Russia's policy again became pro-British.

IV.
UNDER ALEXANDER I AND NAPOLEON I

The Russian occupation reduced to a trickle the flights of serfs from Russia and Prussia, and a great many Lithuanians presently fled abroad. The gentry raised no objections to incoming labor manpower, but disliked the loss of their own serfs. However, the Russian authorities showed little concern over the matter and even less talent either in convincing the fugitives to stay or in detaining them. In 1801 marshals of the nobility petitioned the governor in this matter: the police should handle the arriving or transient migrants more gently and allow them to settle wherever they preferred, rather than forcibly resettle them elsewhere. The petitioners also cautioned the governor that frontier guards should not appropriate the runaways' possessions. In the same year the gentry complained of their "great losses in labor manpower, inasmuch as during the calls of recruits a great many subjects flee abroad."

On September 21, 1801 Tsar Alexander I, without consulting the gentry, decreed that residents within a 100 verst (66 mile - 107 kilometer) wide frontier belt could pay 300 silver rubles in lieu of each recruit due from them. Money was scarce, however, and the gentry petitioned for the abrogation of this ukase. They stated in a long memorandum that the frontier zone suffered heavily from an exodus of young men, and that landlords can neither fill their quota of recruits nor pay the duty in silver, rather than with paper money. When a quota of 1,300 recruits is set — eight to ten thousand youths flee. These fugitives are well received in Prussia, including New East Prussia just across the Nemunas River. Fugitives are resettled in Prussia in places of their own preference, they are free to engage in any trade, and are relieved of the recruit duty up to the third generation. Prior to 1795 men used to flee from Prussia (Proper). This influx had dried up, since fugitives were treated here as deserters and were imprisoned, unless they agreed to enroll as bonded serfs. Some easement was due for such migrants from abroad and for the gentry still paying per capita taxes for men who had fled long ago. The government heeded just one request: that recruits be delivered bodily to county seats, rather than to Vilnius.[10]

The gentry preferred to part with their "revisionary souls," rather

[10] Janulaitis, *Lietuvos Bajorai, op. cit.*, 207-211.

than cash, and attempted to rid themselves of the physically unfit men. The military refused to accept such recruits and insisted on listing freemen as bondsmen. On February 20, 1803, Tsar Alexander I by an ukase acknowledged the legitimacy of freemen: he allowed the gentry to emancipate their serfs, giving them land plots tilled by them, by a "freely negotiated contract" to be verified and approved by the Ministry of Interior, in order to protect emancipated peasants from abuses. The Ministry received a set of guidelines and the law was made applicable throughout the empire. The gubernatorial marshal of Vilnius convoked county marshals and asked them for their suggestions for adapting the rules to local conditions. The gentry requested that the government "points" be published. The moment was ill-timed because of the manpower shortages, and few lords availed themselves of the ukase to release peasants — without their land.[11]

Meanwhile the government verified the gentry's grievances and found that the number of runaways indeed exceeded recruit quotas. Government was losing able-bodied recruits, and the lords were losing their labor manpower. The country was also hurt by the loss of exports to Prussia and the serious shortage of salt imports.

As Alexander I renewed wars with France, the battle lines, formerly in Austria and Prussia, moved ever closer to Russia. The French propagated national liberation and an end to serfdom. Russia countered by the universal mobilization of the militia in 1806 — in ethnically Russian areas: Lithuania and the Ukraine were to contribute money and food stocks. The Holy Synod appealed to the faithful claiming that Orthodoxy needed its defenders, because Napoleon had joined with Christ's enemies, the Jews, and considered himself to be the Messiah. The gentry raised a militia of 600,000 men to defend their homeland — yet many of them were marched abroad to fight, and failed to return. Alexander freed the military from paying debts in wartime, war was being waged abroad, and Russia Proper was spared devastation. The Russian sick and wounded were hospitalized or convalescing in Lithuania, to prevent panic in Russia, while French prisoners of war were ostentatiously marched to Russia in evidence of "the victories" of the gallant Russian armies. Epidemics spread in Lithuania. After the Russian defeat at Austerlitz and the failure of their Prussian campaign, the true Christian Tsar Alexander befriended Christ's enemy and made peace with Napoleon aboard a pontoon anchored in the Nemunas (called Memel in German) River opposite the city of Tilsit (the Lithuanian Tilžė), in

[11] *Ibid.*, 206-207.

1807. The Tsar joined in the Continental Blockade, yet because of his worsened relations with the Russian gentry he dared not announce the peace in Russia. According to Caulaincourt, the military did not eliminate Alexander simply because they feared his heir Constantine more. Meanwhile Alexander engaged in a flirt with Lithuanians and Poles.

After the battle of Eylau in Prussia in February, 1807, Russian General Levin August Theophil Bennigsen, the Hannoverian strangler of Tsar Paul I and later the Military Governor of Lithuania, proclaimed Alexander King of Poland — to ensure the Lithuanian gentry's support in his rear area. Alexander neither confirmed nor disclaimed Bennigsen's step. While in Tauragė, near Tilsit, the Tsar approached General Charles Kniazewicz (1762-1842), the disillusioned former commander of one of the Legions in Napoleon's service. The Tsar proposed to commission him to form a Lithuanian Army to fight on his side against Napoleon, and in return he would reconstitute a Poland out of his own and Prussian-held Polish and Lithuanian territories.[12]

Soon at Tilsit Napoleon reassured Alexander that he would not reconstitute either Poland or Lithuania on a large scale. Nevertheless, a great many Lithuanians continued to flee across the Nemunas to the new Grand Duchy of Warsaw constituted at Tilsit. Russia announced that the left bank of the Nemunas River was a "foreign country" and fixed stiff penalties for crossing the border: a fleeing peasant was to be seized into recruits, the unfit were to be sent as vagabonds for hard labor in fortresses, the estates of fleeing noblemen were to be confiscated. When it was verified that fugitives were mostly gentlemen youths with no properties of their own, a confiscatory lien on the fugitives' shares in parental estates was decreed. The Superior court at Białystok was to review such cases: those involving gentry squires were to be submitted to the Senate for confirmation, those involving the petty szlachta/yeomen were only to be reported.

During the Russo-French negotiations in 1809 Alexander insisted that Poland be not reconstituted in any form. Napoleon procrastinated —and spread the intelligence about the Tsar's demand in Poland and Lithuania. Nevertheless, the Tsar continued his own flirt with several Lithuanian aristocrats about reconstituting a greater Lithuania.

Prince Michael Cleophas Ogiński, one of the leaders of the Lithuanian insurrection of 1794, last Treasurer of the Grand Duchy, later a Napoleonic officer and refugee, and the composer of a marching song which became Poland's national anthem, was disillusioned with

[12]*Ibid.*, 218; Janusz Iwaszkiewicz, *Litwa w roku 1812*, Warszawa 1912, 4-5.

Napoleon and came home. The Tsar restored some of the confiscated estates to the penitent prince and befriended him. Ogiński believed the Tsar — who merely toyed with him while watching the Lithuanians ogle across the Nemunas. The Tsar listened and played coy, promising, yet publishing nothing. In 1811 the Tsar allowed payment of taxes in grain rather than cash — an accommodation beneficial to the needs of his armed forces. In 1812 he reduced per capita taxes to the level paid in Russia. At one point Alexander signed a letter to the Lithuanian gentry written in Polish: the Tsar dictated in French, Ogiński translated, and the Tsar signed the Polish text — and named Ogiński his secretary. Alexander's sole concern was to get more men for his army by forming a Lithuanian Corps, and to provision his forces. Ogiński correctly interpreted the Tsar's intentions, and he argued that as long as recruit quotas were levied — noblemen would enlist only if they saw the Tsar organizing a Lithuanian State.[13]

In April 1812 Alexander I came to Vilnius with his entire government and was well received. Napoleon's army crossed over the Nemunas at Kaunas in June while Alexander was dancing in Vilnius. The Tsar fled with his entourage and ordered a large group of Lithuanian aristocrats to accompany him. As soon as he left Vilnius, Russian troops engaged in their favorite form of warfare: the burning of food magazines, bridges and homes. The Lithuanians who fled with the Tsar could no longer reach his ears. The Russians who had watched their Tsar fraternizing with Lithuanians and Poles and allegedly planning "to dismember Russia," presently deified him.

Napoleon was likewise well received in Vilnius. He met delegations from all social strata, hinted at ending serfdom, and named a Provisional Lithuanian Government. After 18 days in Vilnius he followed his army advancing on Moscow, with three Lithuanian generals on his personal staff. The French cavalry lost most of its horses during the forced march across Lithuania, and Napoleon's only interest in forming a government was to assure a safe rear supply base. Foreign Affairs Minister Maret Duc de Bassano remained in Vilnius as Napoleon's Viceroy, and foreign ambassadors settled here. Commissioner Bignon organized a civil administration. Dutch General Hogendorp was named Military Governor. The French urged the formation of Lithuanian armed units and supply services — on Lithuania's payrolls.

Immediately relations worsened since the French treated Lithuania

[13]Janulaitis, *ibid.*, 219-226.

as a conquered country. They seized scant food stocks and paid no consideration to the needs of inhabitants. Attempts to levy recruits on the Russian model met with stiff resistance. Nevertheless some 19,000 men manned the Lithuanian military formations, paid and provisioned by the country itself. Some 50,000 French deserters of various nationalities were marauding the countryside, and regular French troops behaved no better than the Russians — carousing, robbing, flogging, seizing living quarters. Lithuanian peasants believed the French troopers' talk of liberty. They discontinued their labor for the estates, and some joined the marauding French deserters.

Political leaders wanted a reunion with Poland. The Poles noisily entertained Lithuanian missions and hailed the reunion, yet they would not abolish the frontier and customs tariffs, and refused to supply salt. Lithuanians soon perceived that Poles would not treat them as equals, and they demanded a separate Lithuanian Marshal (Speaker) in a joint Confederation Council. Napoleon decided against this, yet he also refused to incorporate Lithuania into the Grand Duchy of Warsaw. Reunion with Poland ceremonies were staged in all counties, yet no union resulted.

Before long — the avalanche of the disorderly retreating French troops swept across Lithuania bringing epidemics, arson and famine, and leaving thousands of corpses on the roads and in churches. The Lithuanian cavalry escorted Napoleon's cortège from the fording of the Berezina, while Marshals Murat and Ney tried to restore some semblance of a rearguard action among the marauding remnants of the once proud army. The Prussian Corps in Northern Lithuania and Latvia, and the huge Austrian army in southern Lithuania and the Ukraine, stayed out of the fighting. Then both the Prussian and Austrian armies turned against the French. The Lithuanian Provisional Government retreated with the French to Warsaw, Cracow and Dresden — where two faithful Lithuanian gendarmes delivered the remnants of their state treasury. The Government disbanded at Dresden on July 24, 1813, and the surviving Lithuanian troops were taken over on the French payrolls. It behooves to note that, while Warsaw officials jumped on the Russian victory bandwagon, the old men of the Lithuanian Provisional Government declined Alexander's amnesty. They said they had sworn their allegiance to Napoleon, who alone could release them from their oaths.

Tsar Alexander I was back in Vilnius on December 22/10, 1812. Two days later he was persuaded to proclaim amnesty which allowed political refugees two months to return home. The grace period was later extended. During the French invasion, the hallmark of Russian patriotism was to flee and to scorch the earth. After the burning of Moscow the noblemen, nevertheless, were the first to demand indemnity. The Russian gentry feared that the French might rouse their serfs—and, as soon as Napoleon retreated with the Russian army on his heels, the gentry disarmed their serf militiamen at home.

Governor General Levitsky of Vilnius and his Policemaster Oertel, both "yellow" in the war, behaved as ultra-patriotic tyrants with a vengeance against Napoleon's Lithuanian collaborationists. Russian and French deserters and transient Russian troops continued to loot the country. People hid in forests and swamps. The countryside along the main highways was a deserted and scorched wasteland. Russian armies treated Lithuania as an enemy country. Ogiński's documented complaints brought no relief, and once again he became an emigré in Western Europe. Material damage was officially fixed at 87 million silver rubles.

A new census — the Seventh Revision of 1817 — established that Lithuania had lost one-third of its inhabitants since the census of 1811 and that the pattern of population had changed significantly. The only increase of population was shown to have been among Jews in cities.[14]

However, life had to go on.

[14] Janulaitis, *Lietuvos Bajorai, op. cit.*, 261, 268-269.

V.
THE SECOND RUSSIAN OCCUPATION

Back in 1808 Walerian Strojnowski published a book in Vilnius, *O Ugodach Dziedziców z Włośčianami* (About Agreements between Landlords and Peasants), urging the emancipation of the serfs. When a Russian translation of this book was published in 1809, the Russian squires (pomieshchiki) were furious over "the indecent Pole's antagonism to the sacred institution of subjection." However, this idea was well received in Lithuania, except in eastern areas with poor soil and a severe manpower shortage. In southern Lithuania, then a part of the Grand Duchy of Warsaw, serfdom was abolished by the Code Napoleon in 1807 — in name, if not in substance, inasmuch as peasants had not received title to lands they tilled and continued to perform labor and other duties to the estates on a contractual basis. In 1811 Princes Michael Cleophas Ogiński and Xavier Lubecki, and Count Louis Plater submitted to Alexander I their draft of a "Governmental statute for the Grand Duchy of Lithuania" providing for the emancipation of serfs within the decade of 1812-1821.[15]

Alexander I called on General Thaddeus Kościuszko in France. The latter on April 9, 1814, urged the Tsar to grant full amnesty to "Poles," to assume the title of King of Poland with a constitutional system similar to that of England, and "to abolish serfdom within ten years, endowing peasants with ownership title to the lands they tilled." During the Congress of Vienna, Kościuszko on June 10, 1815, wrote to Alexander to thank him for the promises regarding Poland. He continued: "I am a native Lithuanian, Sire, and but few years remain for me to live; however, mystery is shrouding the future of my native land," and he asked for some reassurance.[16] The Tsar failed to reply. Kościuszko then moved to Switzerland where he died on October 15, 1817. By his last will Kościuszko liberated his own serfs and endowed them with lands free from any duties to the estate. However, the Tsar did not permit execution of this will and Kościuszko's serfs in Lithu-

[15] Ochmański, *Historia Litwy, op. cit.*, 155.

[16] K. R. Jurgėla, *Lietuvos Sukilimas 1862-1864 metais*, Boston 1970, 176, citing (Leonard Chodźko) Auguste le Comte d'Angeberg, *Recueil des Traités, Conventions et Actes Diplomatiques concernant la Pologne*, Paris 1862, 599, 700.

ania remained bonded.[17] Memorial services were held throughout Lithuania and the Vilnius gubernatorial dietine asked for permission to bring the body of this "fellow Lithuanian" home and to erect a monument to him. This was refused, and Kościuszko's remains were brought to Cracow instead — at the expense of the Tsar.

Ideas of freedom had spread among the masses. Sons of the gentry and members of the intelligentsia abhorred the institution of serfdom, and peasants remembered the slogans of the French soldiers: "liberty, fraternity, equality." These ideas were in direct conflict with prevalent Russian views. Karamzin, the famous historian, penned a memorandum to his Tsar: "I do not know whether Godunov had done well by taking away freedom from the peasants. But I do know that it does not behoove to return freedom to them now. In those days they had the customs of freemen, today they have the customs of slaves. It seems to me that, to strengthen the State foundations, it is better to oppress the people, rather than give them freedom at an inopportune moment."[18]

In postwar, the surviving serfs and the sick had to fulfill labor duties to the estates, and their masters had to pay per capita taxes at pre-war level regardless of the absence of many of their "souls." Some members of the gentry presently urged emancipation for selfish reasons — in order to be relieved of the burden of feeding their hungry serfs. Just about the time of the new "revision" of 1817, peasants in the neighboring Baltic Provinces of Courland, Livonia and Estonia were given "freedom of the birds" — without land. The dietine of Vilnius in 1818 petitioned the Tsar for "amelioration of the condition of peasants through mutually negotiated contracts of emancipation." In reply, the Tsar praised "the noble intentions of the Lithuanian nobility" and promised to consider the matter. However, Senator Nicholas Novosiltsov prevailed on him in 1819 to deny the petition. He pointed to the reality in the Polish Kingdom: emancipated landless peasants sank into extreme poverty and total dependence on lords.[19] The Tsar squashed the movement and silenced the gentry's dietine on that subject.

The authorities concentrated again on reducing the number of freemen and of proletarian noblemen barred from voting since 1802. The officials insisted on listing free peasants as bonded serfs and thus inflat-

[17] Žmogus (Aug. Janulaitis), *Baudžiava Lietuvoje*, Chicago 1901, 33.

[18] C. R. Jurgėla, *History of the Lithuanian Nation*, New York 1948, 397, citing Henryk Mościcki, *Pod znakiem Orła i Pogoni*, Lwów-Warszawa 1923, 45.

[19] Ochmański, *Historia Litwy*, *op. cit.*, 159; Janulaitis, *Lietuvos Bajorai*, *op. cit.*, 275-276.

ing per capita taxes. The gentry protested that they should not pay taxes for persons they did not own. The officials made it clear that the government had no intention of losing revenues regardless of the legal trifles. Then the gentry shifted in 1820 to an attack on the institution of free peasants by demanding that freemen living on the land 10 years should be bonded. This step failed to arouse any enthusiasm, and once again the gentry sought relief from the tax and the recruit burdens.

Provisioning of the army remained the gentry's burden in peacetime. The government clothed and armed its soldiers but their maintenance was the responsibility of the inhabitants of the area where troops happened to be stationed as, for example, in a frontier area like Lithuania. Soldiers were dispersed on farms and estates rather than being quartered in town barracks. The troops were entitled to receive lodging, kindling wood, candles and straw gratuitously, and were supposed to pay for their meals. Furthermore, the inhabitants were to accommodate and provide for the troops in transit, including vehicles and horses. Lithuania being generally regarded as a border area populated by "restive elements," troop movements were a constant feature of life. Settlements close to highways suffered most, sometimes 20 men were quartered in a single peasant cottage. The troops requisitioned more than they needed, and paid nothing for the stocks. Complaints were ignored by the military — but if complainants were peasants, they were mercilessly flogged. Landlords quite frequently paid the officers to leave: they signed receipts for the officers who pocketed the money they had supposedly paid, in addition to bribes.

When budgetary figures were analyzed, the gentry discovered that, in 1821, a Russian soldier cost the government 48 kopecks (roughly $0.25) annually. This was not an amusing discovery, and protests were raised. Newly promulgated rules required the army to pay for food and provisions, and local residents to provide shelter and straw mattresses. However, the time-honored Russian proverb said, "God is high above, the Tsar so far away" — and reality differed from the law. Army commanders chose the diets for their troops, confiscated stocks carted to markets by poor serfs, and "shamed" the complainants for not understanding "the Russian system."

Alexander I toured his dominions in 1816 and observed his noblemen. Lithuanians had their cultural centers of learning and were deeply conscious of their national, local, religious and class affairs, and had no ambition to serve in Russia. Steeped with centuries-old traditions, they were conscious at all times of being representatives of their country and class, and in meeting the Tsar they were self-respecting, dignified, and well-mannered. Russian nobles "were incapable of uttering a word in the Tsar's presence, they just bowed low abjectly to show their obedience to him. They looked like entertaining maitres-d'hôtel, rather than deputies of the nobility."[20] When class institutions of the nobility were authorized for the entire European Russia, there was no lack of qualified candidates and electors in Lithuania. Noblemen were few in Russia, sometimes as many as elective offices to be filled. The government tolerated occasional discussion of the abolition of serfdom in Lithuania, but squashed any talk on that theme in Russia Proper. Ultimately, officials of the nobility became subservient to salaried officialdom in Russia, while they remained respected and influential spokesmen in Lithuania.

Alexander I abandoned his pose of a liberal monarch in 1819 and turned reactionary. He paid heed to Senator Novosiltsov, his brother Constantine's adviser in Warsaw. Novosiltsov became "strongly enamored of Lithuania" and "lightly and cleverly tossed several suspicions regarding the inclinations and spirit of Lithuanian youths" in Vilnius. Indeed, a "mutiny condoned by the Rector" was detected at the university in 1823. Arrests were made, the Rector was retired, Prince Adam Czartoryski was removed as Curator and replaced by Novosiltsov. The latter installed Pelikan as Rector, "his dastardly creature who spied on youths and filled prisons with them, and who during the insurrection of 1831 was caned on a Vilnius street." The Masons of the Ardent Lithuanian Lodge and student societies of the Filomats, the Filarets and the Philadelphists were disbanded and their members, including Adam Mickiewicz, were arrested. Several professors were fired, about 20 persons were exiled, several hundred youths suffered long imprisonment and tortures for seeking "to develop civic dutifulness and love for one's country."[21] Suggestions for a Lithuanian language chair at the university were rejected.

The Russian occupiers of Lithuania inherited more than 450 elementary and 38 secondary schools, and the Supreme School — the former Jesuit Academy founded in 1569 and chartered in 1579, the oldest university in north-eastern Europe. It was renamed the University of Vilnius in 1803. Subjects were taught mostly in Polish in schools,

[20] Janulaitis, *Lietuvos Bajorai, op. cit.*, citing Baron S. A. Korf, *Dvorianstvo i yego soslovnoye upravleniye za stoletive 1762-1855*, Sankt Peterburg 1906, 436-447.

[21] Ochmański, *Historia Litwy, op. cit.*, 158-160.

in Latin at the university, although elementary Lithuanian grammar, first published in 1775, reprinted in 14 editions by 1796 and 48 more editions by 1864, was used in rural schools. In 1820 there were 430 primary schools with 983 teachers and 21,174 pupils.

Countess Emilija Platerytė / Emily Plateris, 1806-1831, Lithuanian folklorist, captain in the Insurrection of 1831; taking St. Joan of Arc as her model.

VI.
REDUCTION OF THE NOBILITY RANKS

Recruit levies from the ranks of serfs provided the enlisted personnel, and noblemen were to provide the officer corps for the Tsar's armed forces. The Russian gentry readily joined the military and civil services. Lithuanian noblemen, however, were more numerous and yet they had to be coaxed to serve. Only a handful of young gentlemen joined the Lithuanian Corps formed in 1817 under Grand Duke Constantine, the satrap of Poland, and none wanted a civil service in Russia — as long as vacant posts in Lithuania were given to Russians.

The ukase of 1826 restricted the eligibility for elective nobility offices to persons with certain educational qualifications and proofs of nobility, who had performed either military or civil service. The ukase clearly differentiated between the landed gentry *(dvorianstvo)* and the petty yeomanry *(shlyakhta)* listed separately since the revision of 1817. Electoral rights were limited to noblemen owning at least eight serf homesteads. However, tenant noblemen did not readily surrender their franchise and demanded at least a fixed ratio of votes: one deputyship for each bloc of eight yeoman homesteads. Some gentry supported them and the government seemed to be disposed favorably toward extending such voting rights to petty noblemen, yet no law was enacted.

Educational qualifications for elective offices formed no obstacle to Lithuanians. Proofs of nobility were something else. The "ancient noblemen" were listed in "Book Six" dating back at least a century — it was only in 1850 that the government rolled back the "ancient noblemen's" classification to those who proved that their families had been noble a century prior to the royal charter of April 21, 1785. Revenue officials were satisfied with the reference to nobility rolls of 1796, as they were authorized to do by law in 1817.

Dietines complained of the difficulties of obtaining proofs since the removal of the Lithuanian state archives to Russia. "Derivative deputations" *(deputacja wywodowa)* were formed in each gouvernement to screen available proofs of nobility for transmission to the Heraldry Department of the Senate in St. Petersburg. The Heraldry demanded Russian translations of the documents, and costs were prohibitive to poorer claimants. During the Napoleonic wars proofs were examined perfunctorily, and the ukase of 1808 allowed the "derivative deputations" to attest the claims — in effect postponing the final decision. Lower grade officials continued to be named, even after 1831, without the complete proofs of nobility, on the basis of a derivative deputation's certificate supported by an additional document to the effect that the person in question was not entered on the rolls of the tax-paying strata — that one was neither a peasant nor a burgher. Such proofs were to be transmitted to the Heraldry for verification within six months. Those with unsatisfactory proofs could still remain in service, except that their grade was lowered and they had to serve six years before qualifying as commissioned officers.

By 1828 several classes of lesser noblemen were distinguished. Husbandmen of large and small farms, either as owners or tenants, did not differ from freedmen peasants. Some landless hereditary noblemen were servants, artisans, professionals, or minor officials. The exact number of poor noblemen was not known and their doubtful status caused them difficulties with the Russian authorities which had known no such classes in Russia. The numerous poor freemen not subjected to the State had to be reckoned with, inasmuch as legally they were the peers of the landed nobility. They had to be subjected. Yet Russia's foreign relations and the proximity of foreign borders advised caution.

Lithuanian "ground tax noblemen" *(činšiniai bajorai, szlachta czyńszowa)* lived on lands which were not their own and paid a fixed ground tax, like the free peasants. The law of 1810 provided that the status of ground-tax noblemen was to be determined by the Ministry of the Interior. Pending solution, the government handled cases on an *ad hoc* basis. During the war of 1812 a ground-tax nobleman was prosecuted for harboring deserters. Penalty to be meted out depended on the offender's class status. A noble was to be fined 200 silver rubles; if unable to pay, he was to be inducted into the military service or, if physically unfit, exiled to Siberia. In the midst of war, Alexander I had no time to deliberate on the case: he confirmed the sentence applicable to noblemen — thus setting a mandatory precedent. Later, in a case involving a Mohylew area resident, the Tsar ruled that a punishment applicable to noblemen could not be condoned, as the defendant had not proved his claim of nobility.

The ukase of 1824 provided that Lithuanian petty noblemen engaged in urban trades or business and not owning serfs, must be listed as merchants and receive burgher passports. In 1829 Nicholas I urged that verification of nobility claims be expedited. His ukase of 1830 provided that all nobility claimants failing to submit proofs must register as either burghers — without requiring the municipalities' consent, or as royal villagers ("treasury peasants") if land be available.

In 1832 Nicholas I formulated a new class — the so-called "honorary citizens" to be ranked alongside the nobility, and provided rules for expulsion from the ranks of the nobility. "Personal nobility" was conferred on military officers and 9th grade civil officials who were enabled to acquire hereditary nobility upon becoming staff officers or grade 5 officials, and grade 14 to 9 officials received "honorary citizenship," essentially a burgher status. Personal nobility entitling one to own serfs was conferred on the Evangelical Lutheran clergy and recipients of imperial decorations. The ukase of 1832 awarded "honorary citizenship" to university graduates, Academy of Arts graduates, alien scientists and artists, capitalists-manufacturers, and children of honorary citizens.

Finally the Ministry of Finance tabulated the data establishing the existence of four categories of yeomanry or petty nobility: (1) land owners with no serfs or less than three serfs; (2) ground-tax noblemen on leased public, church or gentry estates, and tax-free owners of garden plots and homes; (3) noblemen tenants of estates with serfs; (4) noblemen mortgagees who had lent money to owners and were managing tne farm in lieu of collecting the interest.[22]

[22]Various types and prerogatives of nobility are documented in Janulaitis, *Lietuvos Bajorai*, *op. cit.*, 410-435.

VII.
THE INSURRECTION OF 1831 AND THE AFTER-EFFECTS

Immediately after "the November Insurrection" broke out in Poland, Nicholas I on December 1/13, 1830 proclaimed martial law in Lithuania and by a rescript voiced his trust that the Lithuanian nobility would remain loyal to him. Civil Governor Horn convoked county marshals and demanded supplemental taxes, and these were dutifully voted within six days.

The Lithuanian peasants and petty noblemen revolted in February, 1831. The "manifestoes of the insurrection" differed in the various counties. The nation's freedom based on individual liberty and the equality of all inhabitants was proclaimed in the Raseiniai and Upytė counties. The Telšiai county spoke explicitly of the peasant right to land ownership. Indeed, Samagite peasants expressly stated that they were enlisting "to fight for myself and not for the lord" and inventory duties were discontinued.[23]

After the momentary success of the rebels, Muscovite troops under General Diebitsch were able to maintain their hold on the cities and to overcome the revolt. A Polish relief column arrived too late, and most of the Poles crossed over into Prussia, except the Dembiński task force of about 3,500 Polish regulars and Lithuanian guerrillas who fought their way into Poland. Countess Emily Zyberk-Plater, a Lithuanian folklorist and a guerrilla company commander, died of wounds during the retreat and was buried at Kapčiamiestis in Sudavia. She became the subject of inspired poetry by Adam Mickiewicz, and others, including Louise Anne Twamley.[24]

Russian reprisals were most brutal. In addition to indiscriminate

[23]Jurgėla, *History. . ., op. cit.*, 410-416.

[24]*Ibidem.* Several hundred Polish and Lithuanian rebels were exiled to America on board of Austrian naval vessels, including Alexander Bielaski from Lithuania. Bielaski became Abraham Lincoln's friend and died a hero's death for the Union before Belmont, Mo. in November, 1861, as Captain of an Illinois regiment. Major Joseph Hordynski of the 10th regiment of Lithuanian Lancers (of the Polish relief column) had come to the U.S. with Samuel Gridley Howe's aid and published, by subscriptions, *The History of the Late Polish Revolution.* He detailed the operations of the Giełgud Corps in Lithuania and added a supplement on History of Lithuania. The book was published in Boston in three editions, 1832-1833. The author purchased arms and sailed back to Europe — and perished during an attempt to cross the frontier to Russia.

executions, tortures and arson by troops, the ukase of May 6/18, 1831, placed a sequester on the estates of the "mutineers." During the operations of the Polish relief corps, Nicholas promised an amnesty to those returning voluntarily, swearing their loyalty and receiving a certificate to that effect. The clergy were ordered to report the dates when the Tsar's manifesto was read in their churches. When the rebels retreated, the ukase of October 4, 1831 withheld further amnesties. County marshals were ordered to report the names of "mutineers." The marshals indignantly disclaimed any knowledge thereof. On September 16/28 a Western Committee "for consideration of various proposals regarding gouvernements annexed from Poland" was named by the Tsar. This was to be an independent secret body of six members — five Cabinet ministers and Senator Novosiltsov. It was abolished in 1848 and later restored. It was this body which deliberated upon the problems of petty noblemen, peasants, the reorganization of the school system. It recommended the closing of the University of Vilnius, abrogated the Lithuanian Statute, promoted Orthodoxy, russification and colonization.

The authorities found it most convenient to conscript rebel suspects into the army and their children into military cantonments. The Tsar authorized this by two ukases and directed that he was to be consulted in cases involving noblemen. The Cabinet was soon overtaxed with inquiries from overzealous commanders: too many children were being seized, including noblemen's children who could not, under law, lose their noble status by reason of their parents' crimes. The Cabinet recommended leniency: if masses of noble youths were seized, they would spread contagious spirit of rebellion throughout the armed forces. Available orphanages and schools could not accommodate all, and if those under 12 years of age were allowed to grow up at the side of their parents, they would mature rebellious against Russia. With economy and industry laid in ruins by the rebellion, too many lands remained uncultivated, and the appearance of thousands of beggars would aggravate the situation. The Cabinet recommended that the number of repressable people be limited: temporary conscription would not hurt the army much, children should be dispersed far and wide in the interior.

Nicholas I disliked this softness and wrote: "the gentry are those who own estates or upon whom the rank was conferred after service, while the *szlachta* are but a conglomeration of vagabonds. . . . who roam in idleness and serve others, and compose a most harmful and dissipated class. I hereby confirm my previously expressed will to the effect that, without any exceptions, all the children of these people — who were unmasked, convicted, killed or are missing — be classed as undeniably belonging to the jurisdiction of the military department."[25] The Tsar ordered that in the former territories of the Grand Duchy of Lithuania and in the department of Kiev children of the rebels be seized. All acts of mercy were reserved to the Tsar. Some leniency was later shown to families whose male heads personally tilled their land. When the Cabinet enacted in 1832 a law to banish Podolian petty noblemen to populate military settlements in the Crimea — the Tsar extended the law to apply in all Western areas.[26] Proceeds of the confiscated estates were applied to defray military costs, and structures confiscated in cities were to be turned over to the army.

Efforts were intensified to lure Lithuanian noblemen into military or civil posts in Russia where they could be conveniently watched — and at the same time relieve the shortage of educated officialdom. The dietines requested in 1843 that franchise be restored to those who had taken part in the revolt of 1831. The request was denied. In 1847 some exceptions were cautiously permitted: Governors General were authorized to accept ex-rebels into the civil service after apprising the Minister of the Interior and the Chief of Gendarmerie, and receiving the Tsar's consent.[27]

In 1835 the Tsar ordered a campaign against "the absenteeism" of noblemen from military and civil services. In the Western areas, no one was to be eligible henceforth for elective offices of the nobility, unless he had served at least 10 years in the military or civil service, except those who had served two consecutive three-year terms in elective posts. Vacancies in the nobility's institutions were to be filled by the Ministry of the Interior. In 1836 exceptions were extended to those wounded while in the military service, those who had gained commissions during the hostilities against mutineers, and the holders of decorations. Finally in 1852 Nicholas I imposed an outright *duty* of the noblemen to serve in Russia. Sons of lords owning at least 100 male serfs must enter the military service at the age of 16-18. Those passing the examinations entered the Cadet Corps schools, those failing — were to serve as pri-

[25] Jurgėla, *History. . .* , *op. cit.*, 417-418; Janulaitis, *Lietuvos Bajorai, op. cit.*, 452-3, citing S.M. Seredonin, *Istorichesky Obzor Deyatelnosti Komiteta Ministrov*, III, St. Peterburg 1902, 63, 59-67.

[26] Jurgėla, *ibid.*, 418-419; Janulaitis, *supra*, 454.

[27] Janulaitis, *supra*, 457.

vates with noblemen's privileges. The volunteers passing the examinations could choose their branch of service and their unit. Civil service entrants, except those physically incapacitated, must serve in the interior of Russia. Obligatory tenure was to be five years.

A number of problems arose, including a premonition that too many civil servants from Lithuania might settle in proximate areas. Nicholas I found a solution: in the absence of vacancies in civil service — induct them into the military. Since 1831, close attention was paid to prospective officers' religion and national origin. The 1837 ukase ordered that Western area Catholics desiring to serve in the capital, must first serve five years in the interior of Russia. On his deathbed Nicholas I signed a secret order of February 2/14, 1855: only Russians were to be appointed to police and managerial services on public properties, Russians were to fill all State offices in the Western areas, natives were to be sent to Russia for at least ten years' service.[28]

[28] Janulaitis, *supra*, 462-467.

VIII.
SOCIAL RECLASSIFICATION

The ukase No. 7007 of April 20, 1834 summarized the formal requirements for proofs of the nobility. The basic evidence was to be the *privillegia* (charters) by sovereigns of the Grand Duchy of Lithuania, and attestations from government institutions that one is a descendant of the original grantee. The same rule was to apply regarding family coat of arms and the commissioning of officers. Descendants of municipal officials of the period prior to 1793 were made eligible for the nobility rolls. The right of the Lithuanian Tatars to own land with serfs was reaffirmed in 1838, and young Tatars earning commissions or decorations were deemed to be hereditary noblemen. Children of "personal noblemen" could not be flogged. A central office was established in Vilnius in 1843 to verify claims to nobility arising within the departmental areas of Vilnius, Kaunas, Gardinas and Minsk, and the work was to be completed by 1846. The cut-off term was later extended every few years. Those whose claims were denied — were to be enrolled as either single-homesteaders or citizens (townsmen). Consideration of claims was suspended in 1863. Detailed guidelines regarding the enrollment in other social strata were given in 1856.[29]

Since 1831, the petty noblemen — in the words of Nicholas I "the conglomeration of vagabonds" — had become the principal target for declassification. Large military service quotas were set for them: 10 per 1,100, later 10 per 500 but their service term was cut to 15 years. They were reclassified under various pretexts into the "single-homesteader" and "citizen" strata, or forcibly resettled in Russia. Single-homesteaders and other petty yeomen could not change their domicile. Beside meeting heavy recruit quotas, they paid rent to landlords, per capita taxes to the government, lived in dire poverty — being sustained only by their centuries-old traditions of their being noblemen, masters of their country, former electors of kings, dignitaries and officials. Regardless of their speech at home—they knew they were *Lithuanian* noblemen.

Janulaitis adduces some statistical data regarding their numbers in 1857, when they were still a quarter-million strong:

[29] Janulaitis, *Lietuvos Bajorai, op. cit.*, 467-477.

	VILNIUS GVMT. 1857	KAUNAS GVMT. 1857	GARDINAS GVMT. 1857-1859
Hereditary noblemen	51,900	90,383	ca. 34,182
Personal noblemen	1,557	3,244	4,592
Single-homesteaders	23,324	17,950	11,577
Totals	76,781	111,577	50,351

L. Bičkauskas-Gentvila, a Soviet writer, notes that on the eve of the agrarian reform "the department of Kaunas held the first place in the Russian empire with its number of noblemen. The noblemen made up 9.16% of the entire population of the Kaunas gouvernement, 6.04% of the Vilnius department, 4.69% - Gardinas, 6.03% - Minsk . . . 4.5% - St. Petersburg." According to him, the noblemen of Kaunas area numbered 98,785. Of this number, only 1,019 owned estates with serfs, 34,192 were servants and officials. . . . 9,313 single-homesteaders lived on public lands and 7,629 on the gentry's lands." Liet. Gen. Sergei Gavrilovich Vesselitsky, chairman of the investigative committee for political cases under Governor General Muravyov "the Hangman," recommended in 1863 "to abolish the privileged status of single-homesteaders and the title itself by equating them in all of their duties with presently free peasants." He counted 118,700 single-homesteaders in Kaunas area and "98,785 other noblemen"; 26,706 single-homesteaders and 23,324 other noblemen in Vilnius area.[30]

In 1834 the service tenure of recruits was reduced from 25 years to 20, and some 600,000 conscripts were discharged at one time — to be taken care of by their former masters. Nicholas I noted that these men were around 40 years old, that some were coming home single, others with wives or children, while still others would find adult children at home. The gentry could give these children of ex-servicemen away into cantonments in lieu of providing recruits. Nevertheless, the gentry must take care of the returning ex-servicemen.[31]

The russification drive was pushed cautiously. After the insurrection of 1831 the Polish language was ousted from government institutions. After 1840, signatures of officials were to be subscribed in Russian.

[30]Janulaitis, *Lietuvos Bajorai*, 490; L. Bičkauskas-Gentvila, *1863 m. Sukilimas Lietuvoje*, Vilnius 1958-157; A. F. Smirnov, *Revolyutsionnyie svyazi narodov Rossii i Polshi*, Moskva 1962, 40-41. 371; Jurgėla, *Lietuvos Sukilimas, op. cit.*, 178-179.

[31]Janulaitis, *Lietuvos Bajorai*, 556.

Minutes of the dietine sessions were to be written in two languages, from 1843 — in Russian only. In 1853 the Ministry of the Interior reminded the gentry of the monarch's will: all speeches and all business "in gouvernements annexed from Poland" must be conducted exclusively in Russian.[32] The designations "Lithuanian-Vilna gubernia," "Lithuanian-Grodno gubernia" were dropped in 1840. The Lithuanian Statute — the Code of Laws dating back to XVI century — was abrogated in 1840 and replaced by the Russian Code of Laws. The Medical-Surgical Academy survived until the disclosure of secret societies of students in 1842. A new department of "Kovno" was carved from the western half of the Vilnius gouvernement in 1843. Its first official act was an advertisement for an executioner "with his own instruments," one was hired from Warsaw. The former "Lithuanian gouvernements" became "the Northwestern Country" *(Severo-Zapadnyi Krai).*

The closing of the university in Vilnius did not put an end to "Lithuanian freethinking" as ideas of political emigrés continued to make a deep impact. After much self-recrimination the emigrés in Western Europe became convinced that their insurrections had failed because of the lack of a radical social and agrarian program. The Democratic Society of Paris proclaimed in its manifesto of 1836 that the next insurrection must not be a sorry repetition of the former ones. "The first call to struggle must be: the emancipation of the plebeians, restoration of their title to the lands seized from them, the call to enjoy blessings of independent life by all without differences of religion and birthright." The revolutionary "*Lud Polski*" (The Polish Plebs) of England considered the "common people" to be "the homeland" and demanded a classless society. "The first, the most sacred because based on nature's or more truly God's law, the only untouchable property of man — we deem to be his own strength, his right to use it in a labor of his choice, and then to enjoy the fruits of his labor." A Lithuanian Calvinist, Simon Konarski from "Congress Poland" across the Nemunas River, the former insurrectionist of 1831, returned from France on one of the secret missions to stir a democratic movement. Before his execution in Vilnius in 1838, after much torture, he told his inquisitors: "I will not shed a single drop of my blood for a Poland with a king, even a Pole, rife with privileges." His program for a revolution in Poland and Lithuania was "to end the domination by one of the most powerful states in the world, to liberate serfs with ownership of their land, to en-

[32]*Ibid.*, 572-574.

sure religious, political and social equality, to stamp out privileges and oppression." Louis Mierosławski later preached the like program to delegations of youths from Poland and Lithuania calling on him in France.

Some youths responded. In 1845 the Dalewski brothers formed a secret "Fraternal Union" in Vilnius, renamed the Lithuanian Youths Union the following year. News of the Cracow insurrection and of the massacre in Galicia (1846) aroused both fears and hopes in Lithuania. Peasant disturbances occurred, and Nicholas I noted that "common folks are seething against the gentry" and that Lithuanians were "just waiting to join in the movement, mutiny mongers are constantly on the move."[33] Insurrection was scheduled to erupt in Vilnius and Kaunas on March 28, 1849, yet the leaders procrastinated and the plot was uncovered. Once again dozens of young exiles trekked to Siberia or into the Tsar's armed forces.

The Tsar was beginning to realize the necessity for reforms and for a solution to the problem of serfdom. In 1837 the dietine of Vilnius proposed to name a committee to draft a project for the emancipation of serfs on the Prussian model. Nicholas I ordered the treasury to verify the number of free and bonded peasants, to compare such data with those of the last three previous revisions, and to monitor the gentry's adherence to the inventories. In connection therewith, several estates were taken over from private landlords because of abuses and cruelties in their treatment of serfs. In 1844 Nicholas I decided to impose compulsory "inventories" on private estates — serf taxes were not to exceed one-third of their income and labor duties had to average six days weekly. In 1852 Governor General Bibikov ordered county marshals to monitor the treatment of serfs again and "to save peasants from ill masters." The revision uncovered a mass of abuses. The ukase of 1847 had allowed freedmen to stay on private estates by concluding "freely negotiated contracts for 6 or 12 years." Instead of offering relief, however, this proved to be a measure of oppression, inasmuch as the gentry initiated mass "emancipation" of their serfs, demanded contracts from their "freemen" and ousted those refusing to negotiate. The ousted "freemen," deprived of all of their property, were then enrolled as townsmen. Cities objected, and the law of 1850 authorized such transfers without the consent of municipalities.[34] The crisis deepened.

[33]Ochmański, *Historia Litwy, op. cit.*, 165-166.

[34]Jurgėla, *Lietuvos Sukilimas,* 181-182; Janulaitis, *Lietuvos Bajorai,* 540-541; Bičkauskas-Gentvila, *1863 m. sukilimas,* 48-49, 55.

IX.
CHURCH UNDER THE TSARS TO 1863

Prussia negotiated with Rome, and in 1797 Pope Pius VI created a new bishopric with the see in Vygriai. It merged the Prussian-acquired areas of the dioceses of Vilnius and Samagitia, and the bishop was made dependent directly on Rome. In 1818 its see was moved to Seinai and the diocese was affiliated with the archdiocese of Warsaw.

Russia's Catherine II herself played Pope. In 1772 she banned publication of Papal bulls and other writs prior to their censorship by St. Petersburg. Monastic orders were forbidden to communicate with their superiors abroad. In 1773 she created, on her own authority, a "metropolitan archdiocese of Mohylew," and named Msgr. Stanislas Bohusz Siestrzencewicz Archbishop. She linked the diocese of Vilnius with Latgale and named her handiwork the Bishopric of Livonia. All Uniate eparchies, with the exception of Polotsk, were abolished, their churches were taken over by the Orthodox, and their believers forcibly "re-united" with the Orthodoxy. Catholic church affairs were to be handled by Catherine's *Justizcollegium* which managed the affairs of the Protestant churches.[35]

Tsar Paul I was agreeable to regulating Church affairs in accommodation, but not necessarily in accord with the Papacy. He was considering restoring the Supreme School of Lithuania, the former Academy of Vilnius, to the Jesuits — disbanded elsewhere in the world. He placed church affairs under a "Roman Catholic Department" apart from the *Justizcollegium.* Papal Nunzio Lorenzo Litta came to St. Petersburg in 1797. The following year the Pope sanctioned a Metropolitanate of Mohylew: the Archbishop was to reside in St. Petersburg and his jurisdiction was extended over the Vilnius and Samagitian dioceses theretofore affiliated with the Primate of Gniezno. Two Uniate eparchies/dioceses were also to be allowed. Nevertheless, the noncanonical "department" remained, with Metropolitan Siestrzencewicz presiding over three clerical and three lay members.

The Department was renamed the Roman Catholic College in 1801 by Tsar Alexander I with a recast membership: in addition to the Metropolitan and his two assistants, six delegates from dioceses were to be elected by noncanonical diocesan "consistories" for 3-year terms.

[35] *Lietuvių Enciklopedija,* vol. VX, Boston 1968, 142: Kun, Dr. K. Gečys, *Katalikiškoji Lietuva,* Chicago 1946, 84, 91.

The College was to administer all Church affairs and represent it before the government — without any "outside" interference: meaning by Rome. Roman Catholic "consistories" imposed on the dioceses were run by government-appointed secretaries who had the right of veto regarding decisions of the bodies. "Thus the Russian government imposed on the Catholic Church a collegial form of administration, similar to Orthodox and Protestant church organizations, and acquired full control over the Catholic Church affairs in Russia."[36]

The chair of Catholic theology at the University of Vilnius, reorganized by Alexander I in 1803, was placed within the department of moral and political sciences, and a "dormitory" was formed to be called the Supreme Seminary of Vilnius. Its professors were chosen by University Senate — not by bishops. In 1842 the seminary was moved to St. Petersburg and in 1843 renamed the Roman Catholic Spiritual Academy. All diocesan seminaries were placed under the Academy's guidance and Tsar Nicholas I bestowed upon it the title of an "Imperial Academy."

Since the death of Bishop John Kossakowski of Vilnius in 1808, the diocese was administered on an *ad hoc* basis and had no canonically-named bishop until 1856. "During the period of 110 years (1808-1918) the Vilnius diocese had Ordinary bishops (for only 33 years), and during the other 77 years it was administered by temporary administrators or Capitular Vicars. Bishop Jerome Strojnowski (1808-1815) did not even reside in Vilnius. Archbishop Siestrzencewicz administered that diocese from St. Petersburg between 1816 and 1826. Other bishops entering upon their duties were ousted by the government and deported to interior Russia.

"The Samagitian diocese was more fortunate. Bishop-prince Joseph Arnulf Giedraitis held the see from 1801 to 1835. A well-educated pastor, he strove to maintain schools in every parish. He visited parishes, defended peasants from overburdening duties, planned to establish a central hospital, promoted education, literature and the arts, and gathered at his see in Alsėdžiai a number of authors writing in Lithuanian. He himself translated the New Testament and published it in Vilnius at his own cost." In 1805 the Tsar appointed an Auxiliary — Msgr. Ignatius Giedraitis, who was not confirmed by Rome for a long time. When Bishop Joseph Arnulf Giedraitis died, "Tsar Nicholas I blocked the appointment of a new bishop and between 1844 and 1850 the diocese was administered by Canon Gintyla designated 'Suffragan

[36]Gečys, *supra*, 91-92.

Bishop' by the Tsar in 1840. Nicholas demanded that the Holy See name his appointee the bishop. Pope Gregory XVI noted on the Tsar's letter: 'Gintyllo nunquam episcopus' (Gintyla shall never be a bishop). Similarly, after the demise of Bishop Valančius, for eight years the government did not allow appointment of a new bishop and the diocese was administered by Suffragan A. Beresnevičius."[37]

All Catholic, Evangelical and Orthodox church estates with serfs were nationalized or secularized in 1841-1842, and the clergy thereafter were to be paid nominal salaries for keeping birth, marriage and death records. Former church properties were called "majorates." Janulaitis notes that nominal salaries were not adequate for sustenance: "The Russians calculated that if the clerical profession were made unprofitable, fewer people would become churchmen."[38] On the other hand, according to Ochmański, nationalization of church lands increased the acreage of undistributed state lands. In mid-19th century, "31.5% of the population (222,147 persons of both sexes) in the gouvernement of Vilnius lived on public lands, and 35.2% (202,202) in the gouvernement of Kaunas." Thanks to reforms of 1840-1857, the condition of these people improved somewhat and was much better than that of those on private estates. Around 1860 — in the department of Vilnius, 2,096 lords owned 195,818 male subjects; in the department of Kaunas 1,547 lords owned 174,015 male 'souls'."[39]

In addition to claiming the prerogative of appointing bishops, the Tsars asserted their right to control episcopal communications with Rome. Bishops were not to travel outside the limits of their dioceses without the government's permission. They were not to found new parishes, name pastors and curates, appoint seminary rectors and professors, admit seminarians, confer honors on clergymen, form religious fraternities, establish libraries, publish church calendars and other books —without the government's consent and censorship. In 1842 Pope Gregory XVI published a collection of documents detailing Russian interference in church affairs. This information produced publicity adverse to Russia, and Nicholas I then tried to come to an understanding. A concordat was concluded in 1847. However, it was not published in Russia and thus never acquired a binding legal effect. It provided that

[37]Gečys, *supra*, 93-94; *Lietuvių Enciklopedija* XV, 142-143.

[38]Janulaitis, *Lietuvos Bajorai, op. cit.*, 548-551.

[39]Ochmański, *Historia Litwy, op. cit.*, 167-168.

bishops would be appointed by Popes in agreement with the government of Russia. Bishops canonically dependent on the Apostolic See were to be the sole administrators of their dioceses. They were to name seminary officials and consistory members with the consent of the Ministry of the Interior. In practice, however, Russia never honored the concordat: Bishop Valančius of Samagitia in his report to the Pope for the year 1862 listed the violations on 24 pages. Nevertheless, the concordat enabled the appointment of good bishops. A second concordat concluded in 1882 by Pope Leo XIII and Tsar Alexander III likewise remained a dead letter.

Oppression was intensified after the insurrection of 1831. Monasteries were labeled the nests of Latin propaganda and rebellion: 353 monasteries were shut down in Lithuania by 1893, and only six remained by 1914. Their structures were converted into prisons, army hospitals and barracks, and Russian schools. In 1832 Nicholas I banned uncensored sermons. In 1868 curates and filialists were deprived of the right to say sermons. Only one sermon was to be said Sundays and the police were in attendance to monitor sermons. In one instance the priest read the Gospel about a penitant tax collector beating his breast and begging for God's mercy. The gendarme who understood some Lithuanian reported to the county chief: "I stood by the door and heard the pastor say: 'Look who is standing by the doorway — here the priest pointed at me —he does not even dare to raise his eyes. You know why he had come here. Have mercy on me, beat up that scoundrel.' On hearing this, the people glared angrily at me. I felt it was going to be bad for me and I dashed out from the church." Dr. Gečys notes that the pastor was quite astonished when he was fined a hundred rubles for insulting a policeman inside the church, and the bishop was ordered to transfer this pastor to a poorer parish.[40]

Dr. Gečys itemizes "unconditional injunctions" to bishops and clergy since 1831. They may be summarized briefly: no Catholic "propaganda" (the term also used in the Soviet Constitution) among the Orthodox; no baptizing of children of mixed families where one of the parents is an Orthodox; no marriage ceremony involving an Orthodox party. No confessions and no administering of sacraments to communicants from other parishes and strangers generally, except in cases of serious illness or when the visitor is from afar; a person desiring to go to confession in

[40]Gečys, *Katalikiškoji Lietuva, op. cit.,* 119-120. Rev. Stasys Yla advises that "a recent well documented Rome dissertation by Rev. Vaičiulėnas deals most adequately with the Russian efforts to paralyze the Catholic Church."

a parish not one's own, must present a certificate from one's own pastor that he or she is a Roman Catholic; all such cases must be recorded in special books.

The really heavy blows came after the outbreak of the insurrection of 1862-1864.

Bishop Motiejus Kazimieras / Mathias Casimir / Valančius, 1801-1875.

X.
THE TEMPERANCE MOVEMENT

One of the most remarkable phenomena of the Lithuanian resistance and of the peasants' entrance into the arena of political struggle in behalf of their country, was the great Temperance Movement initiated by Bishop Mathias Casimir Valančius of Samagitia on the eve of the political demonstrations, agrarian reform and the great popular upheaval of 1862-1864. This movement conditioned the toilers to mass action and coordination. According to Dr. Gečys, "Bishop Valančius through his temperance fraternities notably elevated the religious and moral standards of the masses, eased the hard lot of serfs, shielded them from exploitation, penury and debasement, made them useful to their country. . . . Through temperance fraternities he strove to bring the people's strata and classes closer together, to remind them of their obligations, goals, and the common enemy of all. . . . He awakened in their hearts the dormant national awareness which several decades later became the foundation of statehood and independent life."[41]

There was a remarkably high degree of literacy among Lithuanian peasants in a country with practically no public schools. This was achieved by small parochial elementary and catechetic schools in every parish of Samagitia, where the clergy and some noblemen were gradually breaking away from the selfish and self-centered Polish-speaking gentry. The circulation of books and farmer almanacs published in Lithuanian by Laurynas Ivinskis was rapidly increasing, their content and literary quality was improving. This development caused revulsion among some Polonized gentry and townsmen who insisted that the tongue of the common folk was fit only for elementary reading.

Bishop Valančius initiated his drive in 1858 with the call to "Renew the common folk through temperance!" During his visitation of parishes he urged his rural audiences to cease drinking alcoholic beverages. In some parishes he personally administered vows of temperance and enrolled the names of abstainers. Encouraged by his initial success, the bishop in his circular letter of October 11, 1858 urged his priests and members of religious orders: "Lest you should be likened to pharisees who were reprimanded by Christ for placing upon others a burden which they themselves refuse to touch, I voice to all of you, beloved priests in

[41] *Ibid.*, 183.

Christ, my most ardent desire that you yourselves should not drink, should not offer whiskey or rum to others, and thus should yourselves provide the example to be followed by your flocks of the faithful." By a circular dated November 1, 1858 the bishop invited members of the diocesan Chapter and of the Consistory, professors and students of the theological seminary, and his cathedral assistants to join in the temperance campaign. And they did — "with no exceptions," according to Dr. Gečys. "They knew that the bishop in his activities accepted no compromise, no alibi, no exemption on the grounds of birthright or nobility. . . . Whoever did not wish to appear delinquent or be retired early as an emeritus — became active. . . . In his pastoral letter of January 30, 1860 the bishop proudly rejoiced over the diligence and devotion of his clergy in the drive for temperance. . . . The epoch-making drive of the bishop had been won. It was an imposing and wonder-evoking sight to adjacent dioceses, to the widestretched Russian empire, and to the bishop and his clergy themselves. After he had firmly established temperance in the masses, the bishop by a pastoral letter of March 14, 1859 urged the landed gentry to contribute to the noble task — to cease distilling liquor, to close their taverns and join in the temperance movement."[42]

Professor Augustinas Janulaitis, a former socialdemocratic underground revolutionary, approaches the phenomenon from a somewhat different angle. He notes "new winds in Lithuanian writings. Brochures were published. This activity at once encountered the gentry's opposition. . . . They disliked the stirring of the masses. The dream of Daukantas of having a Lithuanian secondary school and enlightened masses could not be realized, of course. The Russian government did not permit a Lithuanian language newspaper, regardless of the strong backing by Bishop Valančius and Prince Ireneus Ogiński. The Government's policies coincided with the gentry's economic interests. Both feared the awakening of the masses. . . . The number of people dissatisfied with landed lords was growing. Parish pastors gradually alienated themselves from lords. The peasants and petty noblemen among the clergy looked askance at great lords. Bishop Valančius cautiously but purposefully strove through his clergy to sway the masses of commoners toward himself and make them his mainstays. With this in view he penned, printed and disseminated booklets in the Lithuanian language. Some clergy were distinctly disaffected with lords, their usage of the Polish language and their publications, and they created their own writings.

[42] Gečys, *ibid.*, 183-185.

Priests were the first to organize the plebs on broad scale when the opportunity presented itself. The form was strictly moral-religious, yet it had social, even national undertones."[43]

The Polish-speaking, -reading and -oriented younger generation of noblemen, army officers, students and youths in general developed a populist outlook not at all opposed to the Lithuanian language of the masses, and a manuscript "newspaper" in Lithuanian made its appearance among students in Moscow. They were strongly influenced by the writings of political emigrés. On the other hand, through his temperance movement Bishop Valančius for the first time aroused and swayed the masses on the broadest scale. No fraternities were ever mentioned. Priests themselves had not realized at first that temperance societies were being formed. When the temperance campaign proved highly popular, fraternity features emerged — rules, medallions, certificates, enrollment books of abstainers in each parish. When the government ultimately enjoined him to disband societies, the bishop was able to say that the movement was entirely spontaneous and religious, and that he had no hand in forming the societies.

Russian authorities and gentlemen brewers may have been amused at first with the peasant and townsmen extravaganza. Suddenly the temperance movement grew like a wildfire engulfing all of Samagitia and the Lithuanian-speaking areas of the diocese of Vilnius, spreading eastward and southward into Whiteruthenian areas and attracting the attention of Russian liberals in St. Petersburg, notably Chernyshevsky and Dobrolyubov who published articles by James Gieysztor and other Lithuanian moderates of the noble class. "Upon the demand of Governor General Nazimov of Vilnius, the bishop on July 25, 1860 presented membership data of the temperance fraternities in the department of Kaunas. Of the 832,243 Catholic inhabitants of 197 parishes, temperance societies embraced 692,000 or 83.2%. Only 140,243 persons or 16.8% were not members. . . . In the Courland department which was part of the Samagitian diocese at the time, temperance membership among the Catholic [minority] embraced 87.1%. . . . At the behest of Bishop Adam Stanislas Krasiński, of the 626,178 Catholics of the Vilnius department — 325,261 or 51.9% joined the temperance fraternities, and in the Gardinas department — of the 193,373 Catholics, 114,640 or 59% joined the temperance movement."

Dr. Casimir Gečys, the most authoritative researcher of the temperance movement, notes that whiskey distillation in the Kaunas depart-

[43] Aug. Janulaitis, *1863-1864 m. Sukilimas Lietuvoje*, Kaunas 1921, 8-9.

ment dropped 46.5% in 1858 and 87.5% in 1859. The demand or sales of whiskey dropped 67.4% in 1859 and decreased daily in 1860. In the Kaunas department "692,000 non-drinkers accumulated savings of over 45 million rubles. In those days this represented a colossal sum. . . . The temperance movement was disastrous for state revenues and distilleries, yet it was socially most beneficient to the country."

Dr. Gečys stresses that "the triumph of Bishop M. K. Valančius was all the greater, since within his diocese he had overwhelmed the real enemies of the people. Some of the latter publicized fabricated 'orders' of the Governor General to drink whiskey, others lowered whiskey prices, still others distributed whiskey gratuitously, and there were those who spread rumors to the effect that members of temperance movements would have to recompense tavern keepers for their great losses. In 1860 Governor General Vladimir Nazimov reported to the Council of Ministers in St. Petersburg: "The living conditions of peasants notably improved in localities dominated by temperance. There is affluence in place of famine; good and warm clothing replaced the rags; the hardly earned kopeck is being saved for dark hours, taxes are paid on time; time and physical strength are utilized for efficient work; the beneficial influence of temperance is obvious even in their health and physical fitness, these basic conditions for their welfare."

The astounding movement unleashed by Bishop Valančius reached St. Petersburg and the Russian interior. "And thus a similar temperance fraternity was formed 9,500 versts away from Kaunas, in the Saratov department on the Volga. The Orthodox clergy of the department of Kaunas, not wanting to remain sideline observers, also began to preach temperance in 1859. The Orthodox Church Synod in a circular letter of September 7, 1859 urged all bishops and diocesan administrators to preach temperance." According to Dr. Gečys, this was an abortive attempt, "lacking in leadership, inner convictions and strength."[44]

The Lithuanian temperance movement seriously hurt excise revenues. Prof. Janulaitis points out that Count Reynold Tyzenhauz, who owned 9,000 serfs in the Vilnius gouvernement alone, had to shut down all of his distilleries, and only three of his 47 taverns remained open. He cites statistics:

Vilnius gvmt.	1858 excise tax paid for	1,072,733 buckets
	1859 excise tax paid for	662,841 buckets
Kaunas gvmt.	1855 excise tax paid for	934,475 buckets
	1859 excise tax paid for	304,970 buckets

[44]Gečys, *Katalikiškoji Lietuva, op. cit.*, 185-189.

In the county of Šiauliai — 35,000 rubles were collected in excise taxes for alcoholic beverages in 1858; five months later — only 500 rubles. According to Janulaitis, "the priests were combatted by excise revenue collectors, Jewish tavern keepers, gentlemen distillers; this was a hard struggle, in part a political struggle against the gentry for influence [over the masses]."[45]

The gentry, enjoying the brewing monopoly and profits from tavern concessionaires, appealed to the government and accused their own Catholic clergy of political incitement. In 1859 Governor General Nazimov officially banned all temperance fraternities within the Northwestern Territory, and the officials went out of their way to promote drunkenness. At Nowogrodek a barrel of vodka was placed across the street from the Catholic church and free drinks were offered — one woman was burned alive in the ensuing revelry of Whiteruthenian peasants. Governor General Nazimov who, as we have seen, was perfectly aware of the beneficial effects of the temperance movement and reported so in his confidential memorandum to the Council of Ministers, presently at Rietavas in Samagitia drank a toast of *krupnikas* (Lithuanian honey liqueur) to the peasants' health and told them that, in the climactic conditions of the country, drinking of vodka was essential to their health, and that Christ Himself drank.

When the government became actively engaged in suppressing the temperance movement, some gentry came to the aid of fraternities. Several gentlemen of the county of Zarasai (Novo Aleksandrovsk) proposed at the county dietine that all distilleries be closed for two years. Soon the wave of pseudo-religious "manifestations" spread, and the drive against drunkenness coincided with the related political struggle.[46] The temperance drive, strongly elevating the Catholic Church influence in Lithuania, did not disappear with Nazimov's injunction order: five years later his successor in the Governor General's chair by a circular order of April 24, 1864 forbade the preaching of temperance from pulpits in the Samagitian diocese and threatened with courts martial and heavy fines.

On the eve of the great political upheaval of 1862-1864, the Lithuanian people were identifiable within three mainstreams: (1) the conservative Polish- and French-speaking landed aristocracy with ready access to St. Petersburg's high society circles and local satraps who —

[45] Janulaitis, *1863-1864 m. Sukilimas, op. cit.*, 9.

[46] Jurgėla, *History of the Lithuanian Nation, op. cit.*, 424-426.

like Muravyov in Vilnius and Berg in Warsaw — likewise corresponded with each other in French; (2) the predominantly Polish-speaking middle class gentry and townsmen whose younger "populist" generation of students and army officers was greatly influenced by political emigrés and the liberal circles of Warsaw; and (3) the Lithuanian-speaking and deeply religious mass of serfs, free peasants, petty noblemen and some middle gentry influenced by Bishop Mathias Casimir Valančius and his disciplined clergy with a populist outlook.[47]

[47] Jurgėla, *Lietuvos Sukilimas, op. cit.*, 20.

XI.

THE AGRARIAN REFORM OF 1861 AND THE "MANIFESTATIONS"

In January 1857 Emperor Alexander II appointed a "Secret Committee to consider measures regarding estate peasants" and in March he named a smaller "preparatory commission to review laws on the problem of serfdom" consisting of Prince Gagarin, Baron Korff, Adjutant General Rostovtsev and State Secretary Butkov. Toward the end of April Rostovtsev prepared a memorandum expressing truly "Western" ideas. He wrote: "No reasoning, educated and patriotic person could oppose the emancipation of serfs. A man must not belong to another man. A man should not be a chattel." This commission recommended gradual emancipation. The Secret Committee approved the general reasoning of the preparatory commission, yet made no conclusions and transmitted the memorandum to the Tsar who was vacationing at Kissingen in Germany. Prince A. M. Gorchakov added Gastenhausen's notations to the effect that "the radical Mazzini party and his friends in England base their principal hopes on a social revolution in Russia. And experience teaches us that this party's leaders are no daydreamers, that they are precise calculators and clever," and the matter cannot be delayed "for centuries." One cannot stop half-way and the government "must act in a reasoned and active manner, lest events overtake . . . and wrest from it concessions which would lead to its fall." The Tsar concurred and enlarged the Secret Committee by adding his brother, Grand Duke Constantine. Finally it was decided "to start with the Western and frontier gouvernements which, because of their abutting on countries where serfdom had been abolished, are better conditioned to accept freedom in the sense of mores and economics." Governor General Nazimov, commissioned by the Tsar, convinced the nobility of the departments of Vilnius, Kaunas and Gardinas to undertake the initiative.

By his rescript of November 20/December 2, 1857, the Tsar was able to answer "the humble petition" of the noblemen of the Lithuanian gouvernements which requested that, rather than revise inventory regulations, peasants be emancipated from the bonded condition and the gentry retain title to their lands. The Tsar lauded the Lithuanian nobility and "allowed" the formation, in each of the three departments, of landlord committees to draft preliminary projects within six months. A "General Committee" in Vilnius was to study the three drafts and prepare an overall draft project within the next six months. Governor General Nazimov likewise praised "the dignity and enlightened wisdom" of the noblemen of his area who were "the first in the entire Russian state to propound a noble way to improve the situation of the peasants." This was the formal stage-managed basis for the so-called Agrarian Reform of 1861. [48]

The most unusual feature of these developments was that while in Russia the liberals and the reactionaries were allowed to publish their views and projects with regard to the proposed reform, no discussion was permitted in Lithuania where the reform had supposedly originated. Lithuanians were obliged to voice their views in the emigré press and in books published abroad.

The most notable voices were those of Oskar Korwin Milewski, the reactionary *(Uwagi nad kwestją włościańską na Litwie* — Comments on the Peasant Problem in Lithuania, Paryž 1858), and of James Gieysztor, the future leader of the insurrection who was generally identified with "Whites" even though the latter dubbed him "Red." Gieysztor spoke up for granting land ownership to peasants *(Głos Szlachcica do swych współbraci o wolności i równości kmieciej* — A Nobleman's Voice to his fraternity regarding peasant freedom and equality, Polznań 1859). The emigré paper in Paris *(Przegląd Rzeczy Polskich* — Review of Polish Affairs) likewise argued that "peasants are aspiring to gain ownership of that which belongs to them . . . and they will get it peacefully with or without the Gentry's consent, through the Tsar or without him. Whoever wants to help his country must extend his hand to the peasants, must give them the land, and must convince them that the Tsar's ukases are but weak echoes of the changes which a reborn independent homeland shall effect for the good of the society."

Finally on February 19/March 3, 1861 Alexander II enacted his Agrarian Reform. Nazimov wired for permission to publish the manifesto in Lithuanian translation, and copies thereof were circulated throughout the countryside to be proclaimed publicly. The reform contained "Local Guidelines regarding landgrants to peasants of the gentry estates in the gouvernements of Vilnius, Gardinas, Kaunas, Minsk and parts of the Vitebsk gouvernement." Special guidance was needed because of conditions in the former areas of Lithuania differing from those in Russia. For instance, while there were communal land-

[48] *Ibid.*, 186-187.

holdings in Russia, peasants here possessed and tilled their own individual plots, their corvées were regulated by inventories, and there were different types of tenancy and servitudes.

The guidelines pertained only to bonded peasants on private estates who tilled their allotted plots. By 1861 private lords owned 69.5% of all the cultivated land area in the department of Vilnius and 74.6% in the department of Kaunas, with three-quarter of a million bonded serfs in the combined area. Landgrant allotments were to be selected by landlords who were authorized to move their peasants and reassign their plots. Peasants were to acquire title to their plots after making payments to the state pro-rated over forty-nine and a half years. Meanwhile they were to continue their corvées and certain duties for nine years in accordance with "regulatory writs" to be negotiated by them with their lords. These rules enabled the greedy to abuse their former serfs by taking away their good soil fields, by depriving them of pastures, timber, kindlewood, fishing and hunting rights which they were to purchase from landlords at prices and conditions set by landlords, and by ousting the dissenters. Conflicts over the gross abuses erupted immediately.

The basic Reform Act did not at all affect other classes of peasants. There were "royal peasants" on public ("treasury") estates — 207,807 in the Vilnius area and 205,523 in the Kaunas department, plus about 20,000 peasants of the "majorates" or former church estates in the Kaunas area and 11,000 in the Vilnius department. 29% of these "state peasants" in the gouvernement of Kaunas and 19% in the department of Vilnius were either totally landless or possessors of just garden plots. There were other types of landless servants and laborers. Finally there were the most wretched proletarians with no property and no assured shelter: the ex-soldiers. In 1862, in the department of Kaunas there were 3,171 men who had served their full term as "recruits," 1,439 children of soldiers, and 3,114 servicemen released into the reserves before their full term of 20 or 25 years was served. In the department of Vilnius there were 3,354 full-term veterans, 3,735 released soldiers and 4,783 soldiers' wives. Only 939 service veterans had small land plots. The rest offered their labor for hire.[49]

Regardless of the actual clauses and guidelines of the reform, peasants believed their own "interpreters" and refused to perform corvées or to sign regulatory writs, believing that they were set free by the Tsar with the title to their personal parcels which they tilled and regarded as their

[49] Jurgėla, *Lietuvos Sukilimas, op. cit.*, 192.

own. Landlords called for "military executions," and Russian troops settled down to live off the land and to beat the peasants into submission. These military executions, 117 in the department of Kaunas alone, accompanied by floggings, canings, robberies, abuses and dispossessions strained peasant "freedmen" to the boiling point. Stubborn Lithuanians would not submit to slave labor, and there were numerous instances of arson and sabotage on manorial estates. By the time of the insurrection only 6.4% of peasants in the department of Kaunas and 9.67% in the gouvernement of Vilnius had signed regulatory writs imposed on them by brute force.

The turbulent socio-economic unrest was aggravated by the simultaneous political unrest of the period of "manifestations." The fever of demonstrations already engulfing Poland was brought to Lithuania by cadets of Mierosławski's Polish Military School in Paris. The first manifestation led by former cadets and their fellow students from universities in Russia occurred on St. Stanislas feastday, May 8, 1861, in St. Stanislas cathedral in Vilnius, where the crowd sang a patriotic hymn. Some students were arrested. However, huge crowds encircling the Governor General's palace, the former Episcopal palace, later called Napoleon's, then Kutuzov's and Red Army Officers Palace, influenced Nazimov to release the detainees.

The fad of manifestations spread rapidly. Manifestations were held under various pretexts — some patriot's or professor's birthday, a death anniversary, a funeral. Fraternization of classes was the vogue in rural communities — where noblemen danced with peasant girls and broke bread with peasants who generally frowned on such frolics during the period of agrarian strife. One huge demonstration to commemorate the union with Poland was arranged on the frontier bridge over the Nemunas River in Kaunas. A crowd from Kaunas, symbolizing Lithuania, met the crowd from across the river, symbolizing Poland, in spite of the fact that police had removed planks from the midsection of the bridge. People in churches sang patriotic — "revolutionary," according to gendarmes — hymns, marched down streets, led pseudo-religious processions. Finally there was a serious clash with the Russian police and troops in Vilnius. The principal "revolutionary" hymn sung by crowds was not identified by the Tsar's police and is not identified by Soviet historians in our time: a refrain calling for the restoration of freedom was sometimes changed into "save us from the Muscovites." Some native officers in Russian army uniforms had been observed taking part in these demonstrations. According to official data, within a four-month period in 1861, there had been 227 manifestations in Lithuania — 116 in Vilnius alone.

In August 1861 Governor General Nazimov proclaimed martial law in major cities and the surrounding areas, and in the entire gouvernement of Kaunas — with the exception of the Russian-colonized county of Zarasai, renamed Novo-Aleksandrovsk.[50] A police regime with summary courts was instituted and additional troops were brought from Russia and stationed in each county. Russian police and soldiers reacted with progressively more brutality, even against crowds of women. Some civil officers of the nobility resigned in protest. The dietines then thanked them for their meritorious services in the past, and thus further antagonized the regime. Appeals in Lithuanian, featuring a cross "broken by the Muscovites in Poland," appeared in various places and some students, priests and civil officials were arrested.

These demonstrations, the martial law and brutal reprisals had achieved their purpose — correctly surmised by Alexander Herzen in his Russian revolutionary magazine, the *Kolokol* (Bell): "With whom shall Lithuania stand? With Poland!" This formulation pointed to Russia's Achilles Heel (in 1861 through 1974 and on): the unreconciled captive nationalities.

[50] Jurgėla, *Lietuvos Sukilimas, op. cit.*, 200-204, citing *Krestianskove Dvizheniye v Belorussii. . . (1861-1862)*, Minsk 1959, 19-31.

Lithuanians in Palanga flee from Red Army invasion.
Painting by Antanas Rukštelė
(Original painting in Lithuanian Art Gallery, Adelaide, South Austrailia.)

XII.
THE INSURRECTION OF 1862-1864

Emperor Nicholas I died during the Crimean War — in which thousands of Lithuanians and Poles fought in the Russian ranks, and other thousands in the Turkish and Allied ranks. Before he died in Constantinople, the great Lithuanian poet who wrote in Polish, Adam Mickiewicz, had spent many enchanted hours listening to "Sultan's Kozaks" singing in Polish, Lithuanian and Ukrainian at their campfires.

In 1856, the new Tsar, Alexander II decreed an amnesty for Polish political exiles and emigrés upon certain conditions, including a statement of "expiation" for their past aberrations. A few months later the amnesty was extended to Lithuanians. About 9,000 Poles came home. Only 43 Lithuanians returned within a year and a total of 353 came home by 1860 — the rest would not "expiate." There were hardened liberals and revolutionaries among the returnees.

Under the new Tsar, universities were allowed to admit more students. Some two thousand "Poles," nearly all from Lithuania, Whiteruthenia and Ukraine, enrolled annually in the universities of St. Petersburg, Moscow, Tartu (Derpt or Yuriev), Kiev and Kharkov and several hundred Lithuanians studied in military and professional academies. Students and army officers maintained close contacts among themselves, and fraternities with "Samagitia" and other chapters were formed in universities. A manuscript newspaper in Lithuanian was published by students in Moscow, and revolutionary literature was available in their secret libraries. Attempts were made to establish liaison with the students of Warsaw and some students traveled abroad to call on popular patriots like Joachim Lelewel, the former professor of the university of Vilnius, and General Louis Mierosławski. Dozens of students enrolled in Polish military schools first established in France and then in Italy. These Lithuanian and "Polish" students in Russian universities trained their Russian colleagues in underground activities, protests and strikes, and during recesses on home leave they distributed revolutionary leaflets to peasants and Russian troops, and arranged manifestations. Several dozen students were detained and sent back to their universities, and the Governors General of Vilnius and Kiev requested that students be denied holiday and recess leaves to their homes.

After the promulgation of the Agrarian Reform, moderates among the gentry managed to convoke an assembly of the landed gentry and were allowed to elect a committee — ostensibly to help in carrying through the agrarian reform. The committee was headed by James Gieysztor from the department of Kaunas. About the same time a circle of "Red" nobles and priests, led by Captain Louis Zwierzdowski, Governor General Nazimov's aide de camp, became active in Vilnius, Gardinas and Kaunas and by the spring of 1862 a "Lithuanian Committee of Action" was formed. Captain Zwierzdowski, being a native Catholic, was soon transferred to Moscow and law graduate Constantine Kalinauskas (Kalinowski, Kalinouski) replaced him at the helm of the "Red" Committee, renamed the Provincial Lithuanian Committee. Soon newsletters were printed in Polish, Lithuanian, and Whiteruthenian. Contacts were established with the Polish Central National Committee whose commissioner Nestor du Laurent was admitted into the Provincial Committee. Throwaway leaflets and newsletters denounced the Muscovite oppression and the abuses connected with the deceptive land reform, preached resistance to recruitment and urged to prepare for an armed insurrection in due time. Embryo units were formed in various places and arms purchasing missions went abroad. The Committee soon became embroiled in a jurisdictional dispute with the Central National Committee, which finally agreed to consult Lithuanians regarding the planned insurrection and its date. The gentry's committee likewise consulted Poland's "Whites" and in December 1862 was reassured that there would be no insurrection at least until the summer of 1863.

The accepted popular version was that the Polish insurrection of January 1863 was precipitated by the conscription for military duty of town revolutionaries, that the call-up of recruits in Lithuania had passed peacefully, and that the Lithuanians revolted some time later. In fact, however, there was a spontaneous insurrection in Lithuania by would-be recruits at least a full month earlier than in Poland — even though it had not been ordered or controlled by the Provincial Committee.

Since most of Lithuania was within the 100-verst frontier belt, a ransom of 300 rubles could be paid in lieu of producing a recruit. According to archival data recently published in Lithuania, no recruits were called in Lithuania after the Crimean War. When the call-up was resumed, however, the Tsar's ukase of September 5, 1862 invoked general recruitment rules within the frontier zones as well. The Governor of Kaunas reported to Vilnius and St. Petersburg that 28 peasant townships had voted to meet their recruit quotas by pecuniary taxes and that some townships had pre-paid the ransom. The Governor warned that peasants would resist the call-up and thus seriously aggravate the general unrest. However, on instructions from St. Petersburg, Governor General Nazimov rejected the argument.

The 1862 call-up quotas were applied to "temporarily dutybound" peasants (former serfs of private estates), state peasants, free people, single-homesteaders, [Russian] settlers and Jews: 5 recruits per 1,000 men, aged 23-27 among state peasants, 21-32 among other classes. Recruits due from public estates were to be chosen by lottery, others by community meetings, and the selectees were to be delivered bodily by January, 1863. However, as soon as lottery drawings began in November 1862, masses of young peasants hid in the forests and entire communities armed with bats and axes defended the selectees. By December 21 armed bands of 10-12 fugitives foraged for food and began liberating the seized recruits from troop convoys. The authorities reacted by seizing more men well in excess of quotas, and the fugitive bands intensified their attacks on armed convoys. Quotas were never filled because of age and physical defects of the seized recruits. Bičkauskas-Gentvila cites these statistics:

	QUOTAS			MEN SEIZED		
	State Peasants	Temporary Dutybound	Single-homesteaders	State Peasants	Temporary Dutybound	Single-homesteaders
Vilnius gvmt	502	838	36	1146	1614	77
Kaunas gvmt	488	745	13	620	1174	19
Totals	990	1583	49	1766	2788	96

On April 8, 1863 the Governor of Kaunas pointed out to the Tsar the difficulties in filling recruit quotas. Hence call-ups in the gouvernements of Vilnius, Kaunas and Gardinas were suspended "until 1864."[51]

In response to the Polish appeal of January 29, 1863, to "Brothers, Lithuanians!", the "Polish Government's Manifesto" was published by the Kalinauskas committee within three days — in Polish, Lithuanian and Whiteruthenian. The opening title stated: "Provisional Provincial Government in Lithuania and Whiteruthenia, in behalf of the Polish

[51] Jurgėla, *Lietuvos Sukilimas, op. cit.*, 228-232.

National Government." The seal read: "Lithuanian Provincial Committee. National Organization." The manifesto was dated "Vilnius, February 1, 1863." Another printed version of the Polish manifesto had a seal: "National Government, Branch Governing Provinces of Lithuania." One Lithuanian version reads: "As of this date there is no longer any slavery: because there is no longer a lord, a nobleman, a peasant, a Jew, we are all brothers and children, equals or alike, both before Lord God and before our beloved Fatherland." Another Lithuanian version reads: "As of this date all husbandmen and other inhabitants of any faith are free like the ancient noblemen." Some versions conferred "nobility" on all enlistees — in order to impress the full meaning of freedom. Peasant landholdings were declared their property with no payments, and the landlords would be compensated by the National Treasury. The landless enlistees, or their surviving families, were to get "at least three *morgen* of land" — six to eight acres.[52]

The first battle between rebels and Russian troops was fought on February 2, 1863 in Sudavia, administratively within the Congressional Kingdom of Poland. Captain Louis Narbutt led his guerrillas into battle in the Vilnius department in February. Boleslas Dłuskis ("Jablonauskis") and Rev. Antanas Mackevičius took to the field in the Kaunas department in March, 1863.

Early in March the "Whites" under James Gieysztor were summoned by the Polish "Red" Central National Committee to take over the Lithuanian Provincial Committee. Kalinauskas alone protested against "the betrayal of the revolution," yet he and other "Reds" readily submitted and performed their assigned duties in the field and in the committee presently renamed "The Branch Governing the Provinces of Lithuania." By the end of May it was renamed "The Executive Branch in the Provinces of Lithuania." Two prominent "Reds," Constantine Kalinauskas and Ladislas Małachowski, became Branch members in June, and after the arrest of Gieysztor on August 12, 1863, to the end of February, 1864, Kalinauskas replaced him at the helm.

Gieysztor had intended that the insurrection start on the same day throughout Lithuania Proper and that the manifesto granting land title to peasants be read in churches in the presence of the assembled gentry. He blames Narbutt, Dłuski and Mackevičius for undue eagerness and the disruption of this plan by taking to the field weeks ahead of the April 1 date set for the insurrection, and for the consequent loss of full

[52] *Ibid.*, 49-50, 238, 264.

effectiveness of a manifesto read on different dates without the presence of the gentry.

One massive strategic campaign was undertaken in April and May, 1863, when the "Palatine of Kaunas" Sigismund Sierakowski, General Staff Captain of the Russian army, arrived from St. Petersburg. He led the campaign under an assumed name of "Dołęga." The triumphant campaign brought together a number of raw guerrilla units. It ended disastrously early in May in a three-day battle near Biržai. The Palatine (Governor) was seriously wounded and taken prisoner. Thereafter the insurrectionists reverted to guerrilla tactics and battled until October 12, 1864.

The struggle was uneven from the start to the end. At no time were there more than 12,000 to 15,000 Lithuanian insurrectionists in the field — armed with scythes, pistols, shotguns and a few rifles taken from the enemy. They fought against tenfold larger units of a trained professional army equipped with telegraph and railroad communications, supply trains, munition dumps, field and hospital services, and including infantry, cavalry and artillery units. In Poland, some 30,000 fairly well armed rebels reinforced regularly by organized units from Austria and Prussia faced 141,000 Russian troops. The accounts of the Russian war minister show that on January 10, 1863 there were stationed within the Vilnius military area 66,482 fighting men — 50 combat battalions of infantry, 36 squadrons of cavalry, 12 troops of mounted cossacks and 120 artillery pieces. By August, 1863, the Russian forces in Lithuania doubled to 123,495. Early in 1864 Russian forces in Lithuania numbered 119 infantry battalions, 24 squadrons of cavalry and 60 "hundreds" of cossacks, and 146 cannon, a total of 144,786 fighting men. According to Bičkauskas-Gentvila, the Russians committed to battle in Lithuania 69 regiments — 9 Imperial Guard regiments, 44 infantry, 6 cavalry, 10 Don cossack mounted regiments and 19 artillery units. Furthermore, there were gendarme and police troops, and rural militia. The latter "sentinel" units included attached regulars —3,778 soldiers and 259 cossacks — and 21,342 foot and mounted militiamen.[53]

Russian official reports claimed that, in 1863, some 5,934 rebels were killed in combat, "more than 733" wounded and 1,361 taken prisoner, while only 261 Russian soldiers were killed, 916 wounded and 18 taken prisoner. Muravyov "the Hangman," Governor General

[53]*Ibid.*, 624-625; L. Bičkauskas-Gentvila, *1863 metų sukilimas Lietuvoje*, Vilnius 1958, 287-288.

since May, 1863 (so nicknamed since his first tour of repression duty in Lithuania during the insurrection of 1831, when he had boasted that he was a Muravyov who hangs others, not one of those who were themselves hanged as "Decembrists") is said to have placed a memorial plaque in an Orthodox church in Vilnius listing the Russian casualties by name. The number is not mentioned — even by Soviet writers. These early official figures would not include several hundred officers and men, native Lithuanians and Poles who abandoned their careers in the General Staff, Imperial Guard and other units and made their way to Lithuania to lead or join geurrilla units, and several dozen Ukrainian and Russian defectors who either perished in battle or were executed by Russian firing squads as deserters.

No statistics are available from insurgent military sources.

In addition to indiscriminate killings of wounded rebels and innocent suspects, the Russian military went through a formality of judicial process: official executions after field court martial sentences confirmed by county commandants, or trials by investigative military commissions reviewed by the Field Auditoriat in Vilnius and confirmed by the Military Area Commander — that is, Governor General. The official list of "due process" executions is as follows:

Kaunas department — 59 executions: 5 Catholic clergymen, 29 or 31 noblemen, 11 or 13 peasants, 2 townsmen, 10 or 11 soldier defectors (including 2 Ukrainians).

Vilnius department — 29 executions: 3 priests, 22 noblemen and officers, 1 peasant, 1 townsman, 2 soldiers.

Vitebsk department (Daugavpils-Dünaburg-Dvinsk area) — 3 Lithuanian noblemen: a count, a student, an officer. (Soviet writers sometimes include 5 Russian soldiers who, in fact, had been tried for criminal offenses not at all connected with the insurrection.)

Gardinas department — 22 executions: 11 noblemen, 5 peasants, 2 townsmen, 1 Prussian subject, 3 soldier defectors. (In addition thereto 3 soldiers of the 5th Don regiment were executed for rapes, murdering a Jewish family and armed robberies.)

Augustavas department (in "Congress Poland") — 48 executions: 19 noblemen, 6 townsmen (2 of them Jews), 15 peasants, 1 priest, 7 soldier defectors with Lithuanian, Polish and Russian names.

Minsk department — 15 executions: 6 civilian noblemen, 3 commissioned officers, 3 townsmen, 2 peasants, 1 soldier-Catholic.

Mohylew department — 8 executions, all noblemen: 7 military officers, 1 civilian physician.

The total number of official executions, "incomplete" according to Polish and Soviet sources, was 184 or 185. Muravyov's collaborator N. V. Berg claimed that the Hangman executed 240 persons.

The sum total of persons exiled to Siberia, interior Russia or imprisoned is not known. In his interim account Muravyov listed the following: executed 128, to hard labor in Siberia 972, to settle in Siberia 1427, exiled to Russia under police surveillance 1529, to Russia to settle on state lands 4096, into soldiers (mostly students) 345, into prisoner troops 864, a total of 9,361. In his other accounts he dwells on his kindness: "only 3500 were sentenced with a loss of their rights, and up to 5000 were exiled to settle on public lands in Siberia, more than 9,000 rebels remained in the country under police surveillance." He accounted only for the period of mid-May 1863 to January 1 or April 1865. Another account of the early 1865 lists: exiled 12,483, left under surveillance 6,024, a total of 18,507. This partial list is preceded by an editorial note to the effect that the Field Auditoriat in its report to January 1865 states "according to incomplete data": total number of repressed 21,712 — priests 294, privileged classes 6,443, commoners 14,976.

The exhaustive documented research by Bishop Paul Kubicki, based on Russian government archives and Church records of Vilnius, Kaunas, Daugavpils and Riga, regarding only the trials of the clergy, shows that a number of priests died in prisons while awaiting trial — in one case, that of Rev. Jonas Rajauskas, as late as 1869. Some files carry notations like the one in the folder of Mons. Juozas Giniotas (Giniatt) charged with "voluntarily handing cash box keys" to insurgent raiders in June 1863, the Field Auditoriat on November 18/30, 1865 noted: "In view of the defendant's demise, it is decided not to pronounce sentence." And none of the people beaten to death or left dying by the Russian "representatives of law and order" are listed in account files. Equally confusing are the tallies of armed skirmishes: varying between 227 and 298, most of them, at least 120, in the department of Kaunas.[54]

This writer's estimates based on various Russian accounts place the Lithuanian casualties and exiles at about 31,000 insurgents and innocent people, like the 1- to 15-year-old "political criminals" listed in the rosters of families exiled from the department of Kaunas. It may be generally summarized that the gentry suffered the most financially, because of the incessant levies of retaliatory "contributions"; the nominal

[54]Various Soviet and Polish data are reviewed in Jurgėla's *Lietuvos Sukilimas, op. cit.*, 626-658, the clery - 552-584.

petty noblemen — by sheer numbers of casualties and exiles; the clergy suffered the highest ratio pro rata. The several dozen burned and leveled villages whose inhabitants were exiled — had been inhabited by petty noblemen or those re-classified as peasants.

In addition to the killed, executed, imprisoned or exiled rebels and the innocents, there were a few thousand escapees abroad. Some people escaped from Siberia — and managed to get as far as the United States.

XIII.
RUSSIAN MOTIVATION OF THE TSARIST ERA

Leonidas Bičkauskas-Gentvila, a Soviet historical writer, concludes his chapter "7. Defeat of the insurrection" with a classic Soviet lie that "the Lithuanian landlords and the Catholic Church actively helped the tsarism suppress the insurrection." He ascribes the contributing cause of its failure to an alleged fact that "the insurrection in Poland and Lithuania had begun earlier than an armed uprising on a scale encompassing the whole of Russia was to start as planned by Russian revolutionary democrats," — who moved only in 1905 and 1917, while in 1863 they just wagged their tongues.

More reliable are the secret memoranda to the "Liberator Tsar" Alexander II penned by his Minister of the Interior, Count Peter Alexandrovich Valuyev and Governor General Mikhail Nikolayevich Muravyov. The reader must be forewarned that their terms "Poles, Polish" were applied to all Lithuanians, Catholics.

On December 13/25, 1862, Valuyev reported about the situation "in the Western country." The Belorussian Soviet Academy of Sciences published his memorandum with underscorings and notations in Alexander's handwriting. It is a lengthy document — 11 printed pages. Valuyev wrote that "palliative" results of the past 30 years show that the methods used were ineffective. The Western country "is united with Russia forever," and no institutions different from those of Russia should be allowed there. "We decreed the dominance of the Russian language. . . . we shut the university of Vilnius. We abrogated the Lithuanian Statute and replaced it with more perfect laws less pertinent to the habits, customs and the reasoning of the population. . . . We subjected the Roman Catholic faith to new restrictions and abolished some of its institutions. Finally, we publicly opposed the Polish element. . . . But we had not essentially improved local administration. . . . we used but one means — force in its various aspects," — with the exception of the more purposeful "reunion of the Orthodox" and the liberation of serfs. Force by itself cannot bring nationalities and religions together, and "Catholicism and Polonism had not lost their original strength," as shown by the recent wave of manifestations. Even at Kiev University which replaced the one in Vilnius, "the student body is motivated by the selfsame spirit which under the present circumstances might have predominated in the former University of Vilnius."

In consequence of the police regime and martial law, "street manifestations nearly ceased, but mental attitudes had not." Emergency stopgap measures based on the premise of intimidation are not enough, a permanent solution is required. The Polish element and Catholicism "cannot be strangled by force alone and cannot be ousted forcibly." The right to emigrate already exists. However, "compulsory emigration based on intimidation is unrealistic" and would require the consent of Poland's Viceroy. It is necessary "to weaken this element and make it accept the idea of irrevocable ties with Russia." It is necessary to undertake the gradual whittling down and absorption of that element and to eradicate all existing obstacles to unification. The hostile element must be divided, weakened, penalized, its material advantages must be eliminated.

"For divisive purposes," Valuyev proposed to re-establish the customs tariff frontier. The Tsar noted: "I do not agree with this." Valuyev also proposed that gouvernement frontiers be altered by transferring some counties "to nearest departments not presently of the Governorship General." As for "preventive measures," Valuyev proposed skillful encouragement of mutual hostility between peasants and lords ("Da," noted the Tsar), and quick-paced development of Russian village schools. "Immediate appropriation of pecuniary support for governmental tserkvas [Orthodox churches] and clergy in the Western gouvernements" would assure the Orthodox Church leadership in education. "In order to combat the influence of customs," it is necessary to have "determination and to demand that the above measures be realized." Governors and top officials should be summoned to St. Petersburg to hear what is expected of them. Catholic churchmen should be told "what the government had done for the Roman Catholic Church and what amelioration could be expected if the clergy would abstain from political activities. Otherwise it would be necessary to halt at once all the advantages to the Latin church."

Valuyev recited various punitive measures, as well as the exploitation of material interests: the martial law, the stationing of troops on the properties "of classes which by their behavior provoke the necessity for such measures or which are taking part in manifestations." The imposition of supplementary taxes and the costs of frontier readjustments, and the unfavorable settlement of the agrarian reform — the withholding of a share of bank bonds, were also proposed. Time acts in Russia's favor. "Regardless of the serious difficulties attending the solution of the Western problem and no matter how long it may take, its final solution must be feasible, because Providence does not pose insoluble problems." [55]

On March 19/31, 1865 Muravyov traveled to St. Petersburg and did not return to Vilnius. Five days later the Tsar accepted his resignation "in principle," and by a rescript of April 17/29 replaced him with General Konstantin Petrovich (von) Kaufmann (1818-1882), "an Orthodox and fully Russian man," according to Nikotin, an official of the Governor General's staff. Muravyov received the Tsar's thanks and the title of Count. In 1866 he was appointed to probe an important political case and died in the same year, at the age of 68. He was buried in Alexander Nevsky shrine cemetery as a Hero of Russia. According to Nikotin, just before leaving Vilnius Muravyov intended to shut the shrine of Madonna of the Dawn Gate. Nikotin strongly approved the project and suggested that Msgr. Żyliński would move the miraculous picture to another church. Nikotin conjectured that Muravyov wished to appropriate the picture for himself. Bishop Kubicki asserts that the Muravyov mausoleum at the cemetery was modeled after the Madonna of Vilnius chapel. Count Valuyev under date of May 22/June 3, 1865 noted in his diary that the newly appointed Governor General Kaufmann intended to blow up the Gate of Dawn shrine in Vilnius. Valuyev added: "What a stockpile of statesmen we have!"[56]

Muravyov's parting shot regarding Lithuania was his "most loyal account of his rule over the Northwestern Country from May 1, 1863 to April 17, 1865" — an opus of 22 pages. "Bearing in mind that the rebellion was simply a consequence of Polish stupidity and our government's policy of appeasement — when I was summoned in May, 1863 to pacify the Northwestern Country, I presented for Your Imperial Majesty's approval a plan to the effect that only energetic measures would restore order, even though this would be disliked in Europe and by some individuals within our own government. . . . Your Imperial Majesty approved my plans of action. . . . The armed rebellion was soon liquidated."

[55] *Krestianskoye Dvizheniye v Belorussii posle otmeny krepostnogo prava (1861-1862 gg)*, Minsk 1959, 37-47.

[56] Jurgėla, *Lietuvos Sukilimas, op. cit.*, 612, citing Paweł Kubicki, *Bojownicy Kapłani za Sprawe Kościoła i Ojczyzny w latach 1861-1915* (3 parts in 8 volumes, Sandomierz 1933-1939), Pt. II, vol. I, 392-406, and *Dnevnik P.A. Valuyeva Ministra Vnutrennikh Del,* v II 1865-1876, Akademia Nauk SSSR, Moskva 1961, p. 45.

In reality, the insurrection was broken at the ill-fated battle of Biržai just before Muravyov's arrival in Vilnius. Nevertheless, he pretended that the rebels were in control of the entire area reaching "into the Belorussian gouvernements, to the old frontiers of 1772." According to him, "police courts invested with the prosecution of political activists were more accurately the caricatures of a weak government." The Catholic clergy were the principal culprits and monasteries the main hideouts for plotters. Native agrarian mediators "were deliberately imposing extreme duties on peasants and inculcating among them a belief that they had received freedom from their former masters, rather than from Your Imperial Majesty, and that oppressive taxes were a consequence of government regulations .... that the entire country is not Russia at all, that it is Polish." The clergy kept records in Polish, disregarded laws, succored the rebellion, Orthodox churches were dependent on their Catholic landlords. "From the beginning of the rebellion the gentry turned away from Russian society and stressed their lack of faith in Your Imperial Majesty's government. ... In brief, I have found the country totally anarchized."

Carrying out the Tsar's will, Muravyov undertook action at once to restore the Army's honor and morale. He made every military and civil commander "responsible for his county, and landlords were made to pay fines in addition to their regular responsibility for disorder in their neighborhood." Fines were "the most effective means to tether the gentry, as they touched their sorest material situation." Fines and contributions were "collected instantly. This stopped mournings, singing, manifestations, bell ringing ... patriotic processions ... and the sending of men into bands. Each parent was made responsible for his entire family and lodgers. Contributions were paid into the State Treasury." The deportation of Bishop Krasiński and "several instances of severe punishment of the guilty clergy soon braked the criminal influence of the clergy."

Muravyov did not recite here, as he had in his "Memoirs," his vow "to start off with priests" and that within a few days of his arrival he confirmed death sentences for three Catholic priests. Neither did he mention that in evacuating petty noblemen, their villages were burned and leveled to the ground and that they were charged with the cost of their transportation into the exile. Muravyov cites that he "severely restricted and controlled all movements" of the inhabitants. He imposed 10% contribution "on all Polish owners of estates and thus deprived them of their ability to succor the armed revolt for which that caste spared no money." He did not boast that he collected from innocent farmers double the value of stocks requisitioned from them by insurgent units, and that village "militiamen" were flogged and fined "for not resisting the rebels."

"General realization that the country's supreme commander's orders would be carried out regardless of anything, prostrated the gentry and all sympathizers of the rebellion." The insurrection itself weakened after the July 1863 arrests of its leaders, and "addresses to Your Imperial Majesty were signed with appeals for mercy. . . . It is true, not all of these addresses were sincere, yet they meant the government's triumph against the revolution, especially since Poles, arrogantly proud in the successes, debase themselves and cringe when failures accompany them." Assassination was attempted against the loyal nobility leader Alexander Domeyko, but the conspirators were soon "detained, sentenced and executed as deterrent examples to others." By August 1863 the Warsaw nationalist government was crushed, the local Lithuanian Branch "with all its palatines and commissioners" was imprisoned, the rebellion petered out, the bands had vanished. Within a year after the Augustavas department (Lithuanian Sudavia) had been committed to his rule, "it no longer looked like a part of the Polish Kingdom, it looked like a Russian gubernia."

"Then, with Your Imperial Majesty's permission, I began by means of kindness and forgiveness to draw other mutineers out of forests and I published an amnesty for those sincerely repentant. In this manner more than three thousand left the bands and swore their allegiance. I exiled to Siberia those who could not be trusted. . . . Few ever went back into the bands."

The rebels switched to guerrilla operations in units of 5, 10 or 15 men. "This created some difficulties. Successful struggle was possible only by levying contributions on those who sheltered and fed them. Not all liked this system, yet this was the only way, and by October the rebellion died, only a small group of rebel bandits remained. . . . To facilitate troop movements and quick transfers, roadside strips were cleared in forests and bogs were drained at the expense of the gentry. This prevented large landholders from building secret underground grain storages to feed the rebels."

Muravyov humbly recalled that he had asked to be relieved of his duties when the rebellion was put down, but that the Tsar ordered him to continue, to revive and strengthen the country's "Russian and Orthodox character." So he tackled the Russian peasantry and brought in new officials from Russia. "I concerned myself with the villagers, the only element loyal to the throne, because the szlachta, gentry and priests will always be our enemies." He promised landgrants to the landless rebels who would return and swear their loyalty, and "several thousands returned from the bands and were given plots." Complaints thereof by "Catholic Polish and German landlords" reached the Tsar. "I knew of this, yet at all times I unwaveringly held to the course set in advance, so necessary for strengthening Russian rule in this country, because only the village plebs and Old Believers [Russian settlers], so ardently cooperating in the supression of the mutiny, are devoted to Your Imperial Majesty. The so-called szlachta, lords and priests have been and shall remain our eternal enemies; no reliance could ever be placed on their loyalty: plotting and deception are the ground rules of their emotions and upbringing. . . . They had betrayed even their Commonwealth's interests and were the cause of its fall."

Then he reviewed financial arrangements for the benefit of the Orthodox — from contributions squeezed from Catholic natives — in order to increase the number of Russian schools, to replace native teachers with Russians, to end the Catholic clergy's "arbitrary activities." He banned the building and repairing of Catholic churches, limited the number of priests in rural parishes and the appointment of pastors, and restricted the travel of Catholic clergymen. He strengthened the Russian element by parceling out confiscated estates among Russian peasants and providing financial benefits and landgrants for Russian settlers and officials. Government posts, especially in police, were taken over by Russians brought from Russia who were assured of a 50% pay supplement to encourage their diligence.

"To those in St. Petersburg who depicted this system as harmful, I have but one thing to say: that Russia, which shed so much of its precious blood during the rebellion, must be guided by its own interests, rather than by some humanitarianism toward the Polish cause. . . . Russia cannot make peace with Polish reveries. . . . Concessions and humanitarianism in this case would be crimes against Russia." Some 3,000 imported Russian officials performed creditably. "It is true that a great many among these officials brought from Russia did not live up to the trust placed in them, which after all happens often in Russia itself. However, such persons were removed. Thus within one year the entire landscape of the country changed. Orthodox churches are built out of fines and contributions funds collected from the gentry and Catholic priests. In this manner more than 100 tserkvas are being renovated or built anew out of these funds."

"As long as the [Catholic] clergy is not made dependent on the government — I have done that already — we cannot depend on the country's moral mood. The Catholic clergy presently does not dare to resist openly . . . it is necessary to levy fines for the slightest infractions. This is the only and obligatory system without which the Polish-Latin propaganda cannot be stopped. . . . I confess that in my actions hitherto, when it was necessary to rush ahead without a glance backward, I had to resort to various measures which, in normal times, would be illegal. Otherwise, we would have been carried out like sleeping babes together with legality. We had found ourselves in such a situation in 1863."

Muravyov boasts that "in Samagitia I even introduced the Russian alphabet for Samagitian and Latvian primers. I distributed Russian prayerbooks replacing the Polish ones formerly used by the Orthodox. I disseminated historical maps and holy pictures of Orthodox saints, distributing more than 100,000 of each. I ordered 60,000 of various prayerbooks. Among the Orthodox I introduced the custom of wearing a cross on the chest. I removed from circulation Samagitian prayerbooks damning the Russian domination. I tossed out subversive textbooks of the local country's history which wrote of Russian aggression and that this country had never been Russian, etc." He commissioned Moscow university professors to write "the history of the local Russian country, offering a prize for the best book. Everywhere I have found displayed things left behind by Kościuszko and other agitators. . . . In a word, all of my efforts were exerted to destroy all that had been invented by the Poles for their own propaganda. This was my goal, and I achieved it."

Muravyov reviewed the files of the investigative commissions and military courts and cautioned that "the very thought of allowing exiles ever to return nullifies the shedding of Russian blood for the cause of our possessions here. I feel dutybound to warn the government regarding this, because more than once that method had borne bitter fruit. Any kindness on the part of our government is interpreted by the Poles as our weakness." The reader is reminded again that "Poles" and "Polish" to Muravyov meant the Lithuanians and all Catholics.

After estimating the numbers of his victims, Muravyov recommended for the future: 1) to retain investigative commissions and a military judicial commission; 2) to bring in Russian officials and endow them with landgrants; 3) to base civilian rule "on the firm foundations of law"; 4) to review and monitor the performance of government institutions and to verify "the correctness of mental reasoning." He recapitulated his own achievements and policy suggestions for the future in seven points. The most important points were — the control of schools by the Orthodox clergy, and good material conditions for Orthodox clergy and teachers. Point 7 states: "Inasmuch as the Roman Catholic clergy were the principal instigators of the rebellion who continually strove to spread revolutionary Polish propaganda calling for the ousting of Russian inhabitants from this country, and since they deliberately built parochial, filial churches and chapels without the secular authorities' permission, even in the midst of Orthodox parishes; it is therefore most urgent to stay alert, lest the past repeat itself. The most special concern . . . must be the annihilation of the Polish element . . . and martial law must be retained. The Polish gentry, szlachta and priests merit no mercy. Laws applying in Russia must not be honored here. . . . The Polish gentry must at all times be perennially assessed contributions.

"I pray to the Lord God that the leading authorities should not guide themselves by European ideas of humanitarianism. . . . Eternal alertness must be maintained over the Northwestern Country, because it cost Russia so much! We shall not be at peace until the Polish element shall be totally crushed there. For this purpose Russian activists are needed and I beg Your Imperial Majesty to pay attention to a steady increase of the Russian element in this country."[57]

[57]Jurgėla, *Lietuvos Sukilimas, op. cit.*, citing *Russkaya Starina* magazine, June 1902, and Polish translation in Kubicki's *Bojownicy Kapłani, op. cit.*, Pt. II, vol. I, 392-406. Muravyov's memoirs — *Zapiski . . . o myatezhe v Sieverozapadnoy Rossii v 1863-1865 gg.* — are found in *Russkaya Starina* monthly vols. 36, 37 and 38 of Nov. 1882 - June 1883. Translations: *Der Dictator von Wilna*, Leipzig 1883; *Pamiętnik Murawiewa ("Wieszatiela")*, Kraków 1902. Walery Przyborowski, in his *Dzieje 1863 roku*, vol. V, Kraków 1910, p. 310 footnote, cites a pamphlet distributed in Russian village schools. "A Dialogue with common people of the Western Russian provinces," completely misrepresenting history, viz., after Napoleon's attack on Russia, the neighbors divided "Poland," the "nest of arrogant and vain Lyakhs" and for more than 50 years the "Poles have enjoyed happiness they had never known before." The Tsar "filled their miserable country with gold and Russian bread, installed order in the courts and defended the poor." The "Poles hate order and peace, they gnashed their teeth like snakes no longer being able to oppress peasants, to abuse the Orthodox religion, to give our temples to Jews . . . to shoot at passersby — in a word, to behave at home and Russian areas as in a forest. They mutinied in 1830, so Tsar Nicholas punished them as they had deserved." And the Illovaisky history textbook alleged that King John Sobieski was a Russian and that Vienna had been relieved in 1683 by cossacks.

XIV.
PATRIOTS – THEIR FAITH AND DEEDS

Reverend Antanas Mackevičius
(1828-1863)

At the age of 12, this son of petty Samagitian noblemen farmers walked to Vilnius and attended a lyceum for six years, earning his board and lodging by performing menial services in a monastery. Then he walked to Kiev in the Ukraine to enter the university. Two years later he returned home, entered the Samagitian seminary and graduated in 1854. He served as assistant and later as pastor of a filial church at Paberžė, mingling with peasants at their weddings, baptismal and funeral functions and zealously defending them from abuses. In the summer of 1862 he visited the shrine city of Częstochowo in Poland and stayed with his fellow Lithuanian, the friar priest Maximus Tareiva, who was later hanged by the Russians during the insurrection. He is said to have met Kalinauskas at Sierakowski's wedding reception in the town house of James Gieysztor in Kaunas. He learned the rudiments of military tactics from Boleslas Kołyszko, graduate of the officers school in Italy, and led his own unit into battle in March, 1863.

According to his parishioner Gieysztor, Mackevičius "lasted to the end as the true tribune of the national-populist idea . . . a nervous entity, ardent, passionate, filled with faith he inspired this faith in the common people who believed him blindly. Whenever his unit was dispersed, he went to his native Liauda, talked to people and led new units into battle. Like Peter the Hermit several centuries earlier had led his fanaticized masses, so did Mackevičius lead his Samagites. If Dłuski in 1863 was a model soldier-guerrilla, Mackevičius was a model insurrectionist revolutionary." Several relatives of Gieysztor served in the Mackevičius units.

Przyborowski called Mackevičius "a demagogue, influenced by emigré Centralization, matured in the theories of Heltman, Alcyat and Mierosławski, yet a sincere demagogue ably expounding his theories in a reasoned manner to captivate the difficult peasant nature and to lead the latter into battle for his homeland's independence. He possessed that simple yet rare good sense. . . . in a great many instances he proved to be an abler and more talented commander than those who had studied and practiced the arts of war."

His legendary fame as the most elusive freedom fighter earned him the nomination (November 3, 1863) as organizer and commander of the armed forces in the palatinate of Kaunas. Poland's Lithuanian "director" Romuald Traugutt in his order to the armed forces cited Mackevičius as the example to all. While making his way to Sudavia across the Nemunas River, he was captured on December 5/17, 1863 and brought to Kaunas.

Mackevičius told his captors: "I love my Lithuania, I dedicated my weak strength to Her." His blind father was brought to his cell. The old man fingered his son's face and reprimanded him for revolutionary activities. The son crossed himself, stood up: "Father, forgive but do not remonstrate. Not all is ended, not everything is lost. Father, my kingdom is not of this world. I shall never regret that I defended my people. I shall suffer here, my reward is due in the life to come."

The Russians learned from him nothing they had not known already. In answer to questions in Russian, he wrote in Polish to the commander of Kaunas: "Honorable Colonel, you order me to disclose my collaborators? Where are they? Could I utilize noblemen, gentry, colleague priests, or youths, or common folk? I say, no. I did not collaborate with manorial lords, as I saw the old Polish szlachta in them, little or not at all concerned with the people. Furthermore, it seemed to be more Polish, least Lithuanian. Therefore I contented myself with expounding my ideas about the people's future, not inciting the common people. I could not collaborate with priests, as many of them either fanatically hate Polonism and are prepared to sacrifice everything for Lithuania by terror and social overturn, or are selfishly concerned with themselves and stooping before manorial steps, or are totally indifferent to everything. I could not exactly utilize the unenlightened folk and mold conspirators out of them. I influenced them in a manner that, without realizing it themselves, they talked of and believed in the possibility of insurrection whenever that should take place in Poland."

In his mocking letter to the Colonel he continued: "My testimony shows clearly that, according to your law, I must expect punishment . . . . Yet if I am guilty, it is only of following a wrong road, not the evil one! Show me my ills and give me enough time to correct them. My thirst for the weal of the people had given me the strength and ability to rouse them, for no other goal than to raise them to the level of awareness and expressing whether they prefer to be united with Russia or with Poland. Such a right already exists in Europe, and it could not be expressed otherwise than by self-liberation. This is attainable by war, and in Lithuania it had to take place through a war in Poland. Such are my further political views. And inasmuch as many conditions for an independent revolution are lacking in Lithuania to win something tenable for the future, I called for massive aid to Poland and demanded help from her for the Lithuanian revolution, to win thereby at least a temporary recognition of civic rights and free land-grants which should raise considerably the people's welfare and, sooner or later, enable them to determine their own future. Kindly consider, Honorable Colonel: are there any machinations herein to grasp the government or elevate myself, as the Commission accuses me? I may not have had the right. However, I am a native of this country and I love it, and I deemed that I had the right. I could not voice my convictions in any newspaper, this is obvious. Unless abroad. But that also would be prosecuted, just as the present result, that is: the insurrection.

"In concluding my testimony I add: if I am guilty, it is of going on an erroneous road, without malice. I assure you that I am not lacking in will to work, to work for the people's happiness. It is up to you, Honorable Colonel, to point the right road to me, and I shall gladly follow it. You pointed to the Penal Code. According to it, I have to die as a commander and as a willful dispensator of death verdicts. I did not dispense death, except in accordance with the letter of the 'Insurrectionist Instruction and Penal Code,' and I used it but once. . . .

"Returning to laws that you, Honorable Colonel, had shown me, I may have insulted the government, yet the monarchial government, emanating from God, must resemble God. God does not doom His wayward children to eternal perdition, unless they do not promise to mend their ways. He does not deny them His grace if they want to right themselves, but forgives them like a father and, as He Himself said, holds the wayward who returned to the right path above those who had no need to mend their ways. Therefore, by applying this to the Imperial court and heart of Alexander II, I await my verdict.

"And I ask you, Honorable Colonel, to send me a Catholic priest that I should prepare to accept the fate meted out to me by God."

His other depositions bitterly denounced injustice, the exploitation of peasants, the venality and greed of Russian officialdom. "Such is the state of my homeland. . . . Unless the administration mends its ways, stops robbing and abusing the inhabitants, another Mackevičius shall arise and complete the work I had not completed. It is beyond our understanding: doesn't Russia have for our country other than the most unconscionable officials? Is my people so unfortunate that nothing remains for it but desperation, nothing regarding the fate of peoples? And yet, this is a people of several million. And a people deserving kindness, if not divine protection then government's, even a Russian one's, because this people is not spoiled to its roots, even though the administration is doing everything to spoil them. These were my motives for the insurrection and these were the considerations which sustained the Lithuanian insurrection ten months. That my views are right, I call as my witness my present situation as a man who had known what he was doing, and what awaits him if he fails."

Anatoly Smirnov cites another letter to Col. Bozherianov-Zherebtsov: "If you don't want a repetition of what had happened, first of all send the noblemen across the Nemunas [river]. Or elevate common people to equality of rights with the nobility. . . . Give Lithuania the [organic] law, give Viceroyship, let one of Grand Dukes settle in Vilnius, and at the same time inquire: do they want to stay with Russia or with Poland? The abuse of force will not help you achieve anything. There shall always be restiveness, always insurrections. These are my last wishes and proposals. I know you will laugh, yet these come from a man who is about to die."

On December 12/24, 1863 the Russian military tribunal sentenced him to death by hanging, and Muravyov twice confirmed the verdict. On December 16/28 the Russians at the gallows offered him mercy in exchange for information regarding the insurrection. Father Antanas Mackevičius answered: "I have done my work, now you do yours."[58]

[58]Jurgėla, *Lietuvos Sukilimas, op. cit.*, documentary quotations - 493-518.

Constantine Vincent Kalinauskas
(1838-1864)

Son of petty nobleman operating a small textile shop, Kalinauskas (Kalinowski in Polish, Kalinouski in Whiteruthenian, Kalinovsky in Russian) studied in Swisłocz and Vilnius, and in 1855 entered Moscow University where his tutor-brother Victor studied medicine. He was expelled for the possession of illegal books — accepting the blame for a colleague — then studied law at St. Petersburg University and, after graduation, worked in a public library. Returning to Lithuania, he failed to get a government job. He hiked around the country and joined the Lithuanian Committee of Action. He edited newsletters in Polish and Whiteruthenian in 1862 and became the head of the Lithuanian Provincial Committee. He argued with Warsaw over the co-equality of the Lithuanian Committee, yet as soon as Poland rose, he published an appeal in Polish: "Brothers! The Kingdom rose up — our people are beating the Muscovite everywhere. Blood flowing on the opposite bank of the Nemunas calls us to arms! Our fight with the annexationist for our sacred rights, for our freedom, is near! Stand together and in concord, and God will help us! God save Poland!"

When the "Whites," at the behest of the Polish "Red" Central National Committee, took over the Provincial Committee and named it the Branch Governing the Provinces of Lithuania, Kalinauskas was the only one to protest in writing: ". . . we accept no responsibility before posterity for errors and wrongs and misfortunes brought upon the

Lithuanian movement by a leadership hostile to the insurrection's spirit and tendencies." Kalinauskas was sent by Gieysztor as commissioner in the department of Gardinas. Later he was recalled to Vilnius and coopted into the Branch. After Gieysztor's arrest in August, he remained at the helm until his own arrest in February, 1864. Living under various aliases and changing his general appearance and the color of his hair, Kalinauskas witnessed every public execution of his fellow fighters.

Gieysztor writes that Kalinauskas faithfully collaborated with him and obeyed the directives. When a death verdict was passed by the Branch on Alexander Domeyko, the leader of the nobility, for collecting signatures of loyalty to Russia, Ladislas Małachowski reported that he had a volunteer to carry out the death warrant. Kalinauskas inquired about the man's name. Gieysztor writes: "When Małachowski stated the name, not familiar to me and unfortunately presently forgotten, he [Kalinauskas] replied: 'I vouch for him that he would do it. However, we cannot allow that.' Małachowski asked why. Kalinauskas said: 'That's a man with a wife and several children, and we have gendarmes to carry out our verdicts.' At that moment I walked up to Constantine, sincerely kissed him and said: 'Oh, you, my dear nobleman!' Kalinauskas was confused, said what's going on here? Amid our colleagues laughing sincerely out of sympathy for Kalinauskas, I explained that he himself is endowed in the highest degree with that weakness, or more precisely the noble heart which he blames upon the nobility, because he refuses to sacrifice a man with a family. Indeed, this weakness is, in my opinion, our people's most precious quality."

His ideas are well known from his *Mužyckaja Prauda* (the Peasant Truth) in Whiteruthenian, which was in parts translated into Lithuanian and Polish, in some cases a year later. After refusing to testify, one night Kalinauskas in prison asked for a pen and paper, and "in excellent Russian" wrote down his "curious" — to inquisitors — views.

In his "annotations" to the military court, Kalinauskas wrote: "Lithuania's historically developed sympathy toward Poland had gained most strength during the Russian domination (a fact which must be given attention) and had overcome circumstances unfavorable to the insurrection, and Lithuania moved. . . . Whoever thinks that Russia's task will be small, is judging superficially, is deceiving oneself. The net knitting us in all classes and binding us to Poland is rooted so firmly in traditions and even in prejudices, that to unknit it, to destroy it and to create something new would require centuries of systematic and prudent efforts. The agitators brought in from all over Russia will accomplish nothing in the matter of union, they will but delude themselves and the government, they will fail and will lead the country, against its own will, to new sacrifices, new national calamities. Until the government will have gained sympathy in the truly enlightened class of the local inhabitants, Russia's word will evoke no response in the hearts of Lithuanians. In my mind, I am guilty not because of my convictions but because of circumstances, and therefore may I be permitted to console myself with a hope that national weal shall yet come. May God permit that our descendants should not have to spill fraternal blood unnecessarily."

In his "Letter from Underneath the Gallows," Kalinauskas wrote from prison: "My brothers, beloved humble peasants! I am writing to you from underneath the Muscovite gallows. It hurts to leave my native soil and you, my dear fellow countrymen. My breast is rending apart, my heart is breaking, but I do not regret my dying for the cause of justice to you. Brothers, accept my words with trust, as they will reach you from the other world, and I have written them having but your well-being in mind. Brothers, there is no greater happiness in the world, than to have wisdom and enlightenment in one's head. But — just as the night and day do not walk together, so the true enlightenment does not mate with Muscovite slavery. As long as that slavery shall dominate our country, we shall have no truth, no well-being, no enlightenment, and we shall be ruled like dumb animals, not for our own welfare, but to our perdition. Therefore, whenever you should hear that your brothers from the environs of Warsaw are fighting for Truth and Freedom, do not remain inactive: seize whatever weapon that might be handy — the scythe or the axe — and rise en masse, keep on fighting for your rights as men and a nation, for your religion, for your native soil. For I say unto you, People, from the gallows: you shall be able to live in happiness only when the Muscovite shall have been removed from your necks."

On March 19, 1864, his turn to die came to the 26-year-old youth. According to Muravyov's collaborator Mosolov, Kalinauskas "walked to his death with firm steps. When he reached the plaza, he stood facing the gallows and once in a while glanced at the distant crowd. When the confirmation was read to him, he began making remarks. For instance, when his name was read: nobleman Victor Kalinovsky, he shouted: 'We have no noblemen, we are all equals!' The policemaster shook his head and asked him to keep silent." Incidentally, Soviet historians substitute the word "tsarist" for Kalinauskas' "Muscovite" or Mosolov's "Russian." [59]

[59] The English translation of the letter was first published in Jurgėla's *History of the Lithuanian Nation, op. cit.*, 460. Other materials and documentation — in the same author's *Lietuvos Sukilimas.*

Sigismund Sierakowski (1827-1863)

Sierakowski was born in a family of noblemen of Lithuanian descent near Łuck in the Ukraine. His father had died in the insurrection of 1830 sabered by the Muscovites. Graduating with honors from the lyceum of Zhitomir in 1845, he enrolled in St. Petersburg University where he befriended Gieysztor and other Lithuanian students. He was detained in 1848 when he attempted to cross over into Austria and was sentenced for life to serve in the convict troops. He served in Orenburg and the Kirghiz areas with Taras Shevchenko and a number of Lithuanians. He tutored officers' children in French, was promoted to Subaltern and pardoned in 1857. He graduated from the Imperial General Staff Academy with honors and was attached as Captain to the General Staff. He befriended Minister of War Milyutin and interested the latter in revising the military code of Peter I and abrogating corporeal punishment in the army. Sent abroad to study military codes and statistics he met Napoleon III, Queen Victoria, Garibaldi — and Polish and Lithuanian revolutionaries. In St. Petersburg he befriended Chernyshevsky, Dobrolyubov and other Russian liberal editors and writers, and also formed a circle of Lithuanian and Polish officers. In 1862 he married a

Lithuanian girl, Apollonia Dalewska. Returning from a trip aboard, he met with the Polish Central National Committee in Warsaw and traveled to Vilnius with Gieysztor who had been consulting with Polish "Whites" in Warsaw.

In March 1863, seeing the emissary from Vilnius who had come to ask him to assume military command in the Kaunas "palatinate," he told the emissary: "You are bringing me a death verdict. However, refusal on your part to participate in the insurrection would show your lack of patriotism, while on my part — this would signify cowardice." He resigned his Russian commission, consulted in Vilnius with other military leaders and went to Kaunas. His plan was to take over the department of Kaunas where people of all classes were most favorably disposed, to seize the undermanned fortress of Daugavpils (Dünaburg, Dvinsk), and meet a ship with volunteers and war supplies from England off Palanga in the Baltic Sea. Holding a secure base in Kaunas, he intended to invade and rouse Latvian and Estonian areas, to help the insurrection in the Vilnius department, and advance through Belorussia northeastward toward Moscow and the Volga — rousing peasants.

Unfortunately, the ship chartered in England encountered difficulties and the expedition ultimately failed. The Daugavpils venture was tipped off by an untimely rising of a small group of noblemen led by young Count Louis Plater in an area settled by Russian Old Believers. Orthodox Belorussian and Ukrainian peasants would not join in the "lords" revolt and deprived the few rebel units of any freedom of movement. The plot in Kazan on the Volga was betrayed by a Russian student. Sierakowski himself was seriously wounded in the three-day battle near Biržai and taken prisoner. An officer escorting him past a group of captives called the insurrectionists "unfortunates." Sierakowski heatedly retorted that "They are the Lithuanian seeds that shall eventually bloom into white blossoms of Freedom!"

His pregnant wife was arrested and exiled. He refused to divulge any in[illegible]mation. Asked about his contacts abroad, he named Napoleon III [illegible]ibaldi — whose intercession in his behalf failed. He told the [illegible] tribunal that he did not recognize Russia's jurisdiction over [illegible]ania. Prince Alexander Suvorov, grandson of the "Butcher of [illegible]" tried to help — in vain: he called Muravyov "a hyena bitten by a [illegible]dog." Sierakowski was hanged in Vilnius at a public execution on [illegible]27, 1863. He shouted a protest against the Tsar's tyranny. His last words were: "Thy will be done."

Boleslas Kołyszko
(1838-1863)

Born in a family of noblemen tenants in Lyda county, Kołyszko studied in Vilnius and in 1860 enrolled in Moscow University. During the period of manifestations in 1861, he asked for a month's leave, went home and distributed leaflets to Russian officers saying, according to gendarme's report: "I ask you, gentlemen, not to confuse political concepts. The Russian people is one thing, Russia's government is another. The latter is our enemy in common. It is the duty of each country's patriot to subvert and to throw off tyranny, otherwise Russia will never liberate itself from its internal chains. And here Russians may confidently count on the energetic and fraternal Polish help." He was returned to Moscow under escort, and there took part in student demonstrations. Facing arrest, he fled abroad and studied at the Polish military school in Genoa and Cuneo. When the school was closed, he returned to Lithuania and trained Father Mackevičius and the latter's aides in military science. When Sierakowski took over, he brought his "Dubysa regiment" of 213 men armed with several carbines, shotguns and scythes, and reported to Sierakowski that his regiment "lacked 105 pairs of boots, underwear and coats." This huge, blond, blue-eyed giant, was captured while escorting the wounded Sierakowski. The investigators reported that "he showed no compunction over his crimes, he voiced liberal ideas instead of clearing himself." His deposition ends with a statement in his own handwriting: "In all of my activities and behavior my purpose was my homeland's weal, and I followed the course which to all and to me seemed to be the best in achieving that goal. Loving my own homeland, I at the same time respected other nations and therefore I have never worked against the Russian state."

According to eyewitness accounts, on June 22, 1863 drums rumbled at the Lukiškės Plaza in Vilnius and an official ordered the former rebel battalion commander to remove his rebel uniform cap as the sentence was read. Kołyszko did not move. The Adjutant seized his cap and tossed it to the ground. The prisoner picked up and dusted his cap, put it back on his head — and with a single blow knocked the adjutant unconscious. According to some, the executioner and his two assistants attacked the doomed man. Kołyszko seized them and juggled them one by one in the air like pinballs, and then quietly stood underneath the noose and allowed himself to be tied. When the officer read the sentence "In the name of His Imperial Majesty" — Kołyszko shot back: "I spit on your imperial majesty." The rope broke because of the giant's weight. He died, when hanged the second time.

Louis Narbutt
(1831-1863)

Son of the insurrectionist of 1793 and a noted Lithuanian historian Theodore Narbutt, Louis studied in Lyda and Vilnius. Arrested in 1849 with other high school members of a secret society, he was publicly flogged in the presence of his parents and schoolmates, and sentenced to life in the convict troops. The bleeding noble youth crawled to his parents' feet and asked for their blessing. "Old father's shoulders sagged, his mother had come a beautiful dark-haired lady and went home a gray-haired old woman," reminisced his sister. Narbutt served ten years in the Caucasus — a tool of the Russian conquest of the freedom-loving mountaineers. He had taken part in 90 engagements, was wounded four times and limped ever since. He was commissioned an officer for his valor, decorated with the Order of St. Vladimir, was discharged a Captain in 1860 and came home.

In February 1863 Narbutt took to the field with 15 men, including his younger brother. He successfully engaged Russian units in a number of skirmishes and eluded massing troops. His own unit was reinforced by young noblemen, students from Vilnius and local peasants. In April his campsite in the forest was betrayed by Russian settlers. Wounded by the first fusillade, he ordered a retreat. As he was being dragged by his fellows, he was wounded again and died in his native forest. His last words in Latin were: "How sweet it is to die for one's homeland. . . ."

Titus Dalewski
(1841-1864)

The scion of a well known family of patriots, brother of Sierakowski's wife, Titus attended University of Moscow and came home as soon as the insurrection began in Lithuania. Gieysztor did not let him "go into the forests" and retained him as his secretary and seal keeper. Later

Titus held the same post under Kalinauskas. He lived in Vilnius under an alias, and when the owner of that passport was detained in Minsk, Titus was arrested and identified. He refused to testify or to betray Kalinauskas. He died before a firing squad in Vilnius on December 30, 1863/January 11, 1864.

There is a letter in the Vilnius archives — written by Titus to Elena Jomantas (Jamont), dated December 22, 1863 and never delivered by Muravyov. Titus wrote: "... The first two days of my imprisonment were tolerable, on the third day they took away everything from me, leaving only underwear. I was brought to a so-called confrontation with Mrs. Syrokomla. Reacting to her requests and imprecations, I had to attest her testimony which sealed my fate. Furthermore, I told the commission that unless they ease my situation, I shall smash my head against the corner of the wall. My face must have looked horrible, my eyes were burning from hunger and cold, my face was covered with dirt, my hands sandy and musty. The commission member was startled and jumped away from me. I returned to my dungeon with the thought of suicide. I was about ready to do that, when they brought me an overcoat and several nailed boards. This was a blessing! Now I am enjoying the rights given all prisoners, inasmuch as I am being tried by a military court. On Monday the field court martial will transmit its verdict in my case to Muravyov — on Tuesday or any next day I will be dead. I experienced no fortune in my life. I shared with my family the misfortune and all the moral sufferings. I loved my homeland and I am pleased to give my life for Her. I leave my family to the care of my nation, because none of us brothers will survive." [60]

[60] Jurgėla, *Lietuvos Sukilimas, supra.*, 535-536.

James Gieysztor
(1827-1897)

In his memoirs written after his return from Siberia to a nearby "Poland" — the Lithuanian Sudavia on the left bank of the Nemunas which had been a part of "Congress Poland" until 1915, the leader of the Lithuanian insurrection notes that one of his close associates, Anthony Jeleński, had testified about him in the fall of 1864. Members of the military commission urged him to confess and thus save others not implicated by the depositions of prisoners. He wrote:

"The evening came, the night. This was the second night so fateful in my life. Many years ago, my personal future and happiness were at stake, the silent self-sacrifice known but to God. I fulfilled my duty, I killed even the hope of personal happiness; yet I never regretted, I could not have acted otherwise. Here the matter concerned the remaining part of what may be dear to a human being: my honor, a good name. Since my infancy I lived only on the love of my country. . . . On the one hand I was called a nobleman, defender of biased superstitions, on the other hand an ardent extremist! Such different and contradictory epithets sustained me. . . . In the citadel I had been prepared to die, even eager to die. . . . I write this with all sincerity. I had not begrudged life, and I had thought so well of my country that I was serene regarding the future of my children. I myself had been an orphan and, thank God, I matured a decent man. . . . Jeleński's deposition shook me. The downfall of a man I had loved and held to be a decent man, the downfall of

[Prince] Nicholas Giedroyć, who was a sort of personification of righteousness, hurt me deeply. I wanted to end this quickly. . . . Yet my conscience spoke differently: . . . Commission members know about two more members of the Branch, won't they use intimidation, won't the arrest of these two lead to other arrests, and hundreds are still free? . . . I decided ten times over and over again one way and the other. . . . I could only help, implicate no one. Yet I would have to write about people who, even though they are sentenced, had not admitted their guilt. . . . I wept and begged God to enlighten me. . . .

". . . Oh, that night — I had not closed my eyes. Lord, even though that night cost me so much and I am leading a hard life to this date, a painful life, I thank Thee for it, because I had won more than a heart, more than a hope of freedom. I had repudiated a certain amount of my country's glory and honor in order to retain inner quietude, to follow the voice of conscience. Lithuania, my beloved, you were a bad mother to me. A great many had died for Thee, yet how many with such self-denial compelled themselves to live and voluntarily to go through torture!

"The next day I asked for paper and wrote my confession! As my determination was born of a pure soul, so God gave me strength, and not for a moment did I violate my people's honor or anyone's interests.

"I concluded that, having studied law, I was well aware of the fate awaiting me, yet I am prepared for it. I touched upon terrorism on the insurgent side. . . . should there be reproachable actions, one must realize that this happened only after General Muravyov's arrival and when the representative of a 70-million people, at the head of an huge army, had not hesitated to employ bloody measures; could it be surprising if a people desperately fighting without weapons . . . should resort to terrorism in retaliation? When my statement was read to the Commission, they did not conceal their conviction that evidently I had written the truth, in agreement with Jeleński's testimony, yet they wanted me to rewrite it, changing the tone. I shot back that this was my conviction and I am only doing my duty. 'But that's obstinacy, you place yourself in jeopardy because of wording, otherwise you might save your life!' Gentlemen, you know well that from the very first moment I had realized that my life is not my own, that it depends not on law, only on General Muravyov's fancy: hundreds of the less guilty people died, some one must state the truth.

"Practically no one had any doubt regarding a death sentence, yet it happened otherwise. I was told that Muravyov was tossing around during the reading to him, yet when it was over he allegedly said in Russian: *khotya odin ne podlichayet* — at least one does not debase himself. I was told this by Dr. Fovelin [Muravyov's physician] . . . . Long daily interrogation began. . . ."

Gieysztor was a firm believer in a dual Commonwealth of Poland and Lithuania — the only member of the Branch to protest against the proposal to secede from the Warsaw Committee and to act independently. He had heard that Commission member Yugan thought well of him, except that "Gieysztor believes in the immortality of the soul and in Poland's future." Commission members admitted frankly that their task was "to doom, to kill, to convict, and also to soil us. 'You know, gentlemen, how history is being written today, and your own children will not recognize you in the script. Your faith — that is self-delusion, you are the Don Quixotes of the 19th century, you believe in truth, justice!' "

After the sentencing and just before the exile to Siberia, Yugan came into Gieysztor's cell to bid him farewell. He asked Gieysztor not to hold his behavior ill. Gieysztor said he wanted to tell him some truths. "More than once you yourself acknowledged to me that our cause is justified, is just. You only pointed out examples of political conditions deforming the concepts of morality. You insisted that a decent person will not take another man's property, yet he will not restore property taken by his father, because that does not burden your conscience. I think differently. I respect the past and the memory of ancestors, and thus I would like to redeem their guilt by my own blood. Let's continue. According to you, our cause must perish forever, because today and in centuries to come the right of might shall rule! You say this is dictated by reason and you are surprised that I, a reasoning person, am blind to this. Yes, my dear sir! A believer sees only what he believes in— this is reasonable to him, because it is just. Yet I too recognize the power of reason and appreciate healthy logic. I charge that you are a monomaniac. . . . Today, you say, there will be no hesitation, there will be a prudent system, flexible, enforceable, and 'Finis Poloniae.' All right, let us reason calmly. There had been no stable system until the present, you say. True, you yourself do not praise today's system, yet there is another, a perfect system, as you think, in your heads (I am not talking about conscience, it must keep silent). Supposing your project of our slow final doom is so wise, so hellishly fatal. . . . No possible changes, no necessary reforms in Russia itself shall change that system dooming us! Excuse me, cold reason is rebelling. . . . Now, Mr. Yugan, we are no longer before the Commission and I ask you to give me your word that you will answer my question truthfully. He gave me his hand . . . In order to inculcate any idea in the masses, it is necessary that the new truth, like a new religion, should nurture itself within man's breast. Excuse me, reason alone is not enough here, faith in that idea is needed also. Tell me, please, within the horde of your activists here, will you find one who would labor for your cause with that self-denial, with that faith with which we go to our death, and in all of Lithuania are there at least a dozen such people who in the interest of their country, disregarding themselves and their careers — who would not be moved by women's tears, by an infant's death, by the voice of one's conscience, by a rich man's purse or the lover's embrace? — Yugan was moved and he walked across the cell. — 'No, I cannot give the word!' — You cannot, and yet you accuse me of a lack of cold reason, of precise calculations, you call us monomaniacs — us, who see numerous armies. . . not noblemen's, but plebeians, voluntarily marching to sacrifice themselves. No, sir, the higher reason must make peace with out faith. How groundless are your theories built on accomplished facts, on force. . . . They do not stand cold reason's criticism and are repellent to your decent selves. Yes, sir, in dying we have your respect also, if a human heart is pulsating in your breast. Yet how difficult will be the moment of death to you, when you look back and see that you have been but a miserable spring in Muravyov's hands!

"Tears involuntarily streamed from my eyes. — I looked up — Yugan also wept. . . . I did not see Yugan again."

"What used to be heroism, today is the fate of many and no longer excites wonder. Not a thirst for glory, but obedience to the voice of conscience guides the behavior of many. . . . History tells us about Regulus, Scevola, and others, about the handful of people defending their homeland. What is that in comparison with the heroism of our children? . . . . What weapons have our people had during the months of combat, under what conditions? Furthermore, how large were their numbers? Compare our defeats — with the French war of 1870! And how much self-denial was shown by our youths during the indagation by commissions, freely confessing that they had gone into the units of their own free will and not letting the menace of death and hard labor intimidate them or to compromise any one! Thousands were sentenced, hundreds died, yet even though they had known our names — who among the fighting youths betrayed us? Still that is a minor thing. Look: when the elders were exiled or imprisoned or let their hands down in resignation, the tireless Constantine Kalinauskas alone continued the conspiracy, intimidated by no one he died for his beloved cause. Famous leaders either perish — or flee abroad, while youths voluntarily, consciously remain in the country. *Constantine Dalewski* repeatedly crossed the frontier risking his life in order to facilitate the escape of others. Others understood their duty differently. To learn the names of the slain fellow nationals . . . frequently mutilated beyond recognition. . . . I name my own cousin *Boleslas* who could have fled abroad, but chose to remain and he perished near Raguva. Even more touching is the example of my other cousin, *Edmund Stengelmeier*. . . . Edmund was lightly wounded (and hid in my Ignacogradas estate. Many peasants knew about this, but they were sincerely friendly to us). Edmund sent his younger brother, *15-year-old Ignatius* abroad and wrote this letter to his mother: 'Beloved Mom, rest assured about Iggie, he is already abroad; as for me, do not hold this against me, Mom, once I had sworn not to lay down arms, I shall not leave the country. But, Mother, please pray to God that He should take us to Himself the sooner, our life is so harsh. And how is James? Edmund.' Is it madness? If this is madness, blindness — it is so beautiful . . . . A few or a dozen days later the 17-year-old boy's prayer was answered. The entire squad perished by Panevėžiukas, in the so-called Royal Forest, and the poor mother had difficulty identifying her child's body." [61]

Young Count *Jaroslaw Kossakowski*, a former officer of the Imperial Guard, returned from France to enlist in the insurrection. When he was captured with the wounded Sierakowski, "the convoy's commander Lieutenant Vongas asked Kossakowski why he, a rich magnate and in good health, did not hide in one of his estates in the area. The young count pressed Sierakowski's hand and said: 'I could not leave my general when he was in misfortune.' " V. Diakov, a Soviet historian, in citing this conversation wrote: "These somewhat naive words were heartfelt and expressed the feeling of respect and loyalty to the commander." Obviously, Diakov has no idea of what a Lithuanian nobleman's *honor* means. . . . Kossakowski was exiled to Siberia.[62]

Besides Stengelmeier, other men of the unit of Father Mackevičius were truly heroes. *Adomas Butkevičius*, a former student of the University of St. Petersburg, was taken prisoner with his skull cleaved, his face shot through, fingers of both hands cut off — yet, according to Smirnov,

[61] Jurgėla, *Lietuvos Sukilimas, op. cit.*, 605-611, citing *Pamietniki Jakóba Gieysztora*, II, Wilno 1913.

[62] Jurgėla, *Lietuvos Sukilimas, supra.*, 296.

during the interrogation he said that he "regrets not being able both physically and morally to complete the undertaken task." He refused to name the insurrectionist government and his student colleagues, and said that he had taken part in the insurrection because of the denial to peasants of "the rights demanded by our times and people." An illiterate nobleman-carpenter *B. Andruškevičius* enlisted in the Mackevičius unit in August 1863, fought in three battles, and refused to testify. *Antanas Jomantas (Jamont)*, another member of this unit and a nobleman, a veteran of many combat actions, "voiced no repentance" when he was captured on July 19, 1864.[63]

[63] *Ibid.*, 509.

Jurgis Bieliakas/Bielinis, 1846-1918, the book-smuggler.

XV.
NATIONAL RENASCENCE

"Renascence, just as birth, is both a continuance and a newness, a living development of a crisis, rather than a resurrection from death," according to Giovanni Papini. "A people's national individuality in its historic evolution acquires different traits or forms. Loss of any of its former characteristics does not end its national identity, except that its individuality suffers, becomes poorer and less articulate. Acquisition of new traits, or development of old peculiarities, at times enriches that identity and makes it more articulate. Renascence, indeed, is neither the birth of a new people, nor the resurrection of a dead people. It marks a historic change or transformation of its national individuality enriched in content and made more distinct."

The Lithuanian renascence of the XIX century was "an excerpt of history, one of its fragments. In order to understand it properly, we must not lose sight of its organic bond tying the national renascence with the wholeness of the people's history." The past should not be "viewed with the eyes of the present," we should not seek in the pre-renascence period "concepts present in the reborn people which had been absent theretofore." Dr. Kajetonas J. Čeginskas, quoted by us above, aptly points out that "the spirit of the times" in a post-Napoleonic Europe created "both an internal Lithuanian crisis and an external threat of Germanization, Polonization and Russification; that is, intensified deliberate efforts to denationalize" Lithuanians.[64]

Wedged between the Western and Byzantine Christendom, Lithuania was the last nation in Europe to accept [Catholic] Christianity. Lithuanian national individuality hardened and survived the two centuries of onslaught by the Teutonic Knights. The Lithuanian expansion eastward encrusted pride and haughtiness upon this people of warriors and administrators. During the several centuries of "Europeanization" in an association with Poland, first the aristocracy and then, from the second half of the XVI century, the common nobility succumbed to the Polish language. The nationalism of the enfranchised classes was sustained by State patriotism jealously safeguarding the equality of Lithuania in the dual Commonwealth with Poland. Cultivation of the Lithuanian lan-

[64]K. J. Čeginskas, "Lietuvių Tautos Atgimimo Pradmenys" (Root elements of the Lithuanian people's renascence) in *Kovos Metai del Savosios Spaudos* (The Years of Struggle for Own Press), Chicago 1957 (77-112), 81-83.

guage, supposedly a deformed relic of the language of the Roman patricians, was neglected. After the dismemberment of the Commonwealth, the onslaught of Russification on Lithuania — on an allegedly "eternally Russian country" because it had used "Russian" language in its statutes before adopting Polish — actually pushed Lithuanians into the arms of Polonization, hastened the process of Polonization and retarded the resurgent native nationalism. In the Russian mentality, Catholicism and Polonism were inseparable and synonymous, and they drummed this alleged synonymity into mentality of the Lithuanian masses. Since the abortive Constitution of May 3, 1791, Lithuania became but a part of Poland in popular concepts, a Lithuanian was but a Pole from the province called Lithuania. Concepts of Polonism and Lithuanianism somehow did not seem to clash in the mentality of the period. Lithuanians writing in Polish crowned Polish literature with Mickiewicz, Słowacki, Syrokomla, Sienkiewicz, and others. The Lithuanian language became identified with the lower strata in the caste system of Russia, yet even peasants sang during the insurrection of 1831 and later, to the tune of the Polish national anthem — the marching song composed by a Lithuanian prince Michael Cleophas Ogiński: "Poland is not lost as long as the Samagites are living."

The XIX century national revival "actually split the former dual Lithuanianism into three types of consciousness. . . . The most numerous was the *traditional* type of national awareness — yielding to alien influence yet not forgetting one's ethnic originality, appreciating and cultivating it, and thus more loyal than the *denationalized* type. The latter decidedly embraced a different nationality and not infrequently was hostile to a new concept of *consciousness* purged of alien influences and overgrowth."[65]

In a XIX century Lithuania Minor, a Lutheran area with a German ruling and urban class, Lithuanians generally were patriots of Prussia and a Gothic alphabet was used in Lithuanian language books and newspapers. In Lithuania Major, a great many Catholic and Calvinist Lithuanians were Polish patriots in their convictions. And then a new species of nationalism based on the cultivation of the ancestral Lithuanian language, pride in Lithuania's great historic role, and the democratization of the society split the Lithuanian people in two: the Lithuanians in language and exclusive loyalty, and the "*gente Lituani, natione Poloni,*" — a term invented three centuries earlier, unjustly im-

[65]*Ibid.*, 111.

puted by some, as Ochmański, to Bishop Antanas Baranauskas whose great Lithuanian poetry had been so instrumental in the process of renascence with whose anti-Polish and anti-religious undertones he disagreed. The first concept ultimately triumphed — even though the painful choice of a nationality was made by some only in 1918 to 1920, after the restoration of a Lithuania independent of its former ties with Poland.

Beginnings of the modern Lithuanian renascence are traced to 1800 —oddly enough, to Thaddeus Czacki's study "About the Lithuanian and Polish Laws," and Rev. Xavier Bohusz's discourse "About the Origins of the Lithuanian People and Language" (1808) prepared at the request of the University of Cracow in connection with the rise of the new science of comparative linguistics. These two events initiated a thence unbroken chain of research into Lithuanian history and language and inspired Michiewicz, Słowacki and other great romantic writers to write, in Polish, on Lithuanian themes of their homeland. Their fellow students at University of Vilnius corresponded, frequently in verse, with their fellow noblemen in the Samagitian dialect. A circle of clergymen and noblemen authors was formed around Bishop Prince Joseph Arnulf Giedraitis (Giedroyć) of Samagitia. Simonas Daukantas initiated a historiography in the Lithuanian language, while his colleague Theodore Narbutt wrote in Polish. This budding movement was disrupted by Russian repressions after the insurrection of 1831. Yet a new stimulus was sparked by Mikalojus Akelaitis, a Sudavian somewhat influenced by Polish positivism, and Laurynas Ivinskis, a Samagite nobleman who published best sellers for farmers — his annual almanacs or calendars between 1846 and 1864.

Meanwhile Bishop Valančius rode the crest with his temperance movement. After the crushing of the insurrection of 1862-1864 to his demise in 1875 he was the unchallenged leader of the Lithuanian people, inasmuch as his diocese embraced also a large part of Auxtaitian (Uplander) Lithuania. Unlike the landed gentry and intelligentsia looking to Warsaw for consolation, hope and spiritual manna, Valančius placed all of his hopes for the survival of the Church and Lithuanianism in the Lithuanian-speaking masses of peasantry and yeomanry. All of his parochial schools were shut down by the regime on the eve of the insurrection, yet his flock was generally literate by that time. He defied the ban on Lithuanian publications by a system of private tutoring and by publishing books in Prussia for distribution in Lithuania through a network of dedicated simple folk. In one of his earliest brochures printed in Prussia he wrote: "The people of Lithuania and Samagitia had not learned Polish in 300 years, because they loved their own language which is especially beautiful. . . . Presently the Muscovite had come to Lithuania, a foreign country. How can they demand that, because of them, this country's people should learn the Muscovite language. Let them first learn Lithuanian, then they will be able to talk to Lithuanians."[66] Father Jonas Katelė (Katėla), pastor of Panemunėlis in the northeastern county of Zarasai, achieved a phenomenal record through the use of manuscript handbooks: by 1881 nearly all of his parishioners were literate, tutored by abler peasants originally instructed by him, and there were more priests like Katelė.[67]

Battle lines were drawn, and the epic struggle over the people's right to publish books in their own language and alphabet began.

[66] Čeginskas in *Kovos Metai . . . supra.*, 98.

[67] Jerzy Ochmański, *Litewski ruch narodowo-kulturalny w XIX wieku,* Białystok 1965, 117; V. Bičiūnas, *Kunigas Jonas Katelė ir jo Laikai,* Kaunas 1934.

XVI.
A PEOPLE'S STRUGGLE OVER THE LANGUAGE RIGHTS 1864-1904

Governor General Muravyov's move against Lithuanian books in the Latin alphabet was inspired by Ivan Kornilov, his Curator of the Vilnius Educational Circuit. In 1864 Muravyov demanded episcopal approval of a religious content booklet to be published by the Government in Lithuanian, in a Cyrillic alphabet. Bishop Valančius examined the text and reluctantly approved it. When soon thereafter Muravyov banned all Lithuanian printing "in Latin-Polish characters," the bishop perceived the scheme. He communicated with the Bishop of Ermland in Prussia and requested that a priest be appointed to serve in the frontier area to assist in publishing books for use in Lithuania. Reverend Zabermann soon settled in Tilsit and acquired a printing shop.

Muravyov's oral order was officially promulgated by his successor, Governor General Constantine (von) Kaufmann on September 6/18, 1865. The order banned any and all publications "in the Lithuanian and Samagitian dialects in Latin-Polish characters" and the ban was applicable throughout the Governorship General. On September 13/25, 1865, the imperial Minister of the Interior, Count Peter Valuyev, by his decree extended the ban throughout the empire. Bishop Valančius, whose residence was moved from Varniai to Kaunas, by a letter dated June 12/24, 1866 notified Governor Nicholas Muravyov, the "Hangman's" son, that Russian characters were improper and totally inadequate to represent faithfully the Lithuanian language sounds.

Valančius summoned a courageous and enterprising young man, Jurgis Bieliakas Bielinis (1846-1918), a resident of a northern county on the border of Courland, who later became the legendary "King of the Book Carriers" — second only to the unglorified trio of priests: Gimžauskas, Sidaravičius and Vytartas. Valančius entrusted 5000 rubles and a number of his manuscripts to the young man who carried his precious parcel to Tilžė/Tilsit. The first eight brochures were printed in Klaipėda (Memel), Karaliaučius (Königsberg) and Leipzig, until Zabermann acquired a printing shop in Tilžė. These brochures were smuggled across the frontier and were distributed far and wide in 1867 and 1868, during the state of martial law which was lifted only in March 1871. The brochures called on the people not to send their children to Russian schools, to refuse to accept books printed in Russian characters and to hide their genuine prayerbooks from the gendarmes. People were forewarned that almanacs printed in Russian characters in Vilnius, ostensibly having episcopal imprimatur, were "replete with matters contrary to the Catholic faith" inserted "after the bishop had signed."

The Zawadzki printing establishment in Vilnius tried in 1865 to reprint older prayerbooks by indicating the original dates of publishing. The ruse was soon detected. The Zawadzki shop was heavily fined and gave up this effort. Enterprising contrabandists, however, facing a heavy demand from customers, in 1865 and 1866 reprinted in Prussia some of the Zawadzki books — reproducing the original publisher's name and dates, as well as the episcopal imprimatur and the Russian censorship permit. When the bishop and Zabermann organized their publishing, some professional contrabandists were at first employed for their unique skills, and a few professionals later assisted the idealists "book carriers." Zabermann in one of his books on his own initiative and without the Bishop's knowledge inserted a panegyric for the Prussian King and a prayer "that God submit you to the rule of our [Prussian] king." This caused trouble a year later, in 1869, when several book distributors were tried, along with the Bishop charged with State treason. In 1888 Zabermann sold his shop to Mauderode and Reylender of Tilžė.

These publications played a tremendous role in arousing the masses to oppose the onslaught of "Russian Orthodoxy, Autocracy, Russian Nationalism" — the motto coined by Minister of Education S. S. Uvarov in 1832 and faithfully upheld until 1915. The number and volume of books printed abroad increased annually. By 1870 several receiving posts were established in the frontier areas and a network of devoted distributors spread. The most efficient organizers were the priests, particularly Silvestras Gimžauskas and Martynas Sidaravičius teamed with a prolific and devoted author-farmer Laurynas Serafimas Kušeliauskas. After the latter's death, Rev. Antanas Vytartas (1863-1932) continued to work almost to the end of the ban in 1904.

After the demise of Valančius in 1875, the book printing, smuggling and distribution was continued by his followers — without a visible or recognized leadership. The entire Lithuanian-speaking population was involved in this struggle led by the clergy and a growing number of laymen, including Prussian Lithuanians, even though most of the Lithuanian-speaking masses in Prussia were generally indifferent to events in "Muscovy" across the border.

The unexpectedly firm and massive resistance surprised the authorities. Panslavism under Russian domination, the Russian historic mission in the face of Western decadence were the dominant ideas in a Russia evolving into an industrialist capitalist nation ruled by reactionaries and the autocracy. With some Russians, like editor Katkov, Russification became their religion. Most of the Russians were not even aware of a Lithuanian nationality. However, the intellectuals and politically active Russians, including Liberals and former Liberals, approved of the Russification policies of the imperial government in general and of the Russification of Lithuanians in particular. The events of 1863 in popular notions were represented as attempts of Polish noblemen to impose severe serfdom, a Jesuit-inspired plot to polonize the Russian population of the eternally Russian land of the Russo-Lithuanian Grand Duchy. The Russian masses were not at all aware of the merciless subsurface struggle of a captive people, abandoned by their own upper strata, to retain their own language and religion, to regain their basic human rights in their own country where even land purchases were denied them, to win the right to pray from their own prayerbooks and to enlighten themselves, to express their views in books and newspapers in their own language and alphabet, to repair their churches, to ornament the roadside and their gardens with crosses — their expressions of the folk arts.

Soon the monopoly of religious content books ended as a new generation of students and intellectuals matured. Lithuanian students in Russian universities published hectographed "newspapers" from 1875. In 1883 *Auszra* — The Dawn — appeared in Ragainė (Ragnit) in Prussia —the first cultural-political newspaper printed for consumption in Lithuania. It was edited by Dr. Jonas Basanavičius, residing in Bulgaria, and a small group in Prussia and across the border in Lithuania calling itself "Lovers of Lithuania." This collectively edited paper avoided severely anti-Russian themes in the hope of gaining legitimacy in Russia, and contained elements of political and economic interests. On the initiative of Prussian Lithuanians — Martynas Jankus, Jurgis Mikšas and others, almanacs-calendars for farmers were published and gained large circulation in Lithuania — just as almanacs in Gothic characters published for Prussian Lithuanians enjoyed good circulation locally. Dr. Georg Sauerwein — "Girėnas" became an important ally of the Lithuanian renascence, particularly in Prussia. A German society for Lithuanian studies was formed — to study and preserve the relics of a vanishing people.

However, the near-idealization of the heathen period of history and occasional articles with Socialist undertones cooled the clergy's support for the *Auszra*, just as its political facelessness antagonized the radical young intellectuals — not to mention the simple farmers who had not understood the themes of the *Auszra.* It ceased publication in 1886. A Catholic *Szwiesa* (The Light) was a short-lived newspaper (1887-8 and 1890). in 1889 a liberal *Varpas* (The Bell) appeared, inspired and edited by Dr. Vincas Kudirka formerly briefly associated with the Polish Positivists. In 1890 a militant Catholic *Apžvalga* (A Review) appeared, followed by the *Tėvynės Sargas* (The Homeland's Guardian). Political appeals and leaflets, ever more radical and belligerent in tone, printed in Prussia and flooding Lithuania, began to worry the Russian authorities. A lesser role was played by Lithuanian newspapers and books published in the United States. By 1890 several ideological and political currents crystallized and matured. By 1896 a Lithuanian Socialdemocratic Party was formed underground, soon (1902) followed by the Lithuanian Democratic Party (farmer-populist with a tinge of socialism) and later by a Christian Democratic Party. The anti-Polish sentiment initiated by *Auszra* was shared by the "parties," inasmuch as a pro-Polish orientation was deemed more menacing than a nearly non-existent pro-Russian one.

Lithuanian scholarly opinion generally discerns three periods in the struggle against the ban on Lithuanian publications: (1) the period of Valančius (1864-1875); (2) 1875 to *Auszra* 1883, with Antanas Baranauskas being the outstanding personality; and (3) 1883 to the lifting of the ban in 1904.

A modern Polish historian, Jerzy Ochmański divides the Lithuanian cultural development into four periods: (1) two centuries of enlightened individuals beginning with Canon Dauksza in the late XVI century, the author of the first Lithuanian book printed in Vilnius, to the publication of elementary primer in 1775 which was reprinted in some 50 editions; (2) the beginning of the XIX century to the insurrection of 1863, the period of patriotic and revolutionary noblemen; (3) "the years 1864-1882 may be called the period of struggle for national culture. Masses of peasants under the leadership of the patriotic part of the clergy with Bishop Valančius at its head managed to resist successfully the Russifying policy of Tsardom, regardless of casualties which were bloody at times. A young generation of peasant intellectuals had grown and matured by 1880 under conditions of a determined muted struggle in defense of the Lithuanian language, Lithuanian books and culture." (4) 1883-1904: the period of 1883-1890 was a period of nationalism accompanied by quickly maturing political currents which Ochmański identifies as "national-democratic, national-clerical and social-democratic workers movement." Professor Stasys Yla calls them "national-Christian, national-Liberal, and national-Socialist Democrats." Ochmański concludes: "In 1890-1905 Lithuania was reborn, a modern bourgeois Lithuanian people was formed which in the revolution of 1905 proved its indomitable will to fight for independence." [68]

[68] Ochmański, *Litewski Ruch. . . op. cit.*, 198-199.

General Muravyov, nicknamed "The Hangman," supervising executions.

XVII.
THE MASSACRE OF KRAŽIAI
1893

In denationalized and Whiteruthenian areas the closings and seizures of the Catholic chapels and churches, and compulsory "conversion" into Orthodoxy in some cases, encountered little resistance from the terrified and illiterate peasants, except in the city of Minsk. In Samagitia —in 1864, when Muravyov ordered the seizure of the church and Bernardine monastery in Tytuvėnai, people filled the church and staged a "sit-in" singing, praying and bearing up under lashing whips. Bishop Valančius praised the people of Tytuvėnai, their "appeals to the mightiest king, their cries and shouts not to take away their church." The bishop exhorted the faithful to gather in and around their churches "and keep the Muscovites away from God's temples," to remain "firm in faith, prepared to bear up under tortures as the ancient Catholics had done."

In 1886, disregarding the concordat concluded with the Vatican in 1882, the authorities demanded that the aged and sick emeriti priests be removed from Kęstaičiai, the church be closed and structures be handed over to Orthodox institutions. As the bishop showed no haste, the police commandeered carts to move the priests and friars. The people, however, refused to surrender their church: they gathered in the church, prayed and sang through nights and days for more than five weeks. They were fed by volunteer parishioners. The police attempted to overturn the mobile kitchen and put out fires — but the women with burning logs chased them away. Finally three "centuries" of mounted Don cossacks arrived, with cartloads of axes, saws and wrecking tools. Mounted cossacks attacked people barring the doorway and lashed the young and the old and the children with whips. Several dozen people were wounded by sabers and horse hooves. Then the Governor of Kaunas arrived. People inside the church and outside ignored the Governor's orders to disperse, and continued to pray and sing.

Finally the soldiers entered the church and dragged the people out one by one. Those resisting were beaten up and detained. Then the priests escorted by cossacks removed the monstrance and the sacred vessels as the cossacks, armed with axes, chopped down altars, holy pictures, confessionals, windows, etc. The people detained at the church yard were released. Father Juknevičius, pastor of the filial church, was exiled to Arctic Russia for five years, charged with inciting to riot.

The most notorious church closing occurred in 1893 — the Massacre at Kražiai. The story may best be told by a disinterested and kind Danish writer Age Meyer (Benedictsen) who published a volume entitled *ET FOLK, der Vaagner, Kulturbilder fra LITAVEN*, Kjöbnhavn 1895. It was published 29 years later in an English translation as *LITHUANIA. The Awakening of a Nation*, Copenhagen 1924. His sympathetic account of the country he had recently visited gave the first insight to foreigners concerning the conditions in Lithuania. We are quoting from the 1924 edition in English.

"These two-three millions of Lithuanians, plain and simple people, without any higher enlightenment, without a spokesman to plead their cause before their oppressor, without a voice strong enough to cry out beyond their frontier of what was going on, these people were hopelessly at the mercy of their arbitrary rulers. The Polish upper classes had . . . too many troubles of their own to think of the affairs of others. The Jews and the Germans had no interest. . . .

". . . The first clumsy move was received with such desperate resistance and defiance that the Russians grew wrath and thought it would be easier to cut the knot than to untie it, easier to pull down all the pillars of Lithuanian nationality and force them to accept Russian nationality. Triumphant Russian reaction sent her hungry flocks down upon the Lithuanian land. The mental bunglers . . . in the schools and Government-Offices were even in Lithuania too insignificant to reap anything but hatred and contempt. Men too incapable and inferior to obtain any position in the home country became teachers in the Lithuanian villages. Former non-commissioned officers, would-be teachers unable to pass their exams, intemperate sons of Russian priests, seedy individuals from different social classes — these were the kind of men who obtained the minor offices in Lithuania. . . . For ten years it pleased the Russians to use Lithuania as a colony for criminals, felons were sent there. . . .

"In order to subdue national feeling the Lithuanians were forbidden to wear their national dress. But what was the good of all this! What was the good of ordering the people to read books printed in Russian letters, what was the good of depriving them of the books they could read! What was the good of Russian teachers and gendarmes, of Russian judges and colonies of criminals, this did not transform the Lithuanians into Russians, the only outcome of all this was hatred and distrust which grew from day to day, and in their church they had a consolidating power strong enough to set every assault at defiance. . . .

"When one comes across national suppression on German soil one feels that it is [in 1895] subject to certain laws and limits, that it respects certain human claims and in any case allows the suppressed ones to air their grievances.

"In Russia it is not so. . . . No church can be built, no bricks inserted, not a wall can be steadied, not even a dilapidated cross by the roadside can be replaced. This decree has become one of the chief weapons against the Roman Catholic Church . . . churches are allowed to fall in ruins, and no new ones are built. The people have not the right to settle their own affairs, nor can they dispose of their common funds, the Russian officers arrange everything for them. The Lithuanians have to witness the one Russian church after the other being built in their country and paid for with their money wherever there happen to be a few Greek Catholics (Russian Orthodox), or wherever by chance there is a Russian garrison. There are now about a hundred (Orthodox) churches in this old Roman Catholic country, and for every year one or more Roman churches are closed and sealed by the authorities as being unsafe, or they are burnt down and must not be re-erected. The peasants then have the choice either of doing without a church, or going to one some distance off, but what is still more important for the Russian rulers is the fact that the priest disappears with the church and his influence is removed, for this makes it easier to draw the people to the Orthodox church . . . priests were forbidden to visit other parishes without permission of the police. In order no doubt to undermine the people's respect for the Church, the police were expressly ordered at the services to read aloud the imperial decrees in Russian; in full uniform, with sword and clanging spurs they thundered out the incomprehensible words over the kneeling congregation. . . . It was decreed at the council of the Governor General to let the police make a search all over the country, and according to a plan agreed upon, the gendarmes made a descent on the Lithuanian parishes.

"The peasants were accustomed to see a couple of policemen watching the churchgoers on holy days — but churchgoers and police had become indifferent, they did not take notice of each other and everything went on in the usual way; but one Sunday the tramping of horses was heard during the service and huge bearded gendarmes dismounted in front of the church. The day of reckoning had arrived, and the peasants in the midst of their singing were filled with fear — it was a case of everyone trying to conceal his treasures — the police seized hymn books and gospels — those who could hurried home through forest and meadow but many were obliged to give up their books — the gendarmes made their way into the farmsteads searching and rummaging, frightening the people by their rough language if any one had ventured to conceal these accursed books which the Tsar himself had prohibited, all books had to be given up, everyone! Although the official robbers only succeeded in finding a part of these books, enough were collected to make a huge *autodafe* in Vilna where the books of poor Lithuanians were transformed into regulation smoke and ashes.

"The offenders did not all escape with merely losing their books, both men and women had to spend months in prison when the gendarme officers happened to be in a bad humor or special circumstances enhanced the offense.

"The war against the Lithuanian language was carried so far that a ukase was issued which simply prohibited parents from letting their children learn to read Lithuanian. If it were found out that the children learned their mother tongue in the homes it meant a fine of 300 rubles, which again meant that only the rich were able to pay it ($150). At the same time judges and other officials were urged to enforce a knowledge of Russian amongst the people. . . .

"The Russians at once encountered the hatred of every one in the country and the contempt of the Polish upper class. Even a simple Lithuanian peasant on the strength of his faith and the word of his priest, felt himself superior to these heretical conquerors, whose representatives in Lithuania, mean and greedy officials, gendarmes, and cossacks did not tend to imbue respect . . . .

"The Government has abolished all the Roman Catholic schools in the whole country, school after school was closed, the pupils dispersed, and too resistant teachers severely punished. With ill advised violence the Russians entirely did away with the old schools in Lithuania, a school in Lithuania was to be like a school in the interior of Russia; in a country where neither socially nor economically it was advantageous to know Russian, this language was all at once to be used exclusively. But the Russian teachers who were sent to replace the Roman Catholic priests and lay teachers were received with such coolness and distrust, that during the first few years the schools were almost empty. As long as the Lithuanians could find teachers for their children outside the enforced foreign schools, they kept them away from the Russian.

"All the Russian village schools in Samogitia in a population of more than a million had altogether 2,444 boys and 89 girls the first year after the suppression of the rebellion and barely half of these were Lithuanian.

"The first teachers from all corners of Russia came to the Lithuanian villages as miserable bread-seekers without knowing the language or customs of the country, and without possessing even the poorest qualifications for carrying out their difficult task, brought the schools into such bad repute, that it had been difficult to raise them again in the eyes of the peasantry."

We are interrupting Age Meyer's story at this juncture to point out that, because of the surprise searches for Lithuanian books and secret schools, clay tiles and bricks with burnt-in Lithuanian alphabet letters were sometimes used for instruction: the police seeking books usually ignored stacks of tiles and bricks — and, at any rate, printed paper books were banned, not alphabet tiles. The most knowledgeable authority on this period of history, Vaclovas Biržiška, notes that the "Lithuanians revived the ancient Assyrian-Babylonian print technique."[69] Teachers in these clandestine schools were itinerants. Let us now continue the Meyer recital.

"Only a year and a half ago (1893) an event took place in Samogitia some twenty miles from the German frontier . . . event of such a revolting nature that the story found its way into the papers all over the world, and perhaps for the first time brought the name of the Lithuanian people to the notice of many. In Denmark special interest was made to attach to the event by the Danish court exercising its influence although in vain to prevent this infamous deed — the closing of the church in Kražiai.

"Now that all the circumstances of the case are brought to light after the verdict of the court at Vilna, the whole affair throws a clear light over the conditions prevailing in Lithuania. The poor victims who gave their blood in the belief they were acting rightly have not given it in vain. They have greatly contributed to open the eyes of many of their countrymen to the wretched position of their fatherland; their blood raised a wave of patriotism amongst the Lithuanians who had emigrated to America and this will assuredly some day benefit their country.

"In the little town of Kražiai was one of the last remaining monasteries which the Russians had spared in Lithuania; a small band of Benedictine monks dwelt there living in accordance with the stringent rules of the Government. An ukase however decrees that when a Roman

[69]Prof. Vaclovas Biržiška, "Pastangos Draudimui Nugaleti" (Efforts to overcome the ban), in *Kovas Metai . . . . op. cit.*, (167-195), 184.

Catholic cloister had dwindled to eight monks or nuns, it has to be confiscated, and the admission of novices is prohibited. In the monastery of Kražiai there were now only eight monks left. The Government through Governor General of Vilna, the former colonel of gendarmes, Arzhevski, gave orders to have the monks removed, the church closed and pulled down, the timber to be used for the building of a Russian school and the land of the monastery to be handed over to the Russian church of the place.

"In Kražiai besides the church of the monastery there was a wooden church one hundred and fifty years old, and so tumble down that the peasants knew its course was about run; they had long ago sent a petition to Vilna praying for permission to restore the church of the monastery without having received any answer. The peasants to begin with could not believe that they were to lose their best church but they soon saw that the authorities were in earnest. One fine day the old monks were removed although they begged that they might be allowed to die in their monastery.

"The priest of the place was ordered to take away the holy vessels within a given time, but now the people interfered. A few chosen men proceeded to Vilna and implored Arzhevski to spare the church. His only reply was that they would be imprisoned if they dared to make any more difficulties. They then went to Tsar Alexander in St. Petersburg and the authorities in Vilna telegraphed to the police of the capital to catch them. By a lucky chance they escaped, succeeded in getting their petition placed in the hands of the Tsar and feeling assured of the success of their mission they returned to their homes. The peasants requested the priests who had come to remove the properties of the church to await the reply from the Tsar. No doubt through some high clerical influence the complaint of the Lithuanians reached Denmark and from there a plea was made for them in St. Petersburg.

"There still came no answer from the Tsar; the priests who only lamely supported the frightened parishioners, were only waiting for an opportunity to carry away the monstrance and the chalice from the sacristy, but the peasants were aware of this and kept watch night and day, two or three at a time, and one morning early the old women overpowered the priest just as he had taken the holy vessels. They bound this Judas and with covered hands they brought back the precious possessions of the church. Then the peasants began to keep up continuous prayers with the priests, until the day when the brutal Governor of Kovno made his appearance in person in order to make an end of the matter.

He arrived in the middle of the night with a band of policemen; he was informed that everything was quiet in the town only some old and young people were in the church praying.

"There was fear and trembling when the arrival of the Governor became known for the people knew what the authorities were like. The women and the children remained on their knees in the church singing hymns, whilst their husbands and brothers with the crucifix and the pictures of the Tsar and Tsarina met the Governor outside the church. They prayed him to spare the church. (von) Klingenberg the Governor answered roughly that all their prayers were superfluous also to the Tsar, that much he could tell them, the church was to be closed and pulled down that night.

"An angry murmur arose amongst the Lithuanians, but the people began to leave the church. Klingenberg all at once gave orders to beat all that came out and to drive out the women and children with the whip. But then the patience of the Lithuanians was at an end. They felt they were maltreated without cause, and indignation seized them all; a hailstorm of stones and pieces of wood fell upon the gendarmes and their chief. Cowards as that kind of men generally are the Governor and his helpers fled into the church, but the peasants broke open the door and (von) Klingenberg with his gendarmes and the Polish priest who was all the time on his side had to take refuge in the loft of the church. He now offered to refrain from taking any further steps with regard to the church, and the spokesman of the peasants requested him to report in writing this night's assault to the Governor General of Vilna. Klingenberg wrote for three hours when suddenly terrified shouts were heard from without: 'The Cossacks.'

"The women and young girls who were again praying and singing in the church shrieked with terror and the Lithuanian peasants made desperate resistance. The Governor climbed down the ladder, his stratagem had succeeded. An order had been sent secretly to the nearest Cossack camp ten miles away: he had been pretending to write his report knowing all the time 300 Cossacks with spears and pistols were on their way. A short and hideous carnage took place that cold and dark November morning, the long lances of the Cossacks tasted blood, these wild fellows rushed into the church, the women were beaten and bound, altars and banners were cut to pieces and the windows smashed.

"A terrified and despairing crowd of peasants were driven on to the thin ice of the river, the ice gave way, some were drowned amidst the coarse shouts and laughter of the Cossacks, some stood in the water until their strength failed them and they went down, most however were dragged ashore and bound.

"The rising was crushed and there was not even a Cossack wounded. The church was sealed and Klingenberg let the Cossacks loose on the little town to catch and bind as many as they could get hold of. The Lithuanian peasants shouted: 'We do not believe that thou art our Governor, we do not believe that the Tsar has refused our prayer' — Klingenberg promptly avenged himself for this offense. The men who were bound were stripped and flogged, in the presence of the women and children, as long as the doctor Vasilenko who tried their pulse found it advisable. 'Perhaps you will know now who is your Governor,' sneered Klingenberg. Lithuanians who escaped have stated that one old woman was flogged to death but this case was not brought before the Court at Vilna, but from what transpired at the proceedings it was ascertained that after they had flogged the men,* their wives and young daughters were handed over to the Cossacks. 'Thanks for your help,' Klingenberg shouted in farewell, 'Teper, dyeti, mozhno gulyat' (Now, children, you can have some fun). The Cossacks' fun in the little town and its environs lasted for several weeks and the fun was as is usual with the Don Cossacks in the land of the enemy and the Grand Turk.

'Death and blood to the sons of the Turk
His lithesome daughters shall be our reward.'

"More than fifty persons languished in jail after this affray for ten months, amongst them seventeen women, two of whom were young girls.

"In spite of all censorship — *not a paper in the whole of Russia was permitted to mention what had happened at Kražiai* — in spite of the desperate efforts of (von) Klingenberg and Arzhevski this terrible misdeed of theirs had not ended in accordance with their plans.

"Their intention was to deport, without the matter being brought before a court of law, the most troublesome of the imprisoned persons, to Eastern Siberia and keep the rest in jail for an adequate number of years.

"As just mentioned this shameful plan did not succeed; for their dastardly deed became widely known, thanks to the Lithuanian papers in Prussia and the best advocates in Russia defended the case of the Lithuanians before the Court at Vilna, where the proceedings had been

*Women were likewise flogged. One woman gave birth to a stillborn baby the next day. A boy of 11 died on the spot after two blows and a kick.

instituted, because the judges were still less independent in Vilna than in the proper jurisdiction of Kovno; this unfairness to the accused prisoners is hardly worth mentioning when it is a question of Russian rule in Lithuania.

"The court passed a 'mild' sentence on the prisoners, varying from ten years' penal servitude to some months, more than half of them being acquitted. The young Tsar Nicholas however annulled the verdict, all being liberated except four. So much was done for very shame, but at the time of writing this book, both these infamous men still [in 1895] fill their important posts, no comment surely is needed." [70]

Dr. Gečys summarizes that at least 27 persons drowned in the river, an undetermined number of people were wounded by swords and shots, 120 were arrested, Klingenberg bid the Cossacks to "Do what you want, just don't touch Jews and Russians." Königsberg and Tilsit papers in Prussia reported the event within two days and called the Russians *Die Söhne der Wildnis.* The official gazette of the Kaunas Gouvernement reported only that four policemen were wounded by rioters, no rioters had suffered. The church at Kražiai was shut down — yet the higher Russian authorities had to reconsider their policy. Klingenberg was soon transferred and such bestial measures were no longer employed.

Rev. Dr. Rapolas Krasauskas notes that Lithuanian resistance induced the Russian government in 1878 to discontinue its quixotic ban on garden and roadside crosses (the ban is back in force under the present Soviet occupation). In 1897 it revoked the decree forcing Catholic pupils to attend services in Russian churches on anniversaries of the Tsar's family, and discontinued the ban on church repairs and construction (the ban was reimposed by the Soviet occupying regime). However, daily prayers for the Tsar's family were continued in schools (presently replaced by courses on atheism and attendance at Communist Party functions).

[70] Age Meyer Benedictsen, *Lithuania, The Awakening of a Nation*, Copenhagen 1924, 190-219; Gečys, *Katalikiškoji Lietuva, op. cit.*, 153-172; P. Klimaitis, ed., *Kražių Skerdynes*, Kaunas 1933; Krasauskas in *Encyclopedia Lituanica*, III, Boston 1973, 184-185; the story of Kęstaićiai — P. Veblaitis, *Kovačsu caro valdžia už Kęstaičių bažnyčią*, Kaunas 1938. On present conditions — see Chapter XXXVIII.

Wounded Lithuanian partisan.

Painting by Antanas Rukštelė

(Original painting owned by Lithuanian Regeneration Assoc., Chicago, Illinois)

XVIII.

THE TUG OF WAR WITH THE OFFICIALDOM OVER THE BAN

On the surface life continued in a typical pattern of a repressed society. Former serfs of private estates paid fixed annual taxes to acquire title to the lands they tilled. The bonded state of serfs on public estates ("the royal peasants") was ended in 1867, and the agrarian reform was generally completed in 1878. Martial law was lifted in 1871, even though large bodies of troops were permanently stationed in the country and regiments of mounted Don Cossacks were roaming constantly. Masses of gendarmes were hunting Lithuanian book smugglers and distributors. Ever more Russian teachers and peasants were arriving to repopulate the several dozen razed villages of yeomen exiled to Russia. Land purchases were restricted to persons of "non-Polish origin" —all Catholics were deemed Poles. Conditions of semi-starvation after the severe crop failures in the late '60s lured migrants to industrial Ruhr in Germany, to England, Scotland, and ultimately to America.

The recruit system was abrogated in 1875 and universal military duty for six years was introduced. This induced young men to "Go West" just before reaching military age. Industrialization made a slow and faltering reappearance. Commerce was stagnant. Railway lines were built for strictly strategic considerations and not for economic reasons. Secondary schools remained only in Vilnius, Kaunas and Šiauliai. In Sudavia, beside a lyceum in Suvalkai, another was opened in Marijampolė in 1867. Therefore, many Lithuanians attended schools in Courland — at Palanga and Jelgava (Mittau). Yet, according to Ochmański, "the conciliatory views of the Young Latvian movement toward Russia which was lending silent support to anti-German efforts, deterred the Lithuanians from imitating their neighbors' methods and [illegible]ms." Sermons and catechization in Lithuanian, rather than in [illegible], made rapid gains after 1870. University and professional edu[illegible]n was available only outside Lithuania — in Warsaw, Tartu, St. [illegible]urg, Moscow, Kiev, Kharkov and Kazan.

[illegible]nteresting phenomenon of the 40-year struggle over the Lithua[illegible] alphabet was the emergence of a non-Samagite leadership. In Sudavia, a part of "Congress Poland," restrictions on land purchases by Catholics were not at all applicable. Serfdom was nominally abolished there by Code Napoleon in 1807. Peasants prospered quickly, acquired lands, sent their children to universities — to Warsaw, and ten annual scholarships were offered by the government to Lithuanians to study in Moscow and St. Petersburg. Therefore, cultural standards here rose faster and Sudavians predominated in the *Auszra*, *Varpas* and other newspaper circles. The great poets of the renascence were Antanas Baranauskas, a mid-Eastern *Aukštaitis*, and Maironis — Rev. Jonas Mačiulis, a *Žemaitis* writing in Eastern Lithuanian dialect.

The Russian regime, officially combatting "Polonism" and seizing Lithuanian language books printed in "Latin-Polish characters," did not ban Polish language newspapers and books printed in "Latin-Polish characters." Therefore, Polish language newspapers and books were printed in Lithuania and were allowed to enter from Poland and abroad. This circumstance speeded up the Polonization of cities and towns, especially in Vilnius and other areas far from the Prussian frontier. The underground Lithuanian renascence proceeded apace, unnoticed and ignored by burghers, intellectuals and the landed gentry. Book smuggling expanded as popular educational and literary works supplemented the diet of religious publications. In 1897 only 16.5% of school-age children attended schools in the department of Vilnius, barely 6.8% in the Kaunas area, yet the census of 1897 showed a literary rate of 41.9% in the department of Kaunas, 37.4% in Suvalkai and 29.3% in Vilnius areas, while in the neighboring Whiteruthenian areas of higher school attendance literacy amounted to 17-25%. Thanks to itinerant teachers, Lithuanians occupied the 4th place in Russia's literacy standards — after the Finns, Estonians and Latvians.

Lithuanian cartoons and political content appeals urged readers to pass them on to others. "The Homeland is calling for help." A Cossack armed with whip was shown chasing a woman: "I am the sower of Orthodoxy sent to Lithuania." A devil seizing prayerbooks by the church, etc. People were roused and treated the Russians with undisguised contempt and condescension. The regime was worried over the ban's boomerang against Russia itself.

Censorship was slightly eased during the Russo-Turkish Balkan War of 1876-7. Young Petras Vileišis, a graduate engineering student, secured from the St. Petersburg censor a permission to publish 5 popular brochures by convincing the censor that the ban applied to "Latin-Polish characters," while his books were written in "Latin-Lithuanian characters" resembling the Czech alphabet. There was a farmer's almanac for the year 1878 among his educational brochures.

Further attempts to gain the local censor's permission were blocked by the intercession of the censorship office in Vilnius, except that Dominican friars of St. Petersburg were allowed in 1878 to reproduce their publication of 1861. In 1879 the Zawadzki printing establishment in Vilnius was allowed to reprint a prayerbook — and more than 50 editions thereafter appeared in Prussia with the Zawadzki name as publishers and with the original 1879 date. Vileišis and a young student Jonas Šliupas tried to get a license for a newspaper *Mūsų Amžius* (Our Age). Their application was seconded by seven Russian academicians and professors, but was denied. Laurynas Ivinskis wrote a booklet for a society for the protection of animals in Rietavas, the estate of the Princes Ogińskis, and Prince Michael Ogińskis secured the St. Petersburg censor's permit in 1881. However, the censor stopped the printing after eight pages had been set. All other individuals' petitions were denied.

In 1879 Professor Baudouin de Courtenay proposed, and the Kazan University agreed, to publish in Latin characters a collection of Lithuanian folk songs compiled by Antanas Juškevičius. Having printed one folio, the printer on his own initiative sent the proofsheets to the censor, and the latter ordered him to stop printing. Courtenay in his memorandum to the university council accused the censor of an illegal attempt to restrict the university's academic freedom to screen its own publications. He argued that Latin characters for Lithuanian texts were used in all scientific works, and that the St. Petersburg censor recently permitted the publication of a number of Lithuanian books in Latin characters. The university council agreed with his reasoning and ordered the printer to complete the printing. Thus three volumes of folk songs were published in Kazan between 1880 and 1882. The Academy of Science of St. Petersburg in 1886 reprinted Dauksza's catechism of 1595, and in 1887 began printing Juška's Lithuanian Dictionary. In 1901-1904 the Academy printed a Crestomathy of Lithuanian texts (two folders) prepared by Professor Edward Volteris. Several Polish and Russian magazines also published some linguistic texts: the censor did not interfere with "official scientific" publications.

Professor Hugo Weber published the Baranauskas poem, *Anykščių Šilelis* (The Grove of Anykščiai) as *Ostlitauische Texte* in Germany in 1882 and sent a parcel of books to the author. The censor in Vilnius held up the parcel. The author, a Monsignor at the time, in his motivated explanation stressed the scientific nature of this publication and pointed out that his poem had been printed with the censor's permit in the almanacs of 1859 and 1860, and was reprinted, with the author's consent, in L. Geitler's *Litauische Studien*; that he wanted to print it in Russia but couldn't, because of lack of proper metal letters. The censor ignored the Monsignor's reasoning. Academician-lexicographer Yakov Grot intervened, and the censor yielded. In 1894 M. Miežinis printed a four-language dictionary, including Lithuanian, in Tilžė, Germany, and the censor allowed its circulation.

Then efforts were made to publish at least some sentences or texts. Rev. Justinas Pranaitis was allowed in St. Petersburg to publish the music scores of his brother's compositions: *Lithuanian Polka* (1893) and *Mazurka for Lithuanian Girls* (1894). Between 1896 and 1900, some concert and play programs were printed in Lithuanian in St. Petersburg and in three cities in Latvia: censor's consent was not required when the police allowed printing, and the local police were not aware of the ban. In 1901 the censor in Vilnius passed a one-page Lithuanian alphabet card — as a "Czech alphabet," and a petition of Vilnius citizens to Archbishop Niedziałowski. The official "Memorial Book of the Kovno gouvernement" for the year 1896 included an article by Professor Kazimieras Jaunius in Russian about the Lithuanian dialects of the Panevėžys County; on the insistence by the noted linguist Lithuanian words were printed in Latin characters. *Praelectio de litteris latinis*, a lecture presented by Jaunius at the Catholic Academy in St. Petersburg in 1899, contained Lithuanian words. Memorial books of the Vilna gouvernement included Lithuanian words in the Matulionis articles on "Lithuanian ethnics in Vilna gouvernement" (1901) and "Names of the fish in Lithuanian" (1903). Directory of the Samagitian Diocese was not allowed, yet the Mohylew Archdiocese in 1902 was allowed to print Lithuanian prayers in Latin letters. Students of Tartu in Estonia attempted to print a Jaunius lecture: one folio was set, then the printer learned of the ban and discontinued the job.

Since 1880 attempts were made to influence Russian public opinion. Lithuanian students in St. Petersburg and Moscow repeatedly wrote letters to editors and articles to the effect that the Lithuanians rejected the Russian alphabet, that their literary program was being blocked, a people is being antagonized, its economic development deterred, etc. Jonas Jablonskis, the future great linguist, published a fictional long list of Russian literary and scientific masterpieces allegedly translated into Lithuanian which could not be published because of the alphabet ban. Several bishops and Prince Ogińskis repeatedly addressed memoranda to the government to repeal the ban — all in vain. The Academy of Science had requested Baranauskas to evaluate a manuscript Lithuanian-Russian Dictionary by M. Gylius, wherein Lithuanian words were written in Cyrillic. Baranauskas in 1878 gave a negative evaluation because of the improper alphabet. Twenty years later, in 1898, the Russian Academy published that evaluation. Several Lithuanians succeeded in presenting their papers regarding the ban at the first congress of Russian "press collaborators" in 1893 — and the congress voted in favor of a revocation of the ban on Lithuanian printing. The Lithuanian Pavillion at the Paris World's Fair in 1900, with its exhibition of banned Lithuanian literature, inspired several articles in Paris newspapers.

The medium of the military postal service was utilized in some instances to transmit "illegal" printed matter. Colonel Vytautas Steponaitis quotes letters published in the contemporary Lithuanian American press by a number of Lithuanians serving in the U.S. forces in China during the Boxer Rebellion. In China they had met Lithuanian officers and men serving in the Russian Army and they supplied the latter with Lithuanian newspapers and books. These publications ultimately reached Lithuania unmolested — by way of the Russian military field postal service from China, as attested by recipients' letters published later.[71] Juozas Tumasonis, for many years the linotypist of Lithuanian language newspapers in the United States, told this writer that as a non-commissioned officer in the Russian Army stationed in Finland during the ban on Lithuanian printing, he regularly received parcels from America and Germany. In one instance, while on night duty at the regimental command post, he was caught reading a book in a "strange" language lacking his company commander's signature. He got the signature by the time he was called to report to the Colonel. Of course, titles and contents of innocuous character were given by him in translation, rather than true contents, when he was called to explain.

By the turn of the century a new method was tried — petitions by township meetings. Stereotype draft petitions were circulated and by 1904 there was hardly a rural township which had not addressed such petitions to the Tsar requesting a revocation of the ban. In Sudavia people insisted on the Lithuanian forms of their names in the records. The authorities at first "rectified" such names by deleting Lithuanian suffixes and later insisted that signatures be given in Russian characters. Peasants and townsmen determinedly refused — and since 1903 the police in Sudavia did not interfere with signatures and store signs in Lithuanian.

[71] Vyt. Steponaitis, *Amerikiečių Lietuvių Kariškos Aspiracijos XIX amž. Pabaigoje* (Military Aspirations of Lithuanian Americans of the end of the XIX century), Kaunas 1927, 71-77.

Since 1897 the Governors of Kaunas and Suvalkai, Governor General Alexander Imeretinsky of Warsaw, the circuit school curators of Vilnius and Warsaw and other officials influenced by Lithuanians, addressed motivated memoranda to St. Petersburg about the harm being done to Russia by the ban on Lithuanian publications and the resulting revolutionization of masses by hostile propaganda from abroad. In 1900 an article in the *Tėvynės Sargas* published in Prussia rebuked the Socialist talk of independence and, on behalf of the conservative Lithuanians, voiced loyalty to Russia and demanded only that Russia respect the Lithuanian people's rights and Catholicism. This article was furiously denounced in the Lithuanian press published in Germany and America. Thirty years later the editor, Canon Juozas Tumas, explained that he had written "that stupid article" violating his own views, as a reasoned necessity impressed upon him by Rev. Juozas Ambraziejus of Vilnius who had friends in the Governor General's office willing to help and looking for some evidence of friendship in a sea of press hostility. Ambraziejus translated the passage and gave the newspaper to his friends who convinced the new Governor General, Prince Peter Svyatopolk-Mirsky who succeeded Governor General Vitaly Nikolayevich Trotsky (dd. in 1901 in Vilnius), to address to St. Petersburg a strong memorandum they had prepared. It urged the lifting of the harmful ban and the legalization of a legitimate Lithuanian press. This memorandum is credited with tipping the scales in the ruling circles.

Finally two trials invalidated the ban. In 1900 Antanas Macijauskas, a student at the Technology Institute of St. Petersburg, printed a "Map of the Lithuanian-Latvian Country," without asking for the censor's permission. All place names on the map were in Lithuanian characters. When the map reached Vilnius eight months later, chief Shakhovskoy of the police press section confiscated the edition and seized 1185 copies. Macijauskas sued him in the Imperial Senate for damages and illegal seizure, alleging that the police action was not justified by any statute of record. On December 14/27, 1902 the Senate held that an executive order banning Lithuanian printing lacked the validity of a law, that Shakhovskoy acted illegally and must pay 12,000 rubles in damages. Shakhovskoy appealed to the plenary Senate. On May 10/23, 1904 — shortly after the imperial manifesto lifting the ban was promulgated — the Senate, Russia's supreme judicial authority, invalidated the ban.

Another trial was deliberately provoked in the same year 1900 by a 25-year-old student of natural sciences. The police chief of Jelgava

(Mittau) in Courland had allowed the printing of Lithuanian posters, in Lithuanian characters, advertising a comedy play. The student, Povilas Višinskis, handed three posters to a shoemaker from Joniškis in the gouvernement of Kaunas and asked him to post them in his town and, if detained, to tell the police where he had received the posters. Shoemaker Brijūnas was indeed arrested, and both he and Višinskis were prosecuted in Joniškis. Their attorney, Longinus Krechin of Šiauliai, a Liberal of Russian extraction, arranged with the judge to find them guilty. Višinskis was fined three rubles or a day in jail. Višinskis deliberately provoked the judge by handing him a poster, and the sentence was increased to 16 rubles or four days in jail. An appeal to a higher instance was lost, as planned, except that the fine was reduced to three rubles. This enabled Krechin to appeal to the Senate. Alongside various arguments in his brief, Krechin advanced a novel claim to the effect that the ban, itself lacking legal validity, had banned "Latin-Polish characters," whereas the posters were printed in "Latin-Lithuanian characters," and there was no statute and no executive decree banning such print. On May 13/26, 1903 the Senate acquitted Višinskis on the ground he had been sentenced under a non-existent law.

Prince Peter Svyatopolk-Mirsky, Governor General of Vilnius, and Governor Peter Veryovkin of Kaunas, being unable to convince the regime by memoranda regarding the harm done to Russia by the ban on Lithuanian alphabet, finally sought out the Tsar during a hunting trip in the Białowież Forest and convinced him. On April 24/May 7, 1904, Emperor Nicholas II by a manifesto lifted the ban on Lithuanian printing.[72]

[72] The events treated in this chapter are documented by Vaclovas Biržiška in his articles in the collective symposium, cited earlier, *Kovos Metai*, 189-194, and the sources indicated in the footnotes. In English — some of these and additional materials are explored in greater detail by Jack J. Stukas, *Awakening Lithuania*, Florham Park Press, Madison, N.J. 1966.

XIX.
RUSSIAN COLONIZATION

The Lithuanian language is the most archaic among the living tongues of the Indo-European family. This indicates a continuity of cultural foundations, character traits and spiritual outlook. Racially, however, modern Lithuanians are not a monolithic people — anthropologically retaining some 74% of the original type in some areas of Samagitia, and only 14-16% in the more recently settled Sudavia and in much traversed areas of Vilnius. There are Baltic, Nordic, Finno-Ugric, Alpine and other types. Inhabitants of cities and towns were mostly descendants of the immigrant merchants and artisans solicited by the rulers in the late Middle Ages — predominantly Germans, Jews, Poles, a few Muscovites, and their intermarriages with Lithuanians were exceptions. Some Prussians, Zemgals and Sudavites-Yathwingians had fled to Lithuania from their homelands which were invaded by the Teutonic Knights or Poles, yet basically these refugees were the same people by race, religion, culture and proximity of language, and only place names and some family names indicate their non-local origination.

Vytautas the Great was a great colonizer of the Ukraine and of the devastated areas of Lithuania. Descendants of the Crimean and other Tatars he had sheltered served Lithuania loyally for centuries in Tatar cavalry units, and Vytautas is still their hero. Those living in compact settlements remained Mohammedans, most numerous in the Ašmena County. After the Lake Melno Peace of 1422 was signed, Vytautas began resettling the vast forest area which had become a no-man's land during the two centuries of the struggle with the Teutonic Order, the former Sudavia called *Wildnis* by Germans. He settled his prisoners of war there, the Pskovians and some Tatars. The area was systematically colonized in the 16th and 17th centuries for economic reasons by Prussian Lithuanians and Germans, Samagites, Eastern Lithuanians, Whiteruthenes and Polish Mazurs. The eastern areas devastated by war and pestilence in the wake of the Swedish, Muscovite-Kozak and Napoleonic invasions, were filled by Whiteruthenes and the frontiers of "Lithuania Proper" no longer represent linguistic borders. Northern Sudavia, part of Prussia between 1795 and 1807 and of "Congress" Poland from 1807 to 1915, became the most Lithuanian area by speech. The Lithuanian language receded westward in the Vilnius area leaving isolated Lithuanian-speaking "islands" in the Ašmena-Nowogrodek-Gardinas triangle. Solid Russian "islands" surfaced in northeastern areas after the suppression of the insurrection of 1831. During the insurrection of 1862-1864, several dozen villages of petty noblemen were razed to the ground, their inhabitants exiled to Russia, and the government systematically colonized Russians in accordance with the program outlined by Muravyov "the Hangman."

As recently as 1938, Tsarist Russia was depicted in Soviet propaganda and historiography as a brutal imperialist and colonialist power. Lately, however, non-Russian nationalities are told that the annexation of Poland was evil, yet the annexation of Lithuania was most beneficial to the Lithuanians. Non-Russians are urged to glorify "the great Russian people," to create "a single Soviet literature and culture," the Russian language is said to be "the second mother tongue" of all, bourgeois nationalism, localism, glorification of the past, relics of native religious "superstitions" are to be combatted, and a "Soviet patriotism and internationalism" identified with serving Russia are inculcated. Since 1972 non-Russian newspapers are filled with "news from the great homeland" —Moscow, Siberia, Uzbekistan, etc. — and "the language of Lenin" is the medium of communication among people of different races. Communism, as interpreted by Lenin and other Russian prophets, is the new religion which brooks no competition from other religions classified as "the opium" or "superstitions."

To the end of the 18th century there had been but one Orthodox church in Vilnius, erected in the 14th century for the entourage of the Orthodox wife of King Algirdas. In 1833, after 38 years of Russian occupation, in the Vilnius gouvernement there were three Orthodox monasteries and four churches with 3,709 communicants, exclusive of army personnel. By building new temples and converting confiscated Catholic churches, Muravyov brought the number of Orthodox temples to more than 100. By the end of the 19th century there were four Orthodox eparchies, including that of Kaunas whose bishop resided in the seized Catholic baroque masterpiece — the Pažaislis monastery.

The late demographer and geographer, Kazys Pakštas, in his article in the Lithuanian Encyclopedia on the Russian colonization of Lithuania, cited the noted Russian historian Vassily Klyuchevsky to the effect that "the history of Russia is the history of a country which colonizes itself" (*Kurs Russkov Istorii*, 1937, vol. I). Pakštas dates the Russian colonization of Lithuania from 1795. It was haphazard at first, it was paced up after 1831 and became systematic after 1863. During the first 65 years of occupation Russian colonization averaged 340 persons per year. After 1864 – in addition to masses of troops, police and government bureaucrats, Russian peasants were settled to replace exiled Lithuanians. A special Land Bank provided financial assistance to settlers. Lest they succumb to Lithuanization, as some Russians had, newcomers were settled in compact communities with their own schools, churches and special privileges. Nevertheless, the newcomers soon ghettoized (in the modern American sense) their settlements. In 1864-1897 some 150,275 Russians were permanently settled – averaging 4,550 annually or 13 times as many as in the previous period. Dr. Pakštas cites Russian (Lebedkin's) statistical data for 1860 and 1897 regarding the number of Russians in Lithuania Proper:

	1860	**1897**
Kaunas gouvernement	4,576	74,500
Vilnius (five Lithuanian counties)	9,625	74,900
Gardinas/Grodno county	8,171	12,900
Suvalkai (five Lithuanian counties)	–	13,100
TOTAL	22,372	249,900

The area included in this account had a population of 3,260,000 in 1897. Therefore, 249,900 Russians comprised 7.67%. Dr. Pakštas continued: "One Russian guarded the political loyalty of 13 non-Russians who were disarmed, barred from even the lowliest government jobs, deprived of their own press and organizations, bereft of the right to purchase land in their own homeland. Russian-populated strategic points . . . cities and railway stations. About 75,000 Russians were settled in cities where places were reserved for their children in secondary schools, to the detriment of the natives. Among the 159,600 inhabitants of Vilnius in 1897–49,933 were born outside the gouvernement of Vilnius . . . about 35,000 were Russian settlers. . . . In 1897 Kaunas had a population of 81,000 among whom more than 20,000 were Russians, mostly military families, because Kaunas was a First Class fortress city. In rural areas compact Russian communities were established in the area of Zarasai-Rokiškis-Brėslauja – about 20,000; in the Lyda County close to 12,000, in Gardinas County about 10,000, and in Ukmergė,

Švenčionys and Trakai counties 9,000 each. Manorial estates confiscated after the insurrections of 1831 and 1863 were distributed to Russian aristocrats — about 20% of all manorial lands. Most of the Russian peasants received landgrants of 20-25 hectare farms supported by public subsidies.

"By the time of World War I the population of Lithuania [Proper] had grown to 4,150,000. . . . Russians may have numbered about 352,750 or 8.5%. Most of them had no spiritual ties with a Catholic Lithuania. . . . About 20% were military and police families, every few years moved to other posts."

Dr. Pakštas notes that the census taken in independent Lithuania in 1923 found 50,700 Russians, and the Polish census in Polish-occupied areas counted about 30,500 Russians, or a total of 81,200. In other words 271,550 Russians had vanished — fled back to Russia when the German armies occupied Lithuania in 1915. Thus the number of Russian settlers dropped from 8.5% to 2.3%. Most of them were landowning peasants.[73] According to the Soviet census, by 1960 the number of Russians rose to 8.5%, by 1970 to 8.6%.

[73]Kazys Pakštas, "Rusų kolonizacija Lietuvoje," in *Lietuvių Enciklopedija*, vol. 12, Boston 1957, 236-238.

XX.
THE LAST DECADE OF RUSSIAN RULE

The Lithuanian masses of peasants and petty noblemen thoroughly disliked the Russians in 1831, even though some of them had never seen any of these *prakeiktos rudinės* — the damned longcoats of the Tsar's army. They did see them face to face during the "military executions" of the agrarian reform period, during the insurrection of 1862-1864, and during the 40 years of seizures of prayerbooks and primers. And they did not like what they saw — people to people.

A markedly literate* and nationality-conscious people surfaced into public life in 1904 and immediately engaged in newspaper and book publishing, organizing credit and consumer cooperatives, theatrical and other cultural activities tolerated by the alien regime. The Lithuanian-speaking intelligentsia was made up of priests, physicians, pharmacists, engineers, attorneys, organists, bank employees — all outside the government. Private schools of music of the Princes Ogiński at Rietavas had maintained a symphony orchestra between 1883 and 1903. The great artist and pianist Mikalojus Konstantinas Čiurlionis received his musical training at another Ogiński school of music at Plungė. An organist school maintained by the Counts Tyzenhauz at Rokiškis had trained a number of composers and choir/orchestra leaders, such as Mikas Petrauskas and Juozas Tallat-Kelpša. Consumer cooperatives were first formed in 1900, and by 1915 there were 161. Commerce was almost entirely in Jewish and German hands. The infant industry was concentrated in the cities, and the industrial proletariat was Jewish and Polish-speaking —the Lithuanian proletariat of half a million landless and farmhands lived in rural areas. By 1900 industrial workers numbered 24,000 or 0.7% of the population, compared with 2.6% in Poland and 1.7% in Russia. Urban and town population constituted 13%. Industrial work hours were from 12 to 14 per day. Artisans worked 13 to 16 hours daily. There was no heavy industry. Some peasants acquired more lands. There was a serious food crisis in 1891 to 1897. Ochmański estimates that 25% of the Lithuanian population had emigrated between 1864 and 1904, mostly to America.

*See Page 130

In a country ruled by the autocracy without an elective representation — political parties were superfluous, yet ideological divisions were present. A first Socialist appeal was published, in Lithuanian translation, by the Polish Socialist Party "Proletariat" in 1883 — *Manipestas artojams* (the Manifesto to Plowmen). Socialist underground circles were formed in Vilnius by Polish and Jewish groups. In 1896 Alfonsas Moravskis and Dr. Andrius Domaševičius formed a Lithuanian Social Democratic Party (LSDP) of 50 members "to gain a Socialist order." In its first program the party aimed at creating "an independent democratic republic composed of Lithuania, Poland and other countries on foundations of a voluntary federation" — obviously excluding Russia. This point was criticized as "nationalistic" by young Felix Dzierżyński, a landed nobleman from the Lyda County who later gained ill fame during the Bolshevik revolution in Russia as the first head of the "Extraordinary Commission" (Che-Ka) of executioners, the secret police. Pressed by Leftists, the LSDP in 1897 adopted a compromise program which rejected an organizational structure on a nationality basis and aimed at making the party that of the native proletariat of all the nationalities of Lithuania, and projecting "a voluntary federation of countries with self-government, legislation and popular administration on the state, country, province and township levels." The program added that "concrete political aspirations are left by the party to the free choice of each member."

Ochmański notes that "the nationalist shade of the LSDP at its birth was all the more remarkable, since its membership at the time was nearly entirely Polish-speaking." Some Polish-speaking members defected and formed a Workers Association *(Związek).* Alongside the LSDP, Jewish Bund and Związek, Joseph Piłsudski formed a "Polish Socialist Party in Lithuania" and tried to subordinate the LSDP to it. The ensuing sharp struggle between Domaševičius (Domaszewicz) and Piłsudski was waged — according to Ochmański — "from Rightist nationalist positions on both sides." In the end the PPSL capitulated. Resident Russians in 1901 formed in Vilnius a branch of the Russian Socialdemocratic Party of about 120 members, to assist in transporting Lenin's *Iskra* ("The Spark") from abroad. The LSDP was depleted by arrests in 1897-99 but recovered by the end of 1899 under the leadership of provincial Lithuanians — Sirutavičius, Daumantas, Janulaitis, Suknolewicz and Kairys who soon organized branches in towns. The LSDP was the only disciplined political underground organization at the time.

Other groupings professing to be "parties" were but loose "currents," exclusively Lithuanian by speech. Kazys Grinius wrote in the Populist *Varpas* in 1896 that Lithuania must be ruled by the Lithuanians themselves and Povilas Višinskis wrote in 1901 in the same newspaper that "our ideal is a free independent Lithuania liberated from alien and native despots." Some Populists attended initial meetings of the Socialists but in 1902 they formed a Lithuanian Democratic Party with the program of a "Free and independent State with regard to other nations and peoples," to be achieved through "direct popular rule" and autonomy, and the distribution of public lands to the landless. A Christian Democratic Party was born soon thereafter.

When a revolution erupted in Russia in 1905 in the wake of military disasters in the war with Japan and of the "Bloody Sunday" massacre in St. Petersburg, the LSDP also moved into action with successful strikes in several cities. In an appeal the LSDP declared its "solidarity with other peoples in abolishing tsardom" and with Russian workers struggling for a constitution. The LSDP demanded abrogation of "exclusive laws with regard to peoples, confessions and castes," liberation of "political and confessional prisoners," security of persons and homes from searches without warrants, universal freedom of speech, beliefs, meetings, associations and strikes, "replacement of the army by a militia." The appeal proclaimed that in a future association of free peoples of Russia "Lithuania shall be a separate State, and its political structure shall be constituted and implemented by a Diet in Vilnius, composed of representatives of the entire population of Lithuania."

The Populists and masses of farmers readily revolted in a typical Lithuanian fashion: various Muscovite officials were collected, placed on outgoing trains — and bidden farewell and good luck in Mother Russia. Township mass meetings demanded the use of the Lithuanian language in schools, government offices and courts, and a legislative Diet in Vilnius. Ochmański notes: "the peasant movement advanced no social-economic demands for the time being." Lithuanian teachers held a congress in Vilnius. By October rural government was in the hands of local Lithuanians: a secret police agent reported that "every Samagite has several copies of proclamations and a loaded pistol in his pocket." By late summer, farmhands staged a number of strikes on the estates. A great political demonstration in Vilnius followed a bloody confrontation between striking workers and Russian troops. Strikes soon followed in other cities. In August Tsar Nicholas II published his edict instituting an advisory legislative Duma, and his October manifesto promised a constitution.

In order to coordinate the activities and to formulate the people's demands, an appeal was published in the daily *Vilniaus Žinios* for a Lithuanian congress of township and city deputies. Dr. Basanavičius with a group of people of various persuasions sent a memorandum to Prime Minister Count Witte demanding "a broad autonomy with a legislative Diet in the ancient Lithuanian capital city of Vilnius, the use of the Lithuanian language in public institutions, and civic rights."

Two thousand deputies from all walks of life, and a delegation of Prussian Lithuanian observers, met in the Municipal Auditorium as a Grand Assembly of Vilnius, within five weeks after the appeal, December 4-6 (November 21-23), 1905. "This meeting, *the only national congress held in Russia in that year*," according to Dr. Alfred Erich Senn,[74] demanded Home Rule with a *Seimas* (Diet) in Vilnius "elected by general, equal, direct and secret ballot, without racial, national or religious discrimination" for all of ethnographic Lithuania (the departments of Vilnius, Kaunas, Gardinas and Suvalkai). The Assembly called on people not to pay taxes, to shut down liquor monopoly stores, not to send children to Russian schools, not to report for induction in the Russian armed forces. It demanded that all school subjects be taught and all official correspondence in township offices be conducted in Lithuanian.

With the Assembly still in session, Governor General Freze published a proclamation in Russian and Lithuanian assuring that the Lithuanian language would be taught in elementary schools, that teachers would be Lithuanian Catholics, that the use of the Lithuanian language would be permitted in the inner affairs of township offices, and that township clerks would be elected by local inhabitants. He urged people to wait until all of the Empire will have been reconstituted on new foundations and legislation will have been passed. A similar proclamation was published by the Governor of Kaunas. The people, however, obeyed their Assembly. The Sudavians promptly proclaimed their reunion with Lithuania.

The organized Populist and LSDP members held caucuses and seemed to predominate in the Assembly, yet the Assembly presidium and committees included some clergy and Rightists, and the resolutions represented a compromise. A separate session of peasant deputies approved

[74] Alfred Erich Senn, *The Emergence of Modern Lithuania*, Columbia University Press, New York, 1959, p. 9.

general resolutions stating: "We, the peasants of Lithuania, firmly believe that we shall live as human beings only when we shall govern ourselves . . . and when all of our country — Lithuania — shall be ruled by the *Seimas* in Vilnius." The wording reflects the language employed by Kalinauskas in 1862-4. Freze's proclamation, according to Ochmański, "was a great victory of the Lithuanian populist revolution." Unfortunately, it was short-lived.

By the end of the year 1905, following the signing of the peace with Japan in August, troops were brought back from the Far East to drown the revolution in blood. Before dispatching "punitive detachments" to Lithuania, the government circulated rumors in Russia about alleged massacres of the Russians there. Martial law was proclaimed in Sudavia and a state of emergency in the departments of Kaunas and Vilnius. Armed detachments terrorized peasants with official robberies under the guise of mass searches. "Gangs of Tsarist officials and police crawled out from their hiding places and like a flock of ravens followed in the wake of troops to wreak venomous vengeance on yesterday's victors, today again — by the grace of the reaction — their slaves," says Ochmański. The Governor General's promises were forgotten, yet the Lithuanian language gained some legitimacy. People were ordered to reinstate the former administration within three days, or else — heavy contributions would be levied and "public enemies" jailed. Several peaceful towns were shelled by artillery. The data of the Vilnius gubernatorial office reveals that there were 187 political prisoners in 1904; 1,303 in 1905; about 2,900 in 1906. The official vengeance sent a large wave of emigrants to America — this time including university students and intellectuals.

According to Senn, "After 1905 the Lithuanian leaders worked strictly within the officially allowed limits of the Russian political system." Ochmański holds that the revolution of 1905 in Lithuania was "so different from the one in Russia and akin to that of Poland." It tied socio-political goals to the national liberation. It had been "an ordeal of fire and baptism of the renascent Lithuanian People. It attested that no amount of violence will be able to tear from the hearts and minds of Lithuanians the indomitable awareness and a will to fight tsardom for the independence and a just social order."[75]

Contemporary leadership was indeed moderate in outlook, realistic in orientation, and inexorably nationalist. The formation of a Christian

[75] Senn, *The Emergence of Modern Lithuania, op. cit.*, 10-11; Ochmański, *Historia Litwy, op., cit.*, 218.

Democratic Party was delayed as the Bishop of Samagitia withheld his approval — while Bishop (von der) Ropp of Vilnius sanctioned (in 1906) a Polish "People's Democratic" group which proved to be violent in its Polish nationalism. Catholics nevertheless formed a number of societies for work among workers, housemaids, students, for book publishing, private schools, etc. Catholic-Nationalist collaboration in a single newspaper proved abortive, and the Nationalists formed a People's Progress Society and published their own magazine *Vairas* (The Helm). Nevertheless, people of diverse ideologies collaborated for common objectives, as in the several graduated elections to the State *Duma* where ideological partisanship gave no advantage.

Quotas were fixed for representation of gouvernements in the Duma, and elections were indirect. Township voters elected their County electors, the latter picked Gubernatorial electors who selected the Duma Deputies. So-called "parties" were lacking structural networks and the means for influencing public opinion in all three venues of these graduated elections. Lithuanian leaders met in departmental conferences to approve candidates to be supported locally, to elect men who would not adhere to Russian ruling parties. Consequently, Leftists were generally favored. When the Polish-speaking groups snubbed Lithuanian overtures, the Lithuanians joined hands with the Jews and acted together in all subsequent elections. The Lithuanians held seven seats in the First and Second Dumas, four were elected to the Third and Fourth Dumas. In each Duma Lithuanian Deputies sided with the opposition. The Russian public heard from the Duma rostrum protests of the Lithuanian people against the oppression, and thus thought of their own condition. Lithuanian Deputies demanded agrarian reform, distribution of lands to the landless, the rights of their language in local administration. They succeeded in legalizing the Lithuanian language in eight city magistracies of Sudavia. The groundwork had been laid in the last Duma for a Home Rule bill, and the Cadet (Constitutional Democrats) Party supported Martynas Yčas, the Lithuanian Calvinist spokesman elected by a predominantly Catholic constituency. The bill was to be debated in March 1917.

Immediately before World War I conditions of life were tolerable under the last Tsar. By 1915, twenty-five Lithuanian newspapers were published. Cultural, economic, professional and scientific societies were developing their activities. A number of private schools were operated by educational societies. The licensing of societies was strictly regulated and editors were penalized for infractions, yet newspapers continued to roll from the presses, and secret societies functioned whenever the government withheld its permission. There was an air of freedom. The Society of Sciences was allowed to send its delegates to America to collect funds for a National Home in Vilnius. Life was marred only in the diocese of Vilnius by the consistent episcopal oppression and intolerance of the Lithuanian language. Only one church in Vilnius was set aside for Lithuanian services, Lithuanian priests were assigned to non-Lithuanian areas, and Polish priests in Lithuanian parishes refused to allow services or prayers "in the heathen tongue."

In 1914 the Teutons collided with the Muscovites, and Lithuania became a battlefield. With the Kaiser preoccupied in Belgium and France, the Tsar's armies under generals bearing German names invaded Prussian Lithuania — and during the brief occupation managed to exile many Lithuanians to Russia, including the family of Martynas Jankus, the farmer-publisher of the period of renascence. A few months later, after "the Second Tannenberg" battle, the Muscovite troops with their wagon trains of the loot were expelled and driven beyond the line of the Nemunas River. The life and economy of Lithuania were disrupted. Warring armies laid waste and drove hundreds of thousands of civilians away from home.

A Lithuanian Committee to Aid the Victims of War was organized, with a seat in Vilnius. It extended its helping hand far and wide, aided by generous contributions of fellow Lithuanians at home and abroad, and by subsidies from the Russian government. The Germans mounted an offensive in 1915 — and on August 18 they seized the fortress city of Kaunas. On September 19 they took Vilnius, and the front was stabilized along the Daugavpils (Dvinsk)-Narocz-Krewo line.

After 120 years of hideous oppression and barbarous misrule, the Muscovites were out of the country. The Teutons arrived.

XXI.
RECONSTITUTION OF THE LITHUANIAN STATE

Early in the war, Deputy Martynas Yčas spoke from the Duma rostrum of the Lithuanian People's hope "to see Russia free and happy after this war" and that "after the smashing of the German forces the Lithuanians, now split in two, will be united under a single Russian banner." This statement resembled the reasoning of the Polish deputy Roman Dmowski who strove for a reunion of all three parts of the dismembered Poland under a single Russian scepter as the pre-condition for reconstituting a Polish State. Šilingas and Malinauskas, "similarly, yet with greater humility and ingratiation typical of the political 'school' of Basanavičius," likened Lithuania to a shining Baltic amber necklace fractured under German pressure, and voiced a belief that "our brethren beyond the frontier" would be liberated and "united with us, because the historic mission of Russia is to be a liberator of peoples." Dr. Senn observes that the Russian government "offered the Lithuanians no sign that their hope would be fulfilled."

The Relief Committee of Vilnius split into two parts: some moved to Petrograd under Deputy Yčas as chairman, others remained in Vilnius under the chairmanship of Antanas Smetona.

On November 4, 1915 the Germans set up a Supreme Eastern Command — *Oberbefehlshaber Ost*, in short called *Ob-Ost*, to provide a military government for the occupied territories. Originally the Ob-Ost area embraced Courland, departments of Kaunas, Vilnius and Suvalkai, and the areas of Gardinas (Grodno) and Białystok. The Suvalkai and Vilnius departments were soon linked into a Vilnius Circuit, and finally on March 15, 1917 the *Bezirks* of Vilnius and Kaunas were merged into a *Militärverwaltung Litauen* with headquarters in Vilnius, under Prince Franz von Isenburg-Birstein.

War and military needs were the sole concern of the Germans, as they were of Napoleon in 1812. All public life was extinguished, newspapers shut, horses and foodstocks requisitioned at will without compensation and with no consideration for the inhabitants' needs. Timber was wasted for road paving and exported to Germany. Deserted estates and farms were exploited by army overseers and forced labor, in effect restoring serfdom in the shadow of summary courts and executions.

Famine broke out in 1916. Gold and Russian currency were withdrawn from circulation and occupation rubles and metal coins were issued. Occupation Ostmarks were later printed with texts in German, Lithuanian, Polish and Latvian. A Lithuanian language newspaper *Dabartis* (The Current Time) was published by the military. In 1917 the publication of a heavily pre-censored *Lietuvos Aidas* (The Echo of Lithuania) was allowed in Vilnius. The military attempted to open German schools run by non-commissioned officers glorifying the Kaiser and Germanism. No correspondence was permitted in Lithuanian. Polonization was aided, most likely inadvertently for reasons of convenience, inasmuch as the German gendarmerie included a great many Poles from Poznania and Silesia, and Polish was the medium of communication with ordinary civilians.

During the years 1915 and 1916, Lithuanian activities in the homeland and abroad centered on relief operations. The informed national opinion was frankly neutral in a war between two oppressors. Lithuanians were serving in both the Russian and German armed forces. Relief was needed for civilians in the homeland, for the refugees in Russia, and for internees and prisoners of war of Lithuanian nationality in Germany, Russia and France. Relief operations on both sides of the war fronts necessitated consultations on neutral soil, and such conferences were held at Stockholm in 1915, at Berne and Lausanne in 1916. A Lithuanian American relief mission of Rev. Dr. Vincas Bartuška and Dr. Julius J. Bielskis was allowed to visit German-occupied Lithuania in the spring of 1916. These contacts on neutral soil were continued throughout the war and facilitated a meeting of minds and the coordination of planning.

This was important when the German policy began toying with the idea of a Lithuanian kingdom united with either Saxony or Prussia. A Lithuanian Information Bureau supported by funds from America was moved from Paris to Switzerland early in the war and it facilitated communication with Lithuania. At home the Relief Committee complemented its membership with persons representative of all political shades, and made every effort to relieve the conditions, to wrest concessions from the Germans, to open Lithuanian schools and to train teachers. Ultimately concessions were wrought, about 1,000 private schools, including teacher seminaries and a number of secondary schools teaching in Lithuanian, were opened. However, the German military occupational regime demanded their licensing annually. The Germans ignored the request to open an university.

Efficient relief operations, the Congressional-Presidential promulgation of a Lithuanian Tag Day in America, the Papal relief aid, intensive Lithuanian publishing and propaganda activities abroad coupled with the dignified refusal to serve in a subservient capacity to the military occupant at home — were impressive signs of an intelligent and unified leadership, mutual adjustment and coordination. The stubborn Lithuanian tug of war with the military occupation authorities also gained friends and good will for the Lithuanian cause in the *Reichstag* circles opposing the militarist camp — in the *Zentrum* Party and among German Social Democrats.

Meanwhile, the all-Lithuanian conferences and the Lausanne Congress of the Oppressed Nationalities in 1916 demanded independence for Lithuania. In January 1917 the Lithuanian National Council in the United States paraphrased the Berne and Lausanne resolutions and demanded that "an united Lithuania be given absolute political independence." The Autonomy Fund, a relief organization in America, in January 1917 changed its name to the Independence Fund.

On the Russian side of the front, the Lithuanians were second only to the Poles in leading the procession of freedom-seeking nationalities. Two secret political conferences were held in Moscow in January and in Petrograd in February 1917. The Lithuanian Deputies of the Duma attended the Petrograd meeting and were instructed to "openly demand from the parliamentary rostrum a broad autonomy for Lithuania." It was agreed that the five major parties form a central political organ to steer "toward the sole objective . . . attainment of independence for the Lithuanian nationality." Concurrently, Lithuanian Deputies told the session of the Central Committee of the Russian Constitutional Democratic Party that the Lithuanians "will never willingly renounce their aspirations for freedom" and that "very undesirable consequences for both the Lithuanians and Russians" would follow if such freedom were denied. On February 21/March 6, 1917 the Lithuanian parties and their Duma Deputies adopted a bold resolution to proclaim in the Duma that "the Lithuanian nation, irrespective of class distinctions, demands the right to decide for itself its political fate and destinies."

On March 13/26, 1917 the political parties formed a Lithuanian National Council which at once demanded self-government and a Constituent Assembly for Lithuania, and set up a "Provisional Administrative Committee of Lithuania" to supervise institutions evacuated from Lithuania. A week later the Council's delegation called on the Presidium of the revolutionary Council of Deputies of Workers and Soldiers, and on the Provisional Government. Chairman Steklov-Nakhamkes of the Presidium agreed that "a free Lithuanian People should determine its own political destinies" and assured the delegates that the Soviet would "energetically undertake to carry the Lithuanian voice into full effect." Prime Minister Lvov "congratulated the orderly initiative of Lithuania" and promised to lay these proposals before the next session of the Provisional Government. However, Lvov's declaration of March 27/April 9, 1917 only disclaimed Free Russia's designs to dominate other peoples or to subjugate them. Soldiers of the front armies began organizing, and the Lithuanian Soldiers Union formed at a congress in Petrograd in May voiced its "amazement and regret" at the Government's inaction with regard to Lithuanian demands.

A National Assembly convened on May 27/June 9, 1917 in Petrograd, with 300 delegates in attendance. Influenced by the chaotic Russian revolution, Liberals joined with the Social Democrats and Populists in opposition to "clericals and bourgeois," and a small group of pro-Bolshevik soldiers threatened to use force. The Catholic and Nationalist majority yielded, and a Liberal Petras Leonas was installed as chairman. In sessions lasting until June 2/15, the Rightists demanded an outright declaration of sovereignty for Lithuania, the Leftists spoke of "the right of self-determination" — only Mykolas Sleževičius, the future Prime Minister, sided with the majority. When the resolution for independence was adopted by 140 to 128 votes, with four abstentions, the Leftists stomped out singing the Marseillaise. In a separate session the left bloc on June 4/17 adopted resolutions similar to the Assembly's, except that the question of independence was reserved for the Constituent Assembly of Lithuania to decide. As a consequence of this disunity, the joint National Council ceased to exist in Petrograd.

The American entrance into the war, reports of thousands of Lithuanian Americans enlisting in the armed forces, the acceptance by Russian revolutionaries of the German Social Democratic slogan of "peace without annexations or contributions," the Russian improvement of this slogan by coupling it with a catch-all motto of unrestricted worldwide "national self-determination," and the spontaneous exercise of self-determination in the Ukraine, Armenia and elsewhere — complicated the situation for the German military in Lithuania. The Ob-Ost had to delude the Zentrum and the Socialdemocratic opposition in the Reichstag that the Kaiser was fighting in self-defense. Independence for Poland was already accepted in principle by all the belligerents. It would be well to control the infectious self-determination by sponsoring it overtly — and binding the "self-determined" peoples to Germany by military and economic conventions.

The Ob-Ost reluctantly yielded on May 30, 1917 to the pressure from Berlin: a *Vertrauensrat* was to be handpicked as an advisory appendix of the Militärverwaltung Litauen. Leading personalities were sounded out. However, the Lithuanians surprised the Ob-Ost by declining to become "trusted councillors" and by proposing that an elective representative body be formed. The Germans tried to play up their flirt with local Poles, but failed to impress the Lithuanians. After additional pressure from Berlin, the Ob-Ost hesitated and consented to the holding of a Lithuanian Conference. Of the 264 elected Parish deputies and nominees of the Relief Committee in Vilnius, the Germans allowed 214 representative Lithuanians from all areas of the country to travel to Vilnius.

The Germans had advertised a forthcoming Lithuanian *Anschluss*. However, the Vilnius Conference of September 18-22, 1917 elected a 20-member Council of Lithuania and unanimously voted for "an independent state of Lithuania" within ethnographic frontiers, with a guarantee of cultural liberty to minorities, and that a Constituent Assembly would "lay the foundations of the State and define its relations with other states."

While the Ob-Ost was nursing its disappointment, nine Lithuanian delegates attended a Congress of the Nationalities of Russia sponsored by the Ukrainian Central Rada in Kiev in October, 1917. The Congress unanimously approved a number of resolutions, including the demand that the Provisional Government of Russia concede the right of Lithuanians to form "a sovereign Lithuanian State" embracing the Lithuanian areas of Russia and Prussia — the only independence resolution voted by the Kiev Congress. Immediately thereafter Lithuanian delegates from Russia, the United States and Switzerland meeting in Stockholm October 18-20, 1917 approved the resolution of the Vilnius Conference and acknowledged the Council of Lithuania the true representative and the supreme authority of the nation.

Returning from Stockholm, Duma Deputy Martynas Yčas, Under-Secretary of Education in the Russian Provisional Government, went to Moscow to attend the All-Russian Pre-Parliament — where Prime Minister Alexander Kerensky spoke "and opened the eyes of our own Leftists." Kerensky, the head of the Russian Democracy, raged against Finland which had declared its independence and total separation from Russia. "Let not Finland deceive itself that this Democracy, which . . .

had stood up for Finland's people, would presently be impotent . . . after our own emancipation from the Tsarist chains. No. She possesses enough strength and enough cannon to turn on Helsinki and, at the same time, other peoples who might be entertaining a desire to separate from Russia." According to Yčas, Kerensky gesticulated, stamped his foot and hysterically pounded the dais with his fists. "Listening to him, the Latvians, Georgians, Ukrainians and we, Lithuanians, realized clearly that there was little difference between the Old and New Russia on the issue of enslaved nationalities. Guided by this realization, the Lithuanian Deputies [of the Duma] and delegates drafted a proper reply to Kerensky, a firm reply declaring our total separation from Russia, even from a Democratic Russia represented by Kerensky. This declaration was read on behalf of all of us by Deputy M(ikalojus) Januškevičius, Deputy Leader of Kerensky's own [Socialist Revolutionary] party."

At this time, on the eve of the Bolshevik uprising, Lithuanian Council (Taryba) delegates were allowed to travel to Switzerland. They were Antanas Semtona of the Right, Jurgis Šaulys of the Liberal bloc, Steponas Kairys of the Social Democrats, and Rev. Justinas Staugaitis of the Christian Democratic bloc, accompanied by Rev. Jonas Maculevičius, better known as Maironis, the great "Poet of the Renascence." In Berne they met American and Swiss Lithuanians and two delegates returning from the Second Stockholm Conference. The Second Berne Conference of November 2-10, 1917, approved the demand of the Vilnius Conference for independence and acknowledged the Taryba of Vilnius as the nation's supreme spokesman. Germany's annexationist designs were denounced, and policies to be followed were outlined.

While the Lithuanians were conferring in Berne, the Soviet of Deputies of Workers, Soldiers and Peasants was swayed by the Bolshevik wing of the Social Democrats. Led by Lenin and Trotsky, the Bolsheviks seized power on October 25/November 7, 1917 and unseated Kerensky. The very next day the Second Congress of Soviets enacted a Declaration of Peace "without annexations and without indemnities". Annexation was explicitly defined as "any incorporation of a small and weak nationality, regardless of the time when such forcible incorporation took place, regardless also of how developed or how backward is the nation forcibly attacked or forcibly detained within the frontiers of the larger state, and finally, regardless of whether or not this large nation is located in Europe or . . . beyond the seas." The process of self-determination was likewise clearly defined in the next paragraph. "If any nation whatsoever is detained by force within the boundaries of a certain state and if that nation, contrary to its expressed desire — whether such desire is made manifest to the press, national assemblies, in parties' decisions, or in protests and uprisings against national oppression — is not given the right to determine the form of its State life by free voting and completely free from the presence of the troops of the annexing or strange State, and without the least pressure, then the adjunction of that nation by the stronger State is annexation, i.e., seizure by force and violence." Lenin, the author hereof, and the Soviet Government thereafter violated both the letter and the spirit of this Declaration. At the time, however, it made good propaganda unmatched elsewhere.

Exactly one week later, on November 2/15, 1917 the Council of People's Commissars, under the signatures of Lenin as Chairman and Stalin as Commissar for the Nationalities Affairs, decreed the Declaration of Rights of the Peoples of Russia which boldly enunciated the right of secession: "2. The right of Russia's nationalities to free self-determination up to seceding and the organization of an independent State."[76]

Oddly enough, a large Lithuanian Conference met at Voronezh in Russia the very next day and sat between November 16 and 19. Its resolutions disclose remarkable intelligence of the Lithuanian political activities in the German-occupied homeland, in the United States, and in neutral countries. The Voronezh resolutions stressed the concurrent and united demand for the independence of Lithuania within its ethnographic frontiers.

On November 22, 1917 the Bolsheviks proposed "an immediate opening of negotiations for peace." Germany accepted a week later, on November 29. On that very day the Taryba delegates returning from Switzerland, stopped off in Berlin where Chancellor von Hertling declared Germany's recognition of the right of Lithuania, Poland and Courland to exercise self-determination. The three Lithuanians — Smetona, Kairys and Šaulys — were received by the Chancellor and General Erich Ludendorff. On December 1, 1917 — the day of the Eastern Armistice — the Taryba officers signed a preliminary protocol at the Berlin Foreign Office. The document promised that in return for German support of the restoration of Lithuania as a State, Lithuania

[76]Max M. Laserson, *The Development of Soviet Foreign Policy In Europe, 1917-1942*, A Selection of Documents, *International Conciliation Series*, Carnegie Endowment of International Peace, New York, January 1943, 10-11, cited by Jurgėla, *Lithuania and the United States: The Establishment of State Relations*, Fordham University, New York 1954 (MS), 29-30. All of the quotations in this Chapter are from this M.S. dissertation.

would conclude military and economic conventions with Germany. A formal declaration to that effect would have to be approved by the Taryba in Vilnius.

In his last published account of the Vilnius phase of the struggle for independence, the late Dr. Jurgis Šaulys, Secretary of the Taryba, recounted that the Lithuanians did not believe in a German victory. At the moment, however, the Allies were deaf to Lithuanian pleas and German arms reigned supreme on the Eastern front. As peace parleys between the Central Powers and Russia and the Ukraine began at Brest Litovsk, the Germans pressured the Taryba to implement the Berlin Protocol. A disinterested researcher, Sir John W. Wheeler-Bennett, cites the authority of the noted German Socialist, Scheidemann, to the effect that the German High Command had made it plain to the Lithuanians that, unless the Taryba accepted the German formula, "the Supreme Command would insist upon the establishment of a new strategic frontier for Germany ... cutting the country in two, and leaving the Lithuanians on the east of it to their own devices."[77]

Dr. Šaulys attested that the Lithuanians procrastinated and played for time. When they finally succumbed to the pressure, they did so in the belief that the German defeat would free Lithuania from the extorted and "unavoidable" terms of the Lithuanian Declaration of December 11, 1917, which proclaimed the independence of Lithuania and, in a separate paragraph, promised to conclude military and economic conventions with Germany.

The Germans wanted the Taryba to send a delegation to Brest Litovsk to communicate Lithuania's self-determination, "omitting in silence, however, the second part" of the proposed declaration. The Taryba declared that it would do so, provided the Germans first answer: "1. When and on what terms the country's administration will be transferred to the Council of Lithuania? 2. When will the occupation army be withdrawn from Lithuania and the opportunity granted to organize a Lithuanian militia? 3. Whether and when the German Government will recognize the restitution of Lithuania's independence?" There was no answer. "However, negotiations and pressures continued until, finally, the formula desired by Germans gained twelve votes, while four members resigned from the Council and the rest abstained from voting." [78]

[77] John W. Wheeler Bennett, *The Forgotten Peace*, New York 1939, 107.

[78] Jurgėla, *Lithuania and the U.S., op. cit.*, 31-34.

The Lithuanians did not go to Brest Litovsk. Kamenev reported to the Soviet about the negotiations he had attended and about "the desire of Poland, Lithuania, Courland, and parts of Eastland and Livland for complete independence and for separation from the Russian State." He said Russia was ready to draw conclusions but would insist on a plebiscite "with the exclusion of any sort of military pressure in any fashion whatsoever." On January 1, 1918 the Petrograd Soviet voted that the free self-determination of Poland, Lithuania, Courland, etc. "is impossible whilst foreign armies remain in them and until the return of the evacuated portion of the original population."

With the Brest Litovsk parleys hanging in uncertainty, Taryba members tried to heal the internal rift. On *February 16, 1918* all twenty members met in Vilnius and signed an unconditional Declaration of Independence severing any and all ties with other states. Carefully calculated steps were taken to apprise the homeland and the world of this fateful decision. The text was set in large type taking up the full front page of the *Lietuvos Aidas.* The paper was printed during the night and dispatched all over the country. Proofsheets were then taken to the Military Censor — who yelled and swore talking to some one on the phone and promptly confiscated the edition — so he thought. While this was taking place, Dr. Šaulys took a typed and signed copy of the Declaration to von Bonin, Counsellor of the Foreign Office attached to the Ob-Ost. Other copies were already on the way to friends in Berlin through clandestine channels within the military.

The local authorities affected complete dumbness but they could not hold their wrath when the suppressed Lithuanian Declaration was printed in three Berlin dailies on February 18, 1918 and Deputy Grübert, Chairman of the Zentrum Party, read it from the Reichstag rostrum and highly commended it to the Government. On March 23, 1918 — after the signing of the Treaty of Brest-Litovsk — Chancellor von Hertling at a reception for the Taryba's delegation,read the Kaiser's writ of recognition of Lithuania's independence based on the declaration of December 11, 1917 *and*, in addition thereto, conditioned on Lithuania's assumption of an unspecified "share of Germany's war burdens, which are promoting Lithuania's emancipation." The Germans would not negotiate any further at the moment — and at home the "recognition" made no difference. Lithuania was able to form a Government only on the Western Armistice Day, November 11, 1918. The Lithuanians received no help from the Germans in organizing armed resistance to the Russian Red Army which invaded at the heels of the retreating Germans.

Details of other developments may be followed in this writer's dissertation and in Dr. Senn's work.

XXII.
THE WAR AND PEACE: 1918-1920

At one point the peace parleys at Brest-Litovsk were broken off because of unacceptable German terms. The Germans ignored Trotsky's formula of "neither war nor peace" and moved inland — as close to Petrograd as Estonia. Lenin pressed for peace on any terms and revealed for posterity the relative value of any treaty signed by a Soviet Government, the mere tool of the Communist Party. The night of February 23-24, 1918 Lenin told the Soviet meeting in the Tauride Palace:

> "The Central Executive signs the peace, the Council of Commissars signs the peace, but not the Central Committee of the Party. For the behavior of the latter the Soviet Government is not responsible." [79]

The signing of the Brest-Litovsk Peace Treaty on March 3, 1918 was preceded by Trotsky's excellent propaganda regarding self-determination in non-enemy empires — obviously the British and French — and by statements of the Soviet and its delegates at Brest-Litovsk regarding the absence of conditions for free self-determination in German-occupied Lithuania, Poland, etc. Vincas Kapsukas, a former member of the LSDP, had been summoned from America to become a minion of the Russian Communist Party and he was on the staff of the Russian peace delegation at Brest-Litovsk.

Lithuania lay well West of the line of territory ceded by Russia. On August 27, 1918, several supplemental Russo-German treaties were signed in Berlin. Among other things, in Part IV of the political treaty Russia of the Soviets renounced its sovereignty over Estonia and Latvia, and confirmed the cession of its sovereignty over Lithuania.[80]

These were, of course, treaties extorted from Russia. However, there was no compulsion in the Soviet Government's inspired action two

[79] Wheeler-Bennett, *The Forgotten Peace, op. cit.*, 261.

[80] *Ibid.*, 427, 429; *Foreign Relations of the U.S., 1918, Russia*, I, 598, 602-617; *International Conciliation*, No. 386, *op. cit.*, 45.

days later: decree No. 698 of the Council of People's Commissars annulling the partitions of the Commonwealth of Poland and Lithuania. Article 3 of the decree enacted in Moscow August 29, 1918, provided as follows:

"Art. 3.—All agreements and acts concluded by the Government of the former Russian Empire with the Governments of the Kingdom of Prussia and the Austro-Hungarian Empire in connection with the partitions of Poland, are annulled and for ever by the present Revolution, in view of the fact that they are contrary to the principle of self-determination of peoples and to the revolutionary, legal conception of the Russian nation, which recognizes the inalienable right of the Polish nation to decide its own fate and to become united.

Signed: Chairman of the Council of People's Commissars:
V. Ulianov / Lenin /
Deputy People's Commissar for Foreign Affairs:
L. Karakhan
Executive Secretary of the Council of People's Commissars:
Vlad. Bontch-Bruyevitch" [81]

These were treaties and decrees signed by "the Central Executive . . . the Council of Commissars" — including Lenin in his capacity of Chairman of the Council of People's Commissars, *not* as head of the Russian Communist Party for whose behavior "the Soviet Government is not responsible."

The Government's master — the Party — disregarded the treaties. "In direct contravention of the terms of the Treaty of Brest-Litovsk, the Bolsheviks continued and, as the opportunity presented itself, even increased their efforts to intervene in Lithuanian affairs. Lithuanian units of the Russian army which were trying to go home were demobilized and disarmed by the Bolsheviks, who in turn set about organizing their own Lithuanian units. The Voronezh Council, which had announced its recognition of the Taryba, was suppressed in March, and the presses of the Council were taken over by the Commissariat of Lithuanian Affairs. In April the Commissariat of Nationalities of the RSFSR ordered its divisions to infiltrate the German-occupied territories of the Russian Empire, and accordingly the Commissariat of

[81] *Polish-Soviet Relations 1918-1943*, Official Documents, Polish Embassy in Washington, Confidential, n.d., p. 71; *Polish-Soviet Relations 1918-1943*, Polish Information Center, New York 1943, pp. 5-6.

Lithuanian Affairs began training special agents."[82]

A Central Bureau of Provisional Communist Organizations of the Occupied Territories, including Finland, Poland and Lithuania, was formed on September 15, 1918, and Lithuanian Section of the Russian Communist Party was formed October 10, 1917. Kapsukas was twice sent to Lithuania on a mission of organizing a Communist Party inside Lithuania. Officially, however, "Kapsukas arrived in Vilnius as a member of the Soviet mission for the regulation of the Soviet Frontiers"[83] — September 22-27 and in November, 1918.

According to Ochmański, propaganda literature printed in Russia was sent with agents into Lithuania "since the beginning of 1918." By March they succeeded in converting some members of the LSDP in Vilnius "into a Socialdemocratic Party of Lithuania and Belorussia, which on September 14, 1918, in an understanding with representatives of the Lithuanian Section of the SDPRR(b) created a Communist Party of Lithuania and Belorussia (Western)." In the Lithuanian language propaganda the tie with Belorussia is usually omitted. The hybrid party held its first "congress" in Vilnius October 2-3, 1918, "attended by 34 delegates representing nearly 800 Party members." These agents, dispatched or recruited by Moscow, decided to follow the example of the Russian proletariat and incite a proletarian revolution in Lithuania. Ochmański notes: "A similar resolution had been approved at the conference of Lithuanian Communists in Moscow at the end of May 1918. However, neither the congress nor the conference preoccupied themselves with enlisting the peasant masses to take part in the forthcoming revolution." Ochmański considers that the so-called Provisional Soviet Government, formed later, erred on two counts: it nationalized land, and "called for volunteers into the army, rather than proclaim a general mobilization. At the moment Lithuanian Communists relied on the armed aid of Soviet Russia." Obviously, the root cause was the lack of Lithuanians: in 1940 less than one-half of some 1600 members of the Lithuanian CP(b) were ethnic Lithuanians, and the percentage of non-Lithuanians among the agents dispatched to Lithuania in 1918 was even greater. This hybrid apparatus serving two geographic and ethnically different areas increased its ranks "three- or four-fold" by the time of another gathering in Vilnius in December 1918. "In Vilnius itself the

[82] Senn, *The Emergence of Modern Lithuania, op. cit.*, 33-34.

[83] Jurgėla, *Lithuania and the U.S., op. cit.*, 36, citing Jurgis Šaulys, member of the Taryba, in *Mūsų Kelias*, Dillingen, Germany, No. 7 (119), February 12, 1948.

Party did not have more than 250 members and candidates."

The Central Committee of this party meeting in Vilnius on December 8, 1918 — "urged by the Central Committee of the SDPRR(b)," according to Ochmański — decided to hasten the revolution by creating a Provisional Revolutionary Government of Workers-Peasants and adopted a manifesto written — or brought — by Kapsukas, "to be published December 16, 1918."

Official Party histories change every few years. The Ochmański book, printed in Poland in 1967, had been joyously greeted in Vilnius at first— and then banned from Lithuania: the author had cautiously described the events of 1939-1940, including the Ribbentrop-Molotov Pacts and the Soviet occupation after an ultimatum— rather than the fictional "restoration of the Soviet power by revolutionary masses" dreamed up by Party "historians."

The version of the Party history printed in the December 1967 issue of the *Komunistas* notes that the CK of the RKP(b), that is: Central Committee of the Russian Communist Party/bolshevik, gave "full assistance through the Central Bureau of the Lithuanian sections of the RKP(b), directed by V. Kapsukas and Z. Angarietis. V. Kapsukas had twice — September 22-27 and November 7, 1918 — visited Lithuania. . . Since the fall of 1918 the entire activity of the CB of the Lithuanian Sections of the RKP(b) was devoted to widening the Party work in Lithuania." On November 10, 1918 Kapsukas reported to the CB in Moscow after his return from Lithuania. The Central Bureau voted: "1) to send more men to Lithuania; 2) to send agitators into the midst of the German soldiers; 3) to take measures to prepare armed forces." Efforts were made to create "the 5th infantry Vilnius regiment of the Red Army" and "agitators" were dispatched throughout Russia to hunt down "workers and peasants born in the Lithuanian gubernias."

This 1967 version of the Party history claims that "the CK of the RKP(b) V. Lenin, helped to decide the form of national statehood of liberated nationalities and their relations with the Russian people. The Communists of Lithuania stood for creating a national state of the Lithuanian people and that this national state unit should enter the RSFSR with *autonomy* rights. The CPL leadership came out against declaring Lithuania a separate independent Soviet republic." The blame for this is placed on "Luxemburgism which, as is known, insufficiently evaluated the significance of the national movement in fighting for the liberation of the worker class." This reference to Rose Luxemburg seems to confirm the impression of the predominance of the non-ethnic urban element in the "Lithuanian" subdivision of the Russian Communist Party. The historical account of 1967 continues that on December 8, 1918 a committee of three was to draft a manifesto of a would-be "Provisional Government" and that its author was Kapsukas, "pupil of the great Lenin," hurrying back to Moscow.

The Central Committee allegedly approved the manifesto the same day, and Kapsukas was "sent to Dvinsk to print the manifesto there." The footnote to this statement reveals that three members were sent to Daugavpils/Dvinsk "to establish *contact with the Red Army units coming to aid*, and to supervise creation of Soviet government organs in Lithuania's northeastern and eastern areas." The history adds that "after consultations with the CK of the RKP(b), the manifesto was printed with the date of December 16, 1918." Lenin was not with the invading Red Army. However, that army had a direct telephone link with Moscow: Kapsukas consulted the CK of the RKP(b) "by a direct telephone line." The history also notes that Kapsukas in his book stated that this date and indication of Vileika as the seat of the revolutionary government "were intended to mislead the counter-revolutionaries"—not to mention generations of the Party faithful.

Dr. Senn had examined available contemporary data and pre-1959 publications. He notes that the "first Bolsheviks from Moscow, sent by the Central Bureau of the Lithuanian sections of the Central Committee of the Russian Communist Party, arrived in Vilnius in April 1918. By July a conference of Communist sympathizers laid the foundations for a 'Social Democratic Workers' Party of Lithuania and Belorussia.' The word 'Communist' was not used at first for fear of frightening of prospective converts, but on August 14 [Ochmański dates it September 14, 1918] the Central Committee of the new party, meeting in Vilna, changed the name to the Communist Party of Lithuania and Belorussia." Kapsukas and Aleksa-Angarietis "together with several other Communists, had arrived in Vilna in the beginning of December with instructions from Moscow. They were immediately co-opted into the Central Committee of the Communist Party of Lithuania and Belorussia. According to Kapsukas himself, the move was made on instructions from Moscow, for in fact the Lithuanian Communists were loathe to declare their independence from Russia. The draft of the manifesto of the government, drawn up by Kapsukas, stressed the need for close bonds with Russia with the proclamation, 'Long live union with the RSFSR.' In reviewing the manifesto, the Central Committee of the Russian Communist Party eliminated the reference to union and also changed the name of the government to the Provisional Revolutionary Workers' and Peasants' Government of Lithuania."

Dr. Senn points out that the Party announcement of December 16, 1918 stressed that this Provisional Government was "responsible only to the Central Committee of the Communist Party of Lithuania and Belorussia," and that the Central Committee in turn had the "rights" of a regional committee of the Russian CP and was "completely subordinate to the Central Committee of the Russian Communist Party." Dr. Senn indicates publication of these manifestoes and other pronouncements in newspapers dated December 22-29, 1918. He notes that Moscow made no effort to hide its role and cites *Izvestiia* of December 25, 1918: "Soviet Russia ... had followed the path of least resistance, namely that of creating independent Soviet republics of Estonia, Lithuania and Latvia." Dr. Senn continues: "In actual fact, the Communist government was only a shadow government. Immediately after its organization on December 8, its members had split up — some remained in Vilna; others, taking the name of the government with them, went to Vileika. Beyond the attempts to gain recognition by the Soviets, this government seems to have done nothing but publicize its program. The purpose of its formation was simply to prepare the way for the Red Army." [84]

This writer, a high school student in Vilnius at the time, never heard of this "government" until the Russian troops were seen on the streets walking arm-in-arm with German Spartakist soldiers on January 6, 1919. All the mouthing on the streets was done in Russian by non-Lithuanians, and the troops were Russians. Some weeks later Polish "Red" units showed up. These crossed over to the Polish lines when the Russians tried to commit them to battle.

All Party histories proudly stress that on December 22, 1918 the Soviet Government promulgated a decree signed by Lenin — in his capacity of Premier: "The Russian Soviet Government recognizes the independence of the Soviet Republic of Lithuania. The Russian Soviet Government recognizes the Soviet Lithuanian Government as the supreme governmental authority of Lithuania, and, until the Congress of the Soviets, [recognizes] the authority of the Lithuanian Provisional

[84]Senn, *The Emergence of Modern Lithuania, op. cit.*, 34-35, 63-65. Ochmański's version — *Historia Litwy, op. cit.*, 248-249. *Komunistas* No. 12 (522), Vilnius, December 1967, 78-79, 84, 94-96, 98-101, 105. Incidentally, the first attempt by the Soviets to interpret history to Lithuanian readers was made in 1957 with the first volume of *History of the Lithuanian SSR* — from prehistory to 1861! The next edition in 1963 dared to extend the history "of the LSSR to 1918."

Revolutionary Workers' Government headed by comrade Mickevičius-Kapsukas." This decree further ordered "proper civilian and military organs of the RSFSR to render to the Soviet Lithuanian Government and its army every assistance in the struggle for the liberation of Lithuania from the yoke of bourgeoisie." This action was ratified the next day, December 23, 1918, by the Central Executive Committee with regard to Estonia, Latvia and Lithuania.

A Party historian, K. Navickas, in the November 1959 issue of the *Komunistas* adds a comment regarding this bastard birth: "The fact that the Government of the RSFSR recognized a young Soviet Lithuanian Republic unmasked the lie of the USA and British imperialists that Soviet Russia allegedly sought rapacious aims with regard to the Baltic countries." On the other hand, Lenin's action in his dual capacity to fulfill his Party's "international obligation" to liberate the people of Lithuania from bourgeoisie without their asking for it, seems to expose as plagiarism the authorship of the more recent "Brezhnev Doctrine" with its application in Czechoslovakia to liberate people from "communism with a human face."

Russian armies lent to a non-existent "Soviet Lithuanian Government" advanced in the footsteps of the homeward-bound demoralized German armies ruled by Soldier Soviets. There was no fighting: the Russians stopped wherever the Germans stopped, keeping a respectable distance. Ultimately the Russian occupation line extended from south of Ventspils (Windau) in Latvia, west and south of Šiauliai to south of Ukmergė, to slightly more than midway between Vilnius and Kaunas, to south of the Varėna-Lyda line. The only resistance encountered by Russian liberators was north of Vilnius where they fought a hastily organized militia of Polish high school and city youths. The claim that "only 500 Red soldiers occupied Vilnius" is dreamed up.

The Lithuanian Army of volunteers was founded on November 23, 1918. The Germans promptly disarmed Lithuanian soldiers venturing into streets with their own arms. On January 1, 1919 the Lithuanian Tricolor displaced the German flag over the Gediminas Hill in Vilnius — and neither the Germans nor Poles intervened. The company of Lithuanian volunteers departed as the Germans withdrew on January 4, 1919. The Russians arrived on January 6. They tore off the yellow and green stripes of the Lithuanian Tricolor and left the red strip fly over the Gediminas Hill — until the Polish army seized Vilnius in April 1919. After the fall of Vilnius, the German troops remaining in occupation by order of the Allied Powers, interfered less in local affairs, and

Lithuanian army and local militia units mushroomed all over the country.

The raw Lithuanian troops engaged the Russians in battle from mid-February. In March 1919 the Germans allowed Polish troops to enter Gardinas where a Whiteruthenian regiment of the Lithuanian army was in process of organization. On May 31 the Poles disarmed this formation. Aided by railway workers, Polish troops unexpectedly descended on Vilnius and seized the city on April 19, 1919. A Lithuanian general offensive was started by the end of April, and the Russians were thrown across the Daugava River by August 28, 1919 — just as the Russian "Whites," a mixed force of well equipped German troops overnight turned into a "Russian" army bolstered by Russian prisoners of war evacuated from Germany, began infiltrating into northern Lithuania and then invaded *en masse.*

This motley force was nominally headed by a Russian Colonel Bermondt-Avalov professing allegiance to the all-Russian Government of Admiral Kolchak in Siberia. The well equipped Russo-German army, backed by the famed "Iron Division" of General Rudiger von der Goltz, attempted to advance into Estonia, allegedly to join the Yudenich army tolerated by Estonia and supplied by the Entente Powers. Repelled by the Estonians, this army assaulted Riga. Beaten off by Latvian units aided by Estonians and a British naval flotilla, the Bermondtist avalanche descended on Lithuania. Units of infuriated Lithuanians were hastily withdrawn from the Russian Red front — the Red Army was still in occupation of Daugavpils/Dvinsk across the river from Lithuanian and Polish lines: the last Lithuanian scouting party crossed the Daugava on January 3, 1920. In a furious campaign the Bermondtists were defeated in a three-day battle at Radviliškis in November 1919. The Bermondtists were saved by the Entente mission headed by French General Niessel. The Lithuanian troops had to stand by as the murdering and marauding "Russian White Army" retreated to Germany by December 15, 1919 — harrassed by local guerrillas defending their families and homes.

Soviet Russia made several overtures for peace to the newly recreated states extending from Finland to Poland in 1919. These countries held joint conferences and preferred to treat with Moscow jointly. However, the Entente Powers, including the United States, favored the Russian Whites and objected to peace negotiations with "the Bolshevists," without offering any aid or *de jure* recognition to the states outside Poland. Finally these states decided to negotiate separately. Peace Treaties were signed by Soviet Russia with Estonia on February 2, 1920; Lithuania, July 12, 1920; Latvia, August 11, 1920; Finland, October 14, 1920. The Treaty of Peace with Poland, signed March 18, 1921, was concluded by Russia and the Ukraine.

In a curious twist of facts, the Soviet Russian treaty of peace with Lithuania states in one article that "Russia and Lithuania had never been in a state of war," even though the document is entitled "Treaty of Peace." A Polish writer, Władysław Wielhorski, notes that he had resided in Kaunas in 1919, that he had read Lithuanian war communiques reporting battles against Soviet Russian armies, had known of the casualties and saw soldiers being treated in the army hospital, and had seen Russian prisoners of war in a camp at Kaunas, and that he was puzzled by that article in the treaty. He conjectured that Lithuania was the only state which had received any payment in gold, and was wondering about the reason. This writer questioned some former members of the Lithuanian Constituent Assembly and diplomats regarding this clause. Most of them were not at all aware of that clause. One diplomat recalled that, on the verge of breaking off the parleys, the Russians had insisted on that wording and the Lithuanians paid little heed to it — while Poland was stretched between Lithuania and Russia.

The Government of Whiteruthenia, or Belorussia, sheltered by the Lithuanian government in Kaunas, lost its asylum. Some of its members emigrated to Russia, others to Czechoslovakia and elsewhere. Whiteruthenian units dwindled to a battalion, then to a company of infantry until the demobilization — but these were units of the Lithuanian regular army, not the Belorussian Republic.

Antanas Juozapavičius (1894-1919), the first officer of the Lithuanian Army killed by the Soviet army during the War of Independence.

Death of Antanas Juozapavičius. —*Painting by E. Jeneris*

Pranas Eimutis (1897-1919), killed by the German Spartakists, while defending the first American Mission in Kaunas.

Povilas Lukšys (1886-1919), the first soldier of the Lithuanian Army killed by the Red Army during the War of Independence.

General Silvestras Žukauskas (1860-1937), Commander-in-Chief of the Lithuanian Army during the War of Independence.

Molotov signs secret document in 1939 to divide Baltic States and Poland.

XXIII.
ERA OF PEACE AND FRIENDSHIP 1920-1939

The Treaty of Peace between Lithuania and the Russian Socialist Federated Soviet Republic signed in Moscow on July 12, 1920 provided: "Article 1. Proceeding from the right proclaimed by the R.S.F.S.R. of all nations to free self-determination up to their complete separation from the State into the composition of which they enter Russia recognizes without reservation the sovereign rights and independence of the Lithuanian State, with all the juridical consequences arising from such recognition, and voluntarily and for all time abandons all the sovereign rights of Russia over the Lithuanian people and their territories.

"The fact of the past subjection of Lithuania to Russia does not impose on the Lithuanian nation and its territory any liabilities whatsoever toward Russia.

"Article 5. In the event of international recognition of the permanent neutrality of Lithuania, Russia on its part undertakes to conform to such neutrality and to participate in the guarantees for the maintenance of same.

"Article 9. The Russian Government shall return at its expense to Lithuania, and shall hand over to the Lithuanian Government, the libraries, archives, museums, objects of vertu, educational supplies, documents and other property of educational establishments . . . removed beyond the limits of Lithuania during the World War of 1914-17. . ."[85]

The Peace Treaty was ratified by the Constituent Assembly of Lithuania elected by secret general ballot under a proportional representation system, which on May 15, 1920 had reaffirmed the declaration of independence. Prisoners of war were dutifully exchanged, a repatriation mission was allowed to function in Moscow and all refugees of various nationalities who wanted to return were repatriated to Lithuania. Only a small portion of the archives and libraries was returned.

On the diplomatic level — relations between the governments remained correct and almost friendly, inasmuch as both Germany and the Soviet Union for their own selfish reasons favored the independence of

[85] *League of Nations Treaty Series*, vol. III, p. 122.

Lithuania — lest Lithuania should fall under the influence of Poland which had been promoting a *cordon sanitaire* and was generally deemed to be the agent of France in the East. Of course, a kind word for Lithuania in her dispute over Vilnius with Poland, helped Moscow to gain a reputation as a champion of small states, of "the rule of reason, of justice and of law" — to use the U.S. statement of July 23, 1940 denouncing the Soviet aggression against the Baltic States. In 1926 Lithuania signed a treaty of nonaggression with the Soviet Union. By a separate note, the Soviet Union reaffirmed the peace treaty including its territorial delineation, and that the "factual violation of the frontiers of Lithuania, against the will of the Lithuanian people, did not change the views of the Soviet Union regarding the territorial sovereignty of Lithuania" fixed in the Moscow Peace Treaty. The nonaggression treaty was extended twice — on April 4, 1934 it was validated until December 31, 1945. Nevertheless, Moscow itself violated this treaty and the territorial guarantees by imposing a "mutual assistance treaty" in 1939. In 1929 the Soviet Union and its Western neighbors adhered to the Kellogg-Briand Pact outlawing war as an instrument of national policy. In 1933 Moscow persuaded its neighbors, including Lithuania, to sign the strongly worded definition of aggression convention initiated and vigorously promoted by Moscow. It included "Article 3. No consideration of political, military, economic, or any other nature can serve as an excuse or justification of aggression."

For many years, there was no exchange of tourists: the only Soviet citizens traveling through Lithuania were diplomats and diplomatic couriers to and from Germany and Western Europe. Commerce was negligible. In the thirties Moscow began sponsoring friendship societies, including tours of Russia by handpicked writers, poets, musicians, newsmen, professors. Some Lithuanian authors were translated into Russian and published in the Soviet Union. A Soviet warship returning from a coronation courtesy visit to Britain called at the Lithuanian port of Klaipėda.

Consequently, on the government level relations were excellent. Lithuania's Minister in Moscow, Jurgis Baltrušaitis, had been renowned as a poet writing in Russian and was popular among Russian intellectuals. Soviet official visitors signing in the guest book at the War Museum in Kaunas penned lofty statements which were publicized in the press. The Lithuanian public was led to believe that whatever Russia had done in the past, the guilt lay on the Tsars, the tsarist system, on the exploiting classes which had for centuries oppressed Russians themselves.

Of course, treaties were signed by governments — not by the Central Committee of the Communist/bolshevik Party, the master of governments. Therefore, the Communist underground was carefully nurtured. Picked youths were secretly brought from Lithuania for training in special Party schools in Russia and shipped back to Lithuania. Clandestine meetings of Communist/bolshevik Party of Lithuania were most frequently held in Germany. Whenever Soviet spies were detected and tried, Moscow had a number of Lithuanian clergymen on hand in its Arctic labor camps and offered to exchange them for convicted spies. One of these traded persons was Antanas Sniečkus, the Communist Party secretary-general for more than 30 years after this Party again became a subdivision of the Soviet K/b Party.

And then came the Hitler-Stalin conspiracy against peace and humanity in 1939 . . . for which Hitler's minions were tried and sentenced by an international tribunal in which Hitler's Soviet partners sat among the judges.

The monument of the Unknown Soldier in Kaunas, destroyed by the communists.

XXIV.
MOSCOW-BERLIN CONSPIRACY vs. PEACE AND HUMANITY

After years of venomous ranting by Hitler against "bolshevism" and by the Kremlin against Fascism and Naziism, mankind was astonished to learn of a "Nonaggression Pact" concluded between Nazi Germany and Soviet Russia. It was signed on August 23, 1939 in the Kremlin by Minister of Foreign Affairs Joachim von Ribbentrop and Chairman of the Council of People's Commissars of the U.S.S.R., People's Commissar for Foreign Affairs Vyacheslav Molotov, in the presence of Stalin, the Soviet dictator and head of the Soviet Communist/bolshevik Party. In view of the stalled Soviet negotiations in Moscow with Britain and France, and the mysterious comings and goings between Moscow and Berlin, misgivings were voiced regarding a possible secret deal. Indeed, the "Nonaggression Pact" included the following:

"SECRET ADDITIONAL PROTOCOL

"On the occasion of the signature of the Nonaggression Pact between the German Reich and the Union of Socialist Soviet Republics the undersigned plenipotentiaries of each of the two parties discussed in strictly confidential conversations the question of the boundary of their respective spheres of influence in Eastern Europe. These conversations led to the following conclusions:

1. In the event of a territorial and political rearrangement in the areas belonging to the Baltic States (Finland, Estonia, Latvia, Lithuania), the northern boundary of Lithuania shall represent the boundary of the spheres of influence of Germany and the U.S.S.R. In this connection the interest of Lithuania in the Vilna area is recognized by each party.

2. In the event of a territorial and political rearrangement of the areas belonging to the Polish state the spheres of influence of Germany and the U.S.S.R. shall be bounded approximately by the line of the rivers Narew, Vistula, and San.

The question of whether the interests of both parties made desirable the maintenance of an independent Polish state and how such a state should be bounded can only be definitely determined in the course of further political developments.

In any event both Governments will resolve this question by means of a friendly agreement.

3. With regard to Southeastern Europe attention is called by the Soviet side to its interest in Bessarabia. The German side declares its complete political disinterestedness in these areas.

4. This protocol shall be treated by both parties as strictly secret.

Moscow, August 23, 1939.

For the Government of the German Reich:	*Plenipotentiary of the Government of the U.S.S.R.:*
V. Ribbentrop	V. Molotov"[86]

[86] *Nazi-Soviet Relations 1939-1941.* Documents from the Archives of the German Foreign Office, edited by Raymond James Sontag and James Stuart Beddie, Department of State, Washington, D.C. 1948, p. 78.

Stalin and Ribbentrop, Hitler's Minister of Foreign Affairs. They conspired to occupy Lithuania.

British and French negotiating missions were still in Moscow when the public part of this Nazi-Soviet "nonaggression pact" was announced. The guarantee of "a free hand" for the USSR in the Baltic States area had been the stumbling block in Moscow's negotiations with London and Paris. On December 5, 1939, the British Secretary of State for Foreign Affairs, Viscount Halifax, stated in the House of Lords: "We have tried to improve our relations with Russia, but in doing so we had always maintained the position that rights of third parties must remain intact and be unaffected by our negotiations. Events have shown that the judgement of His Majesty's Government in refusing agreement with the Soviet Government in the terms of formulae covering cases of indirect aggression on the Baltic States was right. For it is now plain that these formulae might have been the cloak of ulterior designs. I have little doubt that the people of this country would prefer to face difficulties and embarrassment rather than feel that we had compromised the honour of this country and Commonwealth on such issues."[87]

On September 1, 1939 the German armed forces invaded Poland to make "a territorial and political rearrangement of the areas belonging to the Polish state." Sixteen days later the Soviet armed forces invaded Poland from the east to fulfill their share of that rearrangement, and stopped at the line of demarcation of the "spheres of influence" agreed upon in the Ribbentrop-Molotov "Nonaggression Pact." Toasts were raised in the Kremlin to the Russo-German friendship "cemented with the blood" — of the Poles. By September 25 Stalin suggested that it would be "wrong to leave an independent Polish rump state," and that Berlin should waive its claim to Lithuania in return for some Polish territory. Stalin "added that, if we [Germany] consented, the Soviet Union would immediately take up the solution of the problem of the Baltic Countries in accordance with the Protocol of August 23, and expected in this matter the unstinting support of the German Government."[88] Ribbentrop was back in Moscow on September 28, 1939, and signed a "Boundary and Friendship Treaty" — with another

"SECRET SUPPLEMENTARY PROTOCOL

"The undersigned plenipotentiaries declare the agreement of the

[87] Ernest J. Harrison, *Lithuania's Fight for Freedom*, Lithuanian American Information Center, New York, 1945, 18, citing *Speeches on Foreign Policy by Viscount Halifax*, pp. 340-341.

[88] *Nazi-Soviet Relations, op. cit.*, 102-103.

Government of the German Reich and the Government of the USSR upon the following:

The Secret Supplementary Protocol signed on August 23, 1939, shall be amended in item 1 to the effect that the territory of the Lithuanian states falls to the sphere of influence of the USSR (cf. the map attached to the Boundary and Friendship Treaty signed today). As soon as the Government of the USSR shall take special measures on Lithuanian territory to protect its interests, the present German-Lithuanian border, for the purpose of a natural and simple boundary delineation, shall be rectified in such a way that the Lithuanian territory situated to the southwest of the line marked on the attached map should fall to Germany.

Further it is declared that the economic agreements now in force between Germany and Lithuania shall not be affected by the measures of the Soviet Union referred to above.

Moscow, September 28, 1939.

For the Government of the German Reich:	*By authority of the Government of the U.S.S.R.:*
J. Ribbentrop	V. Molotov"

The bargain was sealed with another simultaneously signed "Secret Supplementary Protocol" committing both Governments to stifle the cries of their victims: "Both parties will tolerate in their territories no Polish agitation which affects the territories of the other party. They will suppress in their territories all beginnings of such agitation and inform each other concerning suitable measures for this purpose."[89]

Stalin's successor Nikita S. Khrushchev later revealed the rank-and-file mentality of his people regarding the pacts with the Nazis:

"It hadn't been our fault that we had had to sign the [Ribbentrop-Molotov] treaty. It had been the fault of an unwise Polish government — the government of the Pilsudski-ites, who were blinded by their hatred of the Soviet Union and their hostility to the workers and peasants of their state. . . . So they refused our assistance, and consequently most of Poland fell to Hitler while the Western Ukraine was united with the Eastern Ukraine and its people were given an opportunity to become citizens of the Soviet Union. — Under my leadership we got on with the job of establishing Soviet Power and normalizing the situation

[89] *Ibid.*, 107 — both protocols.

in the lands annexed from Poland. Assisted by Comrade Serov. . . ."[90]

As early as October 3, Hitler's ambassador Count Friedrich Werner von der Schulenburg reported that Molotov wanted that the treaty restoring Vilnius to Lithuania and a German-Lithuanian protocol ceding some territory to Germany be signed simultaneously. Molotov's suggestion seemed to Schulenburg to be "harmful, as in the eyes of the world it would make us appear as 'robbers' of Lithuanian territory, while the Soviet Government figures as the donor. . . . However, I would ask you [Ribbentrop] to consider whether it might not be advisable for us, by a separate German-Soviet protocol, to forego the cession of the Lithuanian strip of territory until the Soviet Union actually incorporates Lithuania, an idea on which, I believe, the arrangement concerning Lithuania was originally based." Ribbentrop likewise disliked Molotov's idea and instructed Schulenburg to "ask Molotov not to discuss this cession of territory with the Lithuanians at present, but rather to have the Soviet Government assume the obligation *toward Germany* to leave this strip of territory unoccupied in the event of a posting of Soviet forces in Lithuania, which may possibly be contemplated, and furthermore to leave it to Germany to determine the date on which the cession of the territory should be formally effected." On October 5 Schulenburg reported that "unfortunately, he [Molotov] had been obliged yesterday to inform the Lithuanian Foreign Minister of this understanding, since he could not, out of loyalty to us, act otherwise."[91]

This meant that the Soviet Union — signatory with Lithuania, Latvia, Estonia and Finland of nonaggression pacts, of the Kellogg-Briand Pact, and of the Definition of Aggression convention authored and vigorously sponsored by the Soviet Union — was ready, as suggested by Stalin on September 25, 1939, to "immediately take up the solution of the problem of the Baltic countries in accordance with the Protocol of August 23rd," as amended by the secret protocol of September 28, "and expected in this matter the unstinting support of the German Government."

[90] *Khrushchev Remembers*, ed. Strobe Talbott, Little, Brown & Co., Boston-Toronto, 1970, p. 143.

[91] *Nazi-Soviet Relations*, *op. cit.*, 112-114.

XXV.
"MUTUAL ASSISTANCE TREATY" IMPOSED ON LITHUANIA

On September 1, 1939, the day Germany attacked Poland, Lithuania invoked its strict Neutrality Law enacted by the Seimas on January 25, 1939.[92] Some reservists were called to active duty to cope with the anticipated influx of war refugees. A nonaggression "treaty" with Germany had been tucked away in a single article of an imposed "treaty reuniting the Memel Territory with the German Reich, thereby settling the questions pending between Germany and Lithuania, and thus paving the way for friendly relations between the two countries," signed on March 22, 1939 in Berlin. It provided: "Article 4. In confirmation of their resolution to ensure the development of friendly relations between Germany and Lithuania, both parties pledge themselves to refrain from using force against each other and not to support the use of force directed against either of them by third parties."[93] As noted earlier, on June 4, 1934, the nonaggression treaty with the USSR had been extended to December 31, 1945. Both Lithuania and the USSR were members of the League of Nations and signatories of the Kellogg-Briand Pact and of the Definition of Aggression convention sponsored by the Soviet Union.

Lithuania firmly resisted German urgings to recover Vilnius from Poland by armed action, and thereby "delivered itself into the hands of the Soviet Union."[94] On September 17, 1939 the Soviet armies invaded Poland and stopped at the Lithuanian-Polish demarcation line. Lithuania sheltered the refugees and interned the fleeing Polish troops.

On September 26, 1939 Estonia received a Soviet demand for an alliance or "mutual assistance" treaty and for the establishment of

[92] This writer had translated it into English at the request of the Lithuanian Legation in Washington for Professor Philip Jessup of the Department of State in 1939. Another, published translation is found in *The USSR-German Aggression Against Lithuania*, New York, 1973, pp. 104-9.

[93] *Documents on German Foreign Policy 1918-1945*, Series D, vol. V, 1937-1939, Department of State, Washington, 1953, pp. 530-1, Note 2.

[94] "By declining to join the war against Poland, Lithuania avoided the status of German protectorate. . .; however, by rejecting German 'protection,' Lithuania delivered itself into the hands of the Soviet Union." *Lithuania Under the Soviets*, Portrait of a Nation 1940-1965, ed. V. Stanley Vardys, Praeger, New York, 1965, pp. 47-48.

Soviet naval and air bases. Soviet military aircraft carried out extensive menacing flights over Estonia. The treaty was signed by Estonia on September 28, the date Lithuania was transferred into the Soviet "sphere of influence," and Latvia was summoned that same day. Latvia signed on October 5.

Minister of Foreign Affairs Juozas Urbšys was summoned to Moscow on October 3, 1939, and was told the principal demands: a mutual assistance pact, the garrisoning of 50,000 Soviet troops in Lithuania — twice the size of the Lithuanian Army. This demand was sweetened by volunteering to return Vilnius to Lithuania. Urbšys flew back to Kaunas the next day to report to the Cabinet. It was agreed in principle to sign a mutual assistance pact, and counter-proposals were drafted: immediate military assistance in the event of an attack on Lithuania or on the USSR across the Lithuanian territory; Lithuania would double its military establishment, would construct defensive fortifications at places mutually agreed on, and both countries would maintain liaison missions of their respective General Staffs to coordinate matters of military collaboration. There was no provision for Soviet bases.[95] A delegation which included Urbšys, Vice-Premier Kazys Bizauskas, Minister to Moscow Ladas Natkevičius, and Brigadier General Stasys Raštikis left for Moscow. They were accompanied by a staff of experts: Ministry's international law counsel Professor Tadas Petkevičius, Director of Economic Affairs Dr. Juozas Norkaitis, ethnologist Dr. Vladas Viliamas, and General Staff Colonel Leonas Rupšys. General Raštikis reported his impressions:

"Crossing over the Latvian-USSR frontier we observed Russian military concentrations. Tanks, armored cars, artillery and trucks were hidden in forests and under roadside trees, well visible from the air. . . .

"At the Moscow airport we were met by protocol officers and the military. . . . The same night around 11 p.m. the Lithuanian Legation received a telephoned invitation to the Kremlin. This late summons surprised us. Only [four] delegation members proceeded . . . by two NKVD automobiles. . . .

"Molotov's office was spacious. A long red-covered table on the left. Several windows on the right, a smaller round table, several leather-covered easy chairs and several straight chairs. A large desk in the rear. With two leather-top chairs. A large portrait of Lenin above the desk. An even larger painting on the opposite wall — Lenin with Stalin at

[95] *Lithuanian Bulletin*, New York, VI, Nos. 1-2, 1948, p. 27.

Stalingrad during the civil war.

"We were met by . . . Molotov, his Deputy — former ambassador to France Potemkin, and Soviet Minister to Lithuania [Nikolai G.] Pozdniakov. . . . We sat around the long table . . . Molotov . . . addressing Urbšys, inquired: 'Well, Mr. Minister, what do you say?' Urbšys propounded the Lithuanian Government's views regarding the Russian demands. . . . Molotov replied briefly, concretely stating separate parts of the Russian demands. . . . The most sensitive item — the Russian demand to establish their military bases in Lithuania. . . . Molotov and Urbšys did most of the talking. Both sides having stated their positions, the meeting adjourned around 1 a.m. . . . .

"The next day [October 8], again after 11 p.m., we met in the same place. Beside yesterday's participants, we saw Stalin. In greeting, he uttered just one word — Stalin — and extended his lifeless hand. Stalin sat down in the place occupied by Molotov the day before, and at once lit up his pipe. — The focal point was the question of Russian military bases. Both Molotov and Stalin argued sharply that military bases are needed for them *vis à vis* the Germans. Urbšys remarked that the Germans should be very sensitive toward the introduction of Red Army bases in Lithuania. Stalin smiled and said: 'Ribbentrop had claimed all of Lithuania, yet we protected you. I will tell you, Mr. Minister, how concerned Mr. Ribbentrop was over you and how he defended Lithuania before us in this very room.' The word 'defended' was uttered by Stalin with bitter sarcasm. Stalin recited that during the Russian negotiations with Ribbentrop and the presentation of conditions, Ribbentrop had been conciliatory and made one concession after another. When the question arose regarding a division of spheres of influence in the Baltic States, Ribbentrop proposed the Daugava River line. 'We did not agree to that,' said Stalin proudly. 'Then Mr. Ribbentrop conceded and offered the Lithuanian-Latvian frontier as the line of the spheres of influence. We did not agree to that either,' — continued Stalin. Ribbentrop then suggested the Nemunas River line. Stalin would not agree to that either. Finally Ribbentrop requested that only a small strip of Sudavia be left to Germany. At this point Stalin asked Molotov to show us the map where a black line marked the frontier running from Kudirkos Naumiestis, along the Šešupė River through Pilviškiai, Marijampolė, Liudvinavas, Krosna to Kapčiamiestis. 'We did agree to that,' concluded Stalin. . . .

"We listened astounded. Urbšys said frankly he did not wish to believe it. Stalin angrily shot back: 'Yes, that is decided, and this matter is ended.' We were greatly moved. Urbšys attempted to protest, yet Stalin interrupted him and would not let him speak."

General Raštikis continues that "Avoiding admission of a Russian army into Lithuania, we offered the Russians a compromise," stated above. However, Moscow would make no concessions whatsoever. At one session Urbšys "in half-jest asked Stalin to have mercy on him, the most unfortunate minister of foreign affairs who must receive and transmit to his Government another ultimatum. Stalin disliked the mention of an ultimatum." At another session, "when Urbšys argued in earnest that introduction of Russian forces into Lithuania would not be compatible with the sovereignty of an independent and neutral Lithuania, Stalin rudely interrupted Urbšys: 'You are arguing too much, young man!' On another occasion Urbšys openly told Stalin: 'You yourself, Yosif Vissarionovich, are a son of a small people and you can understand the sufferings of another small nation which has lost its freedom.' Stalin was silent a moment, and then slowly and coldly replied: 'Yes, I am a Georgian. However, an already Russified Georgian.' "

According to General Raštikis, in view of the uncompromising dictates of the Russians who began making threats and showed their anger, there was a suggestion to break off the negotiations. Finally it was decided to inform the Cabinet in full, and Vice-Premier Bizauskas with General Raštikis flew back to Kaunas. At the Cabinet session it was learned that no German aid could be expected. It was finally decided that negotiations could not be broken off and that some alleviation should be obtained. During their visit to Kaunas, however, Molotov increased the pressure and elevated the pact's duration to 20 or 25 years, which compared ominously with the ten-year duration of pacts with the other Baltic States — renewable for 10 years with Latvia and five years with Estonia.

Raštikis denies allegations that the return of Vilnius was a compensation for acceptance of the Soviet bases. "It is an erroneous view. Practically throughout the negotiations the Soviet applied the same yardstick to the Baltic States. . . . Russian demands presented to Estonia, Latvia and Lithuania were identical. Neither Estonia nor Latvia received any compensation for admitting the Soviet army. The same is true of Lithuania. Neither the Russians, nor the Lithuanians during the Moscow negotiations conditioned their terms: if you will admit our military bases, you shall get Vilnius, if not — you will not get it; or — if you will return Vilnius to us— we will agree to accept your bases, otherwise— No.

"The mutual assistance pact and the return of Vilnius were two different questions and two entirely independent treaties had been prepared. Only later the Russians merged these treaties into one. The admission of Russian garrisons into Lithuania had been discussed entirely separately, without tying it to the return of Vilnius. Lithuania, was obliged to sign a Russian dictated mutual assistance pact because of the conditions prevailing at the time, and not because Vilnius was to be restored to Lithuania. Admission of Russian military bases was *not* the price paid for the return of Vilnius. Lithuania's title to Vilnius was based on the Lithuanian-Soviet peace treaty of 1920 and had nothing in common with the mutual assistance pact. It is true that the Russians had boasted, and are still boasting, that the return of Vilnius was the expression of their benevolence and sympathy toward the Lithuanian People. In fact, however, the Soviet Union robbed Lithuania in that connection. During the discussion of the return of Vilnius, the Russians paid no attention to the peace treaty of 1920 and would not discuss it. They refused to return to Lithuania even the purely Lithuanian areas of Švenčionys and Marcinkonys, the busiest centers of Lithuanian activities."

Dr. Eduardas Turauskas in his non-eyewitness account based on the reports received at the Ministry of Foreign Affairs from its delegation in Moscow, notes the rapidly disintegrating atmosphere of the October 8, 1939 session in the Kremlin. Soviet negotiators made no effort to justify their demands: "Stalin and his aides were clearly impatient and displeased over the delay. Before adjourning for consultations, the Lithuanian delegates inquired about the proposed new frontier with Russia. Molotov pointed his finger at the map, marking approximately the same borders as were later fixed by the pact (restoring to Lithuania only) about one-eighth of the territory formerly occupied by Poland, and disregarding the Soviet-Lithuanian boundary fixed by the Peace Treaty of July 12, 1920.

"Mr. Urbšys and ethnography experts tried to point out that the proposed frontier would exclude the districts settled predominantly by Lithuanians. But the Muscovites would not listen to the arguments. Molotov merely remarked that the Russian people are not yet informed of their government's intention to return the Vilnius environs to Lithuania, while he had personally succeeded in convincing the Belorussian Soviet of the necessity for such action, and that when 'the people' will learn, he is not quite certain about the popular reaction to such 'generosity' of the Soviets to Lithuania."

According to General Raštikis, negotiations in Moscow lasted nearly a full week. The last session of October 9 ended after midnight. After 1 a.m. three documents were signed in Molotov's office: the mutual assistance treaty including the transfer of Vilnius, a secret supplement "which spelled out the number of Russian troops to be stationed in Lithuania, and a map indicating the sections of the Vilnius area to be restored to Lithuania. Urbšys signed on behalf of Lithuania, Molotov on behalf of the Soviet Union. Stalin, Voroshilov and Zhdanov were present at the signing. Snacks were served after the signing. Molotov and Stalin 'swore' that the Soviet Union would not interfere in Lithuanian internal affairs — through its military bases or through the Communist party. Molotov recalled Stalin's statement during the negotiations that it is up to the Lithuanian Government to bring their Communists to order."

Molotov invited the entire Lithuanian delegation and the senior personnel of the Legation to the Kremlin for 4 p.m. — according to Dr. Turauskas for 5 p.m. Raštikis mentions an incident during the sumptious feast, involving Foreign Trade Commissar Anastas Mikoyan. "After much imbibing, Mikoyan argued with Bizauskas seated next to him. Probably desiring to end the Mikoyan-Bizauskas argument, Stalin invited Mikoyan to raise a toast. Mikoyan heatedly spoke of Soviet generosity to Lithuania, even though Communists have no freedom in Lithuania. Mikoyan placed his hand on his breast and said in an excited voice: 'My heart is being stabbed.'

"Toward the end of the feast Molotov and Stalin spoke. Stalin briefly reviewed Lithuanian history. He constantly mentioned the common folk of Lithuania, how much they had suffered from Russian gendarmes, from Polish lords, estate masters and rulers. He spoke of Russian relations with the Lithuanians — omitting the struggles, speaking only of collaboration. Lithuania's security will be truly assured only now, after the signing of the mutual assistance pact. Once again he stressed that the Soviet Union has no intention to interfere with Lithuanian internal affairs. (This was also emphasized by Molotov.) In his talk Stalin sneered at Great Russians who, said he, do not always understand small peoples. Stalin concluded with a wish that Lithuania should again reach the pinnacle of power she had held in the times of Vytautas. This conclusion was rather unexpected."[96]

Several translations are published of the "Treaty on the Transfer of the City of Vilnius and Vilnius area to the Republic of Lithuania and of

Mutual Assistance between the U.S.S.R. and Lithuania," signed in Moscow on October 10, 1939. Couched in niceties hardly reflecting the reality, it provided:

"For the purpose of developing the friendly relations established by the Peace Treaty of July 12, 1920, and based on the recognition of an independent State existence and non-intervention in the internal affairs of the other party; recognizing that the Peace Treaty of July 12, 1920, and the Pact of Non-Aggression and Peaceful Settlement of Conflicts of September 28, 1926, continue to form a firm basis for their mutual relations and undertakings; convinced. . . .; found it necessary to conclude between them the following Treaty. . . .:

"Article I. For the purpose of consolidating the friendly relations between the USSR and Lithuania, the city of Vilnius and the Vilnius area are transferred by the Soviet Union to the Republic of Lithuania and included in the territory of the Lithuanian State; the boundary between the USSR and the Republic of Lithuania being established in accordance with the map appended hereto. . . .

"Article II. The Soviet Union and the Republic of Lithuania undertake to render each other every assistance, including military, in the event of aggression or menace of aggression against Lithuania, as well as in the event of aggression or the menace of aggression against the Soviet Union over Lithuanian territory on the part of any European power.

"Article III. The Soviet Union undertakes to render the Lithuanian Army assistance in armaments and other military equipment on favorable terms.

"Article IV. The Soviet Union and the Republic of Lithuania undertake jointly to effect protection of the State boundaries of Lithuania, for which purpose the Soviet Union receives [is granted] the right to maintain, at its own expense, at points in the Republic of Lithuania mutually agreed upon, Soviet land and air armed forces of strictly limited strength . . . regulated by special agreements. The sites and buildings necessary for this purpose shall be allotted by the Lithuanian Government on lease at reasonable terms [at a reasonable price].

[96] St. Raštikis, "Derybos Maskvoje" (Negotiations in Moscow) in the *Lietuva* magazine, New York, No. 5, Jan.-March 1954, pp. 53-58; Eduardas Turauskas, "Russian Technique vis à vis Lithuania," *Lithuanian Bulletin*, N.Y., v. VI, Nos. 1-2, Jan.-Feb. 1948, pp. 26-27. Sworn testimony of Raštikis in *Baltic States Investigation*, Hearings before the Select Committee to Investigate the Incorporation of the Baltic States into the USSR, House of Representatives, 83rd Congress . . . Part I, Washington, 1954, pp. 374-384.

"Article V. In the event of the menace of aggression against Lithuania or against the USSR through [over] Lithuanian territory, the two Contracting Parties shall immediately discuss the resulting situation and take all measures found necessary by mutual agreement to secure the inviolability of the territories of the Contracting Parties.

"Article VI. The two Contracting Parties undertake not to conclude any alliances nor participate in any coalitions directed against either of the Contracting Parties.

"Article VII. The coming into force of the present treaty shall not affect to any extent [in any way] the sovereign rights of the Contracting Parties, in particular their State organization, economic and social systems, military measures, and generally the principle of nonintervention in internal affairs. The locations of the Soviet land and air armed forces (Article IV of the present Treaty) under all circumstances remain a component part of the territory of the Republic of Lithuania.

"Article VIII. The term of validity of the present Treaty ... (Articles II to VII) is for 15 years [shall remain in force for fifteen years] and unless one of the Contracting Parties finds it necessary to denounce the provisions of the Treaty ... one year prior to the expiration of that term, these provisions shall automatically continue in force [to be valid] for the next ten years.

"Article IX. The present Treaty comes into force upon the exchange of instruments of ratification. Exchange of these instruments shall take place in Kaunas within six days from the day of signature of this Treaty. The present Treaty is made in two originals, in the Russian and Lithuanian languages, at Moscow, October 10, 1939.

Vyacheslav Molotov
Juozas Urbšys "[97]

Finland balked at Soviet demands for a "mutual assistance pact" accompanied by a cession of Finnish territories. Finally Russia openly attacked Finland — after creating a puppet "People's Government of Finland" headed by a Soviet citizen of Finnish extraction, recognizing

[97] Texts slightly differing in English translation may be found in: *War and Peace in Finland*, A Documented Survey, Soviet Russia Today, New York 1940 (ed. Alter Brody, Theodore M. Bayer, Isidor Schneider, Jessica Smith) pp. 112-113; *Baltic States Investigation Hearings*, *op. cit.*, 488-9; *The USSR-German Aggression Against Lithuania*, ed. Bronis J. Kaslas, New York, 1973, *op. cit.*, pp. 149-151; (abridged) *International Conciliation Series, No. 386*, Jan. 1943, *op. cit.*, 74-75 (translated from Russian and compared with Deak and Jessup).

its own creature and marching in its aid against "the illegal government in fulfillment of its international obligation," just as in 1918 Russia marched against Lithuania and in 1968 against Czechoslovakia. On December 14, 1939, the Soviet Union was expelled from the League of Nations by a resolution stating that the USSR had committed an aggression and was "no longer a member" of the League.

Map published by Soviet General Staff in 1939, in which Lithuania is represented as Soviet Socialist Republic.

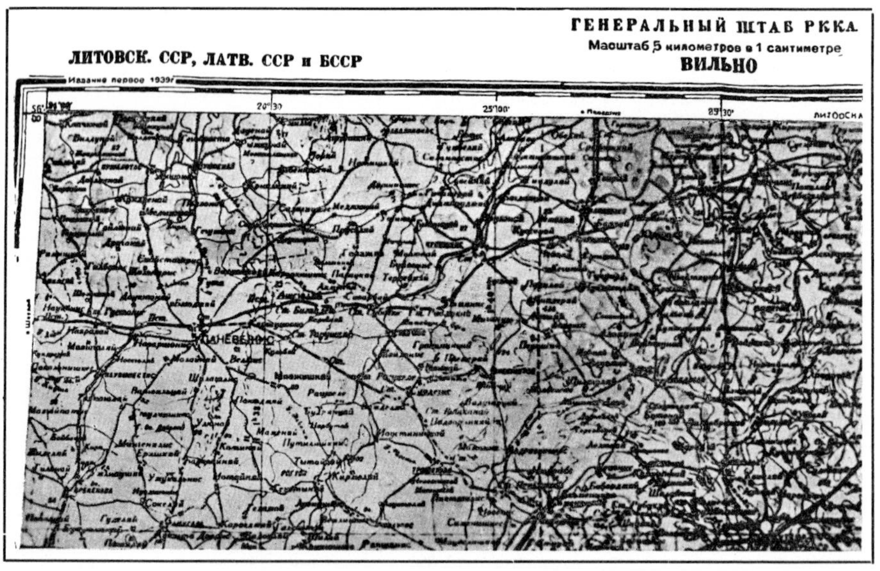

TRANSLATION FROM THE RUSSIAN:

Lithuanian S.S.R., Latvian S.S.R. and B(yelorussian) S.S.R.
First Edition, 1939.
General Staff of the Workers' and Peasants' Red Army
Skale: 5 km to 1 cm
Vilnius

XXVI.
TWILIGHT OF THE INDEPENDENCE

Before and after the signing of the "Mutual Assistance Treaty," the Russians were pre-occupied six weeks with organized looting. Furniture, lighting and plumbing fixtures, carpets and rugs, paintings, machinery, locks, bolts, door knobs and doors, hooks and nails, etc., were dismantled from public and abandoned private buildings. Various experts from Moscow and Minsk institutions rummaged through musea collections, State and memorial archives, libraries, church records, scientific institutions. About 20,000 units were taken from XVI-XIX-century collections of the State Archives, 16,722 from the Muravyov Museum, over 450,000 files from the Governors General Archives, all records and collections of the Evangelical Reformed Synod, collections of the Masonic insignia and records, some Evangelical Lutheran records, all archives of the Uniate and Orthodox churches and their publications, maps and rare books from other collections, concentrating on Lituanica, Vilniana, Masonica and Alba Ruthenica.

These priceless collections were loaded on 68 flat cars and freight cars at the railway depot, taken as far as the Beniakainiai station across the new frontier of Belorussia and dumped on the ground: freight cars were needed to transport other loot. These treasures lay unprotected from elements from October, 1939 to May, 1940 when they were taken to Moscow or Minsk. The NKVD seized additional 9,500 files from the State Archives, 12,000 volumes from the Jesuit Library and 6,500 books and portfolios from the Vilnius City Library — for the Belorussian Academy of Sciences. Some materials were identified in Minsk in 1943 and returned to Vilnius. 7,340 volumes from the Wróblewski Library were never accounted for. The Germans appropriated the antiquities they wanted, including Hebrew collections, some of which were identified after World War II in Scotland, Sweden and elsewhere.[98]

On October 27, 1939, a Lithuanian-Soviet Boundary Protocol was signed in Moscow, "modifying Article 2 of the Russo-Lithuanian Treaty of July 12, 1920 and coming into force on the date" of the

[98] *Lietuvių Enciklopedija*, v. XXXIV (Boston 1966), pp. 239-241.

signing.[99] The very next day, on October 28, Lithuanian troops and civilian relief columns moved into Vilnius and to the new frontier, as Soviet troops retreated to suburban Naujoji Vilnia, one of their bases. As soon as accommodations were completed at the sites designated by mutual agreement, other Soviet troops moved into their new bases.

This is how the situation was described by a Soviet publication in English compiled after the signing of the Peace Treaty with Finland (March 12, 1940) and containing Premier Molotov's report to the Supreme Soviet on March 29 — thus published in New York some time in May, 1940, just as Moscow was engineering the final seizure of the Baltic States:

"Relations between Lithuania and the Soviet Union have in general been closer than in the case of the other Baltic States. By the treaty of 1920 Soviet Russia recognized Lithuanian sovereignty over its ancient capital Vilna, and continued to do so even after it was seized by the Poles a short time later. The Soviet Union has consistently given Lithuania its protection against the Poles, and warned Poland sharply against invading Lithuania at the time of the Czechoslovakian crisis. The establishment of a joint frontier between the Soviet Union and Lithuania by the incorporation into the USSR of Western Byelo-Russia meant a further consolidation of their friendly relations. The mutual aid pact provides military and air bases for the Soviet Union in Lithuania, Soviet military aid for the latter, and returns to Lithuania both Vilna and the Vilna region which were taken under protection by the Red Army after the Polish debacle.

"The gratitude of the Lithuanian people was expressed in a telegram sent to Molotov after the negotiations by Foreign Minister Urbšys;. . .

"G. E. R. Gedye, *New York Times* correspondent . . . by the time the pact with Lithuania was signed he began to change his tune. On October 10 he cabled from Moscow:

> 'In Baltic circles here there is a tendency to deprecate what is considered an exaggeration of the new situation. While appreciating foreign sympathy, it is said that Baltic statesmen feel they know the Russians better than the people of more distant countries and consider that the attacks on Russia over these new pacts, the suspicions entertained of her program and the gloomy views taken of the future

[99] English translation from the Lithuanian version — *The USSR-German Aggression Against Lithuania*, ed. Bronis J. Kaslas, New York, 1973, pp. 151-157. The footnote indicates it was based on a newspaper text, and place names are rather distorted. There was an obvious attempt to reconstruct place names from Russian versions and this was done hurriedly, resulting in distortions alien to local Lithuanian dialects, viz., Elkiškiai, Edunka, etc.

of the Baltic states go rather too far. For one thing, it is said to be assured that none of these states have been in any way threatened by the Soviet Union in the course of the Moscow negotiations. . . .'

"Of the departure of Germans . . . Gedye writes in the same dispatch:

'The departure of the Germans is in no way regretted in the Baltic states, it is said. To the general populace "German" suggests a "Baltic baron" — a member of an unloved class of feudal overlords . . . who are generally considered to have conducted themselves in an arrogant manner as members of a "superior race".'

"After the formation of the new coalition government in Lithuania on November 21 the new Premier, Antanas Merkys, said that his government would continue to fulfill its treaty obligations. . . .

"On January 5 Foreign Minister Urbšys declared that although his country was allied with the Soviet Union, this was in no sense to be interpreted as meaning that Lithuania had become a vassal of her larger neighbor. Soviet troops garrisoned on Lithuanian soil had conducted themselves admirably, he added.

"On March 26, the Moscow *Pravda* published an article discussing Lithuania's improved economic position, which said in part. . . .

"In conclusion it may be said that as a result of the mutual assistance pacts with the Soviet Union, Estonia, Latvia and Lithuania enjoy greater security and prosperity than any of the other small nations in Europe today. Their economic development, healthily rooted in its natural hinterland, the Soviet Union, is no longer subject to the imperialist control which kept them in a semi-colonial state, nor is their trade being withered by the Allied blockade or stalemated by the rivalries of the warring nations. With their independence guarded not only by their own small armies but by Soviet troops, they are safe from all attempts to draw them into the theatre of war."[100]

Let us also recall the two Molotov reports to the Supreme Soviet as published in the Soviet-subsidized publication abroad just before the forcible seizure of the Baltic States.

On October 31, 1939 Premier Molotov reported to the Fifth Extraordinary Session of the Supreme Soviet of the USSR:

"The relations of the Soviet Union with Estonia, Latvia and Lithuania are based on peace treaties concluded with the respective countries in 1920 . . . and ever since then the Soviet Union has invariably pursued a

[100] *War and Peace in Finland*, A Documented Survey . . . 1940, Soviet Russia Today, New York, pp. 70-72.

friendly policy toward these newly created states. . . .

"As you know, the Soviet Union has concluded pacts of mutual assistance with Estonia, Latvia and Lithuania that are of major political significance. . . .

". . . these pacts allow the Soviet Union to maintain naval bases and airfields in specified parts of Estonia and Latvia and, in the case of Lithuania, the pact provides for defense of Lithuanian borders jointly with the Soviet Union. . . .

"Our recent diplomatic negotiations with Estonia, Latvia and Lithuania have shown that we have sufficient confidence in each other. . . .

"The special character of these mutual assistance pacts in no way implies any interference by the Soviet Union in the affairs of Estonia, Latvia, or Lithuania, as some foreign newspapers are trying to make out. On the contrary, all these pacts of mutual assistance strictly stipulate the inviolability of the sovereignty of the signatory States, as well as the principle of non-interference in each other's affairs.

"These pacts are based on mutual respect for the political, social and economic structure of the contracting parties, and are designed to strengthen the basis for peaceful, neighborly cooperation between our peoples. We stand for the scrupulous and punctilious observance of pacts on a basis of complete reciprocity, and we declare that all nonsense about sovietizing the Baltic countries is only to the interest of our common enemies and of all anti-Soviet provocateurs. . . .

"The principles of Soviet policy toward small countries have been demonstrated with particular force by the treaty providing for the transfer of the city of Vilna and the Vilna region to the Lithuanian Republic. . . .

"The Soviet Union agreed to transfer the city of Vilna to the Lithuanian Republic not because Vilna has a predominantly Lithuanian population. No, the majority of the inhabitants of Vilna are non-Lithuanian. But the Soviet Government took into consideration the fact that the city of Vilna, which was forcibly wrested from Lithuania by Poland, ought to belong to Lithuania as a city with which are associated on the one hand the historical past of the Lithuanian State and on the other hand the national aspirations of the Lithuanian people.

"It has been pointed out in the foreign press that there has never been a case in world history of a big country's handing over such a big city to a small state of its own free will. All the more strikingly, therefore, does this act of the Soviet State demonstrate its good will."[101]

[101] *Ibid.*, 114-115.

Thus Molotov ignored the fact that the USSR appropriated for itself most of the Vilnius area, in violation of the Peace Treaty of 1920. His sweet talk of "scrupulous and punctilious observance of pacts" is still the theme of Brezhnev atop the mound of Soviet-violated pacts. . . .

On March 29, 1940 Premier Molotov reported to the Sixth Session of the Supreme Soviet of the USSR, after the signing of peace with Finland. After blaming Britain and France for not making peace with Germany and asserting that "the real aims" of these "principal imperialists powers of Europe" were to make Finland "the starting point of war against the USSR," Molotov continued:

"The conclusion of the peace treaty with Finland consummates the task we set ourselves last year of safeguarding the security of the Soviet Union in the direction of the Baltic. This treaty is the necessary complement to the three pacts of mutual assistance concluded with Estonia, Latvia and Lithuania respectively. Our experience during the six months that have elapsed since these pacts of mutual assistance were concluded enables us to draw very definite, positive conclusions concerning these treaties with the Baltic countries.

"It must be admitted that the treaties concluded by the Soviet Union with Estonia, Latvia and Lithuania have served to strengthen the international position both of the Soviet Union and Estonia, Latvia and Lithuania. In spite of the scare raised by imperialist circles hostile to the Soviet Union, the state and political independence of Estonia, Latvia and Lithuania has not suffered in any way, while economic intercourse between these countries and the Soviet Union has begun markedly to increase. The pacts with Estonia, Latvia and Lithuania are being carried out in a satisfactory manner and this creates premises for further improvement in relations between the Soviet Union and these countries."[102]

Listeners and readers of the Molotov reports wishfully interpreted them as good omens. In retrospect, however, his reference to "further improvement in relations" presaged ominous changes. Indeed, the General Staff of the RKKA (Worker Peasant Red Army) published a map of the Vilnius area with the following top-left title: "*Lithuanian SSR, Latv. SSR and B*(elorussian) *SSR First Edition 1939*," and dossiers were being prepared by the NKVD for genocidal mass exiling, of which we shall read later.[103]

[102]*Ibid.*, 83-84.

[103]Reproduced in *Lithuanian Bulletin*, New York, IV, No. 3, October 1946, p. 23.

Meanwhile Soviet troops at the several bases behaved reasonably well. "But, this attitude of sweet reason lasted only as long as the Soviets were fighting the winter war against Finland. . . . Once the Finns were subdued, the Communists in Lithuania started fomenting strikes on Soviet military base sites; military commanders began complaining to Lithuanians about alleged failures to provide promised food supplies; Soviet soldiers were allowed to mingle with Lithuanian civilians, with whom they would become involved in tavern brawls. At the same time, the Soviets, in a show of strength, transferred substantial military equipment to their bases near Kaunas . . . (late in April 1940). The Lithuanian minister in Moscow, Ladas Natkevičius, reported that 'a black cat crossed the path of Lithuanian-Soviet relations'."[104] "He explained that the attitude of the rulers of the Kremlin had become colder . . . they had started to question him more and more on Lithuania's attitude toward the war, its attitude toward Germany, and its neutrality. Repeated declarations of neutrality by the Baltic States irritated Moscow. On May 16, 1940, *Izvestia* published an article. . .:

> " 'The recent war events (occupation of Belgium, The Netherlands, and Luxemburg) once more proved that neutrality of small states, which do not have power to support it, is a mere fantasy. Therefore, there are very few chances for small countries to survive and to maintain their independence. All considerations of small countries on the question of justice and injustice in relations with the Big Powers, which are in the war "to determine if they are to be or not to be," are at least naive. . . . We should once more remind them that the policy of neutrality of some small countries could not be called anything but suicide.' "[105]

[104] Vardys, *Lithuania Under the Soviets, op. cit.*, 48-49.

[105] U.S. 83rd Congress, Select Committee to Investigate the Incorporation of the Baltic States into the USSR, House of Representatives, *3rd Interim Report*, p. 318.

Antanas Smetona (1874-1944), the first and fourth president of Lithuania.

Aleksandras Stulginskis (1885-1969) the second president of Lithuania.

Dr. Kazys Grinius (1866-1950) the third president of Lithuania.
—Painting by Antanas Rukštelė

XXVII.
THE SOVIET INVASION AND THE ANNEXATION

As soon as Hitler invaded the Low Lands, the Kremlin hastened to complete "a territorial and political rearrangement in the areas belonging to the Baltic States," agreed upon in the first Ribbentrop-Molotov Pact protocol, and its "special measures on Lithuanian territory to protect its interests," as authorized by the secret protocol of the second Ribbentrop-Molotov Pact. The Select Committee on Communist Aggression, formed by the House of Representatives, 83rd Congress, after extended hearings and an examination of voluminous records, reported to the Congress:

"On May 25, 1940, the Soviet Government presented to the Lithuanian Government a note accusing the Lithuanian authorities of the kidnaping of two Soviet soldiers. The accusation shocked the Lithuanians. Until that date they were convinced that the relations with the Soviet Union were good. The Lithuanian Government immediately asked the Soviet Government 'to indicate the persons and authorities which Chairman Molotov had in mind in his statement,' and gave the order to search energetically for the soldiers mentioned in the Molotov statement.

"The next day, the Lithuanian Government informed the Soviet Government that a special commission for investigation of the charges was appointed and expressed its agreement with the Soviet request that 'the representative of the Soviet military command stationed in Lithuania should take part in the investigation.'

"All efforts, however, to clear the case of the alleged disappearance were met with no response from the Soviet Government. Then, unexpectedly, the Soviet Government published a communique on May 30, 1940, 'on provocation of the Lithuanian authorities.'

"Without any delay, the Government of Lithuania sent its Minister of Foreign Affairs, J. Urbšys, to Moscow and through direct negotiations tried to find a way to settle the incident. Molotov agreed to discuss the matter, but only with the Prime Minister. In two consecutive meetings, which took place in the Kremlin on June 7 and 8, the Prime Minister of Lithuania, A. Merkys, tried to convince Molotov that Lithuania had no interest except the cultivation of good and friendly relations with the Soviet Union. Molotov did not pay any attention to his explanations. At the first meeting he attacked the Director of the Security Department and the Minister of the Interior for their hostile attitude toward the Soviet Union. At the second meeting, he reproached the Prime Minister himself for transforming the Estonian-Latvian military convention into a triple military alliance directed against the Soviet Union.

"There was no doubt any longer that Moscow had far-reaching intentions which could endanger the independence of Lithuania. He [Merkys] asked the President of the Republic, A. Smetona, to send immediately a message to the Chairman of the Presidium of the Supreme Soviet of the Soviet Union, assuring the loyalty of Lithuania toward the Soviet Union. He asked also that the Minister of Foreign Affairs should come to Moscow to explain the Lithuanian-Latvian-Estonian relations. Neither the explanation of the Lithuanian Foreign Minister, nor the loyalty message relieved the tension.

"...The Government of Moscow was merely pursuing the plan to implement its secret agreements with Nazi Germany regarding Lithuania....

"On June 14, 1940, Molotov presented to the Lithuanian Minister of Foreign Affairs, at that time in Moscow, the Soviet ultimatum. The Moscow Government accused the Lithuanian Government of kidnaping and torture of Soviet soldiers . . . and demanded:

"1. That the Minister of the Interior, Skučas, and the Director of the Department of Security, Povilaitis, be immediately delivered to the judicial authorities and tried as directly guilty of acts of provocation committed against the garrisons of the Soviet Union in Lithuania.

"2. That a government be immediately formed in Lithuania capable of assuring proper fulfillment of the treaty of mutual assistance between the Soviet Union and Lithuania.

"3. That a free entry into the territory of Lithuania be immediately assured for units of the army of the Soviet Union which will be stationed in the most important centers of Lithuania and which will be sufficiently numerous to assure the enforcement of the treaty of mutual assistance between the Soviet Union and Lithuania.

"Immediately an emergency meeting was called by the President of the Republic. President A. Smetona suggested rejection of the Soviet demands. He urged the organization of military resistance against Soviet aggression. He recommended also that the Government should leave the country and organize abroad for the restoration of the independence of Lithuania. However, the majority of the Cabinet was determined to comply with the Soviet demands in order to prevent the destruction of the country. In their opinion it was impossible in a few hours to organize any substantial resistance against the Red Army. Finally, the President of the Republic agreed to accept the ultimatum and appointed General S. Raštikis Prime Minister. A few hours later, the Lithuanian Foreign Minister, who was still in Moscow, informed the President of the Republic that Molotov considered General Raštikis unacceptable to the Soviet Union and that the Soviet Government decided to send V. G. Dekanozov, Deputy Commissar for Foreign Affairs, to Kaunas to take charge of the formation of the new Cabinet.

"The President felt that under these conditions he could not perform his constitutional duties. He was unwilling to legalize the Soviet extinction of Lithuania's independence. He decided to carry on the struggle for the restoration of Lithuania's independence from abroad and left Lithuania on June 15, 1940. On the same day large military units of the Red Army occupied Lithuania and Dekanozov, Soviet special emissary, arrived at Kaunas. It was his mission to form the new government and to complete the task of incorporating Lithuania into the Soviet Union.

"The first act of Dekanozov was to declare that the Lithuanian Government consider the departure of President Smetona as his resignation and that the duties of President of the Republic would be performed by the Acting Prime Minister, Mr. Merkys [who appointed the Soviet nominee, Justas Paleckis, a Prime Minister and then resigned — and, with Foreign Affairs Minister Urbšys, was deported to Russia. Paleckis claimed the Presidency, and Deputy Premier Vincas Krėvė-Mickevičius assumed the Premiership. In its fuller Third Interim Report, the Kersten Committee added that 'Prime Minister Merkys, while temporarily performing the duties of the President of the Republic, did not and could not legally appoint a new Prime Minister'] . . . .

"On June 18, 1940, Paleckis addressed a message to the Lithuanian nation in which he stated:

> 'In foreign relations the new Government will continue to maintain normal relations with all states. The first task of the Government will be establishment of sincere and friendly relations with the Soviet Union with which Lithuania has a close alliance based on the mutual assistance pact.'

"On June 25, 1940, the Minister of the Interior ordered that the

Communist Party of Lithuania be entered on the register of societies and associations. Thus, the ban on the Communist Party was removed. In connection with this, *Lietuvos Aidas* (Echo of Lithuania) wrote:

> 'The Communist Party which has always fought for the people's interests, will now be the only legal party in liberated Lithuania. There is no place in Lithuania for other parties which for a long time struggled against the people and against the independence of Lithuania.'

"There were officials in the People's government who had confidence in Lithuanian-Soviet friendship and who believed that the Soviet Union would keep its promise to preserve Lithuanian independence. Realizing that they had become victims of an extraordinary fraud they decided to make a desperate appeal to Moscow. On June 24, 1940, the Deputy Prime Minister, Krėvė-Mickevičius, asked the Lithuanian Envoy in Moscow to arrange a meeting for him with Molotov. On July 2, 1940, he was received by Molotov in Moscow.

"[Krėvė] complained of interference in the internal affairs of Lithuania by Dekanozov, the Soviet Legation, and the Red Army. . . . He asked Molotov to discipline the Soviet officials in Lithuania and to conclude a new convention in which Lithuanian-Soviet foreign relations would be stipulated in a more precise manner.

"In a long conversation, Molotov . . . stated:

> 'You must take a good look at reality and understand that in the future small nations will have to disappear. Your Lithuania along with other Baltic States, including Finland, will have to join the glorious family of the Soviet Union. Therefore you should begin now to initiate your people into the Soviet system which in the future shall reign everywhere, throughout all Europe — put into practice earlier in some places, as in the Baltic nations — later in others.' "

[Krėvė-Mickevičius in an interview with this writer recorded at the banquet in his honor in Philadelphia in 1952 and later broadcast by the Voice of America, was overwhelmed with emotion. Krėvė-Mickevičius seized the microphone and said: "In our conversation I told Molotov that Lithuania would never consent to renounce her freedom; that Lithuania, being a Christian country, would never accept a Soviet order. Molotov answered me: 'Had Saint Vladimir tried to persuade his people to accept Christianity, he would have had to wait several centuries. Christianity would not have come. So Saint Vladimir said: All of you, *svolochi*, get into the river and be baptized! And if you won't — I will lop your heads off! Everybody waded into the river, they were baptized and became Christians. We treat everybody that way. We do not bother to persuade — we compel, and anyone who does not submit is destroyed. It shall be thus in every country wherever we shall enter and institute our order. People will have to submit — or perish.' "]

"Realizing the hopelessness of the situation and not willing to participate in the burial of Lithuania's independence . . . Krėvė-Mickevičius upon return from Moscow submitted his resignation (which, however, was not accepted). E. Galvanauskas, the Minister of Finance, also resigned and fled abroad. The leadership was then entrusted to the Communist [Mečys] Gedvilas, Minister of the Interior, who conscientiously carried out the plan drafted in Moscow.

"On July 5, 1940, the Lithuanian Government [with Acting Premier Krėvė on a two weeks' leave of absence] published an official communique to the effect that the elections to the People's Diet would be held on July 14. The next day Paleckis, Acting President of the Republic, published a new electoral law.

"The law [patterned on the electoral law of the USSR, decreed] that the nomination of the candidates should be reserved for the Communist Party and its affiliated organizations. . . .

"On July 7, 1940, the Director of the State Security Department [Antanas Sniečkus, First Secretary of the Communist Party] ordered the liquidation of all non-Communist parties and the arrest of their leaders and active members.

"This left the Communist Party the only recognized party but in order to mislead the voters, it took on the name 'Union of Working People of Lithuania'. . . . The duty to vote was especially emphasized. [Some 2,000 people were arrested on the night of July 11-12.]

"However, on July 14, 1940, very few people voted (15 to 20 percent). Absenteeism was so evident that the Communist Party decided to take some additional measures. On the evening of July 14, the Acting President of the Republic promulgated a decree extending the voting to 10 p.m. on July 15. In it he warned:

'Only the enemies of the people, only the enemies of this new

Lithuania, may stay at home and not participate in the victory march of the Lithuanian people.' "

[Passports of voters were stamped at the polling places. There were no voter rolls. Aliens, including several Americans, had their passports stamped "Voted".] "On July 17, 1940, the Supreme Electoral Commission published: 1,386,589 voters have submitted 1,386,569 envelopes; this represents 95.1 percent of all those who had the right to vote.... For the ticket of the Union of Working People 1,375,349 votes, or 99.19 percent of those who cast ballots, voted. No complaints on irregularity of voting were submitted." [TASS in London published the very same figures on the first day of the "voting."]

"As soon as the Supreme Electoral Commission published the results of the elections, the Communist Party, conforming to Moscow's plans, inaugurated a series of [compulsory] mass meetings. The 'demand of the people' was that 'Stalin's constitution' should be introduced into Lithuania, and that Lithuania become a part of the Soviet Union.

"On July 21, 1940, the People's Diet [and the like diets simultaneously 'elected' and convened in Latvia and Estonia] was convened for its first session [in the theater]. In one hour it adopted the resolution which introduced the Soviet system into Lithuania and declared Lithuania a Soviet Republic. After a brief intermission [the plane from Moscow with the text was late], it adopted the second resolution [deputies seated in the theater seats among Red Army officers and visitors applauded 'the unanimous' resolution which stated, in part, that 'now the people, with the help of the mighty Red Army, have broken the yoke ... and established Soviet rule ... thanks to the Soviet Union'] asking the Supreme Soviet of the USSR 'to admit the Lithuanian Soviet Socialist Republic to the Union of Soviet Socialist Republics as a Union Republic on the same basis as the Ukrainian, Belorussian, and other Union Republics.'

"On August 3, 1940, the Supreme Soviet of the USSR ... decided 'to grant the request' ....

"In the name of the silenced people of Lithuania her diplomatic representatives abroad presented their solemn protest against the falsification of the will of the Lithuanian people to the governments to which they were accredited and unanimously condemned the Soviet aggression and the seizure of their state. [The] protest was sympathetically received and endorsed by the United States where the Lithuanian diplomatic mission continued to enjoy recognition."[106]

On July 23, 1940, Acting Secretary of State Sumner Welles, at the direction of President Roosevelt, released the following statement which remained the official policy of the United States of each successive administration:

"During the past few days the devious processes whereunder the political independence and territorial integrity of the three small Baltic Republics — Estonia, Latvia and Lithuania — were to be deliberately annihilated by one of their more powerful neighbors, have been rapidly drawing to their conclusion.

"From the day when the people of these Republics first gained their independence and democratic form of government, the people of the United States have watched their admirable progress in self-government with deep and sympathetic interest.

"The policy of this Government is universally known. The people of the United States are opposed to predatory activities, no matter whether they are carried on by the use of force or by the threat of force. They are likewise opposed to any form of intervention on the part of one state, however powerful, in the domestic concerns of any other sovereign state, however weak.

"These principles constitute the very foundation upon which the existing relationship between the twenty-one sovereign Republics of the New World rests. The United States will continue to stand by these principles because of the conviction of the American people that unless the doctrine in which these principles are inherent once again governs the relations between nations, the rule of reason, of justice, and of law — in other words, the basis of modern civilization itself — cannot be preserved."[107]

On August 11, 1940 Molotov informed foreign missions of countries represented in Kaunas, Riga and Tallinn about the "admission" of Lithuania, Latvia and Estonia into the Soviet Union, and that he expected such missions to "complete the liquidation of their affairs by August 25, 1940" when their executors "lose their validity," and "diplomatic and consular missions of Lithuania, Latvia and Estonia in other states cease to operate, and transfer their functions, as well as

[106] *Communist Takeover and Occupation of Lithuania, Special Report No. 14* of the Select Committee on Communist Aggression, House of Representatives, 83rd Congress, Washington, 1955, pp. 9-13. The full story is documented in the Committee's Hearings, Part I, and its Third Interim Report.

[107] The Department of State *Bulletin*, July 27, 1940, v. III, No. 57, p. 48.

their archives and property, to" Soviet officials. The American Legation in Kaunas was notified to that effect by the Lithuanian Ministry of Foreign Affairs on August 12.

Without waiting for the conclusion of their farce with "people's diets," Moscow moved early in July to rob the dispossessed countries of their material assets abroad. They failed in some countries: the U.S. froze the assets of the Baltic States as it did the assets of the nations occupied by Germany. Soviet officials kept sending indignant notes — and received firm replies. The Lithuanian Foreign Office called Minister Owen Norem of the U.S. to receive a protest on July 21. The American-educated Miss Magdalena Avietėnaitė read the note to him — and added quietly in English: "Please disregard all of our protests. We do not act independently any more. We appreciate what Washington is doing more than we dare tell. People are listening and I cannot say any more."[108] Norem reported that new "advisors" in the Foreign Office "could not understand our inability to accept the invitation to attend today's meeting of the Seimas. [The informant] expressed deep appreciation of our Government's understanding and treatment."

[108] *The USSR-German Aggression Against Lithuania, op. cit.*, 250-252.

XXVIII.
SOVIET "NORMALIZATION"— THE GENOCIDE

Any and all movements of the Lithuanian Army were banned on the day of the occupation. The army itself was renamed "People's Army," National Guard (Šaulių Sąjunga) was disarmed and mustered out, most of the senior army and guard officers were discharged and arrested. On July 12, 1940, a Lithuanian-born alien, Soviet Army Major General Felix Baltušis - "Žemaitis," was made the Commander-in-Chief of the People's Army. Political commissars named by the Communist Party were attached to all units, and political spying was instituted. Army chaplains were dismissed, soldiers and officers had to attend "political education" classes. When soldiers of the 9th Infantry regiment manhandled their *politruks*, the regimental commander was arrested, the regiment was moved to eastern Lithuania and isolated. As the enlisted men continued to resist, the regiment was mustered out and hundreds of enlisted men were arrested. In August, 1940, the People's Army was reduced to two infantry divisions with some artillery batteries, three cavalry regiments were reduced to one, the air force was limited to a single squadron grounded in Ukmergė, the officers school was dismissed. The two Lithuanian divisions, numbered 179 and 184, were made a part of the 29th Territorial Corps of the Soviet Army, bolstered by several hundred Russian "political leaders" and 5,000 officers and men. During the winter of 1940 some 2,000 men of the Corps "disappeared." In May 1941 the divisions were moved into several training camps and additional Russian officers and men were assigned to the divisions. Simultaneously 271 Lithuanian officers, 33 non-commissioned officers, 15 privates and four civilian employees "disappeared" overnight and several hundred officers were taken "for training" to Russia — never to be heard from again.[109]

The Concordat with the Vatican was voided on June 25, 1940, and property of the churches was confiscated. Church structures were requisitioned for Soviet army needs. Compensation to the clergy of all denominations for keeping birth, marriage and death records was abrogated, pensions to clergymen were invalidated and their personal bank

[109] *Lietuvių Enciklopedija*, XV, 118-119.

accounts confiscated. The teaching of religion was banned. Catholic printing shops and bookstores were confiscated. Religious-content books were removed from school and public libraries and burned, and no religious newspapers or publications were allowed. Catholic and Protestant faculties of theology were closed at the university. Priests were pressured to sign undertakings not to teach religion to children. Only "freedom of the cult" was left: the right to hold liturgical rites — with attendants thereof immediately taken under surveillance. Religious holidays were made working days. Many religious leaders were included in the initial list of 2,000 "public enemies" arrested just before the "People's Diet elections."[110]

The co-operatives were not liquidated at once, yet all private commercial and industrial concerns with an annual turnover of 150,000 litas were taken over by the State. Small shopkeepers and craftsmen were rapidly eliminated through heavy taxation. People's needs were to be served by public institutions — limited to mismanaged stores in larger towns with empty shelves, inasmuch as wholesale distribution became entirely dependent on Moscow and on depleted transport facilities. All means of transportation were nationalized. The postal and telephone-telegraph service was liquidated, and new offices were staffed mostly by Russians.[111]

The People's Diet had decreed a Soviet system and the nationalization of land, factories, banks, etc. After the "admission" of Lithuania into the USSR on August 3, 1940, the "fraternal" Byelorussian SSR "restored" to Lithuania several townships, and the diet itself became Supreme Soviet. Nationalization was a sadistic process of abuse and appropriation of funds into the private pockets of commissars. The nationalization of banks involved the sequestration of most of the savings since the accounts were limited to 1,000 rubles: 38 million rubles were confiscated from 12,000 depositors. Another measure of robbery was the artificial rate of exchange: 10 litas for 9 rubles, even though the bank rate had been 3 to 5 rubles per lita. When the ruble was made the official currency, the 223 million litas in circulation were converted to 200 million rubles, rather than the real value of 700 to 800 million rubles.[112]

[110] *Lietuvių Enciklopedija*, XV, 148-149.

[111] *Ibid.*, XV, 217.

[112] *Ibid.*, XV, 363.

The Bank of Lithuania, railroads, foreign trade became "Union" functions and were taken over by Moscow's "plenipotentiaries" attached to the Government of the Lithuanian SSR. All exports went to Leningrad, Moscow and other Soviet areas — at first in exchange for watermelons "for the famished Lithuania." The administration of the confiscated business and commerce was taken over by the *Vneshtorg* (the commissariat for foreign trade) whose plenipotentiary Morozov assumed his post in Lithuania in July, 1940.

Alien occupational functionaries became the privileged class, and at once there was a housing shortage. Since the larger homes were nationalized, construction was at a standstill: the plans for 1941 published by Premier Mečys Gedvilas projected 1148 new dwelling apartments — one-third of the 1939 rate. The housing crisis worsened with the arrival of the families of the Soviet army, NKVD and civilian ruling class: the government announced that good quarters were needed for "the liberating Red Army and new Soviet institutions." Living space was fixed at nine square meters per adult person. Already in August 1940 the NKVD ordered the mayors of first and second class cities to oust "persons who have no urgent reason to live in cities." Rosters of "non-labor" people embraced clergymen, former house owners, merchants, pensioned persons, families of men employed out of town, the unemployed. They were to be evicted and were to find living quarters by themselves. Production "norms" were increased — on a "voluntary basis" — by voice cote at mass meetings to accept "challenges" from factories in Russia, for the sake of "socialistic competition." Piece-work compensation was instituted — making a "new socialistic virtue" out of the much-condemned capitalistic exploitation: the *Akkord ist Mord.* Living standards rapidly dwindled.[113]

Two-thirds of the Lithuanian population were engaged in agriculture. Therefore, the Soviet *Gau-Leiter* Dekanozov belied the talk of "land expropriation." On June 22, 1940, Minister of Agriculture Mickis assured the farmers: "This land of yours which you had for centuries soaked with your sweat and blood, is yours and shall remain yours." Yet on July 1st, Land Reform Director St. Elsbergas announced a draft bill to nationalize land holdings of religious organizations, churches and parishes; holdings of up to 50 hectares would be left to private owners — "those loyal to the working people." The next day the official daily *Lietuvos Aidas* denounced this news as false and Elsbergas was

[113] *Ibid.*, XV, 364.

fired. The *Farmer's Adviser* in its issue of July 4, wrote: "No one intends and no one is preparing to seize church lands, rectories and monastery farms." The Communist front in its "people's diet" election platform on July 10, 1940 proclaimed: "Do not believe rumors spread by people's enemies, the threats that the people's government would force you to form collective farms and would persecute believers." Agriculture Minister Mickis in his radio speech on election day, July 14, said that "No one intends to force farmers to form kolkhozes."

Yet on July 22, 1940 the "people's diet" enacted a law stating that "all Lithuanian land with its resources, all forests and waters belong to the people, that is: it is state property." Up to 30 hectares were to be left to "private management," the rest was to be distributed to the landless. The decree added: "All attempts to compel peasants to organize into kolkhozes would be severely punished." Retention of private farming was intended to split the farmer class which was to be coerced to give up private farming by heavy taxation and the imposition of levies in produce which were impossible to meet.[114]

On August 14, 1940 Premier Gedvilas told the congress of teachers: "A greatest social revolution is taking place . . . which compels us to revaluate all values. What had been noble and respected yesterday, is ugly today. Everything is changing radically. . . Every teacher, every intellectual must realize that the common folk decided to follow a new road." He exhorted his audience to denounce religious and national "prejudices" and to praise Russia. The state emblem and the cross were removed from walls, and portraits of Stalin, Lenin and Marx appeared alongside several tolerated former non-political leaders, like Vincas Kudirka and Jonas Basanavičius. Teaching of the Russian language was introduced in schools, and evening courses for adults were inaugurated. Classical writers were eliminated from school readers and new Stalinist writers and poets appeared. A verse was eliminated from Kudirka's poem, "My Lithuania! With enemy raging against you, you must become a hydra." New school texts could not be produced overnight — and the People's Commissariat of Education on September 30, 1940 ordered: "It is best to cut out improper sheets" from old manuals. Komsomol and Pioneer units were to be formed in schools and Communist Party *komsorgs* (party organizers) were assigned to all schools. Teachers were ordered to attend courses of the Communist/bolshevik Party history, after classes. The university introduced a separate dis-

[114] *Ibid.*, XV, 364-365.

cipline: the study of the Stalin Constitution. The Lithuanian system of 13 years of elementary and secondary schooling was replaced by a Soviet ten-year system. This meant lowering educational standards, yet it was represented as an effort "to overtake the fraternal Soviet peoples."[115]

The reports of the Museum of Vytautas the Great had documented the efforts to preserve cultural monuments. These labors were nearly nullified by Red Army and Party requisitions of antique furniture and paintings for their use, and the shipping of rare books and historic documents to Russia. Religious art monuments in libraries and musea were systematically destroyed. 423,639 volumes from confiscated stocks of publishing houses in Kaunas alone were destroyed by order of Vassily Procenko, head of the Moscow *Glavlit* — the Supreme Board for Literature and Publishing.

Vladimir S. Semyonov, head of the Soviet delegation at SALT talks in the Johnson-Nixon era, as counselor of the Soviet Legation in Kaunas since 1939 was one of the architects of the takeover and sovietization of Lithuania and, in the postwar years, of East Germany. In 1940 Semyonov and his nominal chief, Soviet Minister Pozdniakov, prodded individual writers to "create" on indicated topics. Most of the writers evaded the orders, and in the spring of 1941 *Tiesa* complained: the writers had not justified the Party's trust reposed in them and had produced virtually nothing about the historic change to a Soviet system. Urged by Semyonov, "President" Paleckis accompanied by a CP Secretary and Arts Board Director, dutifully visited the Writers House and threatened that this negligence would no longer be tolerated. Its Communist manager Petras Cvirka promised to reform his ways — and a special program for writers: lectures on dialectic materialism each Thursday by Russian professors Kashirin and Mursanov, and weekend visits by Stalin laureates from Moscow. Nevertheless, the writers produced nothing of significance — only translations from the Russian.[116]

All the while — thousands of Russian NKVD men, under Gladkov and Bykov, dispersed throughout the country to supervise the compilation of dossiers on "people's enemies" in preparation for "the combat objective . . . to clean up the Lithuanian SSR of the counter-revolutionary and hostile element." CP Secretary Antanas Sniečkus was replaced as head of "security" by Aleksandras Guzevičius-Gudaitis, under Glad-

[115] *Ibid.*, XV, 365.

[116] *Ibid.*, XV, 366.

kov. In February 1941, in emulation of the Nazi "elite corps," the NKVD was split and a new "elite" NKGB was formed: People's Commissariat of State Security under Merkulov, with military forces of its own and titles of "Major of State Security, Lieutenant of State Security," etc. Gladkov became the first NKGB of the Lithuanian SSR.

Party and Komsomol members were security agents ex officio — by reason of their membership discipline. Thousands of people were forced and blackmailed to become informers on their own families and friends. Janitors, bathhouse attendants and hotel employees were the principal victims of pressure to become informers. The secret documents seized by the insurrectionists in June 1941 show the "people's enemies" were: all former members of political parties, "nationalist-chauvinist" organizations — liberals, Catholics, nationalists, socialdemocrats, student activists, national guardsmen; former "political bandits" and volunteers of anti-Soviet armed forces, Tsarist and White army officers, Lithuanian and Polish army judges, former military and civilian policemen, court prosecutors and investigators, prison employees; expelled former Communists and Komsomols; all political emigrés and repatriates; all foreigners, former aliens, representatives and employees of foreign concerns; persons corresponding with people abroad, esperantists, filatelists, boy and girl scouts, former Red Cross employees, former ranking civil officials; the clergy of all denominations, sectarians and "religious activists"; former noblemen, bankers, merchants, hotel-restaurant owners.

At least three NKVD/NKGB orders of the Lithuanian SSR (No. 0054 of November 28, 1940 by NKVD Guzevičius in Lithuanian, No. 0023 of April 25, 1941 by NKGB Gladkov in Russian, and No. 5/2405 of May 17, 1941 by NKGB Gladkov in Russian) — regarding operational "accounting" and dossiers, refer to "Order No. 001223 of the NKVD of the USSR of October 11, 1939," that is: on the morrow of the signing of the Mutual Assistance Pact of October 10, 1939.

Finally, on May 31, 1941, NKGB Merkulov of the USSR ordered NKGB Gladkov of the LSSR "to ready for exiling into remote places of the Union of SSR of the anti-Soviet minded persons." Gladkov and his top aides signed on the face of the order that they had read it. On June 6, 1941, Gladkov issued his own order No. 1/1160 — "Strictly Secret, Highly Urgent, Exclusively Personal" — ordering the County Troykas named by him earlier to execute "the operation known to you" "with precision, intelligently, without noise or panic, in exact compliance with the instructions" of Merkulov. Gladkov enclosed instructions for briefing the involved Party, NKGB and NKVD personnel

— the notorious Secret Order by Merkulov's Deputy Commissar Ivan Serov who later, as head of the KGB under Khrushchev, was wined and dined in London, Washington, and elsewhere. The Gladkov order and Serov's "instructions regarding the manner of conducting deportations from Lithuania, Latvia and Estonia" were both stamped received in Šiauliai on June 7, 1941.[117]

Thousands of railroad freight cars and trucks with NKGB/NKVD troops converged on the Baltic States. During the "Horrible June" night of 13 to 14, 1941, around 4 a.m., trucks picked up "anti-Soviet minded" people and their families — 35,000 from Lithuania alone in the first "operation." The victims were brought to railroad yards where men were separated from their families. After long delays, long trains with human "freight" moved eastward and northward amid cries of children, the wailing of women, and the singing of "God is our Savior and Fortress". . . . Thousands of men were staying away from homes as a routine precaution, and thus some escaped exile. Suspicious of a forthcoming menace, strong-willed men fled into the forests — the NKGB angrily reported armed clashes with "bandits" as early as June 4, 1941.

The people's patience was at an end.

[117]Merkulov's order photo - reproduced in *Lithuanian Bulletin*, No. 9-10 of 1947. Various secret orders of the NKVD/NKGB were published in the *Lithuanian Bulletin*, 1946-1951 and reproduced in the Kersten Committee records: U.S. 83rd Congress, Hearings before the Select Committee to Investigate the Incorporation of the Baltic States into the USSR, House of Representatives, 1953-4, Part I, 407-9, 672-5; 3rd Interim Report, 470-2, 495-7, 511-3, etc.

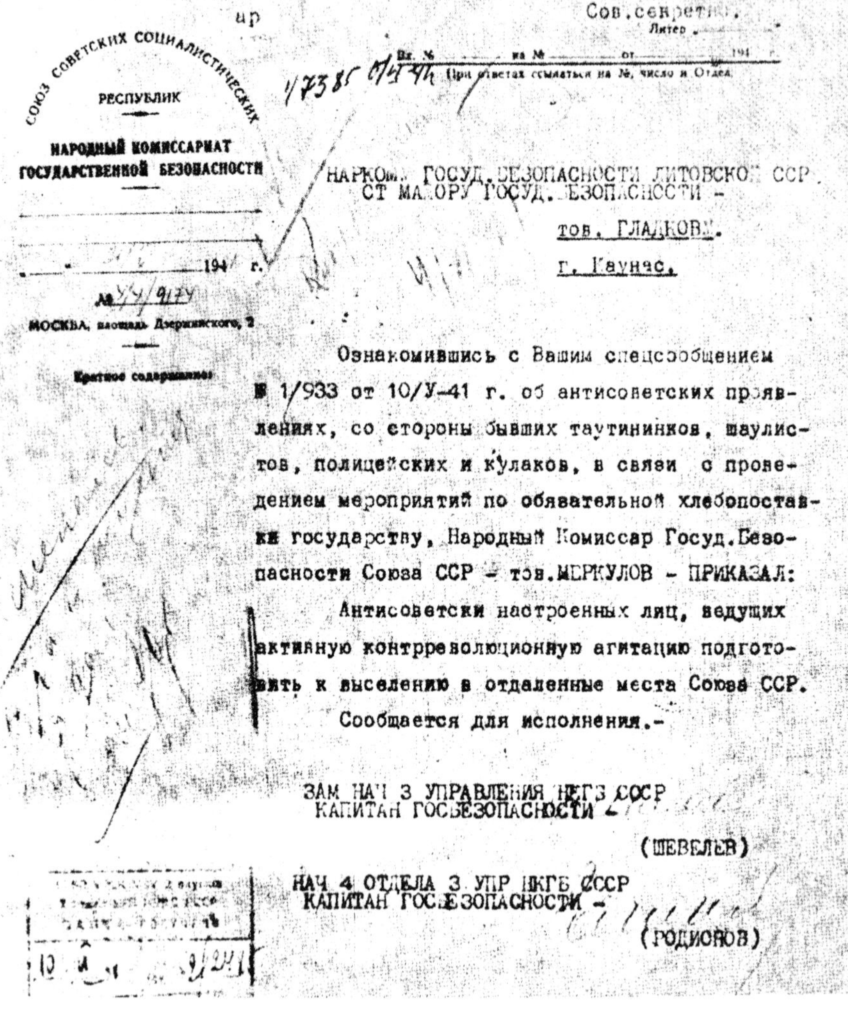

Сов. секретно.

Литер

Вх. № ... на № ... от ... 194 г.

При ответах ссылаться на №, число и Отдел

СОЮЗ СОВЕТСКИХ СОЦИАЛИСТИЧЕСКИХ РЕСПУБЛИК

НАРОДНЫЙ КОМИССАРИАТ ГОСУДАРСТВЕННОЙ БЕЗОПАСНОСТИ

... 194 г.

№ 4/4/9174

МОСКВА, площадь Дзержинского, 2

Краткое содержание:

НАРКОМУ ГОСУД. БЕЗОПАСНОСТИ ЛИТОВСКОЙ ССР
СТ МАЙОРУ ГОСУД. БЕЗОПАСНОСТИ -

тов. ГЛАДКОВУ.

г. Каунас.

Ознакомившись с Вашим спецсообщением № 1/933 от 10/У-41 г. об антисоветских проявлениях, со стороны бывших таутининков, шаулистов, полицейских и кулаков, в связи с проведением мероприятий по обязательной хлебопоставки государству, Народный Комиссар Госуд. Безопасности Союза ССР - тов. МЕРКУЛОВ - ПРИКАЗАЛ:

Антисоветски настроенных лиц, ведущих активную контрреволюционную агитацию подготовить к выселению в отдаленные места Союза ССР.

Сообщается для исполнения.-

ЗАМ НАЧ 3 УПРАВЛЕНИЯ НКГБ СССР
КАПИТАН ГОСБЕЗОПАСНОСТИ

(ШЕВЕЛЕВ)

НАЧ 4 ОТДЕЛА 3 УПР НКГБ СССР
КАПИТАН ГОСБЕЗОПАСНОСТИ -

(РОДИОНОВ)

NKGB Merkulov's Order No. 4/4/9174 of May 31, 1941 "To ready the anti-Soviet minded persons for exiling into remote places of the Union of SSR."

XXIX.
THE INSURRECTION AND WAR

Some of the former public leaders attempted to influence Paleckis by professing their loyalty and advising moderation. However, their pleas fell on the deaf ears of a powerless figurehead of tyranny. From the first moment of the occupation the masses viewed the regime with contempt, fear and derision, and engaged in passive resistance. The monumental show of resistance was the massive boycott of the "People's Diet elections" where only 14-16% of the eligible voters had their passports stamped "Voted" — and enough people managed to stuff the ballot boxes with votes for a fictional character of the comics named *Melchioras Putelė* (Melchior the Suds). The teachers congress concluded its August 14-15 sessions by singing the banned National Anthem and disrupted the Red Army Chorus concert by singing Lithuanian folk songs. Lithuanian soldiers' graves were decorated on All Souls Day. The January 1941 elections to the Soviet were likewise boycotted. *Politruk* (political guidance officer) talks in army units, schools and the university were disrupted. Anti-Soviet folklore developed rapidly, amateur resistance groups of school pupils and youths mushroomed and highly emotional leaflets were scattered all over the country. Soldiers refused to take the oath of allegiance to the Soviet Union. These early efforts are graphically documented in NKGB/NKVD reports published in the *Lithuanian Bulletin* and reproduced in the Kersten Committee reports referred to earlier.

Mature leaders of various resistance groups conferred in Vilnius and on October 9, 1940 adopted the name of the Lithuanian Activist Front. By December 1940, tenuous communications were established with the Lithuanian Activist Front simultaneously formed in Germany by Colonel Kazys Škirpa, the Lithuanian Minister in Berlin prior to the Soviet invasion, whose bold refusal to surrender the Lithuanian Legation to the Soviet Embassy reverberated in world press headlines for a number of days. Counseled by refugee civilian and military leaders, Škirpa formed a clandestine LAF Advisory Council and prepared series of articles and proclamations, the rules for underground resistance and a political program for the re-establishment of a free Lithuanian State, and gained limited approval of some German military leaders. This literature, however, "had little influence in Lithuania, because only a small part of this material could be smuggled into the country," according to Dr. V. Stanley Vardys, the most authoritative researcher on matters pertaining to Soviet-occupied Lithuania.[118] On March 24, 1941, the guidelines for the underground on planning were summarized in the "Directives for the Liberation of Lithuania."[119] The LAF leadership assumed that "there would be a German-Soviet war" — the opportune time for an insurrection against the Soviets and the establishment of a Provisional Lithuanian Government — regardless of German intentions.

The LAF Staff in Lithuania organized a conspiratorial network of "trios" and "fives" linked to one another and the central command through overlapping membership of unit leaders. "A regular member of an underground unit knew only his own group. The rule . . . was to know just what was necessary, and no more, to carry out the assigned task." Dr. Vardys estimates that the network numbered about 36,000 members. Two major centers of command were formed in Vilnius and Kaunas: if one were liquidated, the other would carry on alone. The network was "somewhat impaired" by the mass deportations of June, 1941, but "was not substantially crippled."[120] The hope regarding the future was nourished by the non-recognition of the Soviet absorption of Lithuania by the United States, the major Powers at war with Germany, and by some neutrals. Even the regime of a German-occupied France surrendered the Lithuanian Legation building to the Soviets, yet refrained from a formal recognition of the annexation.[121]

The NKGB/NKVD documents seized by the Lithuanian insurrectionists disclose the details of immature resistance beginning in the summer of 1940, of the arrests and other measures taken by the occupying regime. On April 5, 1941, the discovery of a theft of 500 hand grenades from the police warehouse in Vilnius alarmed the regime. The first armed clash occurred on June 4, 1941. On June 6 the Moscow NKGB referred to Gladkov's report on "the anti-Soviet manifestations in connection with compulsory grain deliveries" and "the exposure and liquidation, in various places of the LSSR, of counter-revolutionary insurgent organizations, which had conducted agitation against grain deliveries and had been preparing a counter-revolutionary insurrection."

[118] *Lithuania Under the Soviets, op. cit.*, 62-64.

[119] Excerpts: *The USSR-German Aggression Against Lithuania, op. cit.*, 321-7.

[120] *Lithuania Under the Soviets*, 65.

[121] Juozas Brazaitis, *Liet. enciklopedija*, XV (357-370) 370.

Moscow wanted more details. Minor incidents in connection with the mass deportations are known from a June 19, 1941 report to Gladkov by the Operative Staff of Kaunas.

In his Order No. 45 of June 21, 1941, Gladkov raved about "a number of instances of banditry." He noted that "a portion of the hostile element, slated for arrest and exile beyond the frontiers of the Lithuanian SSR, went into hiding, passed into outlaw status, and engaged in the formation of bandit groups during the . . . operation of purging of the republic." He cited a clash on June 16 in northern Rokiškis county, a clash with a band of 20 men on June 17 in the Prienai area in the southwest, and "banditry outbreaks . . . recorded in the counties of Šiauliai and Utena" in central and eastern Lithuania. He ordered the commanders "to take into elaboration" the "relatives and persons close to the bandits," to recruit informers, to stage provocatory "escapes" to infiltrate the bandit units, etc.[122]

This last desperate order of Gladkov was probably never received in some areas: at dawn on June 22, 1941, Germany attacked its partner in crimes — and there was a spontaneous insurrection all over Lithuania.

The falling aerial bombs and the thunder of artillery fire electrified the tortured nation and panicked the Russians. City and rural youths, students, factory workers and farmhands, ambushed and disarmed Russian police and troops. The retreating Soviet troops were prevented from destroying bridges and the telephone-telegraph exchange in Kaunas. A brave band of youths seized the Kaunas radio station on June 23 and broadcast the restoration of Lithuanian independence and the formation of a Provisional Government, while Russian troops and tanks were crowding the streets in the vicinity of the radio station. Soviet counterattacks were beaten off by a determined group of rebel youths. Other youths seized several arsenals and liberated political prisoners not yet deported or executed. It is estimated that about one-hundred-thousand people had taken part in the insurrection, including the depleted units of the Lithuanian Army dispersed in several training areas and diluted with Russian personnel. Two thousand insurrectionists were killed in battle, some eight thousand were wounded, and some rebel units were destroyed by German forces not forewarned of the existence of any Lithuanian uniformed or non-uniformed "friendly units."

Colonel Škirpa was proclaimed the head of the Provisional Government. However, the angered Nazi leaders isolated Škirpa and the would-

[122] Kersten Committee's Third Interim Report, *op. cit.*, 472-529. Gladkov's last order is found on pp. 528-529.

be Minister of Foreign Affairs Rapolas Skipitis in Berlin. Several prospective cabinet members were among the mass of deportees. Therefore, the insurrectionists entrusted the Provisional Premiership to Professor Juozas Ambrazevičius, the Minister of Education, and co-opted several other ministers. On June 25, the Lithuanian Provisional Government broadcast an appeal "To the Nation" denouncing the Soviet occupation and oppression, thanking Germany for the "liberation," honoring fallen patriots and declaring that "we wish to be independent, we are determined to sacrifice ourselves and to give all to Lithuania." The Government hastened to complete the reconstruction of the governmental apparatus in the liberated areas of the country, and restored the administrative and educational system of the Republic of Lithuania. Several decrees annulled in part the nationalization of private property and promulgated rules for an orderly restoration of property, lands, industrial and business establishments.

A wave of enthusiasm seized the nation — truly spontaneous worker messages of loyalty greeted the Provisional Government. The indignation over the Soviet outrages deepened as mass executions and tortures became known — the massacre of 412 farmers interned at Pravieniškės for nondelivery of grain quotas; only about 300 of the 12,000 political prisoners in Vilnius and Kaunas were liberated; 76 persons, including secondary school youths, were tortured in an inhuman fashion and then put to death in the Rainiai forest; the medical and nursing personnel treating the wounded Soviet troops were executed at the hospital in Panevėžys; the tongue-cutting, skinning, eye-gouging and bayoneting of a column of some six thousand Lithuanian, Polish and Belorussian prisoners, including small children, during the night of June 26-27 in the Cherveń (Ihumen) forest between Minsk and Mohylew; many, many other bestialities characteristic of the Muscovite troops.[123]

Even though the German troops entered Kaunas and Vilnius in parade formations, as both cities were fully controlled by Lithuanian military commandants, police and civil administration — the Berlin authorities completely ignored the restoration of the independent Lithuanian State. The Führer awarded General von Küchel with the order of the Iron Cross "for the capture of Kaunas," scrupulously refraining

[123]Testimony by two survivors of the Cherveń Massacre — Canon Antanas Petraitis and Colonel Juozas Tumas — Kersten Committee Hearings . . . Part I, *op. cit.*, 409-429. Mrs. Kazimiera Tarvainis testified on her son's fate in the Rainiai Forest and Juozas Miliauskas about the murder of priests — *ibid.*, 364-371. See also the story of another Cherveń survivor: Colonel Jonas Petruitis, *Lithuania Under the Sickle and Hammer*, Cleveland, Ohio, n.d.

from mentioning the role of the Lithuanians. The *Oberkommando* also claimed that the Kaunas radio station was "captured" by a Lieutenant Flohret. Škirpa had been forewarned not to establish any government without German consent, and he "was strongly reprimanded after such a government was created. On June 25, General Pohl, the Wehrmacht field commander in Kaunas, frankly told the representatives of the Provisional Government that he was not authorized to enter [into] any discussions with any Lithuanian government. However, General Pohl, an Austrian, tolerated Lithuanian authorities where these did not interfere with German institutions and policies. He also kept out of the machinations that the SD (Sicherheitdienst) and the Gestapo continuously planned for the removal of the 'stuck bone'." However, in view of the immense support of the people and the sensational popularity of the Lithuanian insurrectionist government abroad, the Nazis decided to dispose of it "by boycotting and obstructing its activities and by pressuring it either to liquidate itself or to enlist into the service of the civil administration (Zivilverwaltung) that was soon to take over the administration of Lithuania." [124]

Communications facilities were denied the Lithuanian Government and various officials from Berlin urged the ministers to disband or transform into an advisory body. Hitler established an "Ostland" embracing the Baltic States and Belorussia. Reichskommissar Heinrich Lohse announced the establishment of a German civil administration on July 28. Still the Lithuanians would not budge. General Commissar for Lithuania, Adrian von Renteln, met with the Government in corpore and urged them to become his advisory council. Finally, on August 5, 1941, the Provisional Government decided to "involuntarily suspend its activities." The ministers placed a wreath on the Tomb of the Unknown Soldier, signed a protest in writing, and dispersed.[125]

It was clear: neither Germany nor the USSR wanted an independent Lithuania.

[124] *Lithuania Under the Soviets, op. cit.*, 69-71.

[125] *Liet. Enciklopedija*, XV, 373-374.

"Captain Daumontas" – Juozas Lukša (1921-1951), one of the chief resistance leaders in Lithuania during the second Soviet occupation.

XXX.
THE ROAD FROM PASSIVE RESISTANCE TO ARMED STRUGGLE

Most of the dozen or so men who had agreed to serve the German Civil Administration in an advisory capacity were motivated by a desire to help their people and to blunt Nazi exploiting measures. Five of them soon resigned, and some died in the Stutthof concentration camp. The Ostland administration's task was to exploit the native manpower and economic resources, and to pave the way for German colonization initiated nearly at once by bringing in German and Dutch settlers. The reinstatement of the Soviet nationalization measures abrogated by the Lithuanian Provisional Government antagonized the population, as did the herding of the Jewish minority into ghetto camps and the classification of people into superior and inferior races. The appeals for labor manpower to work in Prussia gradually turned into demands and finally into a forcible mobilization. The Counselors tried to hold the economic and manpower quotas down. The drive in 1943 for a Lithuanian SS force failed — Lithuania and Poland were the only occupied countries which failed to produce native SS Legions — and the Nazis turned to manhunts among Sunday church attendants.

The rebel Lithuanian soldiers of the former Soviet 29th Corps were given a choice: either to enlist in Home Defense Battalions, or land in prisoner-of-war camps. Twenty-two Home Defense battalions were formed in 1942, ostensibly to protect the country from Soviet parachutists. Within two years only 4,000 to 6,000 men of the original force of 20,000 remained in the country, inasmuch as these battalions were soon shipped to Byelorussia, Ukraine, even Yugoslavia and Italy. Many were killed, others deserted — the Polish Army in Italy had a Lithuanian Battalion made up of Lithuanians deserting to the Allied side.

A conference convoked by Counselors in 1943 agreed to call for the formation of Lithuanian military units to combat the bolsheviks "for the sake of freedom." The Germans censored all references to freedom and published only the call for armed forces. The increasing parachuting of Soviet saboteurs caused German reprisals against the inhabitants of the infested areas — the burning of villages and massacre of the inhabitants. The most gruesome incident was the burning alive of 119 men, women and children of the Pirčiupis village in reprisal for a firing upon

German military cars by Soviet-parachuted saboteurs led by Genrikas Zimanas, who was later rewarded by the Russians with editorship of the principal Party daily *Tiesa* and, finally, of the ideological monthly *Komunistas*.

When all efforts to form Lithuanian SS units failed, the Nazis retaliated against intellectuals, including the Counselors, educators, physicians, clergymen and newsmen. Another conference of 45 prominent Lithuanians was then convoked on November 24, 1943. There was consensus that military units were needed to protect the inhabitants from Russian bandits; that an SS formula was not acceptable to Lithuanians; and that native units must be led by Lithuanian officers. The Germans rejected such a formulation. Finally, on February 13, 1944, after conferences between General Paulius Plechavičius and Ostland SS Chief Jaeckeln and SS Major General Harm, it was agreed that a Lithuanian Task Force *(Rinktinė)* of 20 battalions of volunteers be formed for service within the territory of Lithuania. An appeal was published on February 16, 1944 — and within several days, instead of a few hundred cripples responding to former German mobilizations, 30,000 able-bodied volunteers reported for enlistment in a force of 18,000 men.

This result caused new tensions, rather than a detente. On March 20, 1944, Northern Front Commander Fieldmarshal Model and Ostland SS Chief Jaeckeln demanded that by April 15 General Plechavičius form additional 15 battalions, a force of 9,000 men, for service with the German Army for airfields defense. On April 5, Plechavičius refused. The next day Commissar von Renteln demanded that Plechavičius announce a general mobilization. It was announced — and it failed totally. On May 9 Jaeckeln demanded that the battalions stationed in the Vilnius area be placed at his disposal as German Police Auxiliary units. Instead — the Task Force wearing Lithuanian Army uniforms began demobilizing. On May 15, 1944, Plechavičius and his staff were seized and incarcerated in the Salaspils KZ camp in Latvia. The next day the SS troops attacked the Lithuanian barracks. In some places the men fled into forests, in other places they fought back. Thirteen men were executed in Vilnius that day, 17 more on May 17, and 53 men on May 21. About 3,000 men were seized. 110 men were sent to Stutthof KZ, some to Flossenburg KZ, most of the others were drafted in the Luftwaffe Auxiliary force. The men who escaped — prepared to fight the returning Russians.

The Lithuanian underground resistance began upon the dissolution of the Provisional Government. The Lithuanian Activist Front on September 20, 1941, protested against the imposition of a German civil administration. The Front leader, Levas Prapuolenis, landed in the Dachau KZ and on September 22, the LAF was shut down. Dozens of underground newspapers appeared by the end of the year and several resistance movements were born. By a memorandum dated December 5, 1942, former President Kazys Grinius and Agriculture ministers Jonas Aleksa and Mykolas Krupavičius protested against the colonization, sovietization of farming, and the extermination of Jews — and Grinius was banned from Kaunas, Aleksa and Krupavičius were exiled to Germany under police surveillance. Counselor Vladas Jurgutis, professor of economics, criticized the economic exploitation, and had to resign. When the Chamber of Agriculture pointed out excessive grain levies and Agriculture Counselor Petronis objected to the removal of Poles from farms — Petronis was removed. Education Counselor Germantas refused to sign a decree demanding performance of a labor duty as a precondition for matriculation of students in the universities. He was arrested and died in a concentration camp.

Toward the end of 1943 various underground resistance organizations united into a coalition VLIK: the Supreme Committee for the Liberation of Lithuania, which embraced the former rightist, centrist and leftist political parties, and new formations — the Lithuanian Front, Freedom Fighters, the Nationalist Party, and the Unity Movement. Civil engineer Steponas Kairys, a veteran revolutionary, signer of the 1918 Declaration of the Restitution of Independence, professor of engineering and leader of the Social Democratic Party, was elected Chairman of the coalition. VLIK presented itself to the nation by an appeal dated February 16, 1944 — Lithuanian Independence Day. On April 29, 1944, the underground newspaper *Nepriklausoma Lietuva* (The Independent Lithuania), in an appeal forewarned the people that "the Germans are demanding our sons to be shipped to the West . . . to fight not against bolshevism, but against the British and the Americans . . . who continue to recognize our statehood and where Lithuanian Legations are active. . . . We shall determinedly safeguard our youths for the freedom of the Lithuanian People and State, to deal with the possible return of bolshevism." Soon, however, a liaison courier to Estonia was detained with papers, and six of the nine men of the VLIK Command were arrested in April and May — to be liberated by the American Army at Bayreuth on April 15, 1945. The liberated leaders soon revived the VLIK Mission abroad.

During the Nazi occupation, the Lithuanian resistance was directed against German exploitation and manpower mobilization for military or labor duty abroad. It did not strive to handicap the German war effort against the USSR. The resistance was sustained by the Atlantic Charter of August 12, 1941, promising restoration of the sovereignty to states forcibly deprived thereof. This theme was repeatedly publicized by the underground press. Lithuanian police and civil officials consistently supported the resistance. With the war front once again approaching Lithuania, the SS and Gestapo gained supreme power, and the SS hastened to complete the destruction of Jews interned in ghetto camps: the Nazis liquidated or deported up to 200,000 Jews.

When the Soviet army reoccupied Vilnius on July 12, 1944, and Vilkaviškis on July 31, the German Civil Administration moved to Berlin. It had accomplished few of its objectives: besides Jews, some 75,000 other citizens were deported to Germany for labor and some 20,000 for the Luftwaffe Auxiliary, and six hundred million gold dollars worth of material goods were seized — compared with the Soviet seizure of over two hundred million gold dollars worth. Over 100,000 people fled westward by trains, horse-carts and on foot, as well as nearly the entire population of the Klaipėda (Memel) District whose flight was facilitated by German ships. Some refugees were overtaken by the advancing Red Army. Some of the Lithuanian political prisoners, including Dr. Petras Klimas, signer of the Declaration of Independence and his country's Minister to France, Belgium and Spain, were deliberately abandoned by the Gestapo in Prussian prisons, left to the mercy of the Soviet MVD/MGB.

The war front held stable in northwestern Samagitia until October, 1944. Leaderless Samagites organized some armed units to defend their homes — until the Russians seized Klaipėda on January 29, 1945. A few Lithuanian units kept fighting alongside German and Latvian forces in Latvia until the German surrender in May, 1945. Several hundred Lithuanians fled by boats to Sweden. Those in uniform were interned by Sweden — ten Lithuanians with nearly two hundred Estonians and Latvians were surrendered to Russia, in exchange for Silesian coal, despite mass protests by Swedes and intercession by the foremost personalities of the West.[126]

[126]This review is based mainly on the account of Juozas Brazaitis, formerly Ambrazevičius, head of the Lithuanian Provisional Government of 1941, in *Liet. Enciklopedija*, XV, 374-380. Excellent broader accounts are available in *Lithuania under the Soviets*, *op. cit.*, 66-84, and *Lithuania 700 Years*, ed. Dr. Albertas Gerutis, New York, 1969, 286-296, 331-356 (and several later editions). The battle of the memoranda is documented in *The USSR-German Aggression Against Lithuania*, *op. cit.*, 356-391.

The armed Lithuanians in their homeland's forests now clashed with the Russian invaders bringing their institutions and exacting vengeance on the Lithuanians defending their country's freedom and their families. The guerrilla war began in 1944 and continued into 1953.

Vanagas - the Hawk, U.S.-born Adolfas Ramanauskas (center), Commander of the Southern Area, rose to Generalship. In 1953 he ordered the guerrillas to cease fighting. In 1956 he was held and executed without a trial.

XXXI. THE GUERRILLA WAR *vs.* THE U.S.S.R. 1944 - 1952

The Russians ignored the Atlantic Charter to which they had adhered in writing by undersigning the Joint Declaration of the United Nations of January 1, 1942,[127] and other wartime declarations on Liberated Europe.

MVD units followed on the heels of the Red Army, including a so-called "Lithuanian Division" of non-Lithuanian troops commanded by a genuine Lithuanian officer. Hundreds of people were executed without trial in Vilnius, Svyriai, Kaunas and elsewhere. In addition to former "people's enemies," they had new accounts to square with "Nazi collaborators" — excluding, of course, Stalin and his subordinates. They at once mobilized men of military age, and many men presently fled into forests to join their guerrilla compatriots. Freedom fighters had no choice: they were either to die from tortures or in exile, or go down fighting. No mercy was shown to desperate freedom fighters — or by them to the despoiling invaders.

Dr. Vardys divides the guerrilla war into two periods: the four years of strength (1944-48), and four of gradual decline (1949-1952). The number of active guerrillas at any time varied "between 25,000 and 40,000" according to some, or "an estimated 30,000 active fighters with other thousands ready to join in case of need," according to one of their leaders, young "J. Daumantas" or Juozas Lukša who fought his way to the West with another survivor, wrote his account, went back to Lithuania and died fighting. The patriotic guerrillas faced eight Red Army divisions supported by air force and artillery units, 70,000 MVD and MGB troops, and units of "exterminators" (*istrebiteli*, unaccount-

127 "The Governments signatory hereto, having subscribed to a common program of purposes and principles embodied in the Joint Declaration, dated August 14, 1941, known as the Atlantic Charter. . . . On Behalf of the Government of the Union of Soviet Socialist Republics *Maxim Litvinoff*, Ambassador" — *USSR-German Aggression Against Lithuania, op. cit.*, 476-7, citing *The Public Papers and Addresses of Franklin D. Roosevelt, 1942*, New York, Harper, 1943, pp. 3-5. Recently declassified papers at the F. D. Roosevelt Library include a Churchill cable of March 7, 1942: "The increasing gravity of the war has led me to feel that the principles of the Atlantic Charter ought not to be construed so as to deny Russia the frontiers she occupied when Germany attacked her. This was the basis on which Russia acceded to the Charter." — *New York Times*, June 12, 1972, p. 16. Roosevelt's reaction is not indicated beyond his boast to Churchill on March 18, 1942: ". . . I think I can personally handle Stalin better than either your Foreign Office or my State Department."

ably portrayed in the Lithuanian language propaganda as "people's defenders") made up of local renegades. Between 30,000 and 50,000 patriots were killed in battle. They sold their lives dearly — inflicting estimated 80,000 casualties on motorized Russian units enjoying air support and free communications.

The guerrillas dominated the countryside in 1945-47 and fought pitched battles. Their "main formations . . . according to Soviet sources, could not be broken till the end of 1948," asserts Dr. Vardys, identifying his Soviet sources. Organizational and tactical changes were many, necessitated by the losses suffered and the strategies employed by the enemy. Unification was nominally achieved by the end of 1946, and there was a reorganization in 1949 into LLKS (*Lietuvos Laisvės Kovu Sajudis* — Lithuania's Freedom Struggle Movement), which existed until the end of 1952. The last leader, American-born Adolfas Ramanauskas "Vanagas" (The Hawk) avoided capture until 1956, when he was arrested and executed.

The guerrillas were predominantly young men and women — farmers, workers, high school and university students, some clergymen — led by former junior army officers and non-commissioned officers. Only one general — a much-decorated reservist artilleryman Motiejus Pečiulionis, holder of the French Legion of Honor — declared that he had "but one head, and I shall lay it down for no one but Lithuania." He shared his fate with his "Forest Brethren." He was captured in 1946, spent ten years at Vorkuta in the Arctic, and died in extreme poverty in his homeland. Men who could not maintain a "legal status," dwelled in forest bunkers, others stayed home until called, and they provided foodstocks and intelligence to the fighting units. They were nearly exclusively ethnic Lithuanians and therefore they enjoyed the inhabitants' support.

They were intensely nationalistic and deemed themselves to be representatives of the sovereign Lithuanian State. Many wore Lithuanian Army uniforms, insignia, and decorations. Their underground press discloses their misplaced trust in the Atlantic Charter and other wartime declarations of the "Free World," and they fought under an illusion that the United States and Great Britain would protect their claim to sovereignty, and would send them help; that Britain and the United States might ultimately continue the war against the Soviet Union — "the third party in the war," the former plotter and partner of Nazi Germany. They lacked communications with the West, except for several clandestine missions which fought their way into Poland and crossed over to Sweden. They were contacted by Western intelligence services — whose only interest proved to be military-political intelligence regarding the Soviet military establishment and its intelligence operations, rather than aid to liberation movements. There was no help.

There were few intellectuals and professionals in the forest fraternity, as a great many of them had fled westward. (Credit must be given to those who stayed for the exceptionally rapid training of the much needed physicians, teachers, engineers and scientists in the postwar years.)

According to authoritative researchers, guerrilla leaders "misinterpreted international developments and the intentions of the Western powers." Furthermore, they miscalculated manpower and logistics resources, their chances for a political victory. Without any support from abroad, "a long guerrilla war against the total-war strategy of the Soviets became militarily impossible, especially under conditions of complete sovietization. Strong will, dedication, and support from the population in the long run were insufficient to prevent the destruction of organized partisan resistance. It is therefore not surprising that the partisans lost, after eight years of war. It is rather extraordinary that they were able to fight for such a long time," concludes Dr. Vardys, seconded by Algirdas Budreckis. Dr. Vardys adds that even though the political goal of restoring Lithuania's independence was not achieved, their "dedication to nationalist ideals and objectives seemed to have strengthened national loyalties in Soviet Lithuania. Judging from propaganda initiated after the extraordinary conference of the Lithuanian Communist Party in 1958, the Lithuanian population holds an affectionately patriotic image of the movement, and the regime regards the destruction of this image a necessary prerequisite for successfully shaping the present generation of Lithuanians into Soviet patriots." [128]

Algirdis Budreckis illustrates his account of the guerrilla war with a graphic description of various episodes.[129] He cites the guerrilla oath, their moral and ideological reasoning, and the bestiality of the Soviet "pacifiers." He documents the bitter reaction among the fighters to news received from the West: "They gave us away to death at Yalta, Potsdam. . . . The same mistakes are being repeated. The West does not dare raise a voice in protest against the destruction of a nation, it does not even want to know that we have lost confidence in them, that we

[128] *Lithuania Under the Soviets, op. cit.*, 107-108. The chapter 5 on the Partisan Movement in Postwar Lithuania, 85-108, is comprehensive and well documented.

[129] "Lithuanian Resistance, 1940-1952" and "Liberation Attempts from Abroad," in *Lithuania 700 Years, op. cit.*, 313-392, 394-442, especially pp. 356-392.

are conducting the struggle against their allies." He describes the "Soviet Counter-insurgency." Deputy MVD, Lieutenant General Sergei N. Kruglov came to Lithuania in the fall of 1944 and called a top secret operational meeting of troop commanders. He ordered an intensification of the infiltration of agents into rebel ranks, to identify their leadership and to liquidate their "base of operations." Anyone suspected was to be detained. "Knouts, rubber-covered steel truncheons and bundles of ramrods were to be used to extract information. After interrogation, the friends and relatives of the known bandits were to be exiled to Siberia. Anyone fleeing arrest was to be shot on sight, and the farm or house from which he was fleeing was to be burned to the ground, and its inmates turned over" to MVD/MGB tenderness.

In 1944 the Kremlin established an Organizational Bureau for Lithuania within the Central Committee of the CPSU, headed by Colonel General Mikhail Suslov who wielded the supreme power in the suppression of resistance and re-installation of the Soviet and Party apparatus. This Russian Gauleiter as head of the "Orgburo" directed the armed struggle and provocative "diversion" (subversion) activities in Lithuania. He was later appointed to the Party Politbureau and earned a reputation of extreme "orthodoxy" and "conservatism" among Stalinist hardliners. In Lithuania he was replaced by another plenipotentiary of the CPSU Central Committee — Vladimir V. Shcherbakov.

In February, 1945, [police] Major General Juozas Bartašiunas, nominal head of the Lithuanian MVD, posted a proclamation of amnesty [see the photo reproduction from *Lithuanian Bulletin*, IV, 4, November 1946, pp. 14-15] to freedom fighters who would surrender, repent their "sins" and betray their comrades and the hiding places of men and arms. Some MVD agents were garbed in the Lithuanian Army uniforms of the guerrillas to impersonate freedom fighters and to "smoke out" sympathizers, as well as to blame the guerrillas for the cruelties perpetrated by these agents. Extreme forms of torture,quartering, tongue-cutting, eye-gouging, burying head down in ant-hills, etc., were employed to break the fighters. Mutilated corpses were dumped in town squares — and reactions of passersby were surreptitiously observed in an attempt to identify relatives and friends of "bandits." More than one mother with a bleeding heart betrayed no recognition of her son, to save her family.

Facing hopeless odds, the guerrillas usually applied hand grenades against their own heads to die unrecognizable, to save their families and friends from the representatives of Russian "law, order and culture."

MVD Colonel Burlutsky, one of the commanders dispatched to Lithuania who later defected to the West, testified before the Kersten Committee of the House of Representatives:

"It was like beating the forest for wild game, except that the game was human. Day after day we formed long lines and combed the forests and the swamps, arresting, shooting, burning. If there was any doubt left about escaping from Russia, my experiences in Lithuania put an end to it. Even my well-disciplined soldiers were sickened by their jobs. Often after a particularly grim manhunt I would find them in their quarters half mad with drink; whatever was left of their human feelings were drowned in alcohol." [130]

Nevertheless, the merciless struggle succored by the inhabitants continued. Soviet "elections" were repeatedly disrupted by firing on polling places and execution of forewarned native officials overly dutiful in obeying Soviet orders — some 4,000 Party "activists" died thus. Several massive Soviet offensive operations failed to put down "political bandits." Mass deportations of farmers opposing collectivization were instituted in 1945 through 1950, and mass offensives were repeated again. General Kruglov once again returned to Lithuania in 1950 to deliver the final blow. Regular army units were withdrawn and two MVD divisions completed the manhunts. Most of the guerrillas died fighting, a few surrendered, some managed to establish "legal status." Underground newspapers circulated as late as 1951, when several leaders perished in battles. The struggle died down by 1952. Yet amnesty was publicized in 1955 and 1956 to men still in hiding. In 1957 some persons were held for armed activities. As late as in 1959 three guerrillas were surrounded and killed.[131]

[130] *Lithuania 700 Years, op. cit.*, 383, cf. Kersten Committee's Fourth Interim Report, Washington, D.C., 1954.

[131] The authentic story of the guerrilla war by one of its leaders, Juozas Lukša under one of his "forest fraternity" aliases as J. Daumantas, was written by him in France during his sojourn on a mission: *Partizanai už Geležinės Uždangos* (Guerrillas Behind the Iron Curtain), Chicago 1950. Some extracts are found in K. V. Tauras, *Guerrilla Warfare on the Amber Coast*, New York, 1962. Lukša's story of "Piercing the Iron Curtain," illustrated, was published in *Lithuanian Bulletin*, VI, No. 5-7, May-July 1948. Also: "A Day with the Guerrilla N.C.O. School" *Lithuanian Bulletin*, VI, Nos. 8-10, Aug.-Oct. 1948.

Lithuanian women prisoners in Siberia working in a lumber camp.
—Photograph permission of Mrs. S. Rukas

XXXII. DEMOGRAPHIC CHANGES 1940 - 1970

The Soviet annexation of Lithuania was not merely a transgression of International Law and the comity of nations, as well as another attempt to eliminate an age-long political rival of the Muscovite state. It was an international crime against peace and humanity in violation of Moscow's solemn undertakings under its peace and non-aggression treaties, the Kellogg-Briand Pact, the definition of aggression covenant, the Atlantic Charter, the Four Freedoms, United Nations Charter, wartime declarations to the captive peoples, the Universal Declaration of Human Rights, and the Genocide Convention.

The Soviet annexation is unlike Western colonialism of the era of mercantilism and the colonization of wild, uninhabited or underdeveloped spaces overseas. The North American continent was settled by masses of immigrants of many nationalities who had come mostly of their own volition to seek a better life and freedom, and ultimately formed new peoples and nations enriched by the cultural strains of many peoples and races. The Muscovite rapacity is motivated by lust for expansion and loot. It is characterized by a deliberate genocidal policy accompanying its exploitation of human and economic resources. It signifies an attempt, under a program of Russification and imposition of lower cultural and living standards, to denationalize, mongrelize and assimilate, and ultimately to extinguish viable and dynamic peoples, their languages and cultures, their human and social values developed in a millennium of historic development as sovereign states. The Russia of the Tsars had occupied not only the Arctic and Siberian wilderness, but also subjugated dozens of peoples and nations of higher civilization and culture on Russia's ever expanding Western and Southern fringes, in the Caucasus and in Central Asia. The Russia of the Soviets further expanded its direct rule and created a twilight belt of satellite "people's democracies." In the annexed lands, Moscow is striving to transform its captives into a docile and faceless Russian-speaking "Soviet people," to convert Christian and Moslem freemen into janissaries ruled by Muscovite super-nationalists posing as benign liberators devoid of any superstitions of "localism" and "bourgeois nationalism" — other than Russian. Asian janissaries spearheaded the crushing of Hungary. More recently, Lithuanian, Latvian and Estonian reservists, with their families as hostages at home, spearheaded the Soviet invasion of Czechoslovakia.

As for "Western culture" — Muscovite students abroad at all times strove to master weaponry, technology, physical-chemical sciences and medicine — NOT the arts, metaphysics and inner cultures of the "decadent West." In our times Moscow is still seeking to acquire Western technology — not an interchange of ideas and human contacts. The Sakharov-Solzhenitsyn exchange in 1974 illustrates also the traditional cleavage in the Russian mentality between the Western-minded *Zapadniki* and Slavophiles/Eurasians.

Let us presently note the demographic changes wrought during the three decades of the Soviet occupation of Lithuania.

The last issue of the Lithuanian Statistical Bulletin of 1940 estimated the population of a truncated free Lithuania at 3,032,863 — without the Klaipėda (Memel) District seized by Germany in March 1939. Following the formal annexation of Lithuania in August 1940, the Belorussian SSR restored to Lithuania a few townships with a population of 82,600. Consequently, the population of the Lithuanian SSR at the end of 1940 was 3,115,463. With the Klaipėda District population of 154,000, it would have been 3,269,463. The normal rate of natural increase in Lithuania was 1.3% per annum.

The Nazi occupational authorities added the Svyriai-Ašmena area to the *Generalbezirk Litauen*, with a population of 173,443. The German census of May 27, 1942, indicated the population of Generalbezirk Litauen — without the Klaipėda District — at 2,789,587 of whom 81.1 percent were Lithuanians, 12.1% Poles and 2.9% Belorussians. Some 260,000 Jews in the ghettoes were not included in the census. Should we add 260,000 Jews and 154,000 Klaipėdans, and deduct 173,443 inhabitants of the Svyriai-Ašmena area included in the Generalbezirk but later restored by Moscow to the Belorussian SSR, the gross total population of the entire area designated on Soviet maps as the Lithuanian SSR, would be 3,030,144. This means (3,269,463-3,030,144) a net *loss of* 239,319 people within two years of the Soviet invasion. Only a small part can be explained by the repatriation to Germany of some 55,000 ethnic Germans under a Soviet-Nazi arrangement. The *disappearance* of the remaining 184,319 persons is *attributable only to the Soviet regime.*

The Nürnberg Trial accepted the figure of 136,421 Jews exterminated by the Nazis in Lithuania. The Association of Lithuanian Anti-Nazi Resistants Former Political Prisoners established that of the 29,500 ethnic Lithuanians, political prisoners held in 103 Nazi concentration camps, 6,225 met death in Germany and 7,900 in Lithuania. Adding the 136,421 Lithuanian Jews and 14,125 Lithuanian Christians who died at the hands of the Nazi, the combined total is 164,671 — or roughly 160,000.

An American Communist, Anthony Bimba, the first foreigner shown around Lithuania by the MVD/MGB in 1946, followed the American bourgeois custom and published a book: *Prisikėlusi Lietuva* (A Resurrected Lithuania, Brooklyn, N.Y. 1946). While depicting in glowing terms the happy life under the rays of Stalin's sun in war-torn Lithuania, Bimba reported (p. 31) the findings of a "Special Commission for the Investigation of German Occupation Atrocities." The official toll, itemized by counties, showed 436,535 civilians "murdered by the Germans" and 36,530 "deported to German slavery" — a total manpower loss of 473,065. Indeed, the population of Lithuania hovered around two and a half million in the Soviet statistics of postwar years, the period of several waves of mass deportations and "repatriation" to Poland and Germany, as well as the guerrilla war. Bimba's figures are, of course, gross fabrications: some 160,000 died at the hands of the Nazis, between 100,000 and 200,000 Lithuanian Jews and Christians were liberated by the Allied forces or found refuge in Western-Central Europe. The rest of the missing people died fighting the Russians, were exiled to Siberia or "repatriated" to Poland and Germany.

The Soviet census of 1959 showed the population of Lithuania at 2,711,000. 79.3% were Lithuanians, 231,000 or 8.5% Russians, 230,000 or 8.5% Poles, only 25,000 or 0.9% Jews, formerly the largest minority. The Russians had numbered 65,000 or 2.3% in 1939. The 1959 census listed 175,000 other Lithuanians in the USSR: 32,000 were shown to be in Latvia, none in other Soviet republics — not even in Belorussian SSR which refuses to list Lithuanians and denies schools and newspapers to some 200,000 ethnic Lithuanians. Evidently 143,000 Lithuanians were surviving prisoners in exile.

The census of 1970 showed the population of Lithuania at a nearly pre-occupation figure: 3,128,236, of whom Lithuanians comprised 80.1% — and 158,000 other Lithuanians in the USSR Proper. 84% of the school children studied in Lithuanian-language schools. The number of Russians rose to 268,000 or 8.6%. The population of Latvia rose to 2,364,000 of whom Latvians constitute 56.8% (in prewar years 76%) and the Russians make up 29.8% (in prewar Latvia 13.4%). Estonia in 1970 had a population of 1,356,000 of whom Estonians constituted 68.2% (88% in 1939) and Russians 24.7%. Only 35.9% of Lithuanians understood Russian in 1970. A disturbing note in the census figures is introduced regarding non-Russians whose "mother-tongue" is Russian: some 4% among Latvians and Estonians, 1.5% of the Lithuanians (1970). It is no consolation to know that the Romanov dynasty, Tolstoy, Menshikov or Dostoievsky were "descendants of immigrants from Lithuania."

In January 1974 the population was 3,257,000, and in 1975 - 3,280,000. This indicates an increase of only 24,000 over the 1973 figure, the lowest in postwar years, and an increase of 33,000 in 1974. The urban population in 1975 moved to 56%. Only 47% of the population are males. The population was still short of the 1940 figure — and of the normally expected figure of about 5,000,000.[132]

[132]Calculations are based on the *Lithuanian Bulletin*, Jan.-June 1950; Kazys Pakštas in *Liet. Enciklopedija*, XV (430-450) 446-8; the 1970 Census figures in *Izvestia*, No. 90 (16708), April 17, 1971.

XXXIII. THE RULING CASTE

The Communist/bolshevik Party of Lithuania (LKP/b) was formally a member of the Comintern at least since 1921. However, its Politbureau and most of the Central Committee members were resident in Moscow and the Party underground work in Lithuania was directed by its Moscow Secretariat controlled by the Russian CP/b. For this reason the CPL was affected by all the events in the Comintern and the RKP/b, or CPSU. According to official Party data documented by Dr. Thomas Remeikis, the CPL "never had more than 2,000 members during its underground years. The majority of the membership came from the ethnic and religious minorities — the Lithuanian Jews, the Russians, and the Poles. . . . When the Comintern took an ultra-left course after its Sixth Congress, the CPL almost disappeared, its membership dwindled to about 400." Zigmas Aleksa-Angarietis, Secretary of the International Control Commission of the Comintern and one of the founders of the CPL, perished during the Stalin purges, along with other minor leaders and two prominent Soviet generals — Vytautas Putna and Jeronimas Uborevičius.

"The CPL came out of its underground period with approximately 1,500 members. For a short period it provided the necessary personnel for the transitional People's Government." The hard core were "professional revolutionaries, numbering perhaps not more than 100, who were unquestionably committed to Moscow. They were *the* Party. They were educated in the Sverdlov Communist University, or else received their training from the revolutionary Communists in Lithuanian prisons. This middle level of Party leadership . . . turned out to be basis on which the CPL developed after Lithuania's forcible incorporation into the Soviet Union. . . . Soon after Lithuania's incorporation . . . was formalized by the Supreme Soviet in Moscow on August 3, 1940, the CPL was merged with the Soviet Communist Party (October 8, 1940). Stalin then proceeded to purge the CPL. When he had finished, in the spring of 1941, the CPL had lost about 50 per cent of the underground revolutionaries . . . the native Communists were displaced by officials from Moscow and relegated to secondary positions." [133]

[133] Thomas Remeikis, "The Administration of Power: The Communist Party and the Soviet Government" in *Lithuania Under the Soviets, op. cit.*, (111-140), 113-115.

Of the 4,625 CPL members and candidates — 2,553 fled with the Red Army in June, 1941.[134] Those in Russia, and a few recruits from among the mass of exiles, were drafted for guerrilla activities in German-occupied Lithuania and for the so-called "Sixteenth Lithuanian Division" of the Soviet Army nominally commanded by several Lithuanian officers. Descendants of the Lithuanian exiles of 1831 and 1862-5 and those residing in Russia since World War I, were commandeered into the CPL during the war. By the end of World War II the CPL re-emerged with either 2,851 members and 685 candidates, according to Vytautas Vaitiekūnas, or "some 6,000" cited by Dr. Remeikis.

"Such a Party organization, created in wartime conditions and from politically and ethnically diverse sources, could not be trusted to carry out the sociopolitical revolution that was required to re-establish the Soviet regime after the German withdrawal. The CPL in the postwar years played only a role of apprentice. All real power was concentrated in emissaries from the central organs of the All-Union Communist Party (Bolsheviks). Mikhail Suslov headed a special Central Committee Bureau for Lithuania until the spring of 1946." This Bureau is mentioned only once in an university publication and was graphically described by Colonel Burlutsky before the Kersten Committee. Dr. Remeikis notes that Suslov was succeeded in Lithuania by "a special Central Committee trouble shooter, Vladimir Vasilevich Shcherbakov, and a host of other Moscow-appointed commissars and politicians. It is true that the native Communists occupied the nominal position of power, but behind every one of them, including even the politically reliable First Secretary of the CPL, Antanas Sniečkus, there was a Second Secretary or an assistant from Moscow. Views of local Communists were stifled; the party was completely dominated by Russian *apparatchiki*, who molded the CPL on the All-Union pattern. Such strict political control and dominance by non-Lithuanian cadres in the CPL, as well as in the Soviet (Government) authorities, continued until the death of Stalin and the fall of Beria. In 1949, 50 per cent of the Lithuanian Party's Central Committee consisted of non-Lithuanians. It can be truly said that whatever individuality the CPL came to possess was acquired during the Khrushchev years."[135]

[134] *A Survey of Developments in Captive Lithuania in 1965-1968*, ed. Vytautas Vaitiekūnas, publ. Committee for a Free Lithuania, New York, n.d. (mimeo), p. 5, citing *Komunistas*, 1967, No. 3, p. 75.

[135] *Lithuania Under the Soviets, op. cit.*, 115-116.

It must be added that Stalin's and Beria's fellow-Georgian, Vladimir Dekanozov, who supervised the rape and annexation of Lithuania in 1940, met his dessert before a Russian firing squad along with Beria during Khrushchev's climb to power. Membership in the foreign despoiler's party was deemed treasonable by the patriotic underground, and "about 4,000" overzealous native Communists were killed by guerrillas. Colonel Burlutsky aptly observed in his testimony that native collaborators of the Soviet repressive forces were singled out by Lithuanian freedom fighters.

Dr. Remeikis offers several "significant generalizations on the nature of the CPL." It is "one of the youngest and weakest of the Communist parties of the Soviet republics. Between 1952 and 1956, it had one of the lowest rates of growth. It had and still has practically the smallest percentage of Communists in the population, 2 per cent, as compared with about 4 per cent for the entire CPSU in 1960. As if trying to catch up with the other republic Party organizations, the CPL has since 1956 accelerated its rate of growth very markedly. From 1956 to 1960, it increased over 40 per cent, while during the same time the entire CPSU grew by only about 26 per cent. However, even at that rapid growth rate, it will be at least a decade before the CPL can approach the All-Union percentage. In fact, this may never come, since the CPSU in the last few years grew at a slightly higher rate than the CPL." [136]

In this writer's considered opinion, the "acceleration" of CPL membership was due primarily to two reasons: the final crushing of the guerrilla war and thus the elimination of reprisals against "traitors"; and secondly,— the instinct for self-preservation and for opportunities in life. Admission to universities and professions was denied to non-Communist youths. In the absence of Lithuanians in office — Russian officials were imported, and as long as Lithuanians were a minority in the Party and Government — they had no voice in the decision-making. Party members enjoy special well-stocked stores, modern hospitals and housing, and other privileges of a nobility caste. Membership in the "party" was thus an utilitarian necessity — and soon generated Russian suspicions of "localism" and "bourgeois nationalism," as well as "national communism." As a young Israel immigrant told this writer: "I am told there had been Communists in 1940. Today it's a profession." Severe purges in the Latvian CP and mild purges in Lithuania underscore the Russian concern regarding native CP members. "The promo-

[136] *Ibid.*, 116.

tion of native cadres evidently went further than the Kremlin expected. No wonder Sniečkus had to warn constantly against promoting cadres on a national basis alone." [137]

Dr. Remeikis notes two discernible purges of *non*-Lithuanians in the CPL: one following the 19th CPSU Congress before Stalin's death (November 1952 - March 1953), the other immediately after Beria's liquidation three months later. These purges are "suggested by a series of changes in the top personnel of the Lithuanian Soviet regime and the CPL, changes involving Ministries of Internal Affairs and State Security and a number of deputies of the Council of Ministers. These purges were distinctive in that they affected primarily the lower echelon of the Party hierarchy, and the non-Lithuanian deputies in the government and the Party, and so went almost unrecorded in the press and were scarcely noticed by Western observers. With the elimination of Beria and the consequent expansion of republic jurisdiction, there was, at least in Lithuania, a notable replacement of non-Lithuanian personnel by native Communists. The transfer of non-Lithuanian Communists . . . purges . . . the succession, and natural causes may be considered to be responsible for slow increase" in membership.[138]

Dr. Remeikis discerns a "clash of generations" within the CPL in the '60s among four distinct groups. *1.* Moscow-trained revolutionaries of pre-1940, "highly committed to Moscow, violently anti-nationalist and pro-Russian," numbering "no more than 1500" and greatly influential in high Party posts. This writer is inclined to question the estimate: the CPL had "about 1500" members in 1940, and soon after the incorporation, "about 50%" of such members were purged, and there were natural deaths since. *2.* Between 6,000 and 10,000 members who joined the party during the war, 1941-1945. As noted earlier, Vaitiekūnas cites a membership of 2,851 and 685 candidates as of January 1, 1945. *3.* About 20,000 who joined the party "during the violent postwar years," educated "by the gun" and strongly committed to Moscow. "How this group would react in a crisis is unknown. Politically they appear to be favored to succeed the old revolutionaries in the leadership of the Party. The leadership, however, will be challenged by the fourth group — the post-Stalin Communists, who surpass the wartime and post-war Communists in their technical competence." This *4.* post-Stalin group is called "the new class" by Dr. Remeikis. "In 1960, this group

[137]The above quote is from *ibid.*, 122.

[138]*Ibid.*, 119.

constituted at least 40 per cent" of the CPL membership, "younger people, mostly under forty, educated almost entirely by the Soviet regime. They matured in somewhat stabilized political circumstances and never had to fight for Communism. They grew up in a climate of resurging nationalism and normalization of Party and Government activity. These people have shown as much enthusiasm and concern for the Lithuanian cultural heritage as most of the intelligentsia." The displacement of old revolutionaries by "educated technicians" was so great that Sniečkus repeatedly admonished Party members "to understand the situation and to keep peace." The old revolutionaries among CPL Congress delegates dropped from more than 60% in 1949 to 20% in 1960; wartime and postwar Communists — 18% and 17% respectively in 1949 — rose to 40% jointly in 1960, and post-Stalin Communists rose to 40%.[139]

Dr. Remeikis suggests that "an ethnically homogenous membership influences not only political disposition of the Party but also the operation and autonomy." His reasonable estimate, based on the ethnic membership figures of the CPSU and the membership of the CPL, was that in 1961 ethnic Lithuanians made up 65% of the CPL members. Vytautas Vaitiekūnas traced the growth of the CPL membership from 2,504 in 1941 to 99,173 members and 6,245 candidates in 1968, concentrated in the five largest cities and trained for membership by the Pioneers and the Komsomol. By 1965 — 75% were post-Stalin joiners. The percentage of Lithuanians rose from 61.5% in 1965 to 66.2% in 1968. Female membership climbed to 27.4% by 1968. The number of members with high education rose from 4.5% in 1941 to 19.8% in 1968, and those with a secondary education rose from 18.5% to 51.9% by 1968. At the 1966 CPL Congress 621 delegates were Lithuanians, 211 Russians, 47 of other nationalities and they elected a Central Committee of 131 — including 35 Russians or 26.7%. The percentage of Russians in the Lithuanian Soviet dropped to an average of 20-25%.[140]

The data of January 1, 1973 lists 131,539 members in the CPL — and 96,558 ethnic Lithuanians in the mother CPSU. This would indicate that 96,558 Lithuanians constitute 73%, the 34,981 others — 27%.[141]

Dr. Remeikis notes the remarkable survival of First Secretary Antanas Sniečkus: the CPL to a very significant degree is "a political machine of

[139] *Ibid.*, 119-121.

[140] *Ibid.*, 121-2: Vaitiekūnas, *A Survey of Developments*, 5-9, 55.

[141] *Komunistas* No. 9, (591), Sept. 1973, pp. 7, 9.

Antanas Sniečkus." He had come to CPL Secretariat in 1926, was appointed the First Secretary in 1936 and retained this post under Stalin, Khrushchev and Brezhnev. His principal political characteristic was "his willingness to obey anyone who happens to hold supreme power in the Kremlin" — and, we may add, his excellent orientation regarding the power play in the Kremlin.

Since Stalin's death, Sniečkus and his native crew managed to "evade much of the previous detailed surveillance and control from Moscow and have assumed a great many functions that were formerly carried out by Stalin's *apparatchiki.* Sniečkus . . . has imprinted some of his political characteristics on the CPL." The number of non-Lithuanian "watchdogs" in the Presidium declined from five in 1949, to one in 1961. The "marginal group of Party functionaries — the Russian-Lithuanians or the non-Lithuanians of Lithuania have practically disappeared" — for some time.[142]

Indeed, the stability of the Lithuanian personnel — or rather self-perpetuation in several well-paid posts in the Party and Government — is rather remarkable. Justas Paleckis, a former newsman and Populist Farmer youth leader converted to pro-Moscow sympathies by way of the Lithuanian-Soviet Friendship Society and "cultural exchanges," was a late comer to the Party. He became Acting President, then Chairman of the Presidium of the Supreme Soviet of the Lithuanian SSR 1940 to 1967, when he became President of the Soviet of Nationalities in Moscow after distinguishing himself as head of the Soviet delegations to Inter-Parliamentary Union sessions. He was replaced in the Lithuanian "presidency" by an old revolutionary, Motiejus Šumanskas, the Prime Minister 1956-1967. Another old revolutionary, Mečys Gedvilas, headed the People's Cabinet and became Chairman of the Council of Ministers of the Lithuanian SSR 1940-1956, and since then held the post of Minister of Education. These colleagues of Sniečkus were of ethnic and cultural Lithuanian background. Juozas Maniušis, the Premier since 1967, a Russian-born and Russian-educated Communist who speaks Russian at home, is a stranger among Lithuanian natives with no cultural ties to a people he rules as the executive arm of the Soviet Communist Party.

The most unstable were the "non-Lithuanian cadres, who were more subject to political purges in the CPSU and pushed by native Communists after Khrushchev's rise." A careful distinction between the Party

[142] *Lithuania Under the Soviets, op. cit.*, 122-125.

and government is maintained — yet there is "almost a total overlapping of the Party and government leadership. The entire Council of Ministers is incorporated into the CPL Central Committee." The alleged prerogative of maintaining its own armed forces was never exercised, and even a so-called "16th Lithuanian Division" disappeared after the war. A "Ministry of Foreign Affairs" was formed in 1944 — for tourism, cultural exchanges and propaganda abroad and for the decorative signing of some treaties like the frontier with Poland or trade quotas, alongside the Soviet signatories who negotiated such pacts. The post was vacant 1960-1966, when Deputy Premier Leokadija (née) Diržinskaitė (Mrs.) Pilyushenka was also given the ministerial title for Foreign Affairs.

Dr. Remeikis overly optimistically suggested that "(1) even in the highest circles of the Party an awareness and a quest for realization of national interests is strong and the Kremlin must exert constant pressure to contain such manifestations; (2) . . . purges in the Latvian regime and the Lithuanian intelligentsia make it clear that the Kremlin is not willing to tolerate nationalist deviations even in the interpretation of the national heritage and takes ruthless measures to stamp out all autonomic tendencies; and (3) . . . there is a nationalist segment of the intelligentsia in the Communist Party itself, which actively strives for the enhancement of national values. . . . Neither the Communist bloc nor the West can take the unity of the Soviet Union for granted, despite its façade of unitary centralism." [143]

Sniečkus had mellowed in his old age and gained some popularity at home. The storm for him broke during the Nixon visit in Moscow in 1972 — the self-immolations and youth riots in Kaunas. After the brutal crushing, his Russian watchdog, CPL Secretary Valery Kharazov became visible and loudly vocal. Late in 1973 Kharazov escorted the Moscow emissary Suslov on a post-pacification inspection trip to Kaunas. Sniečkus died early in 1974. With Kharazov in charge, the post-Stalin young protegée of Sniečkus stayed in the Secretariat. But a party hack and ward heeler Petras Griškevičius, a man in his 50s with an education only in the Party School in Moscow, assumed First Secretaryship.

[143] *Ibid.*, 133-140.

Lithuanian women exiles in Arctic Siberia. The photo was provided by a former exile in the Siberian Tundras.

XXXIV.
AGRICULTURE: SERFDOM RESTORED

The Russian Tsarist occupation reduced Lithuania to a backward agricultural country where 40% of the land was owned by large landlords, some of whom resided in Warsaw or Paris and managed their holdings in absentia. Industry had made a promising start in the latter part of the 18th century, and nearly disappeared under the Russian rule which treated the "Western borderland" merely as a strategic defense area — or as a bridgehead for expansion westward. Commerce dwindled since the Napoleonic period as the natural outlets for exports and imports — the ports of Klaipėda (Memel) and Karaliaučius (Königsberg) in Prussia were barred. Jews had always predominated in the urban population, and their number doubled after the huge population losses during the Napoleonic wars and because of the Tsarist policy barring Jews from ethnic Russian areas. The forestry industry, which had helped build and maintain the British naval power, languished and died locally — except for timber rafting down the Nemunas River to new cellulose and paper plants in Klaipėda.

Lithuanians traditionally had lived in individual homesteads amid orchards and gardens, with carved crosses in front of their homes. The agrarian reform of the mid-16th century herded the peasants into crowded villages, yet the petty nobility and other freemen continued to live in individual homesteads. Since the end of serfdom rapid strides were made in agriculture in spite of the hampering effect of the large number of the landless. In Sudavia peasants were nominally free since the imposition of the Napoleonic Code in that part of the "Grand Duchy of Warsaw," since 1815 "the Congressional Kingdom of Poland." The peasants there hastened to abandon the alien village form of life and to move into individual homesteads. By the end of the 19th century other Lithuanians, too, were able to disperse into homestead cottages.

The Agrarian Reform of the independent Lithuanian Republic (1922) limited the size of landholdings and transformed the country into one of smallholder farmers with their own credit, farm machinery, dairy and marketing cooperatives. The landless, smallholders and war veterans received lands and financial assistance, as well as the guidance services of State agronomists. Farming schools and colleges helped to improve husbandry and to introduce limited mechanization. The government promoted the transition from grain cultures to stock-breeding, meat processing, dairying, flax and sugar-beet raising — for export. The initiative of enterprising farmers stimulated the expansion of foreign trade. The gold-based Litas currency provided financial stability, and the State budgets were uniformly balanced.

The late Ernest J. Harrison, the British Vice-Consul, wrote that he had "enjoyed exceptional opportunities of witnessing on the spot much of this astonishing progress, the congenial task of sympathetic observation and inquiry having been facilitated by his professional position and his knowledge of the Lithuanian language, which from the first gave him access to original sources of information and enabled him to dispense with intermediaries. It may therefore be emphatically stated that this record of achievement all along the line affords most conclusive proof of wise statesmanship in key positions which, despite occasional dissensions, succeeded in largely eradicating the survivals of deliberate Muscovite obscurantism bent on retarding national advancement. Thanks to these indefatigable efforts, almost independently of external aid, Lithuania speedily emerged from the slough into which earlier Russian misrule had plunged her, and was already beginning to garner the fruits of enlightened policy in the cultural and economic spheres when the Second World War again involved her in universal catastrophe.

"Hand in hand with these basic changes in the country's national economy signal advances were also made in the sphere of social services which were virtually non-existent under former Russian rule. Measures concerning the care of children, the sick, accidental injury, unemployment and destitution, national health and sanitation were rapidly developed. The progress of the country was such that the general standard of well-being steadily rose. In short, during twenty years of free and independent life the country succeeded, not only in clearing away the debris of 1914-1920 wars, but also in elevating itself to an incomparably higher level in every respect than when it was under alien domination." [144]

When the USSR invaded and annexed Lithuania, the farming population comprised 77% of the total. Farms not exceeding 75 acres constituted 90.2% of the number of farms and 66.2% of the cultivated land. In 1939, farm owners and their families constituted 78.7% of the total farm labor manpower; 21.3% were hired hands. Wages of hired labor

[144] E. J. Harrison, *Lithuania's Fight for Freedom*, 1st American edition, New York, Feb. 1945, pp. 12-13.

constituted only 11-15% of agricultural production costs. Processed foods, butter, bacon, cured pork, eggs, poultry and cattle ranked among the principal export commodities — 69.2% of the total export value for the year 1939.[145]

The so-called "People's Diet" at once limited farm landholdings to 75 acres and nationalized, without compensation, acreage in excess of that norm for distribution "to the landless and smallholders for perennial use." The expropriation act, authorized by Moscow's Pro-Consul Dekanozov, noted: "Any attempt to threaten the private ownership right of the peasants shall be severely prosecuted as injurious to the interests of the people and of the state." This was but a "tactical maneuver" aimed at ruining the production and the self-sufficient Lithuanian farmer, and to create a "class struggle" of the poor peasants against "kulaks." According to a serious researcher, Dr. Pranas Zundė, this purpose was "publicly admitted by the First Secretary of the Lithuanian Communist Party, Antanas Sniečkus, not long after it was carried out, when there were no more farmers who possessed more than 75 acres."

A tax decree of May 14, 1941, levied discriminatory taxes on farmers. A farmer with an annual income of 10,000 rubles was to pay nine times as much in taxes as a farmer with an income of 2,000 rubles. Furthermore, "taxes were estimated not in accordance with the actual annual income, but on the basis of a specified norm of income the farmer was arbitrarily allocated to receive from an acre of arable land or a particular breed of livestock . . . the legislation provided that taxes of farmers with outside income could be increased by an additional 20-50% levy." The second measure of extortion and suppression was the requisitioning of farm products by the state, ". . . out of all proportion to their productive capacity and to the amount of deliveries required from smaller farms. For example, from a 50-acre farm, a farmer had to deliver seven and one-half times the amount of meat [due] from . . . a 12-acre farm. It did not matter whether the farmer was actually engaged in the production of the requisitioned items; he had to fulfill the norm, even if it meant that he had to buy the products for delivery. In this manner, the Communists sought to destroy the kulaks, a category comprising all farmers who worked 62.5-75 acres of land."[146]

[145] Pranas Zundė, "Lithuania's Economy: Introduction of the Soviet Pattern," in *Lithuania Under the Soviets*, *op. cit.*, (141-169), 141-2.

[146] Zundė, *ibid.*, 142-144.

The forthcoming collectivization was indicated by the installation of "farm machinery and tractor stations." Forty-two MTS were set up in the spring of 1941 along with 238 "rental stations" for equipment and horses, and 60 state farms (sovkhozes) embracing 115,000 acres of land. Then the Party "enjoined any further partition of villages into farmsteads, which had been an essential feature of the progressive land reform instituted in independent Lithuania in 1922." Early in 1941 articles appeared in the controlled press regarding an alleged "spontaneous movement of the working peasants into collective farming." The first kolkhoz named in honor of Lenin was formed in January, 1941 — and in March sixteen families began operations with 20 horses and 60 heads of cattle on a 625-acre kolkhoz. The Soviet designs were soon disrupted by the insurrection and war, and the expulsion of the Russian forces. During the German occupation "a small number of farmers regained the land . . . but otherwise the German occupation forces left in effect the Soviet-enacted legislation of land nationalization, and in most instances farms that had been nationalized by the Soviet regime were retained by the Germans as state property under government administration or were turned over to colonizing German nationals."[147]

The Russians returned in 1944 — with the sledgehammer. No foreign newsmen accompanied the troops and the officials brutalized by the war, unlike in 1940, when some American darlings of Moscow descended upon Lithuania to photograph — even for legitimate newspapers — the "spontaneous joy" of the "liberated" Lithuanians. No foreign non-Communist newsmen had accompanied the Russian "liberators" of Finland, Poland, East Germany or Hungary in wartime, or during the peacetime "liberation" of Czechoslovakia from "communism with a human face" by Brezhnev in 1969.

On August 30, 1944, the "Ordinance regarding the Liquidation of Effects upon Agriculture left by the German occupation," decreed by a Russian-repatriated portion of the "Supreme Soviet of the Lithuanian SSR," called for the expropriation of "land seized by German colonists, land that had previously belonged to those enemies of the people who had fled with the German occupation forces, and land left without claimants," viz., deportees to Siberia. Restrictions were imposed on lands left in private possession: 75-acre farms could be reduced to 50 acres, "and in the case of farms whose owners had actively collaborated with German occupational personnel, to 5 hectares" (12.5 acres).

[147] Zundė, *ibid.*, 144-145.

Farmers who had been forced to deliver requisition norms of produce under a threat of execution — were presently deemed to have been "collaborators with the German occupational personnel." The confiscated lands were supposedly to be distributed to Red Army veterans, Soviet guerrillas and persons deprived of their lands by the Germans, and the rest of the land reserves — to sovkhozes, MTS, State use.

The Communists expected a gratitude of the landgrant recipients. However, the peasant and farmer population understood the real Soviet motives. Lacking farming equipment and livestock, they had little use for the land and did not believe that the regime intended to leave land in their private possession for long. By December, 1944, the Council of People's Commissars and the Central Committee of the CPL observed that "too many of the local Soviet and Party organs have underestimated the political significance of a swift re-establishment" of the decrees on landholdings. Grantees were "not grouped around the organs of the Soviet Government," the landless were neglected, leadership was weak and lax in "the appropriation of horses and stock surpluses from the kulak farms and in the mandatory purchase of cows," and in suppressing "attempts to sabotage and resistance by the kulaks," or in providing to grantees protection "from the threats and revenge of the kulaks." The reform, to be completed by February, 1945, continued into 1948. "Between 1944 and 1948, the regime confiscated and redistributed or retained in its own immediate possession, about 34.1 million acres of land." The pulverization or diminution of farm size was intended "to create an agricultural proletariat, heretofore practically nonexistent in Lithuania." Mini-farmers were soon obliged to abandon their landgrants and move into the industrial proletariat in the cities, or to join the kolkhozes, "which was what the Soviet regime had planned." [148]

After some propaganda for collectivization, the onslaught on the "kulaks" began; in Lithuanian, the term "*buožė*" — "the cudgel, bat, club" was used rather than the Russian "*kulak*-fist." On December 12, 1947, the CPL Central Committee decreed regulations defining "kulaks": farmers employing hired hands; farmers who had employed hired labor in the past, during or after the German occupation; "exploiters of outside labor in a concealed form" under the guise of employing relatives; farmers employing seasonal labor or craftsmen; suppliers of animals, seed or machinery under "slaverylike terms"; farmers owning complex

[148]Zundė, *ibid.*, 145-148.

machinery, sawmills or grain mills; purchasers of goods for resale. "Kulak" farm taxes were upped to 250% over the former tax rates, and in 1948 were upped 500% above non-kulak rates. Of course, many found this tax burden unbearable and abandoned their farms.

The first postwar kolkhoz was organized February 26, 1947, in Dotnuva township. Twenty kolkhozes were formed under duress in 1947, and then the drive was extended against self-sufficient smallholders — at first in the form of excessive "deliveries" quotas from "unsocialized" farms. For example, in 1947-8, the State demanded 44 lbs. of milk per acre of cultivated land from an independent farmer and only 11 lbs. per acre from a collective farm. Even though the number of farmers joining kolkhozes was less than one-tenth of one per cent of their total number, the Party and Government proclaimed that, "inspired by the achievements of the farming proletariat in other fraternal republics within the Union, under the leadership of the Communist Party a great many of the poor and middle-income peasants in a number of counties in Soviet Lithuania have begun to organize into agricultural artels — collective farms." On March 20, 1948, organization of collective farms was decreed. By mid-summer 1948 there were 150 totally unproductive kolkhozes. More drastic measures were then decreed — economic coercion, threats, physical repressions and deportations — and soon there were 524 kolkhozes herding over 12,000 formerly free farmers — 3% of the total farm population. This was sufficient for the CPL Sixth Congress in 1949 to affirm "the manifest desire of Lithuanian farmers to organize into collective farms," to abolish private farming.

Recipients of Soviet landgrants were most easily coerced to surrender their unproductive lots. The others resisted the coercion. Farmers refusing to join kolkhozes were placed in forced labor camps or deported to the Soviet Union *en masse*. Party officials are still reluctant to discuss the period of terror — beyond lame admissions of "some violations of the Socialist justice" and occasional revelations in novels and studies regarding "the intensified class struggle and the kulak resistance" allegedly stimulated by rumors that Soviet rule was but a temporary transient phenomenon, by "playing on the religious sentiment" and by alleged Western radio broadcasts "by traitors who had fled abroad after serving the German occupational regime." Much blamed were the patriotic guerrillas — "the bourgeois nationalist underground, bandit gangs," and "kulaks disguising themselves as sympathizers of collective farming and then stirring strife, exaggerating every shortcoming, disrupting the harmony." Nevertheless, the forcible collectivization was completed by the end of 1952 — and the backbone of the guerrilla strength broken — at the cost of several hundred thousand human casualties by death and deportations.

There were more than 8,000 small kolkhozes merging 50 to 80 farmsteads each, when Khrushchev dreamed up an idea of "agrogorod, agropolis" and kolkhozes were joined into larger units and their number dropped to 1,795. In June 1955 Khrushchev himself declared that collectivization in Lithuania and in the Baltic area had been carried on with too much fervor and "many serious mistakes had been made." The campaign for kolkhoz enlargement was thus arrested: their number rose again to 2,185 in 1958 and dropped to 1,867 in 1961 when some kolkhozes were converted into sovkhozes. Dr. Zundė notes that this "conversion of insolvent kolkhozes into sovkhozes served the interests, at least in part, of both the Party and the peasants" formerly left destitute after an entire year's work. Sovkhozes, "a higher form of ownership by the people," were protected and subsidized: 90% of sovkhozes were electrified, in comparison with 24% of kolkhozes. MTS stations were liquidated in 1958, "sold" to kolkhozes at exorbitant profit to the State.

"Poverty and privation became permanent in the lives of farmers forced into collective farms" to work "for contemptibly low wages, and the exploitation of the individual as a source of labor power in collective farming reached proportions that are unknown elsewhere. As late as 1958, the average annual wage of the collective farmer in Lithuania was about 68.40 rubles (new currency) and 452 kilograms of cereal grain." He had to pay 20.2 rubles for a man's sweater, 0.83 rubles for a kilogram of sugar, 2.80 rubles for a kilogram of sausage, 980 rubles for a motorcycle.

The source of sustenance were the garden plots allocated for the private "exploitation" by kolkhoz families, and the few domestic animals left in their private possession — one or two cows, several pigs, sheep, fowl. The sorry state of Soviet agricultural system is vividly exposed by the respective productivity of the kolkhoz/sovkhoz and their "private sector." Dr. Zundė notes that "Although only 5.8% of all arable land is used for these private lots, the comparative weight of the most important livestock production in 1959 was 65.4 for the private sector and only 34.6 for collective and state farms. In the same year, the collective farmers raised 72.4% of the total annual potato crops on the private plots, 86% of the total vegetable produce, and 80% of the total fruit yield." Given the extremely cheap labor manpower and all the agricultural equipment, the kolkhozes and sovkhozes "in most instances failed to produce even the remaining part of that year's production above cost."[149] The situation did not change significantly in 1974.

The twin form of state farming is characterized by excessive bureaucratic personnel or "cadres": 9 to 10% of the farm manpower. They comprise administrative personnel, agronomists, veterinarians, engineers, mechanics, and the omnipresent bullies of the "Party organization" (Partorgs). Fortunately, the educational level of the bureaucracy steadily advanced, replacing some of the brutal Party slave-drivers. The prewar levels of farm output were not reached until 1965 — including both "social sectors" and the private plots. "Progress in agriculture is greatly impeded by state planning in minutest details," from above, relayed by several layers of Party functionaries, and initiative is stifled in the system of forced labor.

"The Lithuanian peasant has regressed a whole century, back to the days when he was a serf on a nobleman's estate. . . . The people have no real incentive to work land which does not belong to them and the fruits of which also belong to the state. . . . In 1968, 420,000 cows and 767,000 pigs were kept on private lots (0.6 hectare each), the produce of which was kept by the tenants, while 414,000 cows and 873,000 pigs were kept by both kolkhozes and sovkhozes combined. On the average one hectare of private land gave 4,138 kg of milk and 879 kg of meat, while collectivized land yielded 412 kg of milk and 85 kg of meat per hectare. Both sectors produce approximately equal amounts of these basic items (54% : 46%), but the ratios of land areas are very different: 3,483,000 ha compared to 272,000 ha (92% : 18%). . . . Collectivization has another negative aspect: it contributes to the destruction of Lithuanian toponymics when new names are given to collectivized farms. In 1958, for example, of 1,133 kolkhozes, 145 were named after individual Russians, such as Lenin, Stalin, Molotov, Kutuzov, Suvorov; 552 farms had Bolshevik names, such as Bolshevik, Communist, Red Flag, October Revolution, Red Star. . . . Old homestead and village names are disappearing as collectivization slowly destroys the age-old treasury of Lithuanian toponyms and spoils Lithuania's heritage."[150]

In brief: collectivization entailed the enslavement of freemen farmers, their pauperization, exploitation, physical and cultural genocide, and the destruction of their country's historic past and place names.

[149] Zundė, *ibid.*, 148-155, citing official Soviet data.

[150] *Encyclopedia Lituanica*, vol. I, Boston 1970, "Collective Farm" (558-562), 561-2.

XXXV.
ECONOMIC COLONIALISM: INDUSTRY AND TRADE

After 120 years (1795-1915) of Russian-sponsored frontier area backwardness, Lithuania emerged the least industrial among the Baltic States. In 1913 — only 3,134 industrial-artisan shops serving their immediate neighborhood were licensed, the most industrial department of Kaunas had 151 establishments employing 6,603 workers. After the devastation of World War I, the evacuation of industrial equipment to Russia and the wasteful destruction and export of timber by the German military, the first census by an independent Lithuania conducted in 1923 showed that only 6.43% of the population subsisted from industrial-artisan employment. The number of licensed establishments rose from 2,474 in 1920 to 16,131 in 1939. Industrial labor manpower rose to 35,063 in 1939, in addition to about 15,000 artisan shops employing one to four persons. According to Lithuanian statistics, industrial output between 1920 and 1940 increased 354.2%. [151]

First Deputy Premier Ksaveras Kairys of the Lithuanian SSR generalized in 1972 that the number of industrial workers "in bourgeois Lithuania" had risen from 23,000 in 1910-1912 to 40,000 in 1940, an increase by 74%, and industrial output increased 260%. In 1970 industrial manpower numbered 414,000 beside — or including — 46,000 engineers and technicians. Capital investment by 1970 amounted to 2.8 billion rubles.[152]

The 1940 Soviet booty embraced banks and industry, including the efficiently managed and profitable food processing industry which accounted for 43% of the industrial establishment. The government held 51% of the stock in several large stock companies practically monopolizing the dairying, meat processing and farm machinery fields in a mixed capitalist economy of Lithuania. Peat mining yielded 100,000 tons of turf annually, and output was projected to one million tons annually for 100 years, enough to supply 150% of the energy requirements. Marsh iron ore resources were too small for profitable smelting. Stone quarries marketed 5.5 million litas ($550,000 in gold) annually, glass

[151] Jonas D. Viskanta in *Liet. Enciklopedija*, XV, 204, 206.

[152] K. Kairys, "Soviet Lithuania — Industrial," *Komunistas* No. 12 (582), 1972, (16-22), p. 17; 1970 data in *Komunistas* No. 9 (591), 1973, pp. 75-76.

1.99 million litas, tiles 0.7 million litas, bricks 100 million litas. The thriving lumber industry satisfied the domestic needs and exported 21.6 million litas-worth. The metal industry with imported raw materials produced machines and parts worth 28 million litas, the chemical plants 25 million litas annually. The hides and furs industry grossed 17.5 million litas in the home market. More fish was imported than processed locally. The textile industry employed over 7,000 workers and its output rose to 68.5 million litas in 1938. The annual production of paper, cellulose and carboard netted 26 million litas.

The late E. J. Harrison noted that the combined value of imports of the four Baltic states in 1938 amounted to $293,756,000 and exports $292,738,000, compared with the USSR imports of $261,758,000 and exports of $259,751,000. The Foreign Commerce Yearbook of 1939 shows that world imports per capita in 1938 amounted to $48.35 in Finland, $25.14 in Estonia, $22.65 in Latvia, $11.00 in Lithuania, $1.99 in the USSR. The exports per capita index figures were $47.05 for Finland, $24.35 for Estonia, $22.55 for Latvia, $13.30 for Lithuania, $1.20 for the USSR. Harrison also noted the discrepancies between the U.S. Department of Commerce data and those of Lithuania: only the goods shipped directly to Lithuania were credited to that country by the U.S., while Lithuania credited to the U.S., the country of origin, machinery and other merchandise purchased through the medium of Denmark, Sweden, Belgium, Germany. Thus the Central Statistical Bureau of Lithuania lists the 1937 imports from the U.S. at $1,230,500, while the U.S. Department of Commerce credits only $510,571 to exports to Lithuania.[153]

The state budgets of "bourgeois Lithuania" were neatly balanced and the litas currency stayed on the gold standard. The state budgets ranged close to 400 million litas, or forty to fifty million in U.S. dollars. In an industrialized Soviet Lithuania all industry, agriculture and services are State enterprises, and annual budgets exceed one billion rubles — with the USSR appropriating 35-40% and "allocating" the rest to the income-producing "Union republic" of Lithuania.

One of the favorite Soviet propaganda themes is to the effect that Lithuania had been merely a colony of the Western "imperialist" powers because of the huge foreign capital monopolies, and that real "sovereignty" was gained only under Soviet colonial rule — dubbed as

[153] Harrison, *Lithuania's Fight for Freedom*, *op. cit.*, 15-16. Other data in *Liet. Enciklopedija*, XV, 204-207. The pre-1940 data do not include the Vilnius area, the 1939 figures exclude the Klaipėda-Memel area.

"the restoration of Soviet power." The Lithuanian Encyclopedia notes that in Lithuania "foreign capital in the hands of individuals and limited companies was not registered. Stock companies engaged in manufacturing in 1939 had 33.3 million litas of foreign capital or 33% of the capital stock total. By states, these investments were credited (in million litas) to: Belgium - 19.8, Sweden - 6.1, Germany - 4.0, Latvia - 1.8, USA - 0.99, other countries - 0.54. Belgian capital owned electrical power stations in Kaunas and Petrašiūnai, Swedish owned the Petrasiunai paper mill and safety match plants and a lumber mill Lietmedis in Kaunas; German capital owned Tilmansas Bros. metal factory in Kaunas and several plants in the Klaipėda area. USA citizens owned the Drobė textile mill and several smaller institutions."[154] The "USA citizens" were not the Wall Street crowd, but former Lithuanian-American tailors, mechanics and workers who invested their savings and managed several textile plants and bus lines in Lithuania.

These figures are not impressive enough to indicate "economic colonialism" by so-called "imperialist powers" — even if the gold-based litas currency be raised 34% in converting to U.S. dollars, viz., $4,500,000 for the 33.3 million litas. On the other hand, the USSR seized *all* banks, native and foreign assets and lands, and subjugated the entire economy and manpower of Lithuania to serve the exploiting needs of Moscow.

By the time the USSR seized Lithuania, the urban population had risen to 17% in 1938 and, with Vilnius, to 23% in 1940. Vilnius had a population of 210,000 (372,000 in 1970, over 400,000 in 1974), Kaunas 154,109 (in 1970 305,000), Šiauliai 31,641 (92,800 in 1970 and 100,000 in 1974), Klaipėda at the time of cession to Germany in 1939 —51,000 (140,000 in 1970). By 1970 the urban population constituted 50.2% of the total — 54% in 1974. The Soviet census shows an urban population increase by 526,000 between 1959 and 1970, while the rural population decreased by 109,000. Prior thereto, in 1952-55, "around 250,000 were liberated from agriculture," to use the term employed by Docent I. Žeberskis.[155] Agriculture now claims 31% of the manpower — "thrice as great a percentage as in the German Democratic Republic." In place of 350,000 farm homesteads, there were 1,321 kolkhozes and 295 sovkhozes in 1972, pending consolidation

[154] *Liet. Enciklopedija*, XV, 208; Lithuania state budgets, *ibid.*, 223 sq.

[155] I. Žeberskis, "Manpower resources in agriculture and possibilities of their employment in industry," *Komunistas* No. 7 (589), 1973, 50, 49.

into 1,129 larger kolkhozes and 279 sovkhozes. "More than half of the urban population moved from rural communities thanks to the mechanization of farming and growing industry and construction," says Party writer Adlys. Of course, the assertion regarding the alleged mechanization as the cause of migration is not true: the poverty had driven the former husbandmen off the mismanaged derelict kolkhozes with their disproportionately large bureaucracy and slave-driving Party idlers.

In 1970 there were only 88 men per 100 women. Adlys adds that Lithuanians constitute 87.1% of the rural population and 73.2% of the urban inhabitants. Adlys, head of the Statistical Bureau, notes that the annual population increase is 38,000 or 1.32%: 88% by natural increase, 12% by immigration, and follows this statement by a curious notation that "the arrivals exceed departures by 51,000." [156]

From the Moscow viewpoint, the industrialization of Lithuania was equivalent to its communization and the destruction of the guerrillas' base of supplies, and it was pushed at a rapid pace. According to Dr. Zundė, "the average annual rate of growth of industrial production in Lithuania in 1946-50 was 37 per cent, whereas the same rate for the Soviet Union as a whole was only 21.8 per cent. From 1951 to 1955, the extent of total industrial production in Lithuania was increasing at a rate of 21 per cent a year, while in the Soviet Union it was increasing only 13.1 per cent a year." In 1959 "the volume of industrial production in Lithuania was 9.1 times that of the 1940 volume, while the equivalent rate for the Soviet Union was only 4.8." Deputy Premier Kairys boasted in 1972 that the industrial output in 1971 was 34 times greater than that of "bourgeois Lithuania" in 1940 and that the entire "prewar annual production level is reached within 11 days." [157]

Because of the foreign planning for the Soviet Union's own needs, the nature of Lithuanian industrial production changed. Between 1939 and 1958 — energy output index dropped, fuel production rose, machinery and metal processing from 4.8 rose to 12.4, building materials output more than doubled, food processing slid down. The emphasis is placed on developing *heavy* industry, or "more accurately, the manufacture of the means of production." Only a small portion of the

[156] P. Adlys, "Certain data of the population census," *Komunistas* No. 6 (564), 1971, p. 56; V. Vazalinskas, "Agriculture: Achievements, Perspective," *Komunistas* No. 6 (564), p. 30; M. Leonavičius, "Large Farms - Clearer Tomorrow," *Komunistas* No. 9 (591), 1973, 44-45; 1974 statistics — *Komunistas* No. 2, 1974.

[157] Zundė, *Lithuania Under the Soviets, op. cit.*, 156-157; K. Kairys in *Komunistas* No. 12 (582), 1972, p. 22.

equipment manufactured in Lithuania is intended for domestic use, the greater part being shipped to the Soviet Union, notes Dr. Zundė.

"Whether it be the turbine factory *Pergalė* in Kaunas, or the metal processing plant *Žalgiris* in Naujoji Vilnia, or the electronics-tube plant in Panevėžys, or a similar factory, their products will be found throughout the Soviet Union, but rarely within Lithuania itself. — The exploitative character of Soviet industrial policy reveals itself even more clearly when the types of industry that were intentionally neglected or prevented from further development are considered." Here he notes that the production of electrical energy steadily lagged behind, light industry and food processing suffered most, native fertilizer mineral industry remained undeveloped. "Manufacture of farm machinery likewise declined and the machinery was imported from the Soviet Union." Pleas to develop or "assign additional agricultural machinery were ignored" by Moscow. Efforts at industrial development were "concentrated primarily on those types of industry whose raw materials, such as metals, etc., must be brought from Russia, the Ukraine, or elsewhere, and whose products are not intended for the Lithuanian market."

Dr. Zundė shows that the indigenous food industry "is treated by Moscow as one of its step-children; it is allocated relatively little capital outlay, it is worst supplied where means of production and power are concerned, yet food products rank first on the scale of exports" to other Soviet republics. The same policy of exploitation is applied to building materials industry. "Despite the shortage of construction materials in Lithuania, nearly the entire productive output of the Akmenė cement factory is shipped off for use in construction outside Lithuania, for Akmenė cement is far superior to ordinary Soviet cement." Giant plants were built to serve the Baltic republics and western Russia, including the Elektrėnai thermodynamic plant near Vievis, "the largest of its kind" in the USSR with the capacity of 1.2 million kilowatts. A large chemical plant was built near Kėdainiai to supply sulphuric acid, mineral fertilizer, anhydrous cement, "utilizing materials from the Kola Peninsula and the Ukraine." The liquid fertilizer plant in Jonava, "the first of its kind in the Soviet Union," uses natural gas piped from the Ukraine and its output is shipped out of Lithuania. He also mentions a vending machine plant with 5,000 workers, a refrigerator plant, furniture and glass factories. "The economic program forced upon Lithuania by the Soviet regime is such that it cannot possibly be met by the existing labor resources in Lithuania and, therefore, it is dependent . . .

on labor imported" from elsewhere.[158]

It is clear that "economic considerations play no part in Moscow's determination to industrialize Lithuania at a rate of speed out of all proportions to Lithuanian labor resources. The only inference to be drawn, then, is that the motives of Moscow are of a purely political nature . . . to unite Lithuania permanently to the Russian sphere, in an economic union and to colonize Lithuania demographically — in short, to Russify and assimilate it. These efforts are conducted under the pretext of improving the national economy." Yet with enough perceptive individuals realizing the threat to the national survival of Lithuanians, the efforts to industrialize "could bear fruit very different from that anticipated by Moscow." [159]

Lithuanian products are exported abroad under treaties arranged in Moscow — and foreign exchange earned is pocketed by the Kremlin.

The Soviet designs to ignore political boundaries of ethnic "Union republics" in consolidating planning economic regions — three in the European part of the Soviet Union and four in Asia — attracted foreign attention recently. In December 1972, in a keynote speech at the observance of the 50th anniversary of the "Union of SSRs," Brezhnev referred to the 15-year plan for long-term economic development and said that future decision-making should be for the good of the country as a whole rather than focus on the interest of individual republics. Professor Viktor V. Kistanov, a planning economist, writing in the *Voprosy Ekonomiki* (Problems of Economics) December 1972 issue, cited a Lenin gospel to the effect that the ethnic composition of population was an important factor in the drawing of boundary lines "but not the only one and not the most important." Existing political boundaries of ethnic republics have often interfered with the desired economic aims. He noted that boundaries had been changed in the past by joint agreement of the republics, and proposals to redraw political internal boundaries were not unusual, as "some form of interethnic association could be economically desirable." Similar statements were made in the April 1973 issue of the *Planovoie Khozyaistvo* (Planned Economy). Theodore Shabad of *The New York Times* and other American correspondents quickly perceived the significance of such ill-disguised assaults on "sovereign" ethnic Soviet Republics which, until recently, have been able to some degree to defend their area interests.[160]

[158] Zundė, *Lithuania Under the Soviets, op. cit.*, 156-162.

[159] *Ibid.*, 168-169.

[160] See *New York Times*, Jan. 3, 1973, May 4 and 5, 1973.

XXXVI.

EDUCATION: "TO CREATE A SOVIET MAN"

When the German armies occupied Lithuania in 1915, they had found no university. Several high schools had been evacuated to Russia, and there were 535 state, 42 municipal and 25 private elementary schools. On the initiative of Lithuanian educators, about 1,000 private schools were founded within a year, and then the military occupational authorities demanded licensing annually. Within the Ob-Ost, or "Greater Lithuania" embracing also the Gardinas/Grodno, Białystok and Suvalkai areas, in the spring of 1918 there were 1,350 grade schools — Lithuanian language 750, Polish 299 (mostly in Grodno-Białystok area), Jewish 164, Belorussian 89, German 81, Latvian 7. There were also several teacher colleges. By Armistice Day in 1918, there were also 20 Lithuanian language junior and senior high schools.

Public education received priority attention in independent Lithuania and, in addition to public and private Lithuanian language schools, there were public and private Hebrew, Polish and German language schools. In 1940, when the Soviets annexed Lithuania without the Klaipėda area, they found 2,743 grade schools with 6,944 teachers and 341,299 pupils, 94 secondary schools in several languages with over 1,300 teachers and 26,500 pupils; five teacher colleges with 88 teachers and 953 students, a Pedagogic Institute, Agricultural Academy, Fine Arts School, Conservatory of Music, an Institute of Commerce, Physical Education School, two universities, a Military Academy and a General Staff College, several theological seminaries, seamanship, technical, specialized vocational schools. Compulsory universal education was instituted by the educational reform of 1936. Grade schools were 4- and 6-year institutions, gymnasia seven years. There were also kindergarten schools, and primary and secondary evening schools for adults.[161]

The first victims of the Soviet occupation were chaplains. Within five days of the occupation Catholic, Protestant, Russian Orthodox and Jewish chaplains were dismissed from schools, the armed forces, hospitals and prisons, and the teaching of religion was banned. On July 25, 1940 ("effective July 6") the Theology-Philosophy Faculty at the university in Kaunas was closed, the University Rector was dismissed, the

[161] *Liet. Enciklopedija*, XV, 764-778.

university was deprived of its name of "Vytautas the Great." Private book publishing was banned. All religious, patriotic and anti-Communist societies, fraternities and clubs were shut down. In lieu of a summer seminar, teachers were convoked on August 14-15 to hear denunciations of the nation's past and its educational system, to listen to the glorification of Stalin the Sun and the Soviet Union. Threats were made that all opposition would be ground to dust. Nevertheless, several thousand teachers concluded the rally by singing the National Anthem.

The school year due to start September 1 was delayed for several weeks. The State coat of arms, crosses and patriotic pictures were removed from school walls, and the National Anthem was replaced by the International. All private schools were taken over by the State. Jewish language schools were closed and their pupils transferred to Lithuanian schools. Schools became numbered institutions — losing their names. Most of the teachers were either dismissed or transferred, superintendents were replaced by Party incompetents. Schools were adapted to a Soviet pattern of 10-year Party tools: elementary four years, secondary six years. Marxism-Leninism and Communist Party history were made compulsory subjects. Russian language and literature courses were introduced, history of Lithuania and Lithuanian literature courses were brutally narrowed and deformed: school texts were seized and "improper pages" torn out. Internal espionage was instituted among teachers and pupils. Pioneer and Komsomol groups were to be formed in each school and "Red Nooks" were instituted — rooms with Soviet leaders' posters and "mottoes" on the walls. These Red Nooks were dubbed "Stalin's Altars" by students. "Komsorgs" (Communist Organizers) were installed in all schools to supervise internal spying.

In the universities, "Komsorg" duties were performed by heads and lecturers of the Marxism-Leninism Chairs — two "professors" and eight instructors were sent to Vilnius from Moscow. Marxism-Leninism was made a compulsory "science" course six hours weekly, two semester course for all students. Professors were likewise ordered to attend indoctrination classes. Some professors were dismissed, some professors and a great many students were repeatedly interrogated by the NKVD, some were forced to become informers. Nevertheless, thanks to the solidarity of the faculty and students the school year 1940-41 was concluded in full. Hundreds of thousands of books from libraries and publishing houses were burned or sent to paper mills, rare books, ancient documents and art objects were systematically looted and shipped to Moscow. During the first wave of mass deportations of June 12-22,

1941, the teaching profession lost 1,089 members — 10% of the total personnel.[162]

The mission of education is the sovietization, "creation of a Soviet man." The educational system is based on polytechnism, collectivism, dialectic materialism, atheism and atheist ideas, proletarian internationalism, Socialist patriotism, friendship of the fraternal Soviet peoples, love of the Soviet motherland, hatred for religion and "people's enemies," and a rigidly biased Communist partisanship -*principialnost.* The political integration of Lithuania was the means to prevent its regression into "localism" and a democratic national State independence. Economic sovietization was to create a "material technical base" for integration under Russian communist rule. Finally, the greatest objective was to sovietize the inhabitants, to shape the "spiritual characteristics inculcating traditions of the revolutionary creators of Communism common to all (Soviet) peoples."

These compulsory "traditions" are to "enhance the oneness of Socialist peoples, to develop common cultural, moral and behavioral ways of life" and to create "an international culture common to all Soviet peoples." The school system is to ingrain loyalty and devotion to the Soviet Union and its Communist Party by encouraging association with Russians in school "international clubs," by glorifying the Great Russian people and its history — and by demeaning the alleged misery of the independent life of a former bourgeois Lithuania and distorting Lithuania's own historic past, and by encouraging using the common "international" Russian language — in Party meetings, Komsomol, Pioneers, schools, administrative offices.

Culture "national in form, socialist in content" — "and international in spirit," vz. Russian — is to bring together various nationalities into a "friendship of fraternal peoples" using common "international" Russian language, translating Russian classics, worshiping Russian heroes, revolutionaries. This requires combat against biased "localism, national limitedness, exclusiveness," private property, all (non-Russian) religions as relics of unscientific anti-social superstitions. Compulsory education of children under a single system of standards and values, the press, radio-television, theaters, cinemas, literature, paintings, sculptures, music, athletic meets, school dances, drama clubs, choruses, "folk festivals" — are the instruments and weapons to be wielded by the Party exclusively, with no competition. There is no room for complaints

[162]*Ibid.*, XV, 778-780.

and no media for expressing dissent.

Teachers are the whipping tools of the Party. Their mission is to rear Communist activists and professional technicians. First Secretary Sniečkus told the teachers in 1940, and repeated ever since: "Every teacher, whatever subject he is teaching — literature or mathematics, natural science or music — is dutybound by honor to apply communistic education based on polytechnism, collectivism, Soviet atheism, Soviet patriotism and hatred for the enemies of the Soviet Union."

Vytautas Vaitiekūnas, the knowledgeable scholar of Lithuanian affairs, explains these Soviet terms. *Polytechnism* means the training of craftsmen and technicians for the Soviet economy, especially industry. *Collectivism* implies the subordination of the individual's rights, aims, interests, convictions and outlooks "to the decisions and directives of the Communist Party, the glorification and sanctification of Communist society, the justification of even the most extreme actions taken by the Party."

Soviet atheism "is remarkable for its aggressiveness and intolerance of other ideologies and has become the official 'religion' of the U.S.S.R. . . . supported and propagated with all the powers of a totalitarian state. The Soviet school is in turn the 'church' of this new 'religion.' The Party demands that 'children be trained atheistically in kindergarten . . . the teacher must foster the student's materialistic world view and educate our youths as real [militant] atheists.' To make certain that all teachers propagate atheism, school administrators organize 'scientific-methodological conferences on questions of atheistic education'; teachers must also attend teacher soirees on questions of atheistic work."

The teacher's duty to the Party does not end in the classroom. He must counteract parental influence regarding religion. He must organize "young atheist circles" to propagate atheistic "thought," to publish "wall newspapers" of atheistic content, lead excursions to anti-religious museums, produce stage plays with atheistic views. He must organize "atheistic seminars" — weekend lectures on atheism, make use of special interest clubs in such subjects as folklore, literature, natural sciences, for atheistic indoctrination. Students of the Institute of Arts in Vilnius must hold shows exhibiting anti-religious works exclusively.

Proletarian internationalism is nothing like the words might suggest: it means "the subordination of one's own nation and country to the Kremlin. Proletarian internationalism is the opposite of proletarian nationalism or national communism, such as that of Yugoslavia, Albania, or China." In effect: proletarian internationalism means Russian nationalism "sucked by a Soviet man with his mother's milk."

Soviet patriotism is the twin of "proletarian internationalism": owing loyalty to the Kremlin alone. A "Socialist patriot," according to the vivid definition by Vaitiekūnas, "proclaims that Lithuania's occupation is liberation; economic exploitation, the 'elder brother's noble assistance'; the destruction of Lithuanian national individuality, the progress of Communist culture. The 'friendship of Soviet peoples' is a device for subordinating all nations to the Russians and ensuring that the leading and deciding role be left exclusively for Russia. . . . To emphasize this Russian primacy, Russia is officially labeled the 'elder brother.' Under the slogan of this type of 'friendship,' the youths are taught . . . that their fatherland is not [their] ancestral Lithuania but the entire Russian-ruled Soviet Union." The teaching of the Russian language begins in the second grade. "Like atheism, all subjects are used for Russification, especially classes in the history and geography of the U.S.S.R. Even the examples in drafting are exclusively Russian: Moscow's squares, the stars of the Kremlin," etc.

"In the University of Vilnius, students specializing in Lithuanian language and literature must take 724 class hours in Russian subjects, i.e. 18.4 per cent of all classroom time." Vaitiekūnas reproduces the table of required subjects and hours for students specializing in journalism – from the University's 1957 catalog. Examination of the curricula reveals a growing "bi-lingualism" in all schools, especially in the universities where hundreds of [Soviet] students are deliberately brought here to study, and Russian lecturers are imported for Leninism and other classes.

Vaitiekūnas illustrates "threefold purges" — of teachers, subjects, and teaching materials (textbooks, maps, etc.). He cites the 1956 edition of "Cultural Construction of the USSR" showing that in the ten postwar years only 13% of all teachers had a higher education, 62.4% had only a general secondary education, in some instances incomplete. In this respect Lithuania "ranked with the lowest Soviet republics. Even the Tadzhik republic had a higher percentage of teachers with higher education: 13.8%." In the school years 1939-1940, there were 8,417 qualified teachers in independent Lithuania. After twelve years of postwar Soviet occupation, there were only 5,507 teachers with pedagogic training.

The curricular purge is evidenced by programs in the new Soviet six-day school week, the 34-36 week school year. Religion, social studies and Latin are eliminated. Lithuanian history and geography are replaced by a few additional hours for the Lithuanian language. Psychology was substituted for the introductory course in philosophy. The hours for history, geography, physical education, drawing-drafting, singing-music, and handicrafts were reduced. A second foreign language (Russian is *not* "foreign") course was extended by three weekly hours, mathematics by 3.5 hours. Three hours a week were added for shop work, seven for practice in agriculture and electrical engineering and the principles of machine operation called "the polytechnic profile." Textbooks are exclusively translations or adaptations of Russian manuals. Problems and examples are Russian exclusively. The Lithuanian Language Grammar contains examples: "The USSR is our motherland. All the peoples of the Soviet Union are helped by the great Russian people. What do the warmongers want? They wish to enslave freedom-loving nations. Forward to the triumph of Communism! Children of the workers in capitalist lands live very miserably. It is good for children to live in the land of the Soviets. Lenin has shown us the road to freedom and happiness. The capital of our motherland is Moscow." These quotations from the Lithuanian Grammar edition of 1957 show the essence of culture — "national in form, socialist in content, and international in spirit."

The teaching of the geography and history of Lithuania is not acceptable to the Kremlin: these subjects are made insignificant chapters in the economic geography of the USSR and "history of the USSR from prehistoric times" (Sic!) — even though the USSR was proclaimed only in 1923. In the few references to the Lithuanian past — "the history textbook is silent about the numerous Russian aggressions against Lithuania; the occupation in the late eighteenth century, for example, is depicted as [beneficial] to Lithuania; the restoration of independence is treated as colonization by capitalist imperialists; the Kremlin's aggression and invasion in 1939-40 is, of course, labeled 'liberation'." Such gross falsification was not deemed adequate, and a revised detailed historical program was decreed by Moscow in 1959. The decree strongly emphasized that the "history program in the secondary schools must . . . inculcate a conviction of the scientific historical development of society leading to the downfall of capitalism and inevitable Communist victory." Since then Lithuanian history became a part of a "continuous USSR history course."

In 1956 Khrushchev decreed obligatory agricultural labor duty during summer recesses for the 9th and 10th year students in schools of general education, and "production teaching" was introduced the next year by making 8th graders leave school to work in factories. This out-of-school education consumed about one-third of the school year, and an additional year was added to schools with production training. In 1958 Khrushchev came out with additional reforms: fifteen- and sixteen-year-old graduates of the eight-year obligatory primary schooling were to be integrated into the productive system. Evening and correspondence classes were to be established for the exploited child labor force — for those desiring additional schooling. No attention was paid to the desiderata of the Lithuanian educators. The child labor was exploited in 1254 lumber processing mills, 962 metalcraft shops and 73 "household cabinets" or carpentry shops.

Most painful for Lithuanians was the ignoring of the constitutionally guaranteed use of the Lithuanian language in schools — by foisting a statutory Article 11 to the effect that "parents have the right to decide in what language their children shall receive instruction." This clause enabled Russian settlers to omit the Lithuanian language classes in schools attended by their children, and to compel Lithuanian children to adopt "the elder brother's language." Thus the culture "national in form, Socialist in content," is being transformed into a culture "Socialist in form, Socialist in content." Since 1961 the CPSU Program came out publicly for a "common international culture for all Soviet peoples," and the culture "national in form" since then is sometimes ostracized as a "relic of insignificant localism of past bourgeois nationalism."[163] The chief ideologist of the post-Stalin period, Mikhail Suslov, in 1973 added a third qualification for culture — spiritual Russification. His formula is "culture national in form, Socialist in content, and international in spirit."

After the fall of Khrushchev, beginning with the school year 1965-66, the seven-year secondary schools were again restored for Lithuanian and Polish language schools, "upon the people's request." The teaching combined with production was abandoned, along with Khrushchev's plan to convert all general education schools into boarding schools, "internats," with student's day strictly planned under the constant supervision by teachers, aimed at eliminating parental influence. Forty-five Lithuanian internats were converted into schools for orphans and

[163] Materials for this chapter were drawn from articles by Vytautas Vaitiekūnas in *Liet. Enciklopedija*, XV, 395 sq., his chapter on Sovietized education in *Lithuania Under the Soviets*, *op. cit.*, 171-196, as well as *A Survey of Developments. . . op. cit.*, 116-127. Other data are from various more recent issues of the *Komunistas*.

for retarded children. The hideous proscription in the University of Vilnius barring "socially alien" children of non-worker classes likewise petered out: significant progress is made whenever Moscow softens its grip. Lately up to 85% of the student body is absorbed by Vilnius University, the Kaunas Polytechnical Institute, and the Institute of Pedagogics. Students insisted and succeeded in retaining traditional caps, student feasts, festivals, "Gaudeamus igitur," and other trappings of the past university life not known in the Soviet Union. And — to the horror of the Komsomol, after decades of atheistic indoctrination, there are still students who, "after receiving A in Marxism, run to churches to thank God."

XXXVII.

LITERATURE AND ARTS: "FOR IMPLACABLE IDEOLOGY STRUGGLE"

"Soviet literature, art, as our entire ideological labor must help educate the people in the spirit of patriotism, to develop working people's conscious pride in their socialist Homeland, the authority of a citizen of the great and mighty land of the Soviets. . . . The Party's 70th anniversary coincides with the exchange of Party documents . . . new Party tickets with . . . Lenin's picture and his immortal words: 'The Party — our epoch's brains, honor and conscience.'" Thus exhorts the Party's theoretical and political monthly *Komunistas* in an editorial, "At the head of the masses," in the August 1973 issue. "Passivity and indifference are not acceptable to the Party." The editorial cites Brezhnev's words about every Communist's duty to be "an active Party combatant. At work, in social life, in science, in private life — at all times and everywhere a Communist must be the Communist," alert, prepared "to repel any aggressive reactionary designs of imperialist circles and any hostile ideological subversion. . . . The Communist Party does not tolerate any expressions of ideology hostile to communism. The Party had many a time forewarned that peaceful coexistence of states with different social orders does not mean a coexistence of the opposing ideologies — socialism and capitalism. In the sphere of ideology the irreconcileable class struggle had been and shall be waged." The editorial then lambasts "bourgeois nationalist traps" and "religious superstitions," as well as "the concept of private property."

Dr. Jonas Grinius, a noted writer and literary critic, notes the "perverted meaning of culture" and concepts of peace, freedom, national self-determination and progress employed by the Soviet media during the Soviet invasion and forcible annexation of Lithuania. The perverted meaning "became clear to writers and artists more slowly perhaps than to the rest of the nation." By the time the Soviet armies re-invaded Lithuania in 1944, "more than half of the writers and artists . . . had fled to the West; Germany, in flames and ruins . . . seemed to them less perilous than Soviet liberation."

He explains the slower realization of a Soviet reality by writers and artists. An engineer's work "does not entail public expression of his thoughts and feelings." A reticent, "merely applauding" engineer may escape his blacklisting by the Party. Writers and artists, however, "have always been faced by a dilemma — either to relinquish their profession . . . or to become propagandists for the Soviet regime. No alternative is possible, for the Soviet regime exercises stricter control over writers and artists than [had] the absolute monarchies of the past. They have to work under conditions of totalitarian encirclement." The press and the publishing houses are owned and operated by the government in behalf of the Party. Works of art are admitted for public display "only after they have been judged and accepted by one or two special committees" named by the Party. "As a rule, exhibits are collective." Written works are censored by the Party and must serve the Party ideology or the political "line." Dr. Grinius cites the report by Antanas Venclova to the Soviet writers' congress in Moscow in December 1954:

"During the early postwar years, the young Soviet [Lithuanian] literature grew and developed in the fierce struggle against the still undestroyed residue of bourgeois nationalism and chauvinism, against the followers of 'pure art,' against the promoters of 'aestheticism' and snobs worshiping the refuse of the Western bourgeoisie and mystics of various shades. The principal representatives of this Fascist-minded 'literature' fled to the West with the retreating Hitlerist troops and now they are serving their new masters — the American warmongers. For some time after the war, their 'ideological henchmen' tried to obstruct the development of our growing Soviet literature, but they were crushed and tossed onto the trash pile."

Dr. Grinius lists a number of writers "tossed onto the trash pile" by incarceration and deportation. Some of them were silenced permanently some had "reformed" to the tune of the shifting ideological dogmatism after atoning publicly for their former aberrations. Among the latter he names the classic writer Vincas Mykolaitis-Putinas, Jonas Šimkus, Kostas Korsakas and — Antanas Venclova himself. Korsakas in his confession noted: "We, of the literary profession, should be deeply grateful to the Party for its constant guidance, for the criticism of our works in accordance with Bolshevik principles, for pointing out to us the proper way of correcting the errors we have committed." Ever since this confession, made in December, 1950, Korsakas became a faithful servant of the Party — authoritative writer, professor, academician, and a rancid gutter agitator.

After Stalin's demise and the accession of Khrushchev individual recantations were no longer required. *Literatūra ir Menas*, the weekly organ of the writers and artists, editorially noted (December 1, 1956) the evils of the "personality cult" and its effects "which must be completely eradicated." Of course, these were merely brave words — no eradication followed. Two months later, Kazys Boruta, the graduate of Soviet concentration camps, wrote that the "criticism" of the personality cult and its effects "has helped to extirpate in our literature and in creative practice the unhealthy manifestations of schematism and stereotypes, which were becoming rampant."

Of course, at no time did the Party intend to abandon its censorship and control over the writers and artists. In February, 1957, President Venclova of the Lithuanian Soviet Writers Union again glorified "the love, the singleminded devotion, and the concern with which the Party has fostered our young Soviet literature, always encouraging it to serve our people. The Party has always taught us to be faithful to the best realistic traditions in the literature of our own and other nations; ... literature that would educate men in the spirit of Communist ideology and morality. This spirit pervades all the pronouncements of the Party on literature and art, and these documents today are still the basic guidepost in our future work. We Soviet writers say this openly to all our friends and enemies: We are proud to be the helpers of our Party."

Dr. Grinius observes that "Socialist realism" must interpret creative material "according to the dialectical and historical materialism professed and preached by the Communist Party," and must serve the political indoctrination — even in human admiration for natural beauty. Writers are salaried State employees — some holding positions in publishing houses and newspapers, some receiving generous largess for their writings with extra pay for membership in various committees. Nevertheless, the Lithuanian literature of the '50s "contributed very little or nothing at all to the development of Soviet prose," and the "level of productivity" was extremely low, the achievements of Communism were "largely ignored." The writers were skeptical of the "thaw" of the post-Stalin period, as were the artists, and they had to be pressured by the Party. Antanas Gudaitis, the Paris-trained painter, complained in 1957 about creative activities "by administrative means, by dictating from above." "All sorts of committees would advise the artist ... on a multitude of little corrections to be made, which essentially directed the work toward naturalism. Such 'methods' have done our painting much harm, they weakened the creative activity of some artists; many of the works from the period in question appear depersonalized, monolithic, lacking in deeper emotional appeal. With such a narrow conception of socialist realism, unpardonably little significance came to be attached to light, shadow, and lineal rhythm as means of expression."

Another artist, Jonas Mackonis, writing in the *Literatūra ir Menas* of October 13, 1956, voiced a longing for at least a public discussion of their craft. He wrote: "It must be said that even when prescriptions were being forced down upon them and taste was dictated from above, our artists held on to a broader and deeper conception of art, although they may have avoided giving it public expression, for fear of being branded formalists. It is commonly known, by now at least, that certain of our painters acknowledged the nineteenth-century works of the Russian *peredvizhniki* [didactic realists], as the only artistic model to be followed, while backstage they were expressing admiration for the painting of Serov, Vrubel, Kontsalovsky, Matisse, and Renoir. Has not the time come for observations of this kind freely to make their way into the press and to be discussed with sincerity and without fear of a possible clash of opinion?" Similar sentiments of writers were voiced nine months later by Vytautas Kubilius. Their demands for new forms were based on "actual changes within Soviet life itself," suggesting that there could be only one question: "Is that which is new significant both intellectually and artistically?" The readers concurred: "We don't want to be directed or led. We have heads of our own."

After the crushing of the Hungarian revolt, the Party editorialized: "We find it inexcusable that, under cover of the criticism directed against the personality cult, attempts are made to negate the whole of Soviet-Lithuanian literature . . . [weakening] the influence of our literature on the reader, on the masses of youth." The term "revisionism" emerged by mid-1957. By the end of the year, Genrikas Zimanas, a member of the Party Central Committee and editor of its daily organ *Tiesa* at the time, wrote: "We all know that the disquieting wave of revisionism, which has risen recently and sought to wash away the foundations of Marxism-Leninism, succeeded in casting some of its poisonous spray on the Soviet people, particularly on some of our literary and artistic workers. . . . Let it be said to the credit of Lithuanian-Soviet writers that they did not produce a Dudintsev in their midst. But the seed of the revisionist onslaught did make its way into our Republic and accomplished its harm. The year 1957 is the year in which this onslaught has been repulsed in our Republic, the year of ideological formation for our literary and artistic workers."

Indeed, the Party blocked the stage production of the *Sukilėliai* (The Insurgents), an opera by Juozas Juozeliūnas. Rector Juozas Bulavas of the University of Vilnius was removed and his management of the department of Lithuanian literature was branded "incompetent." Smilgevičius was dismissed as Minister of Culture because the desire of emancipation manifested itself in the theater and in the State publishing house. The new minister Juozas Banaitis attacked writers, artists, musicians and playwrights for their 1956-57 creations tainted by "individualism." Party Secretary Sniečkus told the CPL Congress in 1958: "Various revisionist tendencies received active support from the Lithuanian bourgeois nationalists who had fled abroad and hired themselves out to American imperialists.' 'He warned: "It is important for every member of the working class to know that anyone who would stir up antagonism toward the Russian nation, anyone who would tear the Lithuanian people away from the Russian people, would be digging a grave for the Lithuanian nation."

Dr. Grinius sees some positive achievement in secondary matters, for instance, the "rehabilitation" of the great writer, Vincas Krėvė-Mickevičius, who died a professor at the University of Pennsylvania in 1954. At the time Dr. Grinius wrote, the "works of a number of deceased writers (Vincas Pietaris, Vilius Storasta-Vydūnas, Šatrijos Ragana, J. Savickis, J. Baltrušaitis, and others) continue to be banned" — which was no longer true by 1974, even though the published writings are highly selective. More original novels were published. Some incarcerated exiles were returned home and allowed to pursue their literary endeavors "on the condition that they publicly renounce and deplore their past and declare their loyalty to the Soviet regime."

The great artist and composer Mikalojus Konstantinas Čiurlionis, "the most important figure in Lithuanian art" (1875-1911), likewise received recognition and a collection of 32 color reproductions was published in Lithuania and East Germany. Theretofore his works were deemed "the expression of individualism and symbolism, and hence decadent art." A group of intellectuals wrote an "Appeal to Lithuanians Abroad," in 1972, urging them to press for the preservation of Čiurlionis paintings "painted on an inferior paper with paints of short duration and his paintings are rapidly aging . . . may not survive till the next anniversary." The appeal states: "There is only one Čiurlionis!" The appellants note that "strangely enough" many Lithuanians are more hopeful of seeing monuments to great Lithuanian personalities somewhere in Chicago, rather than in Vilnius. "Yes, we are telling the truth. No, we are not traitors, enemies of the nation. We want [monuments to] Gediminas in Vilnius, Maironis in Kaunas, Basanavičius in Anykščiai. . . . We believe in our nation, her vitality confirmed by history. We believe in the higher ideals, goodness and beauty, finally in God Himself."

Exhibitions of individual artists are presently allowed. Several painters resident abroad were invited to attend the exhibitions of their earlier works in Lithuania, and some were allowed to show to artist audiences the slides of their own "decadent" works and those of others in the free world. Since 1956 Lithuanian theaters were permitted to collaborate with their Latvian and Estonian counterparts. Lithuanian artists, singers and ensembles are allowed to go on foreign tours with Russian groups to be acclaimed as "Soviet" performers. (At least the Poles are not deceived: they praise Lithuanian groups as such.) Some State prizes are given non-Communists. The much talked-about Lithuanian Encyclopaedia did not appear — but a three-volume "Small Soviet Lithuanian Encyclopaedia" did come out. The several dozen volume Lithuanian Encyclopaedia published in Boston is made available to privileged readers in Lithuania, not the general public. When a researcher requests a certain volume, he must state the part he wants to read — and is given the Xerox copy of the pages required.

In 1962 Eduardas Mieželaitis was given a Lenin Prize in Literature for the collection of his poems in Russian translation — and thereafter the volume was also printed in Lithuanian. Dr. Grinius calls these poems "the rhetoric that passes for poetry," and claims that "the award was made on the basis of something other than the aesthetic value of the poetry."

However, whatever sops may be granted in periodic easements of tensions — the hard line inevitably springs back. Brezhnev's colleague, CPSU Secretary Leonid Iliichev told the writers and artists in Moscow in December 1962: "Without any equivocation, let the following be stated: There never was and there never can be a peaceful coexistence of socialist and bourgeois ideologies. The Party has always fought and will continue to fight the bourgeois ideology in all of its aspects." This self-same theme, as noted in the opening paragraph of the present chapter, was also editorialized in the *Komunistas* of August 1973. It had been the core of Khrushchev's pronouncement of March 1963, and of Brezhnev — after he had signed with President Nixon a "declaration of principles."

Consequently, Dr. Jonas Grinius was quite right in his conclusion penned in 1965: "The Party and the Soviet Government have no intention whatsoever of lifting their encirclement of the writers and the artists. For this reason, the situation of Lithuanian literature and art remains unchanged. The small margin of freedom that had been granted during the thaw has again been narrowed and diminished to accord better with the purposes of the Communist Party and Russian nationalism." [164]

Indoctrination of "Soviet patriotism" was redoubled in Union republics in 1973, along with attacks on sentiments and interests of "localism," on the relics of bourgeois nationalism (other than Russian), etc. Lithuanians are told to glorify Moscow, Russian heroes, Russian military prowess, and the "October Revolution" with which they had no connection whatsoever.

[164] Jonas Grinius, "Literature and the Arts in Captive Lithuania," *Lithuania Under the Soviets, op. cit.*, 197-213. Later sources are indicated in the text of the present chapter. A dissertation by Mykolas Burokevičius, *Lietuvos KP Ideologinis Darbas su Inteligentija 1940-1965* (Lithuanian CP Ideological Labors with the Intelligentsia 1940-1965) is a partisan account of the "struggle" for ideological re-education. It was published in Vilnius in 1972.

The Roman Catholic cathedral of Vilnius before communists' invasion.

The Roman Catholic cathedral of Vilnius (St. Stanislas Basilica) after the communists' invasion. The relics of St. Casimir were removed from the chapel and and the cathedral was converted into an art gallery.

XXXVIII.
THE WAR ON RELIGIOUS HERITAGE

General Data

The religious affiliations of the population of Lithuania, exclusive of the Vilnius area, were indicated in the Census of 1923: Roman Catholics 80.4%, Protestants 9.54%, Jews 7.26%, Eastern Orthodox 2.54%, other Christians 0.09%, other non-Christians 0.09%. Klaipėda District natives were predominantly Lutherans — only 22,159 were Catholics in a population of 153,000. The Polish-occupied Vilnius area was predominantly Catholic.

The general pattern for the country as a whole remained approx-mately the same, as shown by the ratio of nationalities in the Statistical Annual of Lithuania for 1940, exclusive of the Klaipėda District seized by Germany in 1939: Lithuanians (Roman Catholics and some Evangelicals) 80.6%, Jews 7.15%, Germans (predominantly Lutherans) 4.10%, Poles (mostly Catholics) 3.04%, Russians (Orthodox) 2.35%, Latvians 0.6%, Whiteruthenes 0.21%, others 1.86%. These "others" included nearly 600-year-old five Moslem congregations of Tatars and two Karaite congregations.

At the time of the Soviet invasion, the Roman Catholic "Province of Lithuania" in 1940 embraced the Archdiocese of Kaunas and the dioceses of Kaišiadorys, Panevėžys, Telšiai and Vilkaviškis. The Prelacy of Klaipėda was lost to Germany — but in postwar years the Prelacy and the Soviet-administered part of East Prussia, the diocese of Ermland/Varmia, were assigned to the Archdiocese of Kaunas. Parts of the Archdiocese of Vilnius, technically under the Primate of Poland, were restored to Lithuania.

Because of these various political shifts, statistical data by researchers regarding the number of churches and clergy tend to vary. According to Dr. Casimir Gečys, a clergyman of the Vilnius Archdiocese, in 1940 there were 13 bishops and one refugee bishop (of Danzig). Parishioners numbered 2,776,422, the clergy 1,487 plus seven of the Byzantine rite. 470 divinity students and 1,586 members of monastic orders. Priests, including monastics — the Jesuits, Franciscans, Salesians, Marians and Dominicans — numbered 1,646. There were: 1 arch-cathedral basilica (Kaunas), 1 cathedral basilica (Vilnius), 4 cathedrals, 670 Latin rite and

7 Byzantine rite parish churches, 91 non-parochial churches, and 330 chapels. According to Dr. Savasis (an assumed name), "in the two Catholic archdioceses and four dioceses there were 708 churches, 314 chapels, 73 monasteries and 85 convents [950 nuns], with 3 archbishops 9 bishops, 1271 diocesan priests, and 580 monks, of whom 168 were priests. The four seminaries had an enrollment of 470." [165]

Catholic and Protestant theology departments at the University of Vytautas the Great were part of the school of philosophy. There were private primary and secondary Catholic and Jewish schools, publishing houses connected with denominations, newspapers and magazines, religious ecclesiastic fraternities and sororities, organizations of students and intellectuals of Christian and Hebrew ideologies — as well as the Ethical Society and its magazine for liberals and non-believers.

The Evangelical Churches

The Evangelical Lutheran Church had lost 64 parishes to Germany in 1939. Dr. Kristupas Gudaitis, the Superintendent of the Evangelical Lutheran Church of Lithuania in 1938-1941, writes that the communicants of his church in 1940 included 30,000 Lithuanians, 26,000 Germans and 14,000 Latvians affiliated in 55 parishes and filials served by 51 clergymen and administered by an elective Synod. The Evangelical Reformed (Calvinist) Church of Lithuania embraced 15,000 in 13 parishes and filials, ministered by a General Superintendent and 13 clergymen. Dr. Gudaitis probably did not include the Lutherans and Calvinists of the Vilnius area. There were also Baptists, Methodists, Seventh Day Adventists, and Jehovah's Witnesses. These "other Christians" numbered 3,217 to 3,400, including about 1,000 Lithuanians.

Dr. Gudaitis notes that, under the Soviet occupation, the Evangelical Lutheran Synod bowed to the Soviet decrees and formed a Consistory in 1955. There were at the time 26 Lutheran parishes — 21 Lithuanian and five Latvian — with "more than 25,000 communicants," served by 22 ministers and deacons. The Evangelical Reformed Church at a Synod

[165] *Lithuanian Bulletin*, VII, Nos. 1-3, Jan.-March 1949, based on Dr. K. Gečys, *Katalikiškoji Lietuva, op. cit.;* Dr. J. Savasis, *The War Against God in Lithuania*, New York, 1966, p. 13.

in 1957 likewise elected a Consistory for its five parishes ministered by one Superintendent and two ministers.[166]

These figures indicate that 70,000 Lutherans of three nationalities in 55 parishes ministered by 51 clergymen in 1940 — dropped to "more than 25,000" in 26 parishes of two nationalities ministered by 22 ministers and deacons. The number of Calvinists was reduced from 15,000 communicants of 13 congregations ministered by 14 clergymen in 1940 to five parishes ministered by three clergymen in 1957. The losses are explained to some extent by the "repatriation" of some 40,000 to 55,000 persons to Germany as alleged *Volksdeutsche* — Protestants were deemed "Germans" under a Nazi-Soviet arrangement, and non-Protestant spouses were allowed to accompany them—and by escapes westward before the Soviet re-occupation in 1944. Lithuanian Evangelicals of both denominations maintain a number of viable congregations in the United States, Canada and Germany, administered by their respective elected ecclesiastic Synods. Both denominations maintain close contacts and publish books and magazines. Most of the students in the Lithuanian "16th of February" High School in Germany are Evangelicals. The school has a Catholic and an Evangelical chaplain.

Dr. Savasis depicts the oppression of Lithuanian Protestants — the conversion of churches into warehouses, clubs, museums, stables, the desecration of historic cemeteries by conversion to playgrounds, and the billeting of troops in churches. According to him, only ten Evangelical ministers were left and religious services are conducted by laymen, especially in the Klaipėda area where lay preachers had been known. No church was made available to Lutherans in Klaipėda, and "the service was conducted by preacher Bläsner in private homes." Clandestine preachers are full-time kolkhoz farmers. "During the Stalin era, Protestant clergymen in Lithuania were permitted to teach catechism to the children and to prepare them for Confirmation. Since then, however, these privileges had been abrogated, and any attempt 'to spread superstition and to inflict harm on the child's conscience,' as in the case of Catholics, is punishable by law." The 80-year-old minister of the Reformed Church, Adomas Šernas, was forced by moral terrorism to renounce his faith and clerical duties — a few months before his death in 1964.

166 Kristupas Gudaitis, "Evangelikų Bažnyčios Lietuvoje," *Liet. Enciklopedija* XV (166-179), pp. 177-9.

Jehovah's Witnesses

Small secret communities of Baptists and Jehovah's Witnesses sprang up — and membership in these denominations, not registered with the government is considered to be a crime. The oppressed readily sympathize with denunciations of the Communist system as "the work of the devil". The refusal of Jehovah's Witnesses to send children to atheistic schools or to serve in the armed forces is not attractive to the authorities which "find it difficult to put an end to these religious groups, for new adherents are constantly arriving from Russia." A number of Jehovah's Witnesses were tried in open courts and received sentences up to five years in prison. Radio Vilnius in 1962 called them "bandits, traitors, participants in anti-State activity, and serpents in the guise of doves." The broadcast claimed that this sect appeared in Lithuania in 1959 and was propagated by a former "bandit," viz., patriotic guerrilla, and his followers were other "bandits" serving "the loss of freedom" for 10 to 25 years. When they were amnestied, "they joined in a sect which is harmful to their mind and body." A female graduate of medicine was sentenced to four years in prison for inducing a hospital worker, a nurse and a patient, to join the sect. She, Irena Micpovilaitis, could not be persuaded, "not even by the Party and youth organization chiefs, factory heads, or even her sister" and she was convicted for inflicting a "crippling injury on the youth." [167]

In April, 1973, *Sovietskava Litva* reported a month-long trial of nine Jehovah's Witnesses in Klaipėda, sentenced to two to five years of "loss of freedom." Mrs. Kazimiera Volskienė was accused of enrolling "all her children" in the sect. I. Susnys was charged with "annoying methods" in proselytizing. A. Arajus was charged with disseminating Jehovah's "underground publications" in Lithuania, Latvia and the Kaliningrad Oblast (East Prussia). One witness against them was a former sectarian of ten years' standing whose "eyes were finally opened that the activity of Jehovah's sect is very dangerous and of an anti-social character." The Russian newspaper noted that the trial proved "that the preachers of Jehovah's creed forced the believers to renounce civic activities and to ignore Soviet laws by intimidating them with God's punishment."

[167] Dr. Savasis, *op. cit.*, 111-116.

The Jewish Minority

The largest national minority of independent Lithuania — the Jews — had their own denominational establishments, newspapers, publishing houses, theaters, ethnic schools in Hebrew and Yiddish, and famed rabbinical schools. There was a Ministry for Jewish Affairs for a few years, headed by a Jew. They were active in municipal and national political activities, and had ramified networks of boy and girl scouts and athletic youth organizations. They played a great role in the economic and commercial growth of the country, in musical and artistic life, in the medical and other professions.

The Jewish minority is presently nearly extinct in consequence of the Nazi extermination practices, flights to Russia, emigration of the survivors of the slave labor camps in Germany, postwar repatriation to Poland, and direct or indirect emigration to Israel. Only some 25,000 Jews remain in Lithuania, and not all of them are natives.

Jews had predominated in the underground CPL 1920-1940: only 616 were ethnic Lithuanians in a membership of 1,741 in 1940. Relations of the LSDP (Lithuanian Social Democratic Party) with the Jewish Bund had been excellent before and during the revolution of 1905, and thereafter Lithuanians and Jews of all factions formed a bloc in the graduated elections to the Russian Imperial Duma. In 1940, however, the Jews had antagonized the population by greeting the Soviet occupation armies and by their prominence in Soviet "security" organs preparing the mass deportations of the "hostile and socially alien" or "anti-Soviet minded elements." Consequently, some reprisals were unavoidable at the height of the insurrection in 1941. During the Nazi occupation, however, Lithuanian churchmen, statesmen, administration personnel, and rank and file farmers and workers were horrified at the Nazi measures. Protests were raised and Lithuanians facilitated escapes from the ghettoes and sheltered many escapees, especially children.

Genrikas Zimanas, a former teacher of the Lithuanian language and co-author of a Lithuanian grammar in Russian, became a Soviet "guerrilla" leader — one of many parachuted into Lithuania. He is said to have been responsible for the unprecedented burning alive of 119 villagers — including 49 children ranging from babes in arms to under 15 years — of Pirčiupiai by the Germans, in reprisal for a firing by the Zimanas unit on a German military car. Zimanas became a member of the CPL Central Committee, a Deputy to the Supreme Soviet, editor-in-chief of the principal Party daily *Tiesa* and later of the ideological monthly *Komunistas/Kommunist.* English-speaking Zimanas visited the United States and in his talks disclaimed to American correspondents, and in his letters in the American press, any Jewish "bias" or "prejudice" because of his origin. In the past two decades he was the only CPL official expanding on the forthcoming assimilation of national cultures and literature into a single "Soviet" culture and (guess what) language. Unlike Zimanas, some Jews became prominent Lithuanian writers — and some of them were forced to seek emigration to Israel because of their "Lithuanian bias." At least one of the latter is still contributing to a Catholic Lithuanian daily in Chicago and is favorably appraised by the critics of *belles lettres.*

The Academic Committee on Soviet Jewry in New York on October 28, 1968, released a letter — in the original Lithuanian and in an English translation done in Vilnius — addressed to CPL First Secretary Sniečkus by 26 Jewish Lithuanian intellectuals of Vilnius. They noted that "the anti-Israel propaganda by the Soviet press is not intended for internal consumption," yet cartoons in the central press "have revived anti-Semitic passions in a certain part of the Lithuanian (and not only Lithuanian) people." The signers cited instances of discrimination against Jewish students, scientists and communists. "Ten per cent of the inhabitants of Vilnius are Jews," yet none were elected to important Party posts, judgeships, or trade union leadership. "In fact, only a handful of meritorious Jewish revolutionaries of the older generation are still merely tolerated in higher positions."

The letter continues: "We know that the Jewish cultural institutions in Lithuania were destroyed not at the initiative of the Central Committee of the Lithuanian Communist Party. . . . Yet none of us have forgotten the summary punishment of Ceserkas -- violinist, veteran Communist underground fighter, veteran of the Fatherland War -- who had dared (as the Lithuanian clandestine teachers had done in 1863-1905, when the press was prohibited in Lithuania) to teach a group of young Jews the alphabet of their native tongue. He was dismissed from the Party and thrown out from everywhere.

"As for the protection of Jewish cultural monuments, it must be stated that not a single synagogue structure that survived the Occupation has been declared an architectural monument under state protection. Moreover, one of the most outstanding architectural monuments of 16th century Lithuania, the underground synagogue of the Gaon of Vilna . . . was deliberately destroyed and desecrated during the doctors' trial in Moscow in 1952.

"Local authorities, with the obvious connivance or even silent consent from above, are destroying Jewish cemeteries. . . . Tombstones are used as building materials even for the construction of public buildings. The Jewish cemeteries of Sovietsk (formerly Tilsit) or Cherniavski (formerly Insterburg) in East Prussia remained untouched through all the thirteen years of Hitler rule. Only now have they been completely destroyed, and not a trace remains. Quite recently, the Jewish cemetery in Jonava was destroyed without warning (even the foreign radio commented on that). Pink marble from the old Jewish cemetery of Vilnius was used for the pedestal of the Pushkin monument, erected at the foot of the Gediminas Hill in Vilnius. This act of vandalism insults not only the Jews but everyone who respects Pushkin's genius.

"We do not wish to overstate the case. By no means. We know that the situation of the Jews is considerably better in Lithuania than in other parts of the USSR. . . . During the entire postwar period in Lithuania there was only one bloody pogrom, in Plungė in 1958. . . .

"We highly value the Lithuanian Communist Party, the traditional internationalism of its Central Committee, and the national tolerance of the Lithuanian people. Nevertheless, as the chairman of the state security committee, Petkevičius, stated at the plenum of the Lithuanian Communist Party's Central Committee — emigrational tendencies are increasing among the Jewish inhabitants. It is known that if the borders would be opened for emigration today, some eighty per cent of the entire Jewish populace would leave Soviet Lithuania and depart for Israel . . . despite the fact that almost no one among the Lithuanian Jews knows Hebrew any more or observes religious traditions, despite the fact that their present qualifications (most economically active people are employed on service occupations) would not make it easy for them to become integrated into Israel's economy.

"We are confronted with a paradox here. We are not wanted here, we are being completely oppressed, forcibly denationalized, and even publicly insulted in the press — while at the same time we are forcibly kept here. As the Lithuanian proverb goes, 'He beats and he screams at the same time.'

"We are not speaking to you about the noble Communist ideals, about the equality of men and nations, about proletarian internationalism. All these slogans have been thrown into the dust-heap of demagogy long ago. They have been replaced now by one slogan: 'Love for the great Russian people, and what is left from that "love" let us divide up among ourselves.' The authors of this document are appealing only to you, and your colleagues', universal, human, democratic convictions. Do all in your power to put down the menacingly rising wave of anti-Semitism. It is not too late yet. . . .

"The Party has taught us to be watchful, and we have to be watchful now as we write to the Central Committee of the Lithuanian Communist Party. What a painful irony.

Vilnius, February 15, 1968."

This letter was broadcast by the Voice of America back to Lithuania, and in several other languages, and was reprinted in full in the Lithuanian American press. A former Soviet information media editor now in Israel—saved from the ghetto by Lithuanians and raised on a Lithuanian farm — called on the VOA Lithuanian staff in person to tell of the great impression the broadcast had made on him (he was not one of the authors but was quite certain regarding the identity of some) and on his Lithuanian friends. Letters were also received from young Israelis, recent immigrants from Lithuania. The centuries-old Lithuanian Jewish institutions of learning are now honored by names conferred on institutions in Israel and in the United States — not in Vilnius, the former celebrated "Lithuanian Jerusalem," nor in Kaunas or Telšiai, the former sites of the famous Hebrew institutions presently deprived of all institutions, schools, newspapers, theaters, synagogues and books in Hebrew or Yiddish — by the "proletarian internationalists" of the Soviet Russian colonial empire.

The Roman Catholics

THE FIRST OCCUPATION

The greatest martyrdom at the hands of the Soviet occupational authorities was — and is being — suffered by the Roman Catholics of Lithuania, in the words of Pope Pius XII, "the most loyal daughter of Rome in the North of Europe."

The earliest persecution and the NKVD/NKGB attempts to subvert the Church are described by a knowledgeable witness, using the pen-name of A. Trakiškis, in a wartime publication: *The Situation of the Church and Religious Practices in Occupied Lithuania*, New York, May 1944. It was reproduced, with additional data, in the Kersten Committee Hearings Reports. Supplemental data were reported in the *Lithuanian Bulletin* (V, Nos. 1-3, Jan.-March 1949). The postwar martyrdom through 1963 is recapitulated by "Dr. J. Savasis" in *The War Against*

God in Lithuania, New York 1966.

Lithuania was the first Catholic country occupied by Soviet Russia. Unlike Poland and other countries converted into "people's democracies" allowed to exercise their nominal sovereignty and considerable freedom of action in internal affairs, Lithuania after seven weeks of a "people's democracy" status was incorporated into the USSR — 23 years after the Bolshevik counter-revolution of November, 1917, had overthrown the budding Russian democratic revolution.

The Russian Orthodox Church had been dominated by the Tsars since the 17th century and it had never acquired a missionary avocation or zeal. It may have been ostracized by some powers in government and intellectual circles, yet it had made indelible imprint on the character and culture of the Russian masses. The passive Russian religious tradition is still flickering among the masses, and occasionally it bursts into flame among the intellectuals who love their people and their people's culture — Boris Pasternak, Alexander Solzhenitsyn, and others. Churchmen of a traditionally subservient church had suffered persecution and physical extinction, yet ultimately Stalin found it useful to preserve the Moscow Patriarchate and to utilize the "religious superstitions" of the masses in a "Patriotic War" against his former partners in Berlin. A *modus vivendi* was established — and continued into postwar years when churchmen were engaged to attend "Fight against War" and "Defenders of Peace" congresses sponsored by the Kremlin in a cold war to combat American influence and policies abroad.

When the Soviet police machine had taken charge of Lithuania in 1940, the Soviet-bred Russian security men, just fresh from the bloodbath of Stalin's purges and "the liberation of Western Ukraine and Western Belorussia," needed enlightenment regarding this strange country with its rampant "superstitions." They were cautioned in kindergarten terms in the secret orders regarding their observance of the All Souls Day on November 2nd, when masses of people visit their deceased loved ones in the evening and light candles on their graves, and regarding the midnight and dawn masses on days like "the so-called Christmas." One may imagine the trepidation felt by these superstitious brutal watchdogs of the invader observing crowds of people, families with their children, the intellectuals, the poor and the well dressed, flocking into cemeteries and massing into churches that do not look like the Russian tserkvas, to pray and sing and walk in solemn processions. . . . They had been already disturbed by all they had been seeing in this supposedly oppressed and famished country where few people understood "the language of Lenin," where small stores in whatever towns they had been stationed had full shelves and no queues of people, and people were not dressed here in the shapeless, closed-collar attire of the "Soviet people."

Their chiefs had known better. Yet they had been accustomed to having their orders obeyed. It took them nearly a year to prepare rosters of the "hostile and socially alien elements," obviously with the assistance of native Communists and a network of conscripted informers who were to inform on each other out of fear of their own destruction. No pleading with the populace was deemed necessary — they relied on fear, violence, the force of arms, beatings and shootings. State Security Commissar Gladkov boasted to a prominent professor interceding for his son: "We had laid our penes over your independence!"

Chaplains of all faiths were removed from all public institutions, including hospitals and prisons. All publishing houses were seized and "dangerous" religious and non-Communist books were reduced to ashes or made into pulp. All persons formerly active in public life were indiscriminately arrested and violated. All the while — daily, five-day, and weekly *svodkas* were being carefully compiled, until thousands of troops, vans and railway freight cars were brought in to execute Merkulov's orders.

The first phase of this "operation" of mass deportations was violently interrupted by the outraged Lithuanians desperately taking up arms to defend their families, and by the unexpected attack of the Nazi armies. The panicked NKVD/NKGB, and some Soviet Army units, reverted to senseless massacres of thousands of detainees and prisoners — of masses of farmers delinquent in grain deliveries detained at Pravieniškis, high school youths in the Rainiai grove near Telšiai, medical personnel of the Panevėžys hospital, and many other places. The greatest massacre of tens of thousands of people of many nationalities had taken place along the highway from the prison of Minsk toward Cherveń, the former Igumen . . . not because of any revolt or an imminent approach of the Germans, but simply to be rid of prisoners rather than evacuate them from a bombed city . . . a child unable to keep up with his exhausted mother in the column of prisoners . . . the mother is shot, the screaming child is seized by the neck, shot in the head and dumped on his mother's body . . . stragglers indiscriminately bayoneted and shot . . . finally machine-gun crossfire. . . . Those with strong nerves may read the testimony of several survivors — — Canon Petraitis, Colonel Tumas —— in the Kersten Committee Hearings in Chicago, and the memoirs of Colonel Petruitis. The Cherveń affair was the second largest massacre perpetrated by the NKVD/NKGB — after the Katyń massacre of thousands of Polish officers and non-coms, prisoners of war . . . many of them bearing Lithuanian first and family names.

A number of priests, some in their liturgical vestments, were undescribably tortured and executed by the retreating Russians in June, 1941.

THE "LIBERATORS" RETURN

Mikhail Suslov of the Kremlin Politburo arrived with the Soviet armies in the wake of the retreating Germans — to reimpose the rule of a thousand or two self-appointed "leaders" over a three-million strong nation. It took the Russians nearly a decade to overcome the Lithuanian armed resistance, and it cost heavy casualties on both sides and hundreds of thousands of civilian deportees to Siberia and the Arctic. A great many innocent people, including the clergy, were tortured, killed or exiled for alleged suspected aid to "political bandits." When bishops refused to publish appeals to patriotic guerrillas to surrender — Bishop Vincentas Borisevičius of Telšiai was arrested in 1946 and condemned to death. His Auxiliary, Bishop Pranas Ramanauskas, was exiled to Siberia, along with Bishop Teofilius Matulionis of Kaišiadorys and Archbishop Mečislovas Reinys of Vilnius. In 1947 Lithuania was left with but one bishop, Monsignor Kazimieras Paltarokas of Panevėžys, who then settled in Vilnius. (He died in 1958). Theological seminaries were closed, except the one in Kaunas, whose student body was at once restricted to 150, and annual admissions were progressively limited to 25, then 10, lately 5. Attempts had been made, as in Russia, to infiltrate the divinity student body. The seminarians are frequently searched, many professors and administrative employees were exiled — there was only one turncoat in the faculty, Jonas Ragauskas.

The torch of the fight for the freedom of religion — the parent human right of all other freedoms — was gradually taken over by the generation matured under the postwar Soviet occupation. Parishioners stood up for their pastors and repeatedly addressed their petitions in behalf of their constitutional rights, and attempted to get a hearing from the Kremlin. After years of petitioning which had brought no relief, only police reprisals, these dedicated laymen, later joined by younger clergymen, braved all the dangers to establish contacts with Western correspondents in Moscow — whose stories they had heard in Voice of America and other broadcasts — and with Russian intellectuals demanding their human rights and publishing their clandestine "Chronicle of the Current Events." The Russian Chronicle, which published also the stories of the events in Lithuania, was silenced by the KGB in 1973, for some time, as new issues appeared in 1974. The *Lietuvos Katalikų Bažnyčios Kronika* (The Chronicle of the Catholic Church of Lithuania) continues to reach the West, with detailed accounts of the barbarous and barbaric persecution and oppression of the Lithuanian people. The Lithuanian American Community, Inc., performed a valuable service by translating and reprinting most of these materials in the form of annual reports: *The Violations of Human Rights in Soviet Occupied Lithuania, A Report for 1971* (in 1972), *A Report for 1972* (in 1973), *A Report for 1973* (in 1974), and *A Report for 1974* (in 1975).

Dr. Savasis notes that after Stalin's demise the religious situation "took a slight turn for the better," when Khrushchev on November 10, 1954, admitted that brutal anti-religious assaults upon priests and the faithful violated people's feelings. The relaxed guidelines reached Lithuania exactly nine months later: on August 10, 1955 *Tiesa* acknowledged that "many collective farmers and workers who, while engaged in productive work and conscientiously performing their citizenship duties, are still influenced by religious beliefs. Our Party teaches us to be more considerate in our dealings with these people." A year later an academician wrote that "religious belief does not necessarily make bad collective farmers, bad workers, or generally inept citizens," even though greater accomplishments might be achieved "if they did not poison their consciousness with religious superstitions." In December 1956 this academician wrote again that arts owe much to religion, that religion in its modernized form is no obstacle to an educated person. "The technical and scientific progress of mankind can clearly be seen, even in countries where religion has a certain legal status, where scientists are religious men. Conversely, art . . . has sunk to a much lower level, even though the 20th century is noticeably more godless." He concluded that "a religious fanatic and his anti-religious opposite are equally stupid." According to Dr. Savasis, this was "the last article written in *defense* of religion, for it was immediately recognized that the subject was being discussed too freely. Under Moscow's new instructions, religion was again to be attacked, scoffed at, ridiculed."

The post-Stalin amnesties "enabled about 35,000 of about 300,000 deportees to return to Lithuania," others were forced to remain in Russia. About 130 priests returned, "a few remaining voluntarily with the exiles to minister to their spiritual needs." Bishop Matulionis and Ramanauskas returned but were not allowed "to administer their dioceses or communicate with their clergy or the laity," until both died in their restricted areas of residence — Ramanauskas in 1959, Matulionis in 1963. Returnees were never rehabilitated completely.

Two bishops — Julijonas Steponavičius and Petras Maželis — were appointed by Rome and consecrated in 1955, yet within three years Bishop Steponavičius was restricted to a rural town of Žagarė and not permitted by the regime to perform his episcopal duties. Bishop Vincentas Slatkevičius, consecrated in 1957, was also restricted to a rural residence and not permitted to assume episcopal duties. In 1965 Monsignor Juozas Labukas-Matulaitis was consecrated in Rome to head the Archdiocese of Kaunas and the diocese of Vilkaviškis as Apostolic Administrator.[168] Bishop Maželis died in 1966 and was succeeded in Telšiai by Bishop Juozapas Pletkus — who died in 1975 at the age of 80.

ANTI-CATHOLIC DRIVE STEPPED UP

The crude and most vulgar assault on Catholicism was renewed after a brief respite, when Party and Komsomol members were found indulging in religious practices. The Church was blocking the elaborate Muscovite design of integrating and assimilating the Lithuanians into a "Soviet" people in spite of the many years' "combat" on all levels of the society, the thousands of mass meetings and lectures from the same manuscripts, the official ridicule of religious "superstitions" in the kindergartens, schools, theatrical productions, cinema, and the ban on the teaching of the catechism and on participation of persons under 18 years of age in liturgical rites. This writer was told by an American exchange scholar that Lithuanian students in Moscow upon being introduced to him blatantly affirmed that they were Communists and atheists. On Christmas Eve he was invited by one student — and found Christmas decorations there, the traditional Christmas Eve meals, and nearly all students singing carols and hymns. There was silence when he recalled their professions of atheism and Communism. Then one spoke up for all: "Yes, but we are Lithuanians."

[168] Dr. Savasis, *The War Against God. . .*, *op. cit.*, 26-31.

For an unaccountable reason, Party oracles still believe in futile "agitation and propaganda" by paid professionals learning their wisdom from the "Agitator's Notebook" published by the Party. As in matters economic and political, so in matters philosophic and cultural, people are inured to listening to hired mouthpieces and they dismiss such "in the line of duty" talks as lies, even though applause is required. The "Near Eastern Bazaar" tactics of a crudest type make no impression on a people aware of their own distinct national identity, history and culture, and of their militant Church's record in the defense of their national and individual rights. Remembering the events they themselves had witnessed and listening to the Party agitators telling them that their country's independence was overthrown by "a revolution of the working masses against the colonial fascist regime" — how can they believe the same people raving against their religion? Billions of rubles are wasted on "scientific enlightenment" by crude hirelings. However, a Russian proverb says: *Pop svoyo, chyort svoyo* — the clergyman says his piece, the devil does his own.

Under the guidelines on "atheistic education of the masses" — the formation of materialistic philosophy must be "the primary concern of all leading organizations and Party committees" and must "reach every stratum of the population and be appropriate to each group's age, level of education, and interests." "Without exception, all graduates of secondary and technical schools and universities must be deeply convinced and active atheists." 779 groups of professors, teachers, physicians, newsmen, television and literary writers were formed by 1960. In 1962 the Society for Dissemination of Political and Scientific Information claimed a membership of 18,000 — including 13,000 farm activists. The medical profession was ordered to propound that "there are many unhygienic religious practices" — like kissing a crucifix, dipping a hand in holy water. A microbiological laboratory made tests in the Kaunas basilica and reported that water was polluted and microorganisms were swarming on crucifixes kissed by people — the cause of angina pectoris, erysipelas, scarlet fever, abscesses, septemia, heart ailments and other diseases. Teams of doctors toured the country. The radio gloated over a surgeon's report in 1963 that "ten years ago 30 to 50 per cent of hospital patients made the sign of the cross before going on the operation table, this practice was now rarely seen" — thus proving the weakness of religion. On the other hand, doctors were reprimanded for their laxity, their poor attendance at atheist seminars, their permitting secret baptisms of infants and tolerating clergymen visiting in hospitals.

Many hopes of the Party were reposed in a former clergyman, seminary professor Jonas Ragauskas. His *Ite Missa Est* was published and translated into a number of languages, distributed in Poland and in other "people's democracies" with Catholic populations. Yet he was totally ineffective at home. At one time, in Šakiai, when Ragauskas walked into the lecture hall to address collective farmers summoned there by the Party, his audience knelt on the floor and sang the hymn, "*Pulkim ant kelių*" — "let us go down on our knees." This hymn was composed some 170 years ago by a popular poet, Reverend Antanas Strazdas (Drozdowski), and is traditionally sung as the priest approaches the altar to begin the Mass — and is also sung in a Polish translation in Polish-language parishes of the Vilnius diocese. The collective farmers of Šakiai explained to the astounded apostate: "Father, we thought you have come to hold services for us." [169]

CONFISCATION AND DESECRATION OF CHURCHES

Churches are "people's property" to be used subject to the Party servants' whims. About one-half of the churches and most of the chapels were closed under various pretexts — for non-payment of punitive taxes or "rents," non-repair (with materials denied), lack of parishioners, need for other public functions, and some churches were taken over as "architectural monuments." Confiscated churches were converted into libraries, clubrooms, dance halls, restaurants, warehouses.

A modern new church structure in the suburbs of Klaipėda, erected with the government's permission and generously supported by refugee clergymen's contributions from abroad, was seized upon its completion in 1960. The pastor, Reverend Liudas Povilonis, and his assistant, Reverend Bronius Burneikis, were then tried for alleged misappropriation of funds, illegal acquisition of construction materials and speculation in foreign exchange. Photostatic copies of personal letters from clerical contributors abroad were provided by the postal service for use in evidence. The two clergymen and several engineers and public officials who had licensed the structure and provided construction materials, were tried in public sessions. The pastor was sentenced to eight years in prison, his assistant to four years, the laymen received lesser sentences. A Jewish woman in a separate trial in Vilnius was found guilty as an

[169] *Ibid.*, 32-51, also 52-82.

alleged intermediary in the transmission of funds from abroad and a ringleader in paying millions of rubles for dollars deposited abroad. She was condemned to death and executed. The parishioners of Klaipėda repeatedly appealed on behalf of their priests and for the preservation of their church, to no avail. When native workers refused to desecrate the church, the church steeple was toppled by Soviet troops and the structure was converted into a dance hall for the Komsomol.

The most glaring example of barbarism was the fate of a national shrine — the cathedral basilica of St. Stanislas of the Vilnius archdiocese, with the relics of St. Casimir, the Patron Saint of Lithuania, and the coffins of several kings and queens in its vaults, the masterpiece of the great architect of the end of the 18th and the early 19th centuries, Liudvikas Stoka-Gucevičius. The monument of Three Crosses dominating the capital city atop a hill across the stream from the cathedral was blown up, the statuary was removed from the frontal rooftop of the cathedral, and the shrine was converted into a gallery of art and a concert hall — for the organ music. The coffin of St. Casimir was removed from the basilica in the center of the city to the church of Sts. Peter and Paul, the famous monument of baroque art by Italian masters. It is reported by tourists that religious services are held in that church, the new cathedral. At other times it is a "state architectural monument" visited by excursions, including Soviet army personnel with their caps on. The infamous Governor General Muravyov, "the Hangman," had not dared to desecrate the Lithuanian Cathedral — visited and admired by Napoleon I, by several tsars of Russia, and later honored by services held there by Nunzio Ratti who became Pope Pius XI, and by the saintly Bishop Jurgis Matulaitis whose canonization is pending. The bones of Vytautas the Great may still be resting somewhere in the thick walls or vaults of the basilica — the sarcophagus of Vytautas had been secreted in 1656 just before the Muscovite invasion, and was never recovered.

The church of St. Casimir, erected by King Sigismundus III Vasa in 1604, with its spire shaped like the grand ducal crown of Lithuania, had been formerly closed by Tsar Nicholas I. Presently the occupational Communist regime converted this church into an "atheist museum" of a very low taste. The seminary church of St. George, erected by the Princes Radivilas in 1506, became a library (atop burial vaults of the monks). The baroque church of St. Michael the Archangel, erected in 1594 by the Princes Sapieha whose relics are still resting in its vaults, was converted into a home furnishing exhibition hall and warehouse.

The desecration of other famous churches is listed in the work of Dr. Savasis.[170] The Madonna Shrine of the Aušros Vartai, or the Gate of Dawn, and the miniature Gothic art gem of St. Anne escaped the desecration.

THE CLERGY – ATTACKED AND DEFENDED

The Roman Catholic clergy is the occupying regime's avowed "Enemy No. 1." The oppression, defamation and persecution of the clergy is illustrated by Dr. Savasis and documented by quotations from Soviet publications and newspapers. Sectional sub-titles in his chapters reflect the actual charges against the clergy: "Priests violate freedom of conscience. Priests cultivate nationalism. Priests violate Soviet cult regulations, Limitations imposed on pastoral work, Priestly charity is unlawful, Keeping records (of sacraments administered) is unlawful, Outside associations are unlawful. Priests destroy public property, Priests 'coerce' the faithful to make donations, Priests pilfer parish funds."[171] Other indictments not indicated in the sub-titles include the alleged parental admonition to children enrolled in the Pioneers and the Komsomol "not to forget the church." Also denunciation of the alleged installation and use of microphones and amplifiers in churches as "illegal"; of choral singing and religious concerts "to lure people" — even though classic religious music is played and sung in the "gallery of art" by foreign organ and piano virtuosos and native luminaries. The clergy is also accused of "new Church" practices of evening masses, the transfer of religious feast days to "state holidays or days of rest," and the liberalization of fasting. In some instances the relatives and the immediate family of priests are compelled to publish "open letters" in newspapers denouncing the priest(s).

Protests by laymen were occasionally printed — with derogatory editorial comments. When individual clergymen tried to write — their letters were not published. We learn from an editorial reply in a teachers' magazine — to an unpublished letter addressed to the daily *Tiesa* — that Reverend Vladas Šlevas "had suggested introducing the study of

[170] Dr. Savasis, *The War Against God, op. cit.*, 82-85. Some scholars claim that the eastern frontier of Lithuania to 1772, the line of baroque art, marked the cultural frontier of Europe. That line receded in 1920 — and since.

[171] *Ibid.*, 86-106.

religion in schools or else withdrawing the course on atheism. Pupils should be allowed to choose between the two subjects." The writer was soon (in February 1960) transferred to another parish. But when Reverend A. Markaitis voiced his indignation, in a letter to the magazine of writers, over the disparaging and erroneous treatment of the subject of the Middle Ages — the magazine's published reply to an unpublished letter was followed by the priest's shipment to a forced labor camp in Mordovia (in December 1960).

It is different with "ignorant" laymen. A farmer semi-weekly published a letter from a group of kolkhoz women asking "why do they write against God if they say He does not exist? Why no respect is shown to priests? Why do they find fault with parents who bring up their children religiously? It seems to us that without the faith in God and in the immortality of the soul, man would resemble a worthless creature, an insignificant insect. . . . We win awards for our work. We feel that religious faith does not impede one's work; on the contrary, it gives life a noble purpose" (May 1963). A 20-year-old girl wrote boldly that propaganda will not destroy her faith. "As a Catholic I attend church dutifully and see quite a few priests, but I have never met any of the type described in the newspapers. . . . I work and I study. . . . I cannot divide my heart into two parts when it all belongs to the Church. Religion is my very heart, and to take away my religion would be to tear my heart out" (December 1960). She merited a meek response by the ex-priest Ragauskas.

Another agitator was baffled by a 74-year-old pastor of Rikantai whose church was attended by "eighth-grade pupils" with their parents. The pastor prepared children for their first communion, and the agitator vented his anger at school authorities and "the public" who failed "to subdue the priest by their moral force." The agitator walked up to the smiling pastor, Reverend Jonas Kozakas, and talked to him in the orchard. Asked how does he manage to get "so many people" to church, he said: "The believers come by themselves. I do not entice them." Doesn't the anti-religious propaganda interfere with him? "No. When there is an anti-religious concert or meeting in the school or at the club, I change the time of the masses. From their gathering they come directly to the church" (June 1963).[172] This writer has read the same reportage in *Tiesa.*

[172] *Ibid.*, 106-110.

PETITIONS BY THE CLERGY

The reasoning and the manner of activity of the present-day Lithuanian Christians may be readily gleaned from the numerous petitions of parishioners, parents and children. Decidedly more comprehensive were the petitions by the clergy of the individual dioceses addressed not to the ecclesiastic or government authorities in Lithuania but to the Kremlin. Especially dignified was the petition signed in August 1969 by 40 priests of the Archdiocese of Vilnius: a "Declaration" to the Chairman of the Council of Ministers of the USSR (Kosygin), with copies to the Premier of Lithuania and the Church authorities.

In the opening paragraph Lenin is cited to the effect that "every person must have full liberty to freely profess any religion (Lenin's Works, vol. 6, Vilnius 1961)." Lenin is again cited in the next paragraph: "Every person must have full freedom not only to profess any religion he wants, but also to publicize it and to change his faith . . . this is a matter of conscience, and let no one dare to interfere in these matters" (Lenin, v. 6, Moscow 1946). Indeed, note the clerical Leninists, Article 143 of the Penal Code provides penalties for interfering with such rights — "but in reality it is not so." Admission to the only seminary is severely restricted and dropouts cannot be replaced. About 30 priests die every year, only 5-6 are ordained — only 3 in 1969, and many priests must serve two parishes. Seminary candidates are chosen by government officials, rather than by the Church authorities.

In January, 1969, the clergy of the Vilkaviškis diocese petitioned the Council of Ministers of the USSR and in February the petitioners contacted the diocesan administrators, to no avail. The government intervened: two priests — Reverend Juozas Zdebskis and Reverend Tamkevičius — were deprived of their occupational licenses and "are not permitted to perform their priestly duties." The petitioners note that while there had been 12 bishops in 1940, presently there were only two bishops allowed to officiate: one born in 1894, the other in 1895, while two other bishops are banished to distant rural parishes and are not allowed to perform their duties. Vilnius "is not allowed to have its bishop, even though smaller religious communities, f.i., the Orthodox, have their bishop" or equivalent religious leaders.

The clergymen of Vilnius cite restrictions on episcopal visitations and confirmations, the ban on soliciting aid of neighboring pastors to hear confessions, the ban on priests' retreats even though professionals in other fields are allowed to hold their conferences. Government officials "give various directives to priests by word of mouth. It happens that these orders contradict one another," and facts are cited. The Catholics are deprived of "the freedom of the press for their religious needs," they cannot make use of the radio, television, cinemas, schools, public lectures. They lack "the most elementary religious textbooks, prayer-books or other religious writings. In spite of the USSR constitutional guarantee of the freedom of conscience, priests and catechists are forbidden to prepare children for First Communion at their parents' request to educate their children in a religious spirit. Children are permitted "to be examined only singly." Reverend J. Fabijanskas was fined for catechizing, Reverend M. Gylys was confined to forced labor along with Reverend J. Zdebskis. An aged catechist, Miss O. Paškevičiūtė, was sent to a forced labor camp where she died of over-exhaustion. Church-going children are ostracized and abused in schools, are not allowed to serve as altar boys, to sing in choirs, to participate in liturgical processions—and the facts of terrorization are cited. Transportation, even by taxis, is denied to attend church rites, and the garden plot was seized from a named young couple married in a church, who were told: "Let the priest give you land." The sick are denied religious sacraments. Church organists and sacristans are denied their pension rights, etc., etc. The petition concludes with a request to "correct this unnatural situation of the Catholic Church in the Lithuanian SSR and see to it that the Lithuanian clergy and the faithful, as all other citizens, be able to exercise the rights stipulated in the Constitution." [173]

On December 21, 1969, Reverend Liudvikas Povilonis, the former pastor of Klaipėda, whose newly erected church was seized and who himself was imprisoned (born in 1910), and Reverend Romualdas Krikščiūnas (born in 1930), were consecrated in Kaunas as bishops — Povilonis as the Auxiliary of Kaunas, Krikščiūnas the Apostolic Administrator of Panevėžys.

On December 24, 1971 — 47 priests of the Archdiocese of Vilnius addressed their second petition — this time to the Secretary of the Central Committee of the CPSU (Brezhnev) and the Chairman of the Council of Ministers of the USSR (Kosygin), with copies to Premier Maniušis of Lithuania and the Plenipotentiary (Justas Rugienis) of the Council for Religious Affairs. Every signer's name is reported in the *Chronicle of the Catholic Church of Lithuania*, and replies are requested to be sent to Reverend B. Laurinavičius in Adutiškis, Reverend K.

[173] *ELTA Information Service*, New York, release No. 2 (138) Feb. 1970, pp. 4-8; extracts in *The Violations of Human Rights in Soviet Occupied Lithuania, A Report for 1971*, Delran, N.J., 1972, pp. 34-35.

Pukėnas in Nemenčinas, or Reverend P. Blažys in Tilžė of the Zarasai raion, or district.

"The majority of the inhabitants of our republic are believers. They could participate much more actively in the public and political life of our nation if conditions were more favorable to them. The Constitution, the Penal Code, and the international conventions theoretically guarantee to the believers rights equal to those of other citizens." In reality — the number of clergy is continually decreasing, not because of the fault of believers, "but because of the administrative obstacles placed by the government." The appeal recites the unusual constriction of the only seminary in Kaunas, the interrogation and terrorization of would-be entrants by officials and at their places of employment, and those studying outside the seminary are not permitted by the government to be ordained or to assume priestly functions, and the facts are cited. It notes than an official pamphlet for foreign consumption by J. Rimaitis, *Religion in Lithuania* (Gintaras, Vilnius 1971) asserts that "The state places no obstacles in the way of training new priests" (p. 21). Other quotations from Rimaitis are factually countered. For over ten years two bishops are not permitted to perform their duties. Priests who had served their sentences "have to wait for years" before the Council for Religious Affairs permits them to resume their priestly occupation. Lenin's decree of January 2, 1918, permits the private tutoring of children in religion, "yet priests and laymen in Lithuania have been sentenced to forced labor merely for carrying out their canonical duties — preparing children for their First Communion on church premises."

The appeal then refers to "international conventions signed by the USSR on November 15, 1961" entailing a guaranteed right of parents to rear their children in their religion, yet "in our country" the State organs do not allow even passive attendance of children at religious services, though their parents require such attendance. Children are forced to fill out various questionnaires "which do not coincide with the freedom of conscience," they are "ridiculed and even punished for church attendance" and are forced to join anti-religious groups. Adult believers likewise "often suffer for their religious beliefs" — are denied jobs, are threatened and fired, citing the case of a secondary school female teacher, Mrs. Ona Brilienė. "Even after the Supreme Court of the Lithuanian SSR decided that she be re-hired (since she was fired merely for attending church), she was not permitted to work in that town even as a floor sweeper." On the whole, "the conduct of the people's courts in deciding the cases of believers is shocking": the judges are acting on secret instructions "and pass sentences for failure to obey them (for example, the cases of Reverend Šeškevičius in Molėtai, Reverend Zdebskis in Kaunas, and Reverend Keina in Varėna)." Children are interrogated in Soviet courts and are forced to be involuntary witnesses, sometimes "to bear witness falsely (for example, in the case of Reverend Keina on December 7, 1971 in the People's Court of Varėna)."

Six requests are made: to allow the Kaunas seminary to function freely and admit "all the candidates acceptable to the Church"; to honor the constitutional guarantees and allow the printing of prayer-books, catechisms, hymnals, the Bible and other religious books; to allow Bishops Steponavičius and Slatkevičius to perform their episcopal duties "and to permit all priests living in our country (including the Ukrainians) freely and publicly to do their work as priests"; to abrogate the "explanatory text of Article 143 of the Penal Code of the Lithuanian SSR which is in conflict with the international convention signed on November 15, 1961, and with the Constitution of the USSR" and is often abused by the people's courts; to void various secret instructions "which touch upon religious life"; and to review the cases of individuals "sentenced for religious reasons and to acquit them." [174]

AN APPEAL THROUGH UNITED NATIONS

Meanwhile the trials of the clergy and abuses of children in schools evoked a wave of protest petitions signed by thousands of outraged parishioners. Dozens of students from Prienai were maltreated and arrested by the police in Kaunas where their pastor, Reverend Juozas Zdebskis, was tried for catechization. These protests were met by threats and ridicule. Finally, petitions were signed in December, 1971, with an addendum dated January, 1972, under "An Appeal of the Lithuanian Catholics" to be submitted to the Kremlin through the official channels of the United Nations. The memorandum to Secretary General Kurt Waldheim notes: "Our appeal was caused by the fact that religious believers in our republic cannot enjoy the rights set out in Article 18 of the Universal Declaration of Human Rights." Reference is made to a number of petitions addressed to the Soviet Government,

[174] *Lietuvos Katalikų Bažnyčios Kronika*, No. 2, 1972, cited also in *The Violations of Human Rights. . . op. cit., A Report for 1972*, pp. 55-58.

including those from Prienai with 2,000 signatures, Santaika with 1,190 signatures, and Girkalnis with 1,344 signatures of parishioners, sent to Moscow in September-December 1971. No reply had been received, except "by increased repressions toward the believers." Therefore, a new petition signed by 17,053 believers, addressed to Brezhnev, is being submitted to Waldheim with a request to "relay said memorandum, signatures included, to the Secretary General of the Communist Party, Mr. Brezhnev."

This action was at least reported worldwide by the press and by the Russian underground *Chronicle of the Current Events.* The appeal recites the barring of bishops from their duties, imprisonment of the clergy for teaching catechism to children upon parental request, compulsory indoctrination of children in atheism, curtailment of the seminary, appointment of pastors by [Communist] State officials, persecution of believer teachers and non-prosecution of violators of the believers' rights, denial of believers' efforts to restore "churches that have been burned down, as for example in Sangrūda, Batakiai, Gaurė. More instances could be cited."

The Soviet Government is asked "to grant us the freedom of conscience, which had been guaranteed by the Constitution of the U.S.S.R., but which has not been put into practice heretofore. What we want is not pretty words in the press and on the radio but serious governmental efforts that would help us, Catholics, to feel as citizens of the Soviet Union with equal rights."

The January 1972 addendum notes that 17,053 signatures are attached, only "an insignificant portion of religious believers in Lithuania, since organs of the militia and of the KGB have used all kinds of means to interrupt the collection of signatures. Several persons active in the collection of signatures were arrested in Kapsukas, Šakiai, Išlaužas, Kapčiamiestis." Brezhnev is cautioned that "If the State organs will continue giving the same kind of treatment to the complaints of the believers, we will feel compelled to turn to international institutions" — the Pope or the U.N. The memorandum notes the "calamity" of social ills — juvenile crime, alcoholism, suicides, divorces and abortions as a consequence of "compulsory atheistic education" and of an "inhuman way of life deprived of God and religion."

"We are addressing ourselves to you as the highest authority of the Party with a request for most serious and responsible consideration of the facts" and "an appropriate decision." [175]

The original appeal with signatures was shown to some foreign correspondents in Moscow, and a *New York Times* correspondent reassured this writer that he was convinced of the genuineness of the petition he had examined in Moscow. There was no public comment by Secretary General Kurt Waldheim of the United Nations. The Polish monthly *Kultura* of Paris suggested that a high Polish Communist official at the United Nations may have blocked action or publicity regarding this appeal of the downtrodden Lithuanian Christians.

THE PARTY AND KGB REACTION

On March 13, 1972, just about the time the petition through United Nations was getting momentary worldwide attention, Fathers Laurinavičius and Žemėnas, signers of the Vilnius clergy appeal of December, 1971, were summoned by Justas Rugienis, Plenipotentiary of the Council for Religious Affairs and a former security police officer. Rugienis shouted and reprimanded them for signing an appeal in behalf of the exiled bishops and of religious literature. Rugienis was visibly unnerved, called Father Žemėnas "Satan" and "an insolent person." He added: "You may want some day to have seminarians established in the Kremlin." On April 4, 1972, a KGB man called on another signer, Reverend Merkys who had been ousted from the seminary by Rugienis in 1959 and was "illegally" ordained in 1960. The KGB man told Merkys that he would be allowed to work in a parish rather than at the Vilnius arboretum, if he would disclose in writing, in detail, who had ordained him, where his first mass was said, where he had delivered sermons, etc.[176]

Having been unable to converse in a reasonable manner with the shouting Plenipotentiary, Reverend Laurinavičius on July 20, 1972, presented a written reply. Citing his own experiences, he pointed out that there is no "separation of Church and State": the Communist State is interfering with all internal matters of the Church, dictates appointments of pastors, demands that the clergy shoo away children

[175] *Lietuvos Katalikų Bažnyčios Kronika,* No. 1, 1972, also printed in *The Violations of Human Rights . . . A Report for 1972, op. cit.,* 59-63.

[176] *Kronika,* No. 2, 1972, pp. 41-42.

and believers. Citing from the published memoirs of the underground Communists, he noted that "before the war," the way Laurinavičius put it, Communists "wrote, petitioned, collected signatures," and the Pioneers do so at present, "but when priests send a petition to Soviet authorities, their action is interpreted as something sinister and anti-Soviet." The clergy petitioned that Ukrainian priests be allowed to perform pastoral duties, "because the believers in the Ukraine are giving us no rest — they ask us to work there." Article 4 of the Penal Code provides that courts alone dispense justice and mete out punishment, yet two Bishops had been exiled without any judicial process.

Reverend Laurinavičius recites his own experiences with building a church in Švenčionėliai— the years of futile efforts to get a construction permit, the demand for a million rubles for the lumber and the denial of transport facilities. Then he himself "managed to transport one ton of cement to the construction site on my bicycle. I worked hard for four years on this construction. With God's blessing and with the help of good people, the work was completed and passed the State inspection. The church committee then compensated me with the leftover construction materials." With these and the cement purchased by himself, he built a dwelling next to the church — after notarizing his last will and testament devising the house "as the dwelling place for priests who will be working" in this parish. While he was building, a security agent tried to induce him to accompany the agent on a visit to the exiled Bishop Steponavičius "to help in clearing up some questions." When he declined, he was ridiculed in a satire magazine. Rugienis had summoned him in 1962 and claimed that the leftover materials belonged to the State, the parish committee "had no right to compensate workers" for building a church — "its sole right is to pay taxes." The local people's court then confiscated the home he had built.

Reverend Laurinavičius continued that his three "statements" to Prosecutor General Rudenko of the USSR were remitted back to Vilnius, and the answer was that there was no basis to protest the verdict. His fourth appeal found Rudenko to be human: he directed his Deputy Kirienko to protest the verdict. Then the Lithuanian Supreme Court ruled in 1965 that construction materials purchased by the church committee were its property and could be donated to anyone: "a gift is not income for work." [Internal Revenue Service of the United States would phrase it: "a gift is not earned income."] In the absence of any evidence to disprove the use of the priest's own funds, the court annulled the confiscation adjudged by a lower people's court.

Then the case went back to the local court where an arbitrary judge accused the priest of having illegally "enlarged the house" and, indeed, after his expulsion from his home, a small room was added in the attic in order to corroborate the judge. The appeal to the Supreme Court failed: the people's judge had no right to allow an appeal. "This comedy was played in the 20th century. . . . What was my crime?. . . . Why was I robbed of the legacy my parents had left me?"

Reverend Laurinavičius corrobated other statements in the clergy's appeal. He described the desecration of cemeteries by vandals, with no interference by agencies of public order and security. Instead, in December 1971, "two militiamen, the district chairman and some workers arrived at the Jakeliai village cemetery and pulled down a shrine that had stood there for centuries . . . loaded the bricks on trucks and took them away to build stables."[177] Just like the experience of Jews cited in their appeal to Sniečkus, quoted by us earlier. . . .

Meanwhile "investigator for extraordinarily important cases" Vilutis from the Prosecutor General's office of the Lithuanian SSR and other investigators went hunting for people who had signed the appeal to the United Nations and for the solicitors of signatures on the petition. Some important Moscow official, Orlov, whose first name is not known, arrived in Vilnius. Plenipotentiary Rugienis summoned the Bishops and Diocesan Administrators to meet with him and Orlov on April 11, 1972, in the Curia Office of the Kaunas archdiocese.

THE PASTORAL LETTER

Nothing is known of what had transpired in the Curia Office in Kaunas on April 11, 1972 — except that a "pastoral letter" bearing that date and ostensibly issued and sealed by "The Bishops and Administrators of the Dioceses of Lithuania," with no signatures or names, was released to be read from the pulpits of all the churches on Sunday, April 30, 1972, "in place of the sermons scheduled for that day."

The KGB-edited nameless pastoral letter notes that the joy of Easter "is tempered by some serious matters poisoning the Church life, dividing the faithful and causing severe problems" for the Church. After quoting the Scriptures, the letter notes that the "faithful are bound to obey their shepherds" as was reaffirmed by the Second Vatican Coun-

[177] *Kronika*, No. 4, 1972. The full text in impromptu English translation — ELTA Information Service, New York, No. 5 (177), July-August 1973, pp. 7-16.

cil. After some more citations, the letter states: "Thus all of us together: the Pope, bishops, priests and the faithful, constitute the Catholic Church. The essential attributes of Our Church were, and still are, order, unity, harmony, confidence in each other and confidence in the Pope, the Supreme Shepherd and the Shepherd of the separated churches. However, because of the particular historical conditions in which the Church presently finds Herself, certain priests and faithful have taken a cursory and perfunctory attitude toward various matters."

There are certain irresponsible activities: the undertaking of "apostolic work" in disregard of the pastor or even in opposition to him; showing "a completely unreasonable dissatisfaction" with transfers of priests; "irresponsible individuals" appearing near or even inside churches are gathering "signatures on sheets with texts, or even without any text, requesting that the pastor be transferred, that a church be not closed, that a certain priest be appointed" or removed. "These signature gatherers later change or add a text, attaching it to the collected signatures. That is fraud. We are much surprised that there are believers who sign things without knowing what they are signing and without thinking about the possible consequences.

"We must remember that the signing of irresponsible documents affects relations between the Church and State and gives rise to misunderstandings. Such things can bring no good to the Church.

"We wish to remind that each one of the faithful, even more so the priest, must feel his responsibility before the Church and God for one's actions.

"In closing, we wish to exhort you with words from the Second Vatican Council: Let us more zealously promote mutual reverence and concordance within the Church. Let there be unity in things essential and love everywhere! (Gaudium et Spes, 92)."

Of course, the clergy realized at once that the circular was not a regular pastoral letter, since the bishops had no authentic information and their allegations regarding signature gathering were not true. Consultations between a few of the priests must have been held. Within a few days "many priests" received a note:

"Dear Reverend: Days of trial have come upon the Catholic Church in Lithuania and the clergy. All priests were obligated to read on April 30 a letter compromising the bishops, priests and the faithful.

"1. On April 11 Rugienis and a government official from Moscow compelled the Ordinaries to release this deplorable letter.

"2. This letter is slanderous, because the 17,000 believers signed not blank sheets, but under a text known to the entire world.

"3. This letter insults and compromises the finest sons and daughters of the Catholic Church of Lithuania who had the courage to sign the memorandum.

"4. This letter compromises the Ordinaries themselves.

"5. Obedience to Bishops binds the priests only within the [canonical] framework of CIC. No one may obligate a priest to voice a slander.

"6. Conscientious priests will not read this letter regardless of sacrifices they may have to suffer.

"Reverend, we appeal to your sacerdotal conscience: being a messenger of Him who called Himself the Truth, do not bow to the lie and compulsion, do not betray your own People and Church for a bowl of pottage."

THE AFTERMATH

Several days before the pastoral letter was to be read, government officials attending a PTA meeting at the secondary school of Kaunas-Panemunė, complained to parents that some people are signing papers without realizing what they were signing. One said: "If you do not believe us — here is your bishops' letter," and he read aloud the pastoral letter not yet announced in churches. Monsignor Krivaitis, administrator of the Vilnius Archdiocese, is said to have summoned his regional deans prior to April 30 and told them that the Ordinaries were making "strenuous efforts" to publish a catechism, the Bible and Missals. He said, "the West is rotten." When he asserted that signatures on the memorandum sent abroad were "obtained fraudulently," one dean asked for specifics. Monsignor Krivaitis was annoyed: "At any rate, these signatures will not help." Inasmuch as Bishop Labukas had likewise summoned deans individually, the impression was left "that none of the bishops and administrators were doing this on their own initiative." The presence of Party and police agents in churches on April 30 indicates their assignment to verify where the pastoral was read and where it was not.[178]

The clergy's bitterness over this pastoral is disclosed in a *Pro Memoria*, dated "Lithuania, the Month of the Blessed Virgin Mary," or

[178] *Kronika*, No. 2, 1972. Extracts from the pastoral and some notations are included in *A Report for 1972*, pp. 63-65.

May, 1972. There is a notation in the upper right corner: "A Must supplement to the pastoral letter of 11 April 1972."

This remarkable document notes that the "nameless pastoral" was sent out only a week or several days before it was to be read, indicating a "deliberate calculation of not allowing priests an opportunity to consult with each other." Two more scriptural quotations are adduced from John 10 — about the Good Shepherd laying down his life for his flock, and about a thief entering the sheepfold. The note asks: "Actually, who is dividing the Church in Lithuania? Is it the 17,000 believers who had signed the memorandum? No. They are not involving themselves in matters of dogma or discipline. Is it a crime to demand catechisms and prayerbooks, that priests be not jailed for teaching the catechism to children, that displaced bishops be allowed to function and that seminaries accept all those wishing to enter?" The dividers are those "who by publishing dubious 'pastoral letters' are aiding the enemies of the Church and God against those Catholics who are fighting for their rights."

The Pro Memoria refutes various assertions of the pastoral and states that the Bishops had not interceded in behalf of the two displaced bishops, or in behalf of the priests jailed for teaching catechism to children upon their parents' request, and other priests fined for allowing children to serve as altar boys or to participate in a procession. Who loves the Church: those who support it with their contributions and go to prisons, or those "who make false reports for consumption abroad through the atheist press and radio, as Monsignor Krivaitis has done recently." Regarding the lack of confidence, the note asks — who are the irresponsibles: "those who defend the Church, or those who sell out the Church?" The lack of trust in the hierarchy had been caused by their "not quite canonical route to their posts," not quite canonically proper statements on radio, in the press "and in pastoral letters." Bishops returning from Rome first report to Rugienis, "while priests have to be content with brief summaries of the Vatican broadcasts or with articles in the atheist press." The recent consecration of two new bishops was not preannounced to the clergy.

The tactics of Plenipotentiary Rugienis is an effort to divide the Church within itself, and the Curia's bending to the authorities by reassigning or transferring priests to accommodate the officials, is deplored. "From what source does the Curia know about those 'irresponsible' individuals who gathered signatures? Where had signatures been collected without a text? What a poor opinion the shepherds have about their flocks. . . . For everyone knows the fact that the media of propaganda, the blackmail and the employment of administrative power by Lithuania's atheists had not misled the believers. This is attested by the memorandum of the 17,000 believers." The Curia had not seen the signatures—how does it know of a "fraud"? If it had known of and seen them, why did the Curia "wait for the initiative of Orlov and Rugienis?" The Bishops are counseled to visit Prienai and talk to those 2,000 signers defending Father Zdebskis: "When the State interrogated them, they did not disown their signatures."

The pastoral is called "a terrible mistake" and the hierarchy should "issue a new pastoral letter (truly pastoral) and ask the faithful for forgiveness." The two exiled bishops "are revered and loved by all the faithful," and the people "have had enough of those Monsignors who spread the 'truth' about Lithuania's Catholic Church by means of the atheist radio and press" and "pastoral" letters of this last type.

Regarding the effect of petitions on "relations between Church and State," the Pro Memoria asks: "What are they talking about here? About cat and mouse relations?" — other facts of oppression are cited at this point. "What more do we have to lose that we had not lost already? A little personal easement and personal freedom. Blessed are those persecuted for justice's sake, for theirs shall be the Kingdom of Heaven."

The Pro Memoria affirms that "We have the right to expect" unity and love "from those who stand at the helm of the Church. Together let us demand at least as much religious liberty as is reported in the Peasant Newspaper or is exported for consumption abroad (see *La Chiesa in Lituania*)." Admonishing not to publish pastorals of a like type, the Pro Memoria notes that on April 30 "two government officials were in attendance in every church." The Curia likewise had requested information regarding the reading of the pastoral in various churches, as well as who either failed to read or "omitted the atheistic poisonous part," probably presaging further arrests.

Plenipotentiary Rugienis was soon replaced by Kazys Tumėnas, a graduate of the propaganda academy in Moscow and versed in social sciences — presumably a person more civilized in his personal behavior.

The KGB was reinforced with experts from Moscow. Though the Prosecutor General's Office had on file samples of writing of every typewriter sold or authorized in the country, new samples of writing of the enclosed text were demanded. Individual searches were conducted by high officials. Nevertheless, in July 1972 the Catholics of the Archdiocese of Vilnius addressed another petition, with over a thousand signatures, to the Central Committee of the CPSU, "as the supreme authority of the USSR." Additional arrests of priests for catechizing children are reported. Parents are being terrorized for permitting their children to sing in choirs and to take part in religious processions. Deaths of the aging priests are outpacing ordinations, yet admission to the seminary is rigidly restricted. "No such restrictions exist in other countries, our neighbors — Poland, Democratic Germany." The CPSU is requested to put an end to the violation of their rights as citizens, "that no one be punished for teaching religion, and that anyone willing to enter should be admitted to the seminary." The address of the Vilnius Curia is given for replying.[179]

This remarkable story of the petitions and a pastoral letter evoking bitter Pro Memoria, discloses that Moscow, through Orlov, Rugienis and the KGB, replayed in minute details the script originated by Muravyov the Hangman 110 years earlier. Muravyov had forced the Consistory of Vilnius (the bishop had been exiled in advance) and the stubborn Bishop Valančius of Samagitia to issue pastorals of a like content. According to Soviet historians, Muravyov "slightly corrected" the Valančius letter, printed the Lithuanian text and distributed it throughout the country. His gendarmes were ordered to read it in public places and to be present in churches to hear the pastoral read. The insurrectionist underground Committee thereafter, published a firm and impassioned appeal denouncing the "weakness" of pastors at the helm of the Church.

After some 18 months of preparations for the "operation," simultaneous raids and searches throughout the country were made on November 19 and 20, 1973, in connection with "the Case No. 345" regarding illegal religious literature and "production of literature slandering the Soviet order." The searches were most thorough and they centered around rectories, churches, homes of religious intellectuals, students and lay employees of parishes. Even the altars were examined minutely for "secret panels." The searches lasted more than ten hours and in some cases were continued the next day. Prewar and postwar religious literature, thousands of prayerbooks, rosaries, other devotionals, a number of typewriters, homemade printing presses, multiplicators, copying machines and cameras were seized, in some cases entire libraries were removed. Copies of the *Kronika* and Xerox copies of the

[179] *Kronika*, No. 3, 1972.

petition through the United Nations, including signatures, were found and seized.

It is too early to assess the full extent and impact of these massive searches, confiscations, interrogations, detentions and arrests. However, issues Nos. 8 to 18 of the *Kronika* came out *after* this mass "operation." The new issues describe the searches and arrests in considerable detail.

Simultaneously — a record number of 12 youths were allowed to enter the seminary in 1973, and — in the opposite direction — dozens of young folklorists were dismissed or arrested — for such "crimes" as visiting Lithuanian "political bandits" while on assignment in Siberia, for ignoring new "Soviet folklore," and for concentrating on genuine folklore.

A Continuing Story

In mid-August, 1972, foreign correspondents reported from Moscow about an article in a Russian-language (the language most of them can read or have it translated) "Lithuanian" daily, *Sovietskaya Litva.* The article warned against underestimating "the danger of religion adapting itself to present-day conditions" and "making it sound as if religious requirements and Communist norms were compatible. All this calls for intensifying the struggle with religious influences on the minds and feelings" of people — but the crudeness of the campaign might backfire. "Irreparable damage could be inflicted by administrative attacks, by any insult to the sentiments of believers. Wrong methods . . . lead to the intensification of religious fanaticism." The Russian daily continued: "One must not forget that the basic mass of believers are honest Soviet toilers. It is no fault of theirs but a misfortune that they turned up captives of religious prejudices. To help them liberate themselves from the influence of religious ideology is possible only by means of persistent, systematic atheist propaganda. Through individual work, one must produce in them new convictions, new feelings." [180]

Of course, this is only a periodic replay of an old record — for foreign consumption. The raucous most primitive propaganda and terrorization of children and parents in schools and places of employment is accompanied by physical assaults on churchgoers and loudspeakers blaring

[180] Reuters in *Washington Post,* Aug. 14, 1972; *New York Times,* Aug. 15, 1972.

dance and "revolutionary" music as soon as services start across the street in the church. The cruel story of abuse and violence is all the same, the persecution never ceases — only dates, places and names are different. Tsarist Russian border troops and police seized from Lithuanians their prayerbooks published in their language and in their alphabet. The "enlightened" grandchildren and great grandchildren of the tsarist oppressors presently are seizing prayerbooks in any language. Backed by the entire might of the Soviet Union, Soviet Communist Party agitators are waging a ceaseless campaign against human nature and cultural-religious-national heritage of a small good neighbor of Russia, a three million people vanquished by arms and treachery, who are resisting the forcible eradication of their identity.

Language, religion and traditional customs are the three basic attributes of a nationality. For the time being, the Lithuanian language is needed by the Party as a useful weapon or tool in depriving people of their religion and customs. Eliminate the traditional religion and customs associated with that native spiritual heritage — and the basic obstacle to Russification would be gone: all will be "Soviet people" professing the same religion of Leninism, adhering to Soviet "international" customs occasionally spiced with relics of local "self-expression," and all speaking the "international language" — the language of Great Lenin.

The Communist religion can stand no competition from a spiritual rival. For this reason millions of books are printed in the language of a conquered people to subvert their reasoning. A native language is conveniently used for a while in replacing traditional customs by rites of "winter holiday" in place of Christmas, the "spring holiday" replacing Easter, the "summer holiday" instead of St. John's Eve. There are Communist temples with rites for name-giving, marriages and funerals. The sacraments of communion and confirmation are replaced by rites of induction into "Pioneers," confirmation into the Komsomol, and ultimately the knighting into the new class of exploiters — the membership in the privileged nobility and self-appointed "leadership of the toiling masses," the Communist Party.

Abandoned by their own aristocracy and intellectuals, the Lithuanian masses had won their previous chapter in the struggle for their human rights in the period of the ban on Lithuanian printing, 1864-1904. The self-same battle is being waged again. The masses are once again abandoned by the elite of Moscow servants — Party functionaries, scientists, actors, luminaries of arts and literature, intellectuals, teachers, newsmen and hired agitators. The Tsarist oppression was not as crude and as cruel as the Soviet barbarism. It never claimed such masses of victims. The toilers owned the land they tilled. The Tsarists never attempted to subvert words like liberty, democracy, homeland or freedom of religion into antitheses of their meaning: they openly glorified the autocracy, caste system, Russian supremacy and the Orthodoxy — the latter a privileged but not exclusive religion. Preaching other faiths and publications, public processions on Corpus Christi Day, religious funerals, First Communion, etc., were legitimate functions.

Today the battlegrounds are families, kindergartens, various schools, institutions of higher learning — even the language and folklore, and history. Pitted against the armed might and wealth of the Soviet empire are humble men and women, law-abiding, hard-working, concerned with their children's future, dearly loving their native soil, traditions and language.

Children of these humble people are given poor conduct grades in schools for going to church. They are interrogated in classrooms about their parents' religious practice — "deviation in superstitions." They are ridiculed and lampooned in classes by teachers, in corridors by cartoons and hoodlums. They are denied admission to universities. Teachers seize from girls' necks chains with crosses or religious medals, the chains but not the medals are restored after protests. Children are barred from funerals whenever a priest is invited. No religious funeral processions are allowed. Churches newly built after years of effort and obstruction are seized as "public property" or "other public needs." Complaints are answered: "You will get nothing back!" Teachers reprimand parents for decorating their homes with holy pictures —as "pictures of Jews." Buses carrying pilgrims are stopped miles away and drivers are called off. Stations of the cross are destroyed. Teachers and librarians are fired for churchgoing or for baptizing children. Private gardens are seized from couples marrying in churches. Uniformed police and Komsomol hoodlums openly assault people around churches and seize their devotionals. All non-official transit and transport is barred from towns visited by bishops and on traditional local feast days. Priests are not allowed to help neighboring parishes to hear confessions, and are interrogated by the police because of giving communion to masses of people flocking from the neighboring Belorussian SSR left without any clergy. The sick and the dying in hospitals, prisons and armed forces are denied sacraments and the last rites. And yet —

Parents at a PTA meeting ejected a teacher who urged them not to "harm" their children by taking them to church services. Pioneer recruits suggested that a new troop be named after St. John, "the best man in the world." Asked by teachers about persons abandoning priesthood, the pupils answered: "They are either stupid or have no character." People eject policemen behaving disrespectfully in churches. A woman told the police: "Christ had suffered for us. We shall do our bit of suffering for Christ." A barefoot priest carried a heavy wooden cross 30 miles to save it from destruction. A kolkhoz woman being exiled for teaching prayers said: "It is a shame to go to prison for a sin, but I am not afraid of imprisonment for teaching 'Our Father'."

Such is the life in a 20th century "Socialist country" ruled by a nation alien by race, language, religion and culture, by a regime which had signed treaties of peace, friendship, nonaggression, the United Nations Charter, which had ratified the Genocide Convention and the Universal Declaration of Human Rights. A Soviet official at the United Nations, a Lithuanian, said that believers are enjoying "all the freedoms and rights in the Soviet Union," but that atheists need protection in certain countries. . . .

The tragic part is that lately the willing and unwilling minions of the oppression and persecution — teachers, kolkhoz officials, uniformed police, investigators, prosecutors, and "scientific approach" anti-religious agitators are predominantly Lithuanians, bossed by Russians.

Romas Kalanta (1953-1972).
Painting by Antanas Rukštelė

Self-immolation by Romas Kalanta.
Painting by Antanas Rukštelė

XXXIX
CPSU DOGMA: CHOICE I— HOMO SOVIETICUS

Soon after the suppression of the East German and Polish unrest and the crushing of the Hungarian freedom revolution by Soviet tanks, the late CPL First Secretary Sniečkus in a moment of frankness confided: "Either we go with the Russian nation . . . or the chances of the annihilation of the Lithuanian nation. There is no third road." [181]

Let us presently examine Sniečkus' own choice — that of association "with the Russian nation," spelled out in the CPSU Program, the gospel of the Leninist dogmas to be treated as seriously as Hitler's *Mein Kampf.*

The First Program adopted by the Bolshevik Party's Second Congress in 1903, called for the overthrow of the Tsar's autocracy and of the bourgeois system, and for installing a "dictatorship of the Proletariat." According to the CP "science," this program had been "carried out in 1917."

The Second Program, proclaimed by the Party's Eighth Congress in 1919, called for "building a Socialism," as interpreted by Lenin. This was deemed implemented by 1960.

The Third Program promulgated during the reign of Khrushchev by the Twenty-Second Party Congress on October 31, 1961, projected the "building of Communism," or a Communist Society.

Part One propounds general dialectics in eight chapters: "Transition from Capitalism to Socialism — the road of human progress." It includes worldwide projects, such as national liberation movements, industrialization, combatting bourgeois and reformist ideologies, and "Peaceful coexistence and struggle for universal peace." ("U.S. imperialism is the chief bulwark of modern colonialism.")

Part Two deals with "The Tasks of the Communist Party of the Soviet Union in Building a Communist Society." It includes Chapter IV: "The Tasks of the Party in the Field of National Relations" inside the Soviet empire. The Russian and Lithuanian texts make a distinctive use of the word "nation" — not in the sense of a state entity but of a people advanced sufficiently to form a political state. The English translation published by the Soviets in London occasionally fails to differentiate and most frequently employs the term "nation," rather than "a people"

[181] *Tiesa*, Feb. 13, 1958, cited also in *A Report for 1972, op. cit.*, p. 11.

or even "nationality." However, such lapses help to understand why student clubs for mingling with Russians and promoting studies of the Russian literature are called "international," rather than what they are: the means of Russification of non-Russian nationalities. Nevertheless, bearing this lapse in mind, let us follow the Moscow-edited English translation from: "Working men of all countries, unite! THE PROGRAMME OF THE COMMUNIST PARTY OF THE SOVIET UNION Adopted by the 22nd Congress of the C.P.S.U. October 31, 1961. Soviet Booklet No. 83, London, December 1961."

The Chapter IV of the dogma enacts:

"Under socialism the nations flourish and their sovereignty grows stronger. The development of nations does not proceed along lines of strengthening national strife, national narrow-mindedness and egoism, as it does under capitalism, but along lines of their association, fraternal mutual assistance and friendship. The appearance of new industrial centres, the prospecting and development of mineral deposits, virgin land development, and the growth of all modes of transport increase the mobility of the population and promote greater intercourse between the peoples of the Soviet Union. People of many nationalities live together and work in harmony in the Soviet republics. The boundaries between the Union republics of the U.S.S.R. are increasingly losing their former significance, since all the nations are equal, their life is based on a common socialist foundation, the material and spiritual needs of every people are satisfied to the same extent, and they are all united in a single family by common vital interests and are advancing together to the common goal — communism. Spiritual features deriving from the new type of social relations are embodying the finest traditions of the peoples of the U.S.S.R. have taken shape and are common to Soviet men and women of different nationalities.

"Full-scale Communist construction constitutes a new stage in the development of national relations in the U.S.S.R. in which the nations will draw still closer together until complete unity is achieved. The building of the material and technical basis of Communism leads to still greater unity of the Soviet peoples. The exchange of material and spiritual values between nations becomes more and more intensive, and the contribution of each republic to the common cause of Communist construction increases. Obliteration of distinctions between classes and the development of Communist social relations make for a greater social homogeneity of nations and contribute to the development of common Communist traits in their culture, morals and way of living, to a further strengthening of their mutual trust and friendship.

"With the victory of Communism in the U.S.S.R., the nations will draw still closer together, their economic and ideological unity will increase and the Communist traits common to their spiritual makeup will develop. However, the obliteration of national distinctions, and especially of language distinctions, is a considerably longer process than the obliteration of class distinctions.

"The Party approaches all questions of national relationship arising in the course of Communist construction from the standpoint of proletarian internationalism and firm pursuance of a Leninist national policy. The Party neither ignores nor over-accentuates national characteristics.

"The Party sets the following tasks in the sphere of national relations:

"(a) to continue the all-round economic and cultural development of all Soviet nations and nationalities, ensuring their increasingly close fraternal cooperation, mutual aid, unity and affinity in all spheres of life, thus achieving the utmost strengthening of the Union of Soviet Socialist Republics; to make full use of, and advance the forms of, national statehood of the peoples of the U.S.S.R.;

"(b) in the economic sphere, it is necessary to continue the line of comprehensive development of the economies of the Soviet republics, effect a rational geographic location of production and a planned working of natural wealth, and promote socialist division of labour among the republics, unifying and combining their economic efforts, and properly balancing the interests of the state as a whole and those of each Soviet republic. The extension of the rights of the Union republics in economic management having produced substantial positive results, such measures may also be carried out in the future with due regard to the fact that the creation of the material and technical basis of Communism will call for still greater interrelations and mutual assistance between the Soviet republics. The closer the intercourse between the nations and the greater the awareness of the countrywide tasks, the more successfully can manifestations of parochialism and national egoism be overcome.[182]

"In order to ensure the successful accomplishment of the tasks of Communist construction and the coordination of economic activities, inter-republican economic organs may be set up in some zones (notably

[182] "Parochialism" in the Lithuanian text "localism," concern for "local," viz., Lithuanian, interests.

for such matters as irrigation, power grids, transport, etc.).

"The Party will continue its policy ensuring the actual equality of all nations and nationalities with full consideration for their interests and devoting special attention to those areas of the country which are in need of more rapid development. Benefits accumulating in the course of Communist construction must be fairly distributed among all nations and nationalities.

"(c) to work for the further all-round development of the socialist cultures of the peoples of the U.S.S.R. The big scale of Communist construction and the new victories of Communist ideology are enriching the cultures of the peoples of the U.S.S.R., which are socialist in content and national in form.[183] There is a growing ideological unity among the nations and nationalities and a greater *rapprochement* of their cultures. The historical experience of socialist nations shows that national forms do not ossify; they change, advance and draw closer together, shedding all outdated traits that contradict the new conditions of life. An international culture common to all the Soviet nations is developing. The cultural treasures of each nation are increasingly augmented by works acquiring an international character.

"Attaching decisive importance to the development of the socialist content of the cultures of the peoples of the U.S.S.R., the Party will promote their further mutual enrichment and rapprochement, the consolidation of their international basis, and thereby the formulation of the future single worldwide culture of Communist society. While supporting the progressive traditions of each people, and making them the property of all Soviet people, the Party will in all ways further new revolutionary traditions of the builders of Communism common to all nations.

"(d) to continue promoting the free development of the languages of the peoples of the U.S.S.R. and the complete freedom for every citizen of the U.S.S.R. to speak, and to bring up and educate his children, in any language, ruling out all privileges, restrictions or compulsions in the use of this or that language. By virtue of the fraternal friendship and mutual trust of peoples, national languages are developing on a basis of equality and mutual enrichment.

"The voluntary study of Russian in addition to the native language is of positive significance, since it facilitates reciprocal exchange of ex-

[183] The chief ideologist Mikhail Suslov, during his inspection trip to Lithuania in November, 1973, added a third condition: "socialist in content, national in form, and international in spirit," viz. Russian.

perience and access of every nation and nationality to the cultural gains of all the other peoples of the U.S.S.R., and to world culture. The Russian language has, in effect, become the common medium of intercourse and cooperation between all the peoples of the U.S.S.R.;

"(e) to pursue consistently as heretofore the principles of internationalism in the field of national relations; to strengthen the friendship of peoples as one of the most important gains of socialism; to conduct a relentless struggle against manifestations and survivals of nationalism and chauvinism of all types, against trends of national narrow-mindedness and exclusiveness, idealisation of the past and the veiling of social contradictions in the history of peoples, and against customs and habits hampering Communist construction. The growing scale of Communist construction calls for the continuous exchange of trained personnel among nations.[184] Manifestations of national aloofness in the education and employment of workers of different nationalities in the Soviet republics are impermissible. The elimination of manifestations of nationalism is in the interests of all nations and nationalities of the U.S.S.R. Every Soviet republic can continue to flourish and strengthen only in the great family of fraternal socialist nations of the U.S.S.R."[185]

This is a clearcut blueprint for the genocide and Russification of all non-Russian peoples. The various phenomena of exploitation and persecution discussed heretofore — fall into a clear pattern in the light of the dogma cited above, the price of "association with the Russian nation."

[184]The word "cadres" used in the Lithuanian and Russian texts indicates labor manpower generally, rather than "trained personnel."

[185]*The Programme. . . . op. cit.*, 75-77; *Tarybų Sąjungos Komunistų Partijos Programa Priimta TSKP XXII suvažiavime*, Vilnius 1962, pp. 90-93, not differing from the advance *Projektas. . .* Vilnius 1961, pp. 92-95, except that the *Programa* was published by State Publishing House for Political and Scientific Literature, and the *Projektas* by Publishing House of Newspapers and Magazines.

Lithuanian guerrillas disarm a Soviet Union tank unit.

Painting by Antanas Rukštelė

XL.
CPSU DOGMA: CHOICE II — ANNIHILATION

Gradual Russification was Sniečkus' own choice as a faithful *apparatchik* of the CPSU. When in February 1958 he had warned of the "chances of the annihilation," he had in mind the facts of life in the immediate vicinity of his bailiwick: (1) the total annihilation of East Prussia; (2) the strenuous forcible cultural genocide of the native Lithuanian population in the areas allocated by Moscow to the Belorussian SSR; and (3) the purge of the Latvian CP and the rapid pace of the Russian colonization of Latvia under the guise of industrialization and urbanization. Of course, he was also fully aware of the dispersal of the Volga Germans, Crimean Tatars and several smaller nationalities of the Caucasus.

At least since the Bronze Age, the entire southern and southeastern Baltic littoral between the Gulf of Riga and the Vistula River, probably as far as the Oder River, had been settled by closely related tribes later generally classified into three main groups: the Prussians in the West, Lithuanians in the center, and Latvians in the North. Long before the advent of the Slavs and Teutons, these kindred tribesmen had the Goths and Finnic tribes as their neighbors. According to linguists, the oldest form of their common language was spoken by the Prussians. A Lithuanian dialect became distinct by the Xth century A.D., and the Latvian dialect broke off from the Lithuanian by the XIIIth century. The Viking raiders had never established their dominion here, even though one trade route to the Byzantium led over the Daugava (Düna-Dvina) River and some Viking armed trading outposts had been established for some time in the area of the Nemunas and the Vistula estuaries. The island of Gothland had been an important mart for peaceful trade with the West.

The Poles, fairly recent newcomers, made a half-hearted attempt to bring Christianity and enslave the main Prussian-Sudavian areas. When these attempts failed and the Prussians retaliated in kind, a Polish Mazur ruler invited the then homeless Teutonic Order, expelled from the Holy Land, to settle on the Prussian frontier — much to Poles' own regret later. The Teutonic Knights, succored by the Popes, the Holy Roman Empire and hosts of penitent sinners from all over Europe, engaged in crusading raids against the "heathens." The Knights rapidly expanded their conquests and within fifty years, by 1280, reached the Nemunas (Memel-Niemen) River, as their Livonian brethren Knights tried to push southward from the North. The German conquest, however, was stopped in its tracks by the centrally situated Lithuanians who by that time had formed a powerful empire of their own.

The territory subdued by the Teutons and guarded by a vast system of brick and stone castles, was dubbed "Prussia" — regardless of the linguistic peculiarities of the native subjects. A frontier with Lithuania, by then a Catholic country allied with Poland, was negotiated after the great Lithuanian-Polish victory at Tannenberg (1410), and the line agreed to at the Melno Lake camp in 1422 became a permanent Lithuanian western frontier until 1919.

When the Teutonic Knights themselves abandoned Catholicism they had supposedly been bringing at the tip of their swords, they adopted the name of their conquered subjects: a vassal Duchy of Prussia was formed in 1525 with its capital at Königsberg —named the Royal Mount in honor of King Ottokar II of Bohemia who had been crusading here. The Lutheran faith was to be preached in native tongues. Thus three religious booklets were printed in Prussian, and since 1547 a steady stream of books in Lithuanian began rolling off the presses of Königsberg/Karaliaučius until the XXth century. The area between Memel (Klaipėda in the language of the Lithuanian natives) and close to Königsberg was called "Lithuania" in the official records and maps of Prussia. The County of Gumbinnen/Gumbinė was called Lithuanian County, and the name of "Lithuania Minor" (Klein Litauen) was invented for the area where Lithuanian sermons were preached. Preachers were trained at the University of Königsberg whose first Rector was Abraham Kulvietis (Culvensis) from Lithuania (as was its last Rector — Dr. Georg Gerullis, a famous Lithuanian linguist and a high Nazi Party official). The Brandenburg-Prussian union became the Kingdom of Prussia in 1701, and as the Hohenzollerns acquired German areas the name of Prussia stretched to the Rhine.

The Swedish wars waged by three successive rulers of Lithuania and Poland to recover their Vasa dynasty crown of Sweden caused vast devastation in original Prussia, and the Muscovite Tsar Peter's wars against Sweden brought pestilence and plagues to Lithuania and Prussia. Germans — mainly Saltzburg Protestants, Dutch, Swiss and French Huguenot settlers were brought in to resettle the devastated Lithuanian areas of Prussia. Yet the Lithuanian language survived in most of the parishes and at the University of Königsberg, until the rule of the "Iron Chancellor" Otto von Bismarck of Prussia and later of the German Reich. Then the Germanization drive began in earnest, and the number of natives giving Lithuanian as their mother tongue steadily dwindled. The area colonized in part by Swiss settlers gave birth in the 18th century to Lithuanian lay poetry by the great clergyman-poet Kristijonas Donelaitis, in German called Christian Donalitius, the Lutheran pastor of Tolminkiemis. Prussia was the main base of Lithuanian book and newspaper printing during the 40-year Russian ban on Lithuanian literature in the Latin alphabet (1864-1904).

The northern sector of "Lithuania Minor" was detached from Germany by the Versailles Peace Treaty of 1919 and became an autonomous "Klaipėda/Memel District" of Lithuania. It was seized by Hitler in March, 1939.

After the separation of the Klaipėda/Memel area, Germanization efforts were stepped up south of the Nemunas/Memel River, and manifestations of Lithuanian consciousness were forcibly limited, ostracized and stifled. After the advent of Hitler, Lithuanian institutions in East Prussia were shut down, social gatherings were attacked by Nazi "fighters." Several thousand historic Lithuanian place names were replaced in several decrees by German names — in most cases by translating into a German equivalent, viz., Pilkalnis/Pilkallen into Schlossberg.

In 1939 East Prussia had 2,488,122 inhabitants. During World War II the British and Soviet air raids pulverized Königsberg in 1944 and destroyed its historic landmarks. The Soviet armies invaded in January, 1945. Masses of people fled, perished or were deported to Russia, other survivors sought shelter and food in Lithuania. At the Potsdam Conference the area of East Prussia was split into two "areas of administration" along the Vyžainis-Braunsberg line just South of Königsberg. The southern and western areas were entrusted to Polish administration, the area north of that line was entrusted to Soviet occupation and administration. Stalin had argued that this area was ethnically Lithuanian. Indeed, in Königsberg one could have viewed more Lithuanian names of storekeepers than in Kaunas, except that the owners of these names no longer understood Lithuanian and were German nationalists. The Prussian statistics up to World War I showed roughly 150,000 indicating Lithuanian as their mother tongue, there had been "Lithuanian" regiments of the Prussian royal guard, and an express train named the "Lithuanian."

The Russians did not wait for a peace conference to confirm their claim to northern East Prussia entrusted to Soviet administration at the Potsdam Conference. All the Geneva Conventions, declarations of principles, Four Freedoms, humanitarianism, etc., were ignored by Russians and Poles, while the other "principled" war victors looked the other way. The Russians at once expelled or exiled all the natives. The rubble of Königsberg was renamed Kaliningrad and the Soviet-occupied area — championed by Stalin as ethnically Lithuanian — became Kaliningradskaia Oblast (April 7, 1946) linked with Leningrad. The surviving natives, including 20,000 Prussian refugees in Lithuania, were shipped to East or West Germany. A massive colonization of the area by Russians and Belorussians followed: the Soviet Census of 1970 showed a population of 732,000 in Kaliningradskaia Oblast, Russian in speech, including 23,400 Lithuanians — said to be returnees from hard labor camps of the Arctic. Only Russian schools and institutions are functioning.

The seven centuries of German rule had never completely Germanized the area. The Russians accomplished complete Russification within several years. There is no native population. *All* of the place names received Russian names. Thus Tilžė/Tilsit — the center of Lithuanian cultural and publishing activity — became Sovietsk; Gumbinė/Gumbinnen, the former seat of the Lithuanian County, became Gusev; the battlesite of Rūdava/ Rudau is now Melnikov; Isrutis/Insterburg became Chernyakhovsk; the famous Krantas/Kranz of the narrow land strip is Zelyonogradsk; Ragainė/Ragnit - Neman; Pilkalnis/Pilkallen/Schlossberg became Dobrovolsk; Trakėnai/Trakehnen, the home of the horse breed of that name, became Yasnaia Polyana, probably to insult the memory of Leo Tolstoy. Tolminkiemis/Tolmingkehmen is either Illinskoy or Chistyie Prudy. During the observance of the 250th anniversary of birth of the great Lithuanian poet Donelaitis, the USSR issued a memorial postage stamp in honor of this "Soviet" poet, the Lithuanian Lutheran pastor of Tolminkiemis in Prussia. A large delegation of Lithuanian scientists and Party officials went to Tolminkiemis to open a memorial plaque (with Russian and Lithuanian inscriptions) and told the gaping Russian Soviet people of Chistyie Prudy of "your great poet, your hometown."

In the area entrusted to "Polish Administration," the Poles likewise would not wait for a peace treaty to formalize their compensation for territories "in Eastern Poland" lost to the USSR. All place names were Polonized, natives for the most part were expelled to Germany except those admitting their Polish or "Mazur" origin. The vacated lands were settled by "repatriates" from territories seized by the USSR, including "repatriates" from the Lithuanian SSR. The area was formally incorporated into Poland.

Even though the Soviet CP Program proclaims the right of every citizen to speak any language and to bring up one's children in the language of one's choice — there are *NO* non-Russian schools in Kaliningradskaia Oblast. In fact, in all of the Soviet Union there is *not one* Lithuanian language school outside the Lithuanian SSR, and it is said that Polish language schools exist only in Lithuania.

Regardless of the complete extinction of old Prussia — from the maps, the annihilation of its inhabitants and traditions and original place names — the Soviet propaganda to Lithuanians continues to rave against the "German aggression abetted by Roman Popes, German colonization of Lithuanian areas of Prussia, Germanization," etc. — and about the stubborn Lithuanian resistance to Germanization — "aided by the Great Russian people." In discussing the 40-year "tsarist ban" on Lithuanian literature, it is impossible to avoid mentioning the Lithuanian printing activities in Tilžė and Ragainė, but there are no such towns to be found on maps.[186]

The Soviet Census of 1970 lists some 150,000 Lithuanians outside the Lithuanian SSR. Some 40,000 are listed in the Latvian SSR, yet *none* are shown in the compact Lithuanian areas seized by Stalin in 1939 and incorporated into the Belorussian SSR — unless they are the "other" 52,000 beside the Russians, Belorussians, Poles, Ukrainians and Jews. The story of the genocide in progress is best told by "An Appeal of the Lithuanians in the Belorussian SSR."

The appeal notes that at least 50,000 (up to 250,000) Lithuanians remained in the Western areas of the BSSR with Lithuanian-speaking majorities — Apsas, Gervėčiai, Rodūnė, Nočia, Varanavas, etc. Lithuanian teachers and intellectuals were terrorized into leaving. Those who studied in Lithuanian schools in the Lithuanian SSR — could not return home. The population census showed not a single Lithuanian in the BSSR. "Only recently *Mokslas ir Gyvenimas* (Science and Life) reported the existence of 8,400 Lithuanians in the BSSR and 10,700 in the Ukrainian SSR." The appeal notes that Lithuanian schools, kindergartens, clubs, reading rooms, were tolerated under Polish rule after World War I. "Since 1944, after the return of the Soviet rule, no Lithuanian schools are permitted. All Lithuanian cultural institutions, permitted under Polish rule, were not permitted to re-open. Russian language schools were opened in place of the Lithuanian schools. The

[186] General data — in any standard encyclopedia. The *Encyclopedia Lituanica* contains valuable information under "Lithuania Minor, Königsberg, Donelaitis, Literature," etc.

inhabitants petitioned the authorities to no avail. Petitions with 1,000 signatures were dismissed as 'too insignificant.' Professor Tadas Ivanauskas, who seconded these efforts from Vilnius, was told that the numbers of Lithuanians were 'figments of your own imagination.' People who send their children into neighboring schools within the Lithuanian SSR are penalized," — their private gardens are taken away from them and no animal feed is allotted to them. A kolkhoznik who sent his children to a school in the Lithuanian SSR — was assigned by kolkhoz chairman Lovchenko, a Russian from Smolensk, to a brickworks seven kilometers away: "When you have to travel 7 kms daily to work, you will know where to send your children to school."

During collectivization, Lithuanian farmers were not allowed to join with their fellow nationals. Lithuanians are mandatorily listed as Poles or Belorussians in their passports. The Church was completely eliminated by not allowing replacement of the deceased or aged priests. Performance by visiting Lithuanian ensembles is severely restricted — permits must be secured from several level authorities of both "republics." Children of parents who speak Lithuanian or Belorussian at home, are encouraged to speak Russian. "Already there are children who go to confession in Lithuania and use the medium of Russian." Baptismal and family names — just as place names — are mutilated and deformed in the vital records: Jonas Jočys - Ivan Yoch, Motiejus Balsys - Matvei Bols, etc.

No Lithuanian language newspapers are delivered to anyone in the BSSR — not even to Party officials, and postal authorities refuse to issue money orders for subscriptions in Lithuania. The appeal stresses that people in their own homeland have no rights and are doomed, "just as happened before our very eyes with the Prussian Lithuanians. We are struggling for a life worthy of a human being. We cry: Help us! SOS!" [187]

Furthermore, there are increasingly shameless attempts by Belorussians to claim the very history of Lithuania. An edition of the historic First Lithuanian Statute — in Russian, with a Lithuanian historian listed as an alleged editor — boldly speaks of alleged "Belorussian" lawmaking. A glossary of Lithuanian words found in the original Statute is attached — as a dictionary of "Belorussian" words translated into Russian . . . .

When more "Union" ministries were turned over to "republics," that

[187] *A Report for 1972, op. cit.*, 29-33, contains some extracts.

is, to local administration, the Latvian authorities which had hitherto not known what was being produced across the street from a plant under local control, presently discovered that even though Latvians were producing more goods of the best quality than any other republic — they were being lambasted to produce more and better. When Berklavs and other young Latvian Communists inquired "what's in it for us" in 1959, and as they objected to the development of heavy industry and argued for a Latvian-oriented industrial development — the Latvian CP apparatus was severely purged and the leadership was replaced by Russian-oriented "loyalists" raised in Russia. At the same time Sniečkus warned the CPL against "a one-sided view toward the questions of nationality policy."

Monument for P. Lukšys, the first Lithuanian soldier who died in the Wars for Lithuanian independence, 1919.

XLI.

THE "THIRD ROAD": HUMAN RIGHTS AND SELF-DETERMINATION

Spectacular escapes — and attempts to escape — to freedom in the 1970's, as well as violent and non-violent protests against the continuing enslavement indicate a third road preferred by the new Lithuanian generations.

Radioman Simas Kudirka of the Soviet fishing fleet ship *Sovietskaya Litva* (Soviet Lithuania) moored alongside a U.S. Coast Guard cutter *Vigilant* in the U.S. territorial waters off Gay Head, Martha's Vineyard, Massachusetts, decided to seek asylum in the United States. On November 27, 1970, he jumped on board the USCG ship. The United States was, and is, a signatory of the United Nations Covenant on the Status of Refugees. Kudirka was treated well by guardsmen — but the officers in charge of the area, in Washington, and in the Department of State, reaching to the White House staff, were bored and indifferent bunglers, and the ship's commander was ordered by his superiors to surrender "the Soviet seaman" to the Russians.

A crew of Russian bullies was allowed to board the USCG ship, to beat Kudirka into unconsciousness in plain view of the uniformed and supposedly red-blooded American crewmen, and to drag the tied and pummeled man into the Soviet boat. Kudirka was hurriedly shipped to Lithuania. His knee had been crippled by beatings and for months he lay bedridden in prison. At his trial six months later he spoke warmly of "ordinary Americans" on board the *Vigilant*, but the decisions at Teheran, Yalta and Potsdam allowed enslavement of entire nations and "in the eyes of the American military administration I, as a Lithuanian, was the legal property of Brezhnev, the heir to Stalin, and should be returned to him."

As other incidents, this one too might have gone unnoticed — except for the presence of a ship-owner of Latvian extraction among the negotiating American fishermen — and he told the world. It is enough to say that President Nixon personally voiced his "outrage." Some of the Coast Guard misfits were allowed to retire, new instructions on refugee handling were issued, poor seamen of the *Vigilant* had to suffer derision at the hands of civilians for quite some time, the press in general was outraged and a subcommittee of the House of Representatives under Representative Wayne L. Hays conducted open hearings on the case and filed its report. In addition thereto, a young newsman of Lithuanian extraction took time off his job to write a well-documented book, *The Day of Shame.*

The story kept coming back ever so often in dispatches from various "severe regime" prisons in Russia — and three to four years after the event a strong voice was raised in Kudirka's behalf in Congress by Senators and Representatives who hardly agree on any other matters. This writer, at Congressman Hays' request, had examined Kudirka's papers and notes left behind on the USCG *Vigilant* and was impressed with the seaman's wide-ranging curiosity and his devotion to his family, but he did not realize what a really *great* man this little seaman is. Obviously, at the outset his life was saved by the worldwide publicity and outrage. Kudirka himself did not believe that he would live to stand a formal trial. At his trial he acted and spoke with utter dignity, conviction and effectiveness. Thanks to Voice of America and other radio broadcasts to Lithuania — Kudirka acquired devoted friends in Lithuania who followed every development in his case and reported to the Russian *Chronicle of Current Events* and to Western correspondents in Moscow.

It appears that Kudirka was rushed back from Martha's Vineyard to Lithuania and tried for treason on May 18-19, 1971, by a so-called "Supreme Court of the Lithuanian SSR." Kudirka declined to accept an assigned counsel because the latter "could not defend him truthfully without jeopardizing his own life and position." Kudirka stated flatly: "I do not consider myself guilty since I did not betray my homeland, Lithuania. I do not consider Russia, called the Soviet Union today, as my homeland." He said he had decided to defect because of social and national injustice being done to Lithuania. He minced no words: "I am not a criminal. My decision to go abroad does not contradict the United Nations Declaration of Human Rights or even the Soviet constitution. Therefore, I consider myself completely innocent. However, I know very well that my fate has already been decided by the security organs." And he told of the KGB officials who had come from Moscow to "reeducate" him in prison and urged him to denounce "bourgeois nationalism." But Kudirka told them that he was relinquishing his own personal freedom for the sake of his real homeland Lithuania. "Six months in solitary confinement had given me sufficient time for deep reflection." There had been two prisons in Vilnius under the Germans, seven under the Soviets, "overfilled until 1955." "Now we are destined to die a slower death — assimilation. However we don't want to die" — and he mentioned guerrilla losses and mass deportations. "*The new generation intends to follow the road of their fathers.*"

A death sentence had been threatened to him and "I believe this promise will be fulfilled. I am a devout Catholic. Therefore, if the Supreme Court sentences me to death, I would request it to invite a priest to give me the last rites of the Catholic Church." The presiding justice pretended he could not comprehend "what are you talking about." Kudirka requested them — "Do not persecute my mother, my wife, and my children. I ask you not to harm them."

Before his sentencing, Kudirka told the court: "I have nothing to add to what I have already said, only one wish, more specifically a request both to the Supreme Court and the Government of the Soviet Union: I ask that you grant my homeland, Lithuania, independence." The presiding judge asked the humble sailor how he visualizes an independent Lithuania, and the latter said: "An independent Lithuania, in my opinion, has a sovereign government and is not occupied by any army. The government has a national administration, its own legal system, and a free democratic system of elections. The laws of other countries are not binding on this government, as the laws of Russia are here today. An independent Lithuania would not be dominated by the Russian language as it is today. I would like to see that there be no more trials, such as mine, in Lithuania."

The presiding judge asked him if he implied that "the present court was not democratic and was illegal?" Kudirka shot back: "Of course, inasmuch as the trial is taking place behind carefully screened windows and closed doors, with Russians on guard. In a democratic trial, anyone who wished would be permitted to attend. If I betrayed my homeland, then why are you afraid to show the public a traitor? Let the public itself judge me. Unfortunately, the courtroom is empty. Beside my wife and a few Chekists, I see no one. There are also a few guards, but they don't know the Lithuanian language and don't know what we are arguing about."

The sentence was: ten years at hard labor in a strict regime camp, and confiscation of his personal property. And so the police removed his furniture, a rug, and a radio set from his apartment — worth 700 rubles.

Kudirka was not aware that his relatives did not yield to KGB pressure to sign statements regarding his alleged mental abnormalcy. Doctors of the city of Vilnius, headed by Chief Psychiatrist Gutman, also resisted the KGB pressure.[188] Serving his time in different camps, Kudirka with other prisoners, signed several complaints and appeals for civil and human rights. Jewish, Latvian, Lithuanian, Ukrainian and Russian fellow prisoners used the first opportunity to tell Lithuanians and foreigners of the high esteem the little ex-seaman enjoyed — *and* of his need for additional rations, as the camp administration deprived him of the canteen privileges.

And then — a miracle. His mother happened to be American born — in May, 1974, her U.S. citizenship was formally recognized and a U.S. passport was issued to her. Kudirka himself had a right to derivative U.S. citizenship . . . and, thanks to the intercession by President Nixon, later by President Ford, Kudirka was released and allowed, with his mother, wife, daughter and son, to come to the United States late in 1974.

Just before Kudirka's "leap heard 'round the world," a prominent young linguist, Professor Jonas Kazlauskas disappeared near his apartment in Vilnius on October 7, 1970 — in company of two broad-shouldered types. Six weeks later it was announced that his decomposed body had been dragged from the Neris River, a medical report was prominently published, and the professor, a CPL member, was buried as a notable person — except that Party bigwigs were absent. His scientific accomplishments were evaluated for months.

It appears that Professor Kazlauskas had been invited to lecture at the Pennsylvania State University and he intended to go, but Moscow turned down the invitation without bothering to consult him. He protested vehemently — and then was seen being led away by two burly Russians. It was rumored that Kazlauskas had been taken to a mental hospital near Moscow — and in effect murdered there and then dumped into the Neris. This mysterious event brought home the insecurity of intellectuals and the use of psychiatric confinement to silence dissidents. This belief was reinforced when it became a public secret a few months later that Dr. Gutman and his colleagues in Vilnius had refused to be parties to branding Kudirka insane.

Two Lithuanians — Pranas Brazinskas, 46, and his son, Algirdas, 15, made the first successful mid-air hijacking of a Soviet domestic air-

[188] *Attempted Defection by Lithuanian Seaman Simas Kudirka*, Hearings before the Subcommittee on State Department Organization and Foreign Operations. . . House of Representatives, 91st Congress, 2nd Session, Washington, 1970, and *Report*. Algis Rukšėnas, *The Day of Shame*, David McKay Co., New York, 1973. Trial data in *A Report for 1971*, *op. cit.*, 18-26. Rep. Robert P. Hanrahan, *The Congressional Record*, November 15, 1973.

liner to escape from the Soviet Union on October 15, 1970; they diverted an Aeroflot liner from Soviet Georgia over the Black Sea to Trebizon in Turkey. Both asked for a political asylum. Unfortunately, when the pilot tried to upset the hijackers by diving, a gun went off and a stewardess was killed. The Brazinskas duo were held for trial in Turkey. Moscow dispatched two "student escapees" on a similar route to Turkey — piloted by one of the pilots in the Brazinskas flight. The Turks were not fooled by executioners-in-disguise, and the "refugees" went back to the Soviet Union. Moscow used every imaginable pressure on Turkey to extradite the Brazinskases for an alleged homicide "in Soviet air space," and a permanent legal staff was maintained at Ankara to follow every move in the case, which was repeatedly adjourned to await ever-new "evidence" promised by Moscow. Brazinskases were freed under an amnesty promulgated in 1974 — and the USSR, never much painstaking for legality, appealed the release as not legal; an amnesty is applicable to persons already sentenced and could not apply to persons awaiting trial. Young Brazinskas is now fluent in Turkish, he learned English, and became a budding Lithuanian poet.

A 34-year-old construction engineer Vytautas Simokaitis and his wife Gražina, on November 9, 1970, attempted to divert an Aeroflot liner on the local Vilnius-Palanga run to fly across the Baltic to Sweden. The couple was overpowered and tried "for treason." The engineer was sentenced to death and his wife to three years at hard labor. On an appeal, his sentence was reduced to 15 years at hard labor — thanks to the simultaneous trial of "Leningrad Jews" who had tried to hijack a plane for eventual flight to Israel by way of Sweden: the worldwide publicity helped to commute death sentences.[189]

A number of seamen, including Lithuanians, jumped Soviet ships off Canada, Greece and West Germany. They said the Soviet captains made a big splash over the surrender of Kudirka by the Americans, and other escapees avoided being handled by the Americans.

On Sunday afternoon, around 1 p.m. May 14, 1972, in a small park in front of the State Drama Theater in Kaunas — where the last act of the subjugation had been staged 32 years earlier — a nineteen-year-old Romas Kalanta set himself on fire. This son of CP members told the police who tried to put the flames out: "Do not save me — I am dying for the Freedom of Lithuania." He lived several hours in the hospital where he refused to be interrogated. He kept repeating: "I am perishing

[189] Summaries in *A Report for 1971, op. cit.*, 62-64.

for the Freedom of Lithuania." A mass of flowers buried his coffin in his parents' home. The funeral was pre-announced for 4 p.m. Thursday, May 18. Fearing a demonstration by fellow students, the police ordered a secret burial two hours earlier than pre-announced. This precipitated two days of bloody demonstrations and riots.

On Thursday, May 18, 1972, from early morning people crowded into the theater park and tried to place wreaths on the site of self-immolation. The police, in mufti, were busy taking photographs of demonstrators. A long column of youths tried to march on the Kalanta apartment in the suburbs. Then the news of a secret burial broke. With their arms linked, youths marched from the apartment site to the theater park, shouting: "Freedom, Freedom for Lithuania!" The youths besieged the Party's City Executive Committee across the street from the park. A Party official spoke to them — and was interrupted by screams of a woman being dragged into a police van with her arms twisted behind her back. The massed police charged the crowd, plying their truncheons. The youths turned into the park and stood their ground. At the immolation site — a tall youth climbed on the bench, said that Lithuania was enslaved and must fight her oppressors. A second youth spoke, then a third — with the police taking pictures. Suddenly the police charged, belaboring the youths with their truncheons. The youths did not flee — they turned on the police. Making their way out into the Freedom Boulevard, they formed themselves in orderly columns and marched toward the police headquarters, chanting the slogans of freedom. At the former Garrison Church, now an art gallery, a large detachment of police troops blocked them. One youth climbed on a church column and hoisted the Lithuanian Tricolor — and the crowd sang the long-forbidden National Anthem: "Lithuania, Our Homeland, the Land of Heroes." They were not able to sing to the end, as the troops began seizing the leaders. Again charged by truncheon-wielding police troops, the crowd marched back to the theater park, and dispersed.

Crowds were milling in the park since early morning the next day. The police troops refrained from beating, just insisted that they keep moving. By 4 p.m. the police decided to get the people out of the park, and belabored with their truncheons anyone near the park. Suddenly troop carrier trucks converged on Freedom Boulevard, filled with gas-masked paratroopers armed with automatic weapons and tear-gas grenades. When the soldiers and the police charged, the youths struck back with stones, and the wailing of ambulance sirens soon filled the air. A dead youth lay on the ground until midnight. A 12-year-old boy with blood trickling from his mouth also lay on the ground. An elderly woman struck by the troops was carried unconscious into a store. People urged the police to put her in an ambulance, the police shot back: "Let her croak." The police and troops kept kicking the youths being dragged into the police vans, being especially cruel to the long-haired ones. One girl was dragged by her hair. A few fires flared up — the courthouse, the bank, the Philharmonic Hall and several other buildings were set on fire. A police motorcycle lay burning, shop windows were shattered, a dead policeman with a knife in his chest lay on the Mayakovsky Street. A large number of injured police and troops were in hospitals for treatment — a much larger number of injured people were hiding in their homes, afraid to admit their injuries.

People were still milling around on Sunday, but the police kept arriving at intervals and herding the nearest people into the vans. After a brief interrogation, a great many youths were shipped to Vilnius "for investigation." The less culpable youths were herded into the Police Headquarters yard, roughed up with truncheons and then allowed to go home. Most of the "long hairs," including some girls, were shaved bald by the police.

The Kaunas youth riots were widely reported by foreign correspondents from Moscow — during the Nixon visit there. The "official" view was reported on TV on May 19 by the "mayor" of Kaunas. He said that a judicial-medical panel investigated the suicide of Romas Kalanta, born in 1953. After analyzing the data, including the testimony of the suicide's parents, teachers and friends, the board determined that "Romas Kalanta was mentally ill and committed suicide while in the state of this illness." He added that certain irresponsible adolescents attempted to disturb the peace, and such violators are being brought to "administrative and criminal responsibility."

Hundreds of people were arrested and beaten up. Five months later the authorities announced the conviction of eight "juvenile delinquents," born between 1947 and 1954: a stagehand Vytautas Kaladė, a student Antanas Kačinskas, technology student Rimantas Baužys, a 24-year-old packer Kazys Grinkevičius, student Jonas Prapuolėnaitis, student Juozas Macijauskas, and a printing shop apprentice Virginia Urbonavičiūtė. They were called "hippies" who had allegedly demonstrated shouting "Freedom, freedom for hippies," and they were sentenced to various short-term imprisonments. Nothing was said regarding the hundreds of other youths taken to Vilnius for "investigation."

It had been reported by some Lithuanian sources that the self-immolation had been planned in advance of President Nixon's visit to Moscow to attract his attention to the lot of the victims of "Great Power deals," that lots had been drawn — and Romas Kalanta had drawn the lot, and that youths from Latvia and Estonia had been alerted in advance and had taken part in the Kaunas demonstrations. If President Nixon or Secretary of State Kissinger had noticed the event while drafting with Brezhnev another "Declaration of Principles,"— no public announcement was made.

Self-immolations in South Vietnam had been repeatedly publicized by TASS. The Lithuanians, however, more probably were influenced by the more recent self-immolation of Jan Palach, a Czech youth protesting against the Soviet military invasion of Czechoslovakia — for which thousands of Lithuanian, Latvian and Estonian reservists, with their families left hostages at home, were mobilized. For a while this alien form of protest threatened to become national.

Within a few days after Kalanta's self-immolation, a hospital attendant Stonys, born in 1949, and three of his friends, hoisted a Lithuanian Tricolor in Varėna on May 28, 1972. The friends of Stonys were seized, and the next day Stonys set himself on fire in the town plaza. He died on June 10 in a military hospital. The funeral was closely guarded by the KGB and police.

On June 3, 1972, a 60-year-old worker Andriuškevičius burned himself in Kaunas, in the park in front of the theater where Kalanta had set himself on fire, and for the same reason. Andriuškevičius died the next day in an army hospital. On June 10, 1972, a 62-year-old worker Zaličkauskas tried to burn himself to death in Marijampolė/Kapsukas. He was taken to a military hospital — and nothing further was ever reported regarding him.

In July, 1972, the Western news agencies reported from Moscow the story printed in the Russian underground *Chronicle of Current Events* (No. 26 of July 5) that at the international handball championship games in Vilnius, June 11-18, 1972, Lithuanian students responded noisily to each encounter — cheering every foreign team, whistling when the Soviets were winning, and not standing up for the Soviet National Anthem. The KGB seized many spectators, about 150 medical and other students. Many were released in 15 days, the fate of others is not revealed.[190]

At midnight on May 19, 1973, the anniversary of Kalanta's self-immolation, a group of young men and women carried a 100 kg wooden

[190] *A Report for 1972, op. cit.*, 17-27.

cross to the Hill of Crosses near Meškuičiai. The cross was decorated with symbolic ornaments: a heart pierced by two swords — with a Swastika on one hilt and a pentagonal Red Star on the other. Two students from Šiauliai were arrested by the KGB along with Mečislovas Jurevičius, born in 1927, a former "bandit." Asked about his earlier encounter with "Soviet law" — why was he tried, the latter answered: "For Stalin's errors." The KGB man yelled: "Stop slandering Stalin! You could use a Stalin now." After a gruelling twenty-four-hour interrogation, the investigator let him go and said: "We know that you carried the cross in Kalanta's honor." Sixteen-year-old Virginijus Ivanovas was expelled from the school of music of Šiauliai. Student E. Mištautas was likewise subjected to a long interrogation.[191]

An article in *Tiesa*, "Kieno balsas?" (Whose Voice?) (March 17, 1974), disclosed a trial for "activities incompatible with Soviet laws" of a retired roentgenologist, Dr. Izidorius Rudaitis, who had allegedly received "foreign currency" from an American tourist, Dr. Balys Matulionis, to be used for activities "toward the liberation of Lithuania." His co-defendants were students of the Polytechnical and Medical Institutes of Kaunas — Aloyzas Mackevičius, Vidmantas Povilionis, Antanas Sakalauskas and Šarūnas Žukauskas — all listeners to "foreign broadcasts" and readers of "anti-Soviet literature." They were all accused of reproducing and disseminating anti-Soviet literature, and of stealing four typewriters from a Kaunas high school. The *Tiesa* article affirms that these defendants "have been sentenced" — but the sentences are not disclosed. "This trial is a painful phenomenon in the life of our society, the more so since, with the exception of Rudaitis, the defendants are all young people." [192]

A related article in the *Komjaunimo Tiesa* (Komsomol Truth) of March 30, 1974, warns about the forthcoming release of an economist, graduate of the Vilnius University, Antanas Terleckas. He is said to have listened to "slanderous" foreign broadcasts and "in 1956-57 joined a small band of political renegades formed in Vilnius, headed by a traitor of the Fatherland who had returned from his place of punishment. These adventurers tried to enmesh young people in their provocations. . . .the poisonous seeds of nationalism and anti-Sovietism." *The*

[191] ELTA Information Service, No. 3 (182) May-Fune 1974, 2, 9-11, citing the Catholic *Kronika* No. 9.

[192] *ELTA, supra*, pp. 14-15. These youths were in the list of prisoners handed by Sen. James L. Buckley to the Minister of the Interior Scholokov late in 1974, see: *Congressional Record*, December, 1974, S-22428-22434.

Chronicle of the Catholic Church of Lithuania (No. 9) reveals that Terleckas, employed in a confectionary, was arrested on May 24, 1973, and charged with "misappropriation of state property." Terleckas withstood the torture of interrogations and was then placed in the psychiatric ward of the Lukiškės prison hospital in Vilnius. Finally he was tried on December 19,1973. The only witnesses against him were two confessed thieves who were granted immunity in exchange for their false testimony against the head of the department. "For humanitarian reasons" the judge sentenced Terleckas to one year "loss of freedom" under a severe regime and credited against this sentence his seven months' imprisonment before trial. The judge justified his "humanitarianism" by the defendant's poor health and the tragic situation at home — a gravely ill wife and three young children.[193]

The Lithuanian Tricolor was raised in a number of places the night of February 16, 1974. Leaflets, "Russkies Out of Lithuania!" "Freedom for Lithuania!" were distributed by high school students in Šiauliai. The Tricolor was raised over the schools of Jurbarkas — by Komsomol members.

In the midst of strained tensions at the end of November, 1973, immediately after two days of mass searches, the chief ideologist Suslov brought to Lithuania the "Order of Friendship of Peoples" conferred upon the Lithuanian SSR. Accompanied by his successor in Gauleiter's office, Valery Kharazov, and the ailing First Secretary Sniečkus, Suslov paid a visit to "pacified" Kaunas. During the presentation ceremonies Suslov stressed "the most important decision" of the 24th Congress of the CPSU "to steadfastly continue to strive for the further cohesion of all Soviet people in their common task, the building of Communism," and repeated all the tasks cited by us in an earlier chapter from Part Two, Chapter Four of the Party Program "of international Leninists." Suslov stressed that agreements "with many Western states, including the United States," consolidate "the international legal recognition of the principle of peaceful co-existence" and of "the permanence of the existing frontiers." Praising the "switch toward detente" as benefiting the USSR and "world socialism," Suslov blasted the "reactionary forces" for dragging out "a decayed scarecrow of a Soviet military threat" and the "absurd and foolish attempts to interfere in our affairs" by "adventurist" demands for concessions by the USSR. Then he dissected "imperialism's ideological subversion," etc. — The foreign

[193] *Ibid.*, pp. 4-6, 15-16.

news media interpreted this Conquistador's ravings as "selling detente policy in Lithuania" or "muting Republic's nationalism."

Suslov's successor in the Gauleiter's post in Lithuania, "Second Party Secretary" Valery Kharazov on this occasion gave a long-winded "report" to the Central Committee of the CPL, with First Secretary Sniečkus in the audience. Kharazov called for implementing the CPSU decisions in view of the "still present backwardness" of people influenced by imperialist propaganda and evildoers among the anti-Soviet elements arousing "distrust among citizens of various nationalities," and smearing "the great combat achievement — the indestructible union and fraternal friendship of the peoples of the USSR." Kharazov ordered the same old medicine or love potion: the intensification of atheistic "education" and more aggressive "leadership" in executing the Party's decisions. "Our press media, radio and television must guide themselves more by the central media of our Party — the newspaper *Pravda.* From its pages the primary organizations learn the Party views on labor, principling, new forms and methods of work." He concluded by echoing his master's Suslov words: "Let me voice the conviction that Party organizations, all Communists of the republic shall close their tight ranks around the CPSU Central Committee, shall more strenuously implement the decisions of the XXIV Congress of the Communist Party of the Soviet Union." [194]

Western correspondents in Moscow recalled Suslov's inspection trip and Kharazov's tough "report" — in connection with the demise of Sniečkus in January 1974. Michael Parks of the Baltimore *Sun* surmised that the death of Sniečkus "may have removed a formidable obstacle to a Kremlin-oriented drive to reshape Lithuania's political and economic apparatus of old cronies" of Sniečkus. Moreover, security officials were tracking down the equipment used to produce underground political and religious tracts, and "telephone conversations between Lithuania and other parts of the Soviet Union are carefully monitored." [195]

However, the gradual transmutation of his native country into a Russian-oriented culturally and linguistically "Soviet people" was Sniečkus' own choice as a faithful CPSU apparatchik since 1920. Kharazov became voluble and verbose since Suslov's inspection trip. In place of a young protégé of Sniečkus, a relatively unknown Party hack was named the First Secretary to assist Kharazov — Petras Griškevičius. Since Suslov's visit, and Kharazov's "report," an overall increase

[194] *Tiesa,* Nov. 24, 1973.

[195] *The Sun,* Jan. 24, 1974, A-4.

of Russian authors in the Lithuanian language media of the CPL is noticeable. Yet the suddenly exaggerated "Soviet patriotism" is repulsive to the natives.

The year 1973 most prominently disclosed the bitter, unrelenting Lithuanian struggle for their basic human rights. Some beautiful personalities were unveiled — with no help from all those courageous defenders of human rights anywhere on the globe, with the exception of sacrosanct confines of the Soviet colonial empire. Another great spirit locked in a frail tortured body victimized by Soviet "law and order combatants," surfaced through the medium of the Russian *Chronicle of Current Events*, later complemented by Lithuanian sources: Liudvikas Simutis.

Liudvikas Simutis, born in 1935, was apprehended in 1955 as an underground guerrilla and was sentenced to death, but the Supreme Soviet of the USSR commuted the sentence to 25 years of strict regime labor camps — the equivalent of a death sentence. On July 20, 1970, Simutis appealed to the Presidium of the Supreme Soviet of the USSR to commute the remainder of his sentence because of his failing health and the fact that the armed struggle in which he had participated was over. He explained why he, as thousands of other Lithuanians, had fought against the Soviet regime. Simutis argued that if the Stalinist terror has indeed been condemned and the Soviet system is changed, it was pointless to keep him imprisoned, even though he adheres to his anti-Soviet views: he considers that he, as well as his nation, were victims of Stalinism, and should be freed upon the condemnation of Stalin.

The Prosecutor General's office of the USSR rejected his unrepentant appeal and informed him there was no basis for reconsidering his case.

Simutis again appealed to the Presidium of the Supreme Soviet of the USSR on December 10, 1971.

"I was five years old when they showed me the corpse of my father. One side of his face was swollen blue. The other side was bloody. His eyes were gouged. The skin of his arms and legs was white, peeling from the body, boiled. His tongue was plucked and pulled out with a string. His genitals were crushed — I was told that later. Next to my father lay similarly mangled corpses. The wailing of my mother and of many people I had not known. The damnation of the Bolsheviks. I had never heard that word until then." This was in June, 1941 . . . .

Simutis continued that, five years after World War II, deadly fighting was still going on in his country. The (North) Vietnamese were assisted not only by the Soviets: no one helped the Lithuanians defending their native land. "Almost all the decent people of the world (if it is possible to call them decent after all this) looked on in silence as the Lithuanians were slaughtered by Soviet soldiers."

"I knew that Lithuanians, *our* people, were in the LLKS, while the Soviet soldiers spoke to me in an incomprehensible, alien Russian language. I knew that there was no revolution in Lithuania, that the Red Army had come to our land and without our invitation proceeded to impose its own order, and that this is called occupation. I knew, I certainly knew that it was not the LLKS struggle which led to such a fury, because the LLKS had not existed when the Chekists were boiling my father's arms, crushing his sexual organs.

"I wanted to live, to study, and to play. But what sort of a life is it when the body of a murdered neighbor lies in the street for three days and no one is allowed to bury him? What kind of studying could it be when your school friends, one after another, stop appearing in school — they were carried off with their families to Siberia in nailed-down railroad freight cars. What kind of play is it when adults are wailing?

"I could not stay on the sidelines. I could not. My anti-Soviet struggle was honorable, not egotistic. . . .

"I was captured in 1955 after three years of intense anti-Soviet activity. I was taken while I lay flat on my back in a hospital with a backbone malady, according to the medical prognosis committed to a hospital for three years. I was in a cast, and could not walk. Such circumstances of my capture did not imbue me with respect toward the Chekists, did not encourage me to change my views regarding the Soviet Government. . . .

"I believe in the triumph of justice. This does not mean that I could see nothing positive in the Soviet system. . . . I am only emphasizing that I was not and did not become a criminal; that my tenure in prison did not contribute to the solution of my antagonism toward the Soviet Government. There is no reason to expect that the situation could change in the near future, for the gap between the official line of the Soviet State and the concrete situation here is very deep. I cannot adequately monitor the changes outside, as long as I am securely isolated from them. . . .

"I understand that, having come out with a gun against the Soviet Government, I had to be arrested by the Chekists and kept in prison a certain time. However, I do not understand why am I being starved in prison and why was I degraded in various ways. Besides, at this time —

when the struggle is over, we had been subdued — my continued imprisonment is becoming purposeless. Especially since my health recently deteriorated. I am still fit to work and could earn a living at this time. In the immediate future, under prison conditions, I may become unemployable. Then my liberation would be more bitter than a death in prison." [196]

It is clear from the testimony of great men like Kudirka, Simutis, Kalanta, Zdebskis, Bubnys and other selfless men and women, that the Soviet-reared younger generations of Lithuanians believe in the road to Freedom and Self-determination followed by the preceding generations.

[196] Various publications in Lithuanian, and *A Report for 1972, op. cit.*, 36-39; U.S. Senator James L. Buckley, "Report on Russian Trip," *Congressional Record*, Dec. 19, 1974 (S-22428 - 22434) S-22431, 22434.

XLII.
MANKIND'S RESPONSIBILITY

The kind reader of the preceding pages had a condensed panoramic view of the experiences of the Lithuanian people at the hands of Muscovite Russia.

Reeling under the massive assaults by their Slavic and Teutonic neighbors, the Lithuanians managed in the XIII century to form an unified state of their own. Their unification was helped by the stout resistance of the Prussian and Latvian kinsmen. Small groups of other kinsmen in the Smolensk and the Oka river areas near Moscow were assimilated by the Slavs. However, by the end of the 14th century, when the Lithuanians accepted Roman Christianity, there was still a need to found several Lithuanian Catholic parishes far to the east of Vilnius.

The Lithuanian empire failed to recover Prussia and Livonia yet it blocked the Teutonic *Drang nach Osten.* Maneuvering for space and manpower reserves during more than two centuries of resistance to the Teutonic drive, the Lithuanians had brought under their rule all of present-day Belorussia and most of the Ukraine. However, to the inhabitants of the Ukraine and Belorussia the Lithuanian administration meant a liberation from the heavy Tatar yoke. The Lithuanians followed the rule: "Destroy nothing ancient, impose nothing new." In 1323 King Gediminas had sent letters throughout Germany inviting knights, merchants, artisans and farmers to settle in his country and enjoy self-government. Gediminas told the West that he allowed different religious denominations in his realm — "we all worship one God" *(omnes habemus unum Deum).* Heathen Lithuanians lived alongside their Christian subjects, and in Vilnius there were Catholic and Orthodox churches. Later, all Lithuanians became Catholics. Yet Tatar and Karaitė prisoners of war and refugees were settled in Lithuania Proper and allowed to retain their respective faiths — and the memory of Vytautas the Great was revered among Lithuanian Mohammedan Tatars until World War II. The Tatars were granted the status of nobility, and elite Tatar Cavalry units served loyally as late as in the Insurrection of 1831. Jews, expelled from elsewhere, settled in Lithuania and were warranted religious freedom and the franchise in municipal administration. This religious tolerance, extraordinary for that age, may have inspired the sentiments of Roger Williams, the founder of the Colony of Rhode Island and Providence Plantations.

The rulers of Vilnius retained local princes in the annexed "Russian" areas as vassals, alongside the Lithuanian garrisons. Later, during the Lithuanian Crusade against the Golden Horde, some twenty of these princes perished in the Battle of Vorskla (1399). This enabled Vytautas to replace the princes with his own appointive governors, the Palatines, and thus bring about a more compact unification of his vast state. Jogaila's charter of 1387 limited the political franchise to Lithuanian Catholic noblemen. This caused malcontence among noblemen with Orthodox wives and the few princely converts to Orthodoxy. However, the Orthodox soon gained full equality — "as long as they are of the Christian faith of either rite," and the Orthodox Ruthenes became patriots of Lithuania.

Ultimately, the Grand Duchy of Lithuania evolved into a democracy of noblemen, who elected their ruler, judges, Diet deputies and local officials. In fact the principle of *nemine dissentiente* at the Diets and Dietines degenerated into a *liberum veto*, presently the prerogative of the five permanent members of the United Nations Security Council.

There was no censorship of books and writings — something the Muscovites could not comprehend. In 1654 the Muscovite envoy Pushkin demanded the burning of books allegedly insulting his ruler and the tearing out of pages derogatory to his country. This demand could not be met. In the modern USSR even great authors cannot publish their books or articles, ordinary citizens cannot receive books from abroad, Xerox copies of individual pages of Western encyclopaedias are given to Party members writing dissertations, pages are torn from Soviet encyclopaedias when certain powerful personalities fall into disgrace.

The late Colonel Ignacy Matuszewski, a Warsaw editor and a reserve officer, had managed to save Poland's gold from the Nazi invaders in 1939. However, because of his former association with the post-Piłsudski "regime of Colonels," he was not called to active duty by the wartime Polish Government-in-exile. During the World War II years he wrote in the New York Polish daily, *Nowy Świat* many well-reasoned articles — prefaced with a note, required in wartime, that he is a registered foreign agent, viz., a reserve officer, and that a copy of each article is filed by him with the proper federal bureau. In a number of his articles Matuszewski vigorously championed Lithuania. In one article he posed Cain's words regarding Abel: "Am I my brother's keeper?" Matuszewski told his fellow Poles: Yes, you are! A millennium of history molded different human types with differing world outlooks, in Muscovy — and in Poland and Lithuania, Poland's faithful historic partner. This writer never met Matuszewski — whose Warsaw newspaper had proclaimed in 1938: "Commander, lead us on to Kaunas!" However, Matuszewski's cogent and dispassionate reasoning in wartime induced this writer to translate a number of these articles for the Lithuanian weekly *Amerika* of Brooklyn.

Indeed, during the millennium, traits of character, outlooks and traditions developed differently in Lithuania and Muscovy. Lithuanians love flowers and trees, flower gardens and hand-carved chapel crosses adorned their individual homesteads, while crowded single-street Russian villages were bare of arboreal vegetation. To Lithuanians — the woodpecker is many colored, the world-under-the-sun is even more varicolored. To Russians — the world is either gray, or white. The Lithuanians are attached to their ancestral birthplaces with their orchards, gardens, streams and birds. The Russians aspire to seek a better life, and loot, "beyond the horizon." Russian revolutionary emigrés in the West admired architectural monuments — to be moved to Russia upon the destruction of the decadent Western civilization. The Soviet occupants systematically looted Vilnius before surrendering the city to Lithuania in 1939. They removed even door knobs and electrical fixtures — as later they meticulously dismantled factories in Germany and Manchuria, and then left the machinery and the looted art rust and rot alongside railroad tracks in Russia. Russians sent abroad traditionally study the military science, technology and medicine, not the Western philosophy or political science.

As opera lovers must be aware, the "Iron Curtain" was not a 20th century invention: it had long been in existence along the pre-1772 Lithuanian-Muscovite frontier. In *Boris Godunov*, spectators see an inn on that frontier — one door opening into Muscovy, the other into Lithuania, and hear the Tsar order the hermetic sealing of the frontier: not a hare should run across nor a bird fly over the border. In the modern USSR, entire areas are closed to foreigners. Western books and "decadent art" slides are seized by customs officers. Western books in Academy libraries may be read only by a few privileged Party people. Foreign broadcasts are jammed or otherwise interfered with, viz., by shutting off the power during the broadcast of an undesirable commentary. German repatriates state that, in factories, the Lithuanians openly discuss VOA newscasts. The Russians working alongside them bitterly complain over their condition and blame "the government." Yet, when talk turns to foreign affairs — they profess their utter ignorance: "the

Government knows best." Some people assert that the discontented Russians would rebel only upon hearing that "the enemy" was in a neighboring village — and would then square their personal accounts with the officials, kill animals, burn down public structures and the vegetation, loot the stores.

Russian music, enriched by Ukrainian folklore, is universally liked. Individual Russians are mostly kind and sympathetic people. They had never had a chance to experiment with a democratic order — and they certainly deserve the chance. Their neighbors covet no Russian territories and hope that, under a democratic system, the Russians would learn to value their own human and civic rights — and to respect the rights of their neighbors, and would live at peace with themselves and with their neighbors. For the greatest security of any people lies in the love and respect of their neighbors. Unfortunately, in matters political — even a Solzhenitsyn tends to prefer authoritarian rule, rather than a popular democracy. Russians are charming as performers in arts. Yet armed Russians *en masse* tend to become power-drunk, unbearable, cruel, lustful — as witnessed by millions of Europeans in the final stages of World War II.

Ancient Lithuania, later in an association with Poland, shielded Europe from the Mongol invasion and from Muscovy, and protected Russia from the Teutonic onslaught. The line separating Eastern and Western civilizations ran along the eastern frontier of Lithuania and Poland. Then the "Big Three" — Frederick "the Great" of Prussia, Maria-Theresa "the Great" of Austria, and the German ruler of Russia, Catherine "the Great," opened Europe to Muscovy by dismembering "Poland," that is: the Commonwealth of the Kingdom of Poland and the Grand Duchy of Lithuania. In Lord Acton's words, this was an unprecedented international crime: a sovereign Christian nation was totally extinguished, rather than temporarily occupied.

Gradually Russia mellowed, ruled by autocrats employing "the Mamelukes" — Baltic German barons (and pseudo-Barons) who in certain periods accounted for the majority of Governorships and Generalships, and at the imperial court represented the "Western façade" of Russia. After the revolution of 1905, life became quite bearable in Russia — much to be envied by people living under the post-1917 revolutionaries.

In 1920-1939 the frontier of civilizations ran along the eastern borders of Finland, the Baltic States, Poland, and Romania. During World War II, the "Big Three" — Churchill, Roosevelt and Stalin —

moved the frontier of civilizations to the center of Europe, in violation of all their wartime pledges and professed principles. Of course, membership in the USSR ruled by "international Leninists" is at all times open to willing, or unwilling, West European nations thus far protected by NATO, should they ever drop their vigilance and allow themselves to be seduced by the sweet talk and duplicity of Moscow spokesmen of detente.

Consequently, the East-West line is by no means final in Europe. The Europeans or Americans closing their eyes and shutting their ears to the plaints of the Estonians, Latvians, Lithuanians and others may yet wake up with more "Soviet republics" or "People's democracies" well West of the present line. In 1974 Solzhenitsyn assessed that cultural exchanges might be banned in protest, or indignation, over a sudden conquest of Europe. This great Russian humanitarian and a patriot heard of the American and European reactions to the violations of the Indochina pacts, after so many American and other lives and billions of dollars had been sacrificed there.

Indeed, we must realize that we *are* our "brother's keepers" and must admit no exceptions: we cannot build our happiness, security and well-being in isolation over the graves of Lithuania, Vietnam, Hungary, Korea, etc. The sufferings and the spilling of innocent blood, be it of Jews, Arabs, Latvians, Tibetans, Cambodians, Albanians or others, are international crimes, and the victims of such crimes deserve the sympathy and assistance of all humans. Justice was not served at the Nüremberg Trials, where some Nazi conspirators against peace and humanity were tried and sentenced by judges including the fellow conspirators of the doomed Nazis. The perpetrators of the massacres of Katyń, Cherveń, Vinnitsa, Pravieniškis, Rainiai, etc., etc., sat in judgment over the mass murderers of Auschwitz, Buchenwald, etc. The renaming of *katorga* hard labor prisons for political dissenters — into "corrective labor camps" or "camps with a strict regime," should not blind us, our "brother's keepers," into complacency regarding the fate of thousands upon thousands of innocent people doomed for the teaching of the *Our Father*, for the love of their own nationality, their belief in human rights, and reasoning independently from the "Party."

Immanuel Kant, the great son of Prussian Lithuania, in his introduction (*Nachricht eines Freundes*) to Christian Gottlieb Mielcke's Lithuanian-German and German-Lithuanian Dictionary published in Königsberg in 1800, championed the preservation of the Lithuanian language in schools, churches and community life. Kant wrote that, besides the beauty and the characteristics of this language, the Prussian Lithuanian "more than his neighbors is imbued with a sense of personal dignity," he is accustomed "to speak to his superiors as his peers, he is sincere and loyal." Similarly impressed was the great French geographer, Elisée Reclus, who wrote during the Insurrection of 1863. He noted that the Lithuanians fought in the defense of their land "with the frenzy characteristic of peace-loving races when disturbed," and that they are "refined, intelligent, full of imagination and poetry, strong in the sense of their personal dignity."

These assertions were certainly proved by the Provisional Lithuanian Government's protest to the Nazis in 1941, the patriotic guerrilla war of 1944-1952, by Simas Kudirka and the clergy, and by the account of Liudas Simutis to the Supreme Soviet regarding his motivation in fighting against the occupant. He wrote of the complacency of the West: "Almost all the decent people of the world (if it is possible to call them decent after all this) looked on in silence as the Lithuanians were slaughtered by Soviet soldiers." This is a serious charge by a freedom fighter who had suffered so much "in peacetime." Unfortunately, his opinion is not fanciful. It applies equally to conditions of today, as to those of 1944-1952, or 1955 — the year of his capture in a cast at the hospital.

At the Conference on Security and Cooperation in Europe, convoked at the insistence of the Soviet Union for the sole purpose of legitimizing the frontiers imposed by Soviet conquest, European statesmen tended to look away from the stark reality of Soviet colonialism right in their midst: in Estonia, Latvia and Lithuania. Non-European participants, viz., the United States, seem to be willing to concede the Soviet demand for the sanctity of "the present frontiers" which were never fixed by freely negotiated peace treaties of the nations concerned, or by legitimate self-determination, or by racial affinities or truly founded security grounds.

Washington spokesmen disregard their own professions of the policy of non-recognition of the Soviet annexation of the Baltic States — of the fruit of the Hitler-Stalin conspiracy against peace and humanity for which Ribbentrop was hanged, with Stalin's approval. In answering inquiries from concerned voters and Members of Congress, the selfsame officials who endorse the basic article about the sanctity and inviolability of the "*present* frontiers in Europe," hastily reassure that there is no change in the policy of nonrecognition of the absorption of the Baltic States by the Soviet Union. They note "the basic U.S.

approach to CSCE is to insure that the conference emphasizes substance over atmosphere . . . avoid the implication of formal recognition of the territorial status quo in Europe." They quickly follow up their mis-statement with words about their lofty desire to "increase the flow of communications" across frontiers — a freer movement of ideas and people which should alleviate the lot of Balts. Then they reassure that the United States would *not* sign any commitment *against* the exercise of self-determination — presumably in Kingdom come.

Self-determination was exercised by the Baltic Peoples in 1918-1920. Their sovereignty was recognized by *all* the participants of Conference on Security and Cooperation in Europe — including the Republic of Germany, the parent of the new "federal" Germany and of a "democratic" Germany. The sovereignty of Lithuania, Latvia and Estonia was attested by their membership and creditable performance in the League of Nations — which in 1939 expelled the USSR for its attack on Finland, the host country of the European "Security" conference. Self-determination was re-confirmed, if needed, by the Lithuanian Insurrection of 1941, the guerrilla war of 1944-1952, the protests ever since — and by the mass of political prisoners deported far from Lithuania.

Recognition of the illegal "present frontiers," coupled with an unwillingness to commit the United States *against* the exercise of self-determination in unnamed areas *in the future* (the draft anticipates some frontier changes by "bi-lateral agreements" between the parties concerned) — is *not* a non-recognition of the Soviet "devious processes whereunder the political independence and territorial integrity of . . . Estonia, Latvia and Lithuania were to be deliberately annihilated." It is an illusory and self-deceptive attempt to "cover up" (to use a post-Watergate phrase) the Soviet rapacity and collusion with the Nazis. This would not even silence the Kremlin ravings against "the imperialists" (the U.S.), and the Kremlin pose of championing the "self-determination" and "liberation from colonialism" anywhere — except in the areas seized by the USSR. According to the Kremlin, the Balts in 1940 exercised their self-determination by "restoring the Soviet power" and allegedly "welcoming" the liberating Red Army. As in Dante's hell — one may enter (the USSR), voluntarily or otherwise, but cannot leave.

In connection with the Helsinki-Geneva "security conference," let us recall the oral testimony of the late Secretary of State John Foster Dulles before the Kersten Committee on November 30, 1953. Secretary Dulles stated (the italicizing is ours):

"... we must *be sure that the captive peoples know* that they are not forgotten, that we are not reconciled to their fate, and, above all, that *we are not prepared to seek illusory safety for ourselves by a bargain with their masters which would confirm their captivity.*

"These, Mr. Chairman, I can say to you, are our purposes. We have not forgotten the *Atlantic Charter* and its proclamation of 'the right of all peoples to choose the form of government under which they will live.' We still share the wish expressed in that charter, 'to *see sovereign rights and self-government restored* to those who have forcibly been deprived of them.'

"This is an hour when it is particularly important that our Nation's dedication to these principles should be made manifest. We approach a possible *meeting with* the representatives of *the Soviet Union.* I can assure you that we welcome opportunities to settle specific disputes between us to end, if possible, the race in armament, particularly atomic armament, and to reduce the risks of war.

"Let me also assure this: *We do not look upon the conference table as a place where we surrender our principles, but rather as a place for making our principles prevail. That is our resolve* — a resolve which I am confident is backed by the Congress and by the people of the United States."

Congressman Charles Kersten called this testimony of Dulles "a manifesto of faith in human freedom — in these peoples and all peoples." [197]

This is a far cry from the "basic approach" of the U.S. delegates at Helsinki and Geneva in 1974 and 1975. Furthermore, the joint communique of President Eisenhower's meetings with Khrushchev-Bulganin and representatives of Great Britain and France, stated that Eisenhower had brought up the problem of the Baltic States — and evidently found the ground sterile. The communique was printed in full in the capitals of the "Big Four." Incidentally, the Vilnius newspaper *Tiesa* spaced out the reference to the Baltic States.

Thereafter, the 89th Congress in 1965 and 1966 unanimously enacted a joint resolution No. 416 urging the government to direct the attention at the United Nations and "at other appropriate international forums," to the denial of self-determination for the peoples of Estonia, Latvia and Lithuania, and to bring the force of world opinion to "bear on behalf of the restoration of these rights to the Baltic peoples."

[197] *Baltic States Investigation, Hearings . . . Part I, op. cit.*, p. 4.

The communiques of the United States-Soviet summit meetings in 1972, during the tragic events of protest in Lithuania which rated a deceitful briefing of the foreign press by Soviet spokesmen, and in 1974, make it clear that the conference table was not at all used "as a place for making our principles prevail." The statement of principles in common with Brezhnev, signed by President Nixon in Moscow, was immediately interpreted by Brezhnev, and by Suslov in Lithuania, as benefiting the USSR and "world socialism," and consolidating "the international legal recognition . . . of the permanence of the existing frontiers."

It is well to remember that when American Presidents — Woodrow Wilson, Franklin D. Roosevelt and others — spoke of principles regarding "all the people everywhere," etc., their domestic audiences paid little heed — some even dismissed the "campaign oratory." But the unintended audiences in German- or Russian-occupied countries treated these professions seriously, like the Gospel or the Scriptures.

Let us consider the principles of national self-determination which had liberated so many countries from the German, Austrian-Hungarian, Turkish and Russian empires. An average person does not realize that Wilson's "14 Points" did not embrace a principle of self-determination beyond the reference to the settlement of frontiers of Poland and Yugoslavia. The Fourteen Points were conditions of peace to the enemy — the Central Powers. The Points reacted to the sweeping mottoes of the Bolsheviks proclaiming peace without contributions or annexations, and a worldwide self-determination. In the view of President Wilson, his "Points" were conditions for the enemy to negotiate, not for the Allies, like Russia. Secretary of State Lansing on June 30, 1919, in Paris, met with the Ukrainian delegation representing the Petlyura Government and Galicia which sought a recognition for the Ukraine — a country which then had a government, armed forces and territory under its administration. Secretary Lansing told the delegates that "self-determination would govern the transfer of any Ukrainian from one country to another."[198] The United States at the Paris Peace Conference in 1919 steadfastly opposed a recognition of Estonia, Latvia, Lithuania, the Ukraine — and initially of Finland — as interference in Russian affairs. Samuel Eliot Morison, the U.S. representative on the conference's Baltic Commission, resigned in protest against this policy.

[198] Jurgėla, *Lithuania and the United States: The Establishment of State Relations*, MS, Fordham University, 1954, p. 177, citing *Paris Peace Conference*, XI (1945), pp. 253-255.

Morison claimed that this policy contradicted both the interests of the United States "and principles for the vindication of which the United States was supposed to be waging war," and that "the right of conquest is the only right Russia possesses over these non-Slavic peoples." However, Russian ambassador Bakhmetiev was consulted by the United States at every point, and nothing was done to dispel worldwide illusions that "self-determination" was a Wilsonian Point.

The Atlantic Charter, the Four Freedoms and declarations to the occupied or liberated nations were not pronouncements limited to post-June 1940 frontiers in Europe and did not make an exception of the Baltic States — and, as we just noted, in 1953 the United States held the Atlantic Charter applicable to the Baltic States. The populations in Soviet-German-Soviet occupied Lithuania, Latvia and Estonia were confident in their belief that these declarations were meant to apply to their countries.

The cold contempt by Liudas Simutis, the freedom fighter captured while he lay on his back in a cast in a hospital, is truly meaningful. The genocide in East Prussia violated every known principle of American and Allied policy, yet — who among the "decent people" protested? The inspiring words about freedom and the principles and human rights should not be employed as "con game" to be gambled away at the conference table.

In April 1974 the United Nations Special Committee on the Question of Defining Aggression approved an eight-article Draft Definition of Aggression. It is the very same definition which the Soviet Union had sponsored for decades and which the Soviet Union had signed in its covenants with Lithuania and other neighbors, members of the League of Nations. The 1974 draft version was embellished with some additions sponsored by new nations of Africa. Litvinov had spoken for the "sanctity of treaties" and of this Definition of Aggression — prior to the Ribbentrop-Molotov Pacts. After the seizure of the Baltic States and parts of Finland, Poland, Germany, Romania and Czechoslovakia, Vyshinsky and Gromyko resumed the theme of "sanctity," while brushing aside "slanderous" reminders of the Hitler-Stalin deals. Presently, Moscow, with the blessing of the other signatories of the Atlantic Charter, etc., put forward a demand at the Helsinki-Geneva conference to sanctify the Ribbentrop-Molotov deal: to recognize the permanence of the "present frontiers." The "decent people" wish only some "freer movement" of ideas and people — that is all — in exchange for the recognition of the Soviet loot. Yet even that price is annoying to Moscow which tolerates no heresies or dissent within its empire held together by brute force.

Some nine or ten American, Canadian and Swedish citizens attempted to remind the "decent people" sitting in Helsinki at the Conference on Security and Cooperation in Europe (CSCE), about the *missing* members of the European Community just south of the Gulf of Finland: Estonia, Latvia and Lithuania. They distributed their memoranda to the delegations and the press. At the behest of the Soviet Union, the Finnish police arrested these spokesmen for the European conscience. Secretary William Rogers of the United States interceded in their behalf. These spokesmen of conscience were then released, "gagged" — and taken to the airport to leave Finland. Thus the "freer exchange of ideas" could not take place at the seat of this conference. When the voice of conscience, or dissenting views, may not be heard at an international conference allegedly seeking security for the European states and peoples — while the violators of treaties and covenants, the only imaginable potential aggressors, are allowed to assert their sanctimonious dedication to the sanctity of treaties and human rights and frontiers — we are back in the Dark Ages, regardless of our spacemanship, technology and lip service to the rule of reason, of justice and of law in international relations.

In 1943, sixty-six Swedish intellectuals in a joint appeal noted that the political, cultural and economic achievements of the Estonians, Latvians and Lithuanians during the two decades of independence between two world wars had won for them "the admiration of the world and clearly demonstrated their state-building ability." The Swedish intellectual elite in a statement made during the war, when the Baltic States were under a German military occupation, noted that "the conscience of the world" could never be reconciled with a sacrifice of these small peaceful nations "to the imperialistic interests of the great powers." This would constitute a crime "against the high-minded principles which were proclaimed in the Atlantic Charter which promised freedom and self-government to all nations that have been deprived of them by force. We, the undersigned, claim for the Baltic nations the inalienable right to live their own free life." [199]

Former Asst. Secy. of State Adolf A. Berle, Jr., speaking to the students of the College of Free Europe at Strasbourg in August, 1956, recalled that some people claimed that the captive countries in Europe

[199] August Rei, *Have the Small Nations a Right to Freedom and Independence?*, London, 1946, pp. 27, 32.

"had been conquered and would be held by the strongest empire in Europe . . . it would be impossible to change that fact . . . that a decade of Russian military domination would crush the youth . . . wipe out their national culture. We proposed nevertheless to do the impossible. . . . We insisted that young men would still see visions and that old men would still dream dreams. We claimed that while states and governments could be captured, the minds of men would always look toward the light." Berle continued that "It is clear that Estonians, Latvians, Lithuanians, Poles, Hungarians, Czecho-Slovaks, Romanians, Bulgarians and Albanians insist on controlling their own lives and creating governments of their own choice. Already these people are morally and intellectually citizens of the free world."

Dr. Berle pleaded also for the cause of the "Russians who are bound to us by ties of race and by the common bond of humanity. They also are entitled to freedom from fear. . . . I have thought sometimes that our object might be a demilitarized frontier between mid-Europe and the Soviet Union, so that both the Soviet Union and mid-Europe might be free of the fear that some army would cross a border. . . . All we want of their rulers is that they attend to their own affairs. What we want of their people is friendship and understanding." Of Russia's neighbors Dr. Berle said:

"We are not speaking of countries which are to become free later. We are discussing countries which are free now, in the sense that their peoples are members of the free world. It is the governments of Poland, Czechoslovakia, Hungary, Estonia, Latvia, Lithuania, Bulgaria, Albania, Rumania, which are captive. The peoples of these countries do not recognize these governments, and know them for what they are: handfuls of frightened men, supported only by Russian soldiers and Soviet secret police, in fear of assassination or exile. These governments are really besieged garrisons in government palaces. The men and women outside are free and have begun to know it." [200]

Salvador de Madariaga warned in 1959 that "The people of the United States will need all of their reserves of common sense in order not to be carried off their feet by the shallow commentators, tired intellectuals and blasé columnists who kept telling them that, after all, the cold war has lasted long enough and some arrangement must be found since, Hungary or no Hungary, the Soviet Union had been the first power on earth to hit the moon. This is no fancy. It is a terse

[200] Address by the Honorable Adolf A. Berle, Jr., Cours d'Ete 1956, College de l'Europe Libre, Strasbourg Robertsau.

expression of the muddle-headed defeatism into which many people have been thrown by weariness, indifference, prosperity and an unfortunate reluctance to look awkward facts in the face." [201]

Richard M. Nixon, the former Vice President of the United States and the loser in the presidential election of 1960, affirmed in 1966 that Russia's objectives were still the same, except that "the Soviet leaders, as a result of the confrontation in Havana, are now aware of the great risk of self-destruction if they pursue the policy of world conquest rashly." [202]

As President, Nixon disappointed many of his electors when he retreated from conservatism in his domestic policies and, with his principal adviser on security,— an admirer of Metternich, embarked on spectacular moves in foreign policy which in certain areas contradicted his formerly voiced views. An era of (fictional) detente was inaugurated built on the foundation of trusting the Kremlin establishment whose members have learned to smile for the press photographers yet never retreated one step from the Ribbentrop-Molotov deal as improved at Yalta, Potsdam, Helsinki and Geneva. Like Metternich, he never realized that the Achilles Heel of multinational empires is the nationalism of the subject nationalities,— which ultimately extinguished Metternich's own empire, and may yet splinter the Soviet empire. Nationalism of the subjugated nationalities is the nightmare and the main fear of the Politburo — in a country where the minority, at most the slight majority, the Russian nationality is bullying, defiling, exploiting and oppressing the large and small and splinter nationalities under the rule of "international Leninists." That submerged nationalism is a force more powerful than nuclear arms. It is the only force which can split the Soviet Union into its elements without a war. It is not at all understood by professional Kremlinologists of pro-Russian and pro-Big Power orientation. Their analytical efforts are directed at interpreting the various speeches of members of the Kremlin establishment — some of which are made deliberately to befuddle our Kremlin watchers waiting for the convergence and evolution of Communism into some form of democracy. They should rather read and re-read and never forget the Third Party Program of the CPSU and glean realities therefrom.

Meanwhile, ordinary people should retrieve and speak up for true decency — in matters international as in domestic. They should demand

[201] Alfreds Berzins, *The Two Faces of Co-Existence*, New York, 1967, p. 286.

[202] *Ibid.*, citing *U.S. News and World Report*, Oct. 3, 1966.

such decency from our elected officials and their appointees administering the foreign policies and destinies of our country, or the policies of our Allies, or of the "non-aligned" countries. Lithuania, Latvia and Estonia have no lesser a right to the restoration of their sovereignty and freedom within the family of independent nations — than the people of Norway, Malta, Indonesia, Uganda, Finland, etc., etc.

We *are* our "brother's keepers." We should remember Abraham Lincoln's cautioning words: "A house divided against itself cannot stand. I believe this government cannot endure permanently half-slave and half-free." (June 17, 1858.)

BIBLIOGRAPHY OF REFERENCES
(Cited)

Acta Patriarchatus Constantinopolitani, ed. Miklosich et Müller, Vindobonae, I - 1860, II - 1862.

d'Angeberg, le Comte de-, *Recueil des Traités, Conventions et Actes Diplomatiques concernant la Pologne*, Paris, 1862.

Attempted Defection by Lithuanian Seaman Simus Kudirka, Hearings before the Subcommittee on State Department Organization and Foreign Operations. . . House of Representatives, 91st Congress, 2nd Session, Washington, 1970 — and *Report.*

Baltic States Investigation, Hearings before the Select Committee to Investigate the Incorporation of the Baltic States into the USSR, House of Representatives, 83rd Congress, 1st Session, Part I, Washington, 1954. [See also: *Third Interim Report* and *Special Report No. 14*, and *Second Interim Report.*]

Bartnicka, Halina: *Polskie szkolnictwo artystyczne na przełomie XVIII i XIX w. 1764-1831*, Ossolineum, Wrocław, 1971.

Bartoszewicz, Kazimierz: *Dzieje Insurekcji Kościuszkowskiej*, Wiedeń, n.d. (1909).

Berzins, Alfreds: *The Two Faces of Co-Existence*, New York, 1967.

Bičiūnas, V.: *Kunigas Jonas Katelė ir jo laikai*, Kaunas, 1934.

Bičkauskas-Gentvila, L.: *1863 m. Sukilimas Lietuvoje*, Vilnius, 1958.

Bimba, Antanas: *Prisikėlusi Lietuva*, Brooklyn, N.Y., 1946.

Buckley, James L.: "Senator James L. Buckley on Russian Trip," *The Congressional Record*, Dec. 19, 1974, S-22428-22434.

Čeginskas, Dr. Kajetonas: "Lietuvių Tautos Atgimimo Pradmenys," in *Kovos Metai dėl savosios spaudos*, ed. Vytautas Bagdanavičius, Dr. Petras Jonikas, Juozas Švaistas Balčiūnas, Chicago, 1957.

Daumantas, J.: *Partizanai už Geležinės Uždangos*, Chicago, 1950.

Department of State *Bulletin*, v. III, No. 57, July 27, 1940, Washington.

Documents on German Foreign Policy 1918-1945, Series D, vol. V, 1937-1939, Department of State, Washington, 1953.

ELTA Information Service, New York, Information Bulletins (indicated dates in footnotes).

Encyclopedia Lituanica, vol. I, Boston, 1970; v. III, 1973.

Engelhardt, Leo: *Zapiski Lva Nikolaievicha Engelhardta*, Moskva, 1866.

Foreign Relations of the United States: *1918 Russia*, vol. I; *Paris Peace Conference*, vol. XI.

Gečys, kun. Dr. Kazys: *Katalikiškoji Lietuva*, Chicago, 1946.

Gieysztor, Jakób: *Pamiętniki Jakóba Gieysztora*, II, Wilno, 1913.

Golubinsky, E: *Istoria Russkoy Tserkvi*, II, Moskva, 1917.

Grydzewski, Mieczysław: *Na 150-lecie Rzezi Pragi*, Londyn, 1945.

Gudaitis, Dr. Kristupas: "Evangelikų Bažnyčios Lietuvoje," *Lietuvių Enciklopedija*, XV, Boston, 1968, pp. 166-179.

Halifax: Speeches on Foreign Policy by Viscount Halifax, cited by

Harrison, Ernest J.: *Lithuania's Fight for Freedom*, New York, 1945.

Hordynski, Joseph, Major of the 10th Regiment of Lithuanian Lancers: *The History of the Late Polish Revolution*, 4 editions, Boston, 1832-3.

Iwaszkiewicz, Janusz: *Litwa w roku 1812*, Warszawa, 1912.

Janulaitis, Augustinas: (Žmogus) *Baudžiava Lietuvoje*, Chicago, 1901; *1863-1864 m. Sukilimas Lietuvoje*, Kaunas, 1921; *Lietuvos Bajorai ir jų Seimeliai XIX amž. (1795-1863)*, Kaunas, 1936.

Jurgėla, Constantine/Kostas R.: *History of the Lithuanian Nation*, New York, 1948; *Lithuania and the United States: The Establishment of State Relations*, MS dissertation, Fordham University, New York, 1954; *Lietuvos Sukilimas 1862-1864 metais*, Boston, 1970.

Khrushchev, Nikita S.: *Khrushchev Remembers*, ed. Strobe Talbott, Boston-Toronto, 1970.

Klimaitis, P., ed.: *Kražių Skerdynės*, Kaunas, 1944.

"*Komunistas*" monthly, Vilnius — issues indicated in footnotes.

Korf. Baron S.A.: *Dvoryanstvo i yego soslovnoye upravlenie za stoletiye 1762-1855*, Sanktpeterburg, 1906, cited by Janulaitis.

Kovos Metai del savosios spaudos, ed. Vyt. Bagdanavičius, Dr. Petras Jonikas, Juozas Švaistas-Balčiūnas, Chicago, 1957.

Krestianskoye Dvizhenie v Belorussii (1861-1862), Minsk, 1959.

Kubicki, Paeł: *Bojownicy Kapłani za Sprawę Kościoła i Ojczyzny w latach 1861-1915*, 3 parts in 8 volumes, Sandomierz, 1933-9.

Lamb, Harold: *The March of Muscovy*, Garden City, N.Y., 1948.

Laserson, Max M.: *The Development of Soviet Foreign Policy in Europe 1917-1942*, International Conciliation Series, Carnegie Endowment for International Peace, No. 386, New York, 1943.

League of Nations Treaty Series, vol. III.

"*Lietuva*" magazine, New York, issues indicated in footnotes.

Lietuvių Enciklopedija, Boston, vol. XV (1968), XXXIV (1966).

Lietuvos Katalikų Bažnyčios Kronika, issues 1-15; printed issues 1-7, Chicago, 1974.

Lithuania 700 Years, ed. Dr. Albertas Gerutis, New York, 1969.

Lithuania Under the Soviets, Portrait of a Nation, 1940-1965, ed. V, Stanley Vardys, New York, 1965.

"*Lithuanian Bulletin*," New York, issues indicated in footnotes.

"*Memorabilis et perinde. . .*" DVACI (Venice), 1583.

Meyer, Age (Benedictsen), *Lithuania, The Awakening of a Nation*, Copenhagen, 1924.

Mościcki, Henryk: *Pod znakiem Orła i Pogoni*, Lwów-Warszawa, 1923.

Muravyov, Graf Mikhail Nikolievich: a) *Der Dictator von Wilma*, Memoiren des Grafen M. N. Murawjew, Leipzig, 1883; b) *Pamiętnik Murawiewa ("Wieszatiela")*, Kraków, 1902; c) "Zapiski . . . o myatezhe v Severozapadnoy Rossii w 1863-1865 gg.", in *Russkaya Starina*, vols. 36, 37, 38, November 1882 - June 1883.

Nazi-Soviet Relations 1938-1941, Documents from the Archives of the German Foreign Office, edited by Raymond James Sontag and James Stuart Beddie, Department of State, Washington, D.C., 1948.

Nufer, Friedrich: *Friedrich Nufers Schicksale während und nach seiner Gefangenschaft in Warschau unter den Polen and Russen*, Posen, 1795.

Ochmański, Jerzy: 1) *Historia Litwy*, Wrocław, 1967; 2) *Litewski ruch narodowo-kulturalny w XIX wieku*, Białystok, 1965.

Pakštas, Kazys: "Rusų Kolonizacija Lietuvoje," *Lietuvių Enciklopedija*, XV, Boston, 1957, pp. 236-8.

Pamiatniki Drevne-Russkago Kanonicheskago Prava, Russkaya Istoricheskaya Biblioteka, Sanktpeterburg, 1908, vols. 6 & 26.

Paris Peace Conference... State Department, vol. XI, Washington, 1945.

Petruitis, Col. Jonas: *Lithuania Under the Sickle and Hammer*, Cleveland, Ohio, n.d.

Polish-Soviet Relations 1918-1943: a) Polish Embassy in Washington, n.d.; b) Polish Information Center, New York, 1943.

Polnoye Sobraniye Zakonov Rossiiskoy Imperii, volumes cited by Janulaitis, *Lietuvos Bajorai ...*

Programme of the Communist Party of the Soviet Union, The Adopted by the 22nd Congress of the C.P.S.U., October 31, 1961. *Soviet Booklet* No. 83, London, November, 1961.

Przyborowski, Walery: *Dzieje 1863 roku* (5 vols. 1897-1910), vol. V, Kraków, 1910.

Raštikis, Stasys: "Derybos Maskvoje..." *Lietuva*, New York, Jan.-March, 1954, pp. 53-58.

Rei, August: *Have the Small Nations a Right to Freedom and Independence?* London, 1946.

Roosevelt, Franklin D.: *The Public Papers of ... 1942*, New York, Harper, 1943.

Rukšėnas, Algis: *The Day of Shame*, David McKay, New York, 1973.

Russkaya Istoricheskaya Biblioteka, Sanktpeterburg, vols. 1908.

"*Russkaya Starina*" magazine, 1882-3.

Savasis, Dr. J.: *The War Against God in Lithuania*, New York, 1966.

Senn, Alfred Erich: *The Emergence of Modern Lithuania*, Columbia University Press, New York, 1966.

Seredonin, S. M.: *Istorichesky Obzor Deyatelnosti Komiteta Ministrov*, Sankt-Peterburg, 1902.

Seume, J. G.: *J. G. Seumes Sämmtliche Werke*, Leipzig, 1837.

Smirnov, Anatoly Fillippovich: *Revolyutsionnyie suyazi narodov Rossii i Polshi*, Moskva, 1962.

Sruogienė, Dr. Vanda Daugirdaitė: *Lietuvos Istorija*, Chicago, 1956.

Steponaitis, Vytautas: *Amerikiečiu Lietuvių Kariškos Aspiracijos XIX amž. Pabaigoje*, Kaunas, 1927.

Strojnowski, Walerian: *O Ugodach Dziedziców z Włościanami*, Wilno, 1808.

Stukas, Jack J.: *Awakening Lithuania*, Madison, N.J., 1966.

Šaulys, Jurgis, in "Musų Kelias," Dillingen, Germany, No. 7 (119), February 12, 1947.

Tarybų Sąjungos Komunistų Partijos Programa, Priimta TSKP XXII Suvažiavime, Vilnius, 1962 (preceded by a *Projektas*. . . Vilnius, 1961).

Tauras, K. V.: *Guerrilla Warfare on the Amber Coast*, New York, 1962.

Trakiškis, A.: *The Situation of the Church and Religious Practices in Occupied Lithuania*, New York, 1944.

Turauskas, Eduardas: "Russian Technique vis à vis Lithuania," *Lithuanian Bulletin*, New York, VI, No. 1-2, 1948.

"*U.S. News and World Report*," October 3, 1966.

The USSR-German Aggression Against Lithuania, ed. Bronis J. Kaslas, New York, 1973.

Vaitiekūnas, Vytautas: *A Survey of Development in Captive Lithuania in 1965-1968*, New York, n.d.

Valuyev, Peter: *Dnevnik P.A. Valuyeva*, Ministra Vnutrennikh Dyel, 2 vols., AN SSSR, Moskva, 1961.

Vardys, V. Stanley: see "Lithuania Under the Soviets."

Veblaitis, P.: *Kova su caro valdžia už Kęstaičių bažnycią*, Kaunas, 1938.

Violations of Human Rights in Soviet Occupied Lithuania, The, A Report for 1971 (1972), 1972 . . .

War and Peace in Finland. . . by "Soviet Russia Today," New York, 1940 (ed. Alter Brody, Theodore M. Bayer, Isidor Schneider, Jessica Smith).

Wheeler-Bennett, John V.: *The Forgotten Peace*, New York, 1935.

Yablochkov, M.: *Istoria dvoryanskago soslovia v Rossii*, Sanktpeterburg, 1876.

INDEX